Memoirs of a Maverick

Memoirs of a Maverick

The First Fifty Years (1941–1991)

Mani Shankar Aiyar

JUGGERNAUT BOOKS
C-I-128, First Floor, Sangam Vihar, Near Holi Chowk,
New Delhi 110080, India

First published by Juggernaut Books 2023

All photographs courtesy Mani Shankar Aiyar's personal archive

Speeches on p. 285 and p. 286 have been reproduced from Lok Sabha Debates with the permission of the Hon'ble Speaker, Lok Sabha

10 9 8 7 6 5 4 3 2 1

P-ISBN: 9789353451738
E-ISBN: 9789353451721

Typeset in Adobe Caslon Pro by
R. Ajith Kumar, Noida

Printed at Thomson Press India Ltd

Contents

Preface

The origins of these memoirs lie in a suggestion made by Chiki Sarkar, founder and publisher of Juggernaut Books, in November 2015 at a reception-banquet on the lawns of my residence when she took me by surprise by saying I really should write up the story of my life. Sonia Gandhi, who was the chief guest at the banquet, backed the idea – largely, I think, because she had no further plans for me in politics. For my part, not having achieved anything spectacular, I could not immediately envision why anyone should be interested in a record of my undistinguished years. But Chiki and her commissioning editor at the time, Nandini Mehta, persisted until their enthusiasm began infecting me. To them, therefore, goes the credit or debit for inspiring this two-volume exercise in reminiscences and the companion volume on Rajiv Gandhi's premiership and after.

While writing it, two songs of my youth have kept buzzing in my head: 'Those Were the Days' and 'My Way'. The first, sung by Mary Hopkin, produced by the Beatle Sir Paul McCartney in 1968, when I was twenty-seven, has remained in my heart since as a kind of summing up of my dreams for myself:

Those were the days my friend,
We thought they'd never end,
We'd sing and dance forever and a day,
We'd live the life we choose,
We'd fight and never lose,
For we were young and sure to have our way.

And its closing lines:

Oh, my friend, we're older but no wiser
For in our hearts, the dreams are still the same.

The lyric is an English version by Gene Raskin of a Russian romance, 'Dorog Dlinnojou', composed by Boris Fomin with words by Konstantin Podrevsky. The lines seem to sum up the running theme of my eighty-two years.

And as Frank Sinatra sang to lyrics composed by Paul Anka and others:

I've lived a life that's full,
I travelled each and every highway,
And more, much more,
I did it my way.

Yes, I did it my way. Hence the title *Memoirs of a Maverick*. A maverick is defined by most dictionaries as 'an unconventional thinker, independent-minded, one who blazes their own trail'... something of a lone wolf, eccentric in their own way.

The inordinate length of this trilogy is the result of N. Venkatraman having joined my staff in 1992 and, over the next three decades, having assiduously archived every scrap of paper relating to me and my doings, then producing them before me in endless succession as I wrote till I lost all control over the length of these memoirs. His fidelity has substantially augmented my recall. To him and to Chandran Pottanatt, my wife's principal assistant, who helped Venkat with the archiving, as well as to Manish Bhatt, the other faithful member of my staff, go my deep gratitude for providing me the raw material for this journey of eight decades.

During a seven-year hiatus when Venkat went off to work with a Congress minister (2009–16), Gulshan Lal Bali filled in to begin with, and then Vandana Seth served a six-year stint during which she contributed original research, kept the archives up to date and taught me uses of the laptop of which earlier I had no inkling. After Chiki proposed this autobiography, Vandana urged me to start writing instead of moping around at the fading away of my political days. To her too, grateful thanks. I also gratefully acknowledge the contribution of a very bright young man from Jammu and Kashmir (and a

Dosco to boot!), Naushad Qayyum Khan, who interned with me, 2015–16, and has since acted as an intelligent sounding board for much of my thoughts and is an impressive source of information on his home state. He has grown into one of my closest companions.

Many friends of long acquaintance have helped out along the way: Chandrashekhar Dasgupta, alas no more, my college friend and IFS colleague whose engaging wit, usually at my expense, lights up many an episode and provides the scaffolding of my intellectual development (a *guru dakshina* he totally rejected as his views had grown in a radically different direction to mine); Talmiz Ahmed, who joined me in Baghdad in 1977 and for forty years has remained true to his salt, backing me to the hilt, fighting my battles, assisting in every way, especially with the brilliance of his intellect, his treasure trove of knowledge and fetching good humour; Sati Lambah, with whom I worked in Pakistan and whose contribution on the backchannel to resolving issues related to Kashmir will continue to outlive him; Ronen Sen, Rajiv Gandhi's favourite foreign policy aide, whose remembrances often run contradictory to my own; V. George, private secretary to both Rajiv and Sonia Gandhi, who retrieved some documents and refreshed my mind on several key dates and sequences by looking up his diaries for the Rajiv period; Wajahat Habibullah, an old school friend, whose book on Rajiv Gandhi preceded mine; to my nephew, Vidya Shankar Aiyar, an authority on nuclear disarmament and a never-failing source of encouragement; to the Parliament House Library for their well-indexed store of newspapers and other journals and their ever-helpful staff; to Raminder Singh who has gone out of his way to look up records of the Union debates in the Cambridge University library; and to Sunil Binjola, director (operations) in the South Asia Foundation-India that I chair for having taken time off to prepare this work's website of footnotes and endnotes. The reader is invited to read the footnotes to find what has otherwise had to be left out to keep the length of the book within reasonable limits. Vir Sanghvi deserves special mention for his solidarity through thick and thin all these years (and the numerous five-star gourmet meals to which he has generously hosted me).

Two senior associates who have been unstinting in encouraging me along are former external affairs minister K. Natwar Singh and former foreign secretary Maharajakrishna Rasgotra. To them my respectful thanks. In the same category would fall former Jammu and Kashmir governor N.N. Vohra. Other friends who have jogged my memory include former defence secretary and defence minister of Pakistan Salim Abbas Jilani; former Pakistan high commissioners to India, Humayun Khan and Ashraf Qazi Jehangir; former minister, prolific writer and 'foeman worthy of my steel', Javed Jabbar; and my friends Zia Khaleeli and Sameera Naved in Pakistan. I also acknowledge the encouragement and memory-pushing I have received in writing these lines from my Cambridge friends, J. Krishan Kumar, Tim Lankester, Rahul Khushwant Singh, Ajit Singh and former chancellor of the exchequer, Norman Lord Lamont of Lerwick. A special mention is warranted of my Trinity Hall colleague, Khurshid Kasuri, who became for five eventful years (2003–08) Pakistan's foreign minister, undoubtedly the best India has ever had. I have also greatly benefitted from a telephone conversation with Air Vice Marshal (retd) Arjun Subramanian.

I wish to particularly thank Chiki Sarkar and her amazing team – Devangshu Datta, Devangana Ojha, Yashika Dudeja, Rimli Borooah and Arani Sinha, who toiled endlessly over the overlong manuscript to make it more readable. I admire their punctiliousness and persistence.

No work of this magnitude can be undertaken without support from the family. Suneet has consistently displayed the truth of the slogan emblazoned on one of my T-shirts: 'Daddy Knows a Lot, but Mommy Knows Everything'. She has maintained my emotional equilibrium for half a century by gently pulling me up when I despair and gently pulling me down when I float on air. No one has been more persuasive in getting me to get on with the job of writing this book instead of finding arguments not to do so.

My daughters – Suranya, Yamini, Sana – have been founts of inspiration and moral support in everything I have undertaken, including this book. Their individual and collective wisdom far exceeds mine. It is to them I owe a lot of course correction as I churned out these 4,00,000 words.

To their husbands, my sons-in-law – Uday Walia, Adarsh Kumar and Vipin Narang – I have turned for enlightenment on specific points. Adarsh is principally responsible for repeatedly coming to my rescue when this manuscript hit the rocks of my computer ignorance. To all of them, I give thanks.

I also give thanks to my six grandchildren – Uma and Kabir; Rukmini and Raghu; Ishaan and Leela (aged fourteen to six) – who, I hope, will read and absorb this story of their grandfather and carry it to future generations of the family.

I must also mention my brother Jam (Swaminathan Aiyar), the renowned journalist, and my sister Tara, for their contribution to getting the first few chapters of these reminiscences right when we were being brought up together by a mother (Amma) who left an indelible impression on us. My cousin Kartik Pashupati deserves thanks for finding a number of family photographs.

And where in all this do I fit in the Covid-19 pandemic? Somewhere – for, after all, if there had not been these prolonged lockdowns, this book would perhaps not have seen the light of day.

Finally, I give thanks to Nayantara Sahgal, the novelist and political commentator, a favourite niece of her 'Mamu', Jawaharlal Nehru. She has dedicated a book she has written on Nehru's foreign policy to me for 'speaking the same language' as that great man. I have never received a more flattering compliment. So, reciprocally, I dedicate this work to her.

Mani Shankar Aiyar
12 January/5 June 2023

Begun at:
Silver Sands/Boat Shack,
Candolim Beach,
Goa, India

Ended at:
22, Atherton Road, Brookline,
Boston, MA, US

A note on the QR codes

1. For each chapter a QR code is given that may be scanned to access detailed footnotes and endnotes.

2. Scan this QR code to know more about some of the book's featured photographs.

1

The First Twenty Years

1941–1961

My birth certificate

When Pakistan's President Pervez Musharraf visited Delhi in 2003, he enquired whether he might be provided with his birth certificate. The municipal authorities failed to retrieve the record while he was in town and it was only months later that the certificate was sent to him. So, when I arrived at my birthplace, Lahore, in July 2008, I couldn't help getting into a little mischief. I was there as the minister for Panchayati Raj, at the head of a fifty-five-member delegation to attend an India–Pakistan conference on local self-government hosted by the Pakistani minister concerned, Daniyal Aziz.

In response to the boasting of the mayor of Lahore, Mian Amer Mahmood of the Jama'at-e-Islami, that they had digitized all their records, I enquired if they could retrieve their birth records for 1941. 'Yes, sir,' came the reply. I then asked if they had the records for April 1941. With just a hint of hesitation they answered that, of course, they had the records for April 1941.

'In that case,' I went on, 'would you have the records for the 10th of April 1941?' Intrigued, they replied they were sure those would be available, but why did I want to know? Because, I answered, that was the day I was born here in this city and I would like to test if they could get my birth record quicker than Delhi had been able to find President Musharraf's.

Next morning there was a suppressed air of excitement when I went down to the conference. I found a large envelope staring at me when I sat at my designated place. I cautiously opened it and found a duly certified photocopy of my birth record, retrieved literally overnight by the Lahore Municipal Corporation. I joined enthusiastically in the applause at this telling proof of the Lahore corporation authorities outclassing their Delhi counterparts.

There was one detail, though, that puzzled me. I was recorded as having been born on the 9th, not the 10th, of April 1941. It then struck me that my mother had often told me that my time of birth was 12.24 a.m., just after midnight. So, while she had been admitted to the hospital in labour on the 9th, she wanted me to know that my date of birth was actually the next day. Astrologers may please note. They may also note that during World War II, clocks had been moved half an hour ahead. So, I may actually have been born on the 9th, not the 10th, in terms of today's Indian Standard Time – and definitely on the 9th in terms of today's Pakistan Standard Time.

This confusion over my time of birth would appear to have confused my stars as well, which perhaps accounts for the ups and downs of my maverick life!

Mention of World War II brings me straight to the cause of my conception. It is a longish tale.

Amma

My mother – Amma, as I called her, and Bhagyalakshmi or Bhagyam, as the world knew her – was orphaned at the age of eight. Her mother died in 1917 giving birth to her fourth child. Her father remarried for the strictly utilitarian purpose of having someone to look after the children, and then himself died the following year, within months of his second marriage, in the infamous global influenza epidemic of 1918.

Tragedy had already struck the family earlier. The eighteen-year-old husband of his eldest daughter, Alankaram (who was then thirteen), died within six months of her marriage. Knowing well the dreadful fate of child widows in rural Tamil Nadu, my grandfather, who was far more enlightened than most men of his time, had her admitted to a school for child widows in Madras (now Chennai). This was run by a remarkable woman, Sister Subbalakshmi, who was herself a child widow.

For several months – perhaps more than a year after she was orphaned

– Amma and her two little brothers were farmed out to various members of the extended family who treated them little better than domestic servants. I think all of us – her children – were traumatized by Amma's description of being savagely struck on the head by an irate relative-employer with an iron ladle that split her crown. She had to walk miles every day to reach the doctor who treated her wound. The scar remained starkly visible, and as children, we would be consumed by a ghoulish desire to see it, even as we dissolved in tears upon listening to the sorry story, no matter how many times we heard it.

Deliverance appeared in the shape of an angel, Sister Subbalakshmi herself. She had learnt from Alankaram about her younger sister and the two almost-infant brothers. My sister tells me Amma was about to be married off to a fifty-year-old man, but Amma herself never told me this, though I knew there was a lot of 'women's only' talk between mother and daughter from which male children were excluded.

Sister Subbalakshmi arrived in Shulamangalam village (which is in Thanjavur district, in my former constituency), quite literally kidnapped the frightened ten-year-old and marched her off to the nearby Pashupathikoil railway station. The suddenly deprived relatives turned up in full force at the station to snatch back their ward and unpaid servant. Amma told us how she cried when the lady of the house threatened to jump in front of the engine if the child were not restored to her, but Sister Subbalakshmi held her firmly by the arm and told her not to be bullied by empty threats. The train lurched and started. The relative wisely desisted from suicide.

Next day, Amma found herself a scholarship student at Sister Subbalakshmi's home for child widows. The scholarship was Rs 5 a month and generously provided by a 'rani of Andhra', though Amma never discovered her royal benefactor's actual name. When, subsequently, the 'rani' died, the Ramakrishna Mission took up the financial responsibility, and that is how Amma came to live in the Ice House on the Madras Marina, where the Vivekananda Foundation is now headquartered. Amma's only regret was that when all the other children went home for their holidays, she was left all alone in the hostel.

It was at school, I think, that a lifelong rivalry started between my mother and Alankaram *periamma* (Tamil for 'elder mother'). That sibling rivalry embittered Amma's life, though the two sisters remained close despite differences.

Amma turned out be a competent but not brilliant student (in contrast to her elder sister who did not know what 'second position' was). She steadily passed her exams and made it to the prestigious Queen Mary's College to read for a BSc degree in chemistry. Having got her degree, she joined the Madras Education Service and was posted to Visakhapatnam. The officials who had come to the railway station to receive her were quite bewildered to find themselves landed with a single woman aged twenty and still unmarried. Where could they put her up? Someone suggested the vice chancellor of Andhra University be approached as he had a huge house with most of the rooms unoccupied. The vice chancellor agreed to take in Amma. He was none other than Dr S. Radhakrishnan who, decades later, as president of India, was to prove a fundamental turning point in my effort to make a career in diplomacy.

In the meantime, Alankaram *periamma* shone as the brightest star of her class at Lady Hardinge Medical College in Delhi. In consequence, she won a full set of Shakespeare's plays that now has pride of place on my library shelves. That led to her securing a scholarship to go to England to obtain her MRCOG (Member of the Royal College of Obstetricians and Gynaecologists) degree.

Amma goes to England

Amma, still unmarried at close to thirty, determined that she too must get to England, and get herself a teacher's training degree (she had only an LT – Licentiate of Teaching – by way of teaching qualifications). But from where was she to get the money? She herself had next to nothing. Her distinguished sister was disinclined to help. But Alankaram had assisted at the birth of the first son of a renowned customs officer, A. Sattanathan, who generously loaned Amma the money to travel to England.

Amma quit her teaching job and took a Lloyd Triestino liner to an Italian port (probably Brindisi) from where she was to proceed by an overland train to London. She sailed from Bombay (now Mumbai) in the last week of August 1939. When the ship docked at Suez, the passengers learnt that World War II had broken out. As their destination was Italy, and Italy was an Axis power, passengers were in a panic as to whether, as British Indian subjects, they should risk disembarkation at an Italian port and find themselves interned for the duration of the war, or just get off the ship at Port Said the next day.

Amma spotted the renowned Gujarati industrialist Ambalal Sarabhai among the first-class passengers. She decided that if he stayed on board at Port Said, she would continue the journey, but that if he got off, so would she. In the event, Ambalal Sarabhai got off and Amma followed suit. After some days of waiting in Port Said, Lloyd Triestino took her to Massawa, a small, flea-bitten port in what is now Eritrea, which was then under Italian colonial occupation. (My brother, Swaminathan, has been there on a World Bank mission, and I ardently wish to visit when I can.)

Amma hung around Massawa for several anxious days until another liner picked her up and sailed to Colombo. From Colombo, she took a train to Madras. But on the way, her trunk was stolen, and the only worldly possession she was left with was the sari she was wearing. She was back at her starting point within less than a month of her departure, with no foreign teaching degree, no job, no possessions, no prospects and a huge debt to pay off.

At this moment of ultimate wretchedness, she was left with no option but to accept her sister Alankaram's invitation to go to Delhi and try to pick up the tattered threads of her life. It took a little persuasion by her sister but Amma reluctantly agreed to catch the Grand Trunk Express. Alankaram then wrote to say that a friend of hers would meet Amma at the first of Agra's two stations – Raja ki Mandi and Cantonment – and that if she wished, she could visit the Taj Mahal with him. Amma was somewhat aghast at this daring suggestion but when the 'friend' turned out to be thin, bespectacled and less than an inch taller than her own five feet one, she decided to risk it.

All went well until they reached the fort where Shahjahan had been imprisoned by his son, Aurangzeb. Aurangzeb had attempted to compensate for this incarceration by providing his father with a small mirror through which Shahjahan could see a reflection of his beloved wife's tomb. It was obligatory for tourists to take a peek at the legendary mirror. The trouble was that both Amma and the 'friend' were too short to raise themselves to the required height. So, when he offered to lift Amma up by the waist for a look-see, my mother was horrified at his insolence. She never told me, however, whether she eventually accepted the offer. At any rate, they were married a few months later – and thus, I owe my birth to Adolf Hitler. For had he not invaded Poland, I would never have been. Was it worth taking humanity to the slaughterhouse just so I could be born?

My parents' wedding was both unusual and a disaster. It was unusual because it was held in the bridegroom' s house, not the bride's, for my poor mother had neither home nor family to 'give her away'. It was a disaster, because they had hardly entered the nuptial chamber when my father announced that he had really wanted to marry my mother's sister. It was a blow from which the marriage never recovered. Nevertheless, four children followed in quick succession: me; my brother Swaminathan on 12 October 1942; my sister Tara on 29 February 1944 (Leap Year's Day); and my youngest brother, Mukundan, on 19 September 1945.

Following the traditions and customs of the day, I was given a name that combined the names of my paternal and maternal grandfathers – Venkataraman and Subramanian – into Venkatasubramanian. Horrified at the baby being burdened with such an unwieldy name, Alankaram *periamma* insisted on a nickname: either Ravi (the rising sun) or Ajit (the unvanquishable). Amma modestly chose the latter. So, I am now easily able to identify those who call me Ajit as close family or people who have known me since infancy. Later, when I was around eight, I imitated Napoleon and crowned myself 'Mani', the usual diminutive of Subramanian, which is the name by which all but my immediate family know me.

Similarly, my brother, known to the world as famed journalist Swaminathan Anklesaria Aiyar, is 'Jam' within the family. As an infant, he not only had a large head and outsize ears, but when he was learning to crawl, would also push along objects that came in his way instead of going round them. Thus, he initially came to be nicknamed 'Jumbo the Elephant' that, over time, got shortened to 'Jam'.

It was this salutary experiment with long Tamil names that led to my sister being simply called Tara (requiring no diminutive) and my youngest brother 'Mukundan', sometimes abbreviated to 'Mukund' or, on northern tongues, 'Mukand'.

Life in Lahore

How did this Tambrahm family come to be living in Lahore? The story has its roots in the political turbulence of Tamil Nadu in the 1920s. My father was the third son. He stood to inherit at most a tiny share of the ancestral lands. Appa too had shed his given name – Pattabhiraman – and switched to the much simpler 'Sankar'. He decided to get himself a profession. So he graduated in physics in 1927 at the age of twenty from Pachaiyappa's College, Madras, the first in his family to get a degree.

One of Appa's college contemporaries was C.N. Annadurai, who went on to found the Dravida Munnetra Kazhagam (DMK) in 1948. Annadurai became the first Dravidian chief minister of the state in 1967, and remains revered evermore by the people of Tamil Nadu as '*Anna*' (elder brother). Annadurai was one of the social reformers instrumental in ending the Brahmin domination of Tamil Nadu (then the Madras Presidency). Until the mid-1920s, Brahmin domination in the civil services, education, the judiciary and the Bar, and other avenues of government employment had been absolute. Notwithstanding their minuscule 3 per cent share in the Tamil population, Brahmins secured fifteen out of sixteen places in the Indian Civil Service (ICS) between 1892 and 1904; held twenty-one of the twenty-seven engineering positions selected through competitive examinations; constituted 67 per cent of those receiving baccalaureate degrees from Madras University; and overwhelmingly dominated the legal fraternity, the judiciary, academia and journalism.[1]

The political movement of the Justice Party and the far more effective 'Self-Respect Movement' of the great 'Thanthai Periyar' (E.V. Ramaswamy Naicker) meant that, upon graduation, my father found that, as a Brahmin, few or no job opportunities were available. Thus his fond ambition of becoming a clerk in the railways was stymied. Infuriated, he took a train that would take him as far as he could get from Madras. (Perhaps if he had been born later, I would have been a Canadian!) He got off at far-distant Lahore where another Aiyar, P.N.S. Aiyar, had preceded him nine years earlier and set up a firm of chartered accountants and income tax advisers in 1918.

Appa was appointed an articled clerk at Aiyar & Co. and took no time at all to become a living legend in his profession. Such was his reputation that it used to be said – quite apocryphally, I think – that he could recite any

1 S. Narayan, *Dravidian Years*, Oxford University Press, New Delhi, 2018, pp. 2–3. For more details, scan the QR code on p. 43.

clause of the Income Tax Act backward to the astonishment of any income tax officer challenging him!

His clients were from all over Pakistan, ranging from Peshawar to Karachi, the most prominent being the Dalmia family that owned the biggest cement factory in the region. Appa loathed Ramakrishna Dalmia, the much-married rake, as much as he adored his younger brother, the pious Jaidayal Dalmia. The cement factory was so renowned that when I was posted to Karachi half a century later in 1978, one of the well-known bus stops was still called the Dalmia Cement bus stop, though the company had been nationalized and its name changed after the 1965 Indo-Pakistan war.

Appa specialized in the Income Tax Appellate Tribunal and won many a forensic battle for his clients. While his professional life flourished, his late marriage (he was thirty-three when he married) was fizzling out. Amma found almost any excuse to spend as little time with her husband as possible. Therefore, since Alankaram had been transferred from Lahore to Akola, in what was then called the Central Provinces & Berar, Amma went to her elder sister's for support during childbirth. Thus, while, I was born in Lahore, Swaminathan (Jam) and Tara were both born in Akola. Our stays in Lahore were intermittent. Simla (now Shimla) was where the Income Tax Appellate Tribunal would sit in the summer, giving my mother another opportunity to get away from her husband on the pretext of keeping house for him on his frequent forays to Simla on work.

In consequence, I have hardly any personal memories of Lahore. I had a favourite toy leopard that I seem to remember, though that is probably only from a photograph shown to me often (and included in the photo section of this book). I am told I loved the sobriquet by which I was known – 'Sher Khan'. When I got married, I learnt that at least one branch of my wife's family had also lived in Lahore's Laxmi Mansions, our home in the city. So, I may have caught my first glimpse of my brother-in-law-to-be, Tejbir Singh, from my pram. I have since been often to 44, Laxmi Mansions (as it is still called), and it is so familiar that I can easily imagine what it must have been like to be nurtured there.

Alas, I think I have now (in May 2018) made my last visit. Number 44 is still standing. Dr Malik, who owns it – and has always been a most gracious host – runs a clinic there. Nevertheless, I am almost certain that Mammon will, sooner than later, lay a finger on the building, as he has to the two other wings, and I will not be seeing it again. However, the image of my first home is now so firmly implanted in my mind and photographs that I can always recall it.

To return to the chronology, after having three children in the north, my mother announced that she must have at least one child in the south and moved with all the children to Madras, where Mukund was born. Having dallied in the south for several months, she took us off to Simla for the summer of 1946. Family lore has it that I insisted on seeing the winter snow and so this provided her an excuse to stay on in Simla. Winter turned to summer; we continued staying in Simla. Thus it came about that when, in mid-August 1947, the country was partitioned, my father found himself in Pakistan while the rest of the family was in India!

My mother told me years later that my father was considering taking Pakistani citizenship because much of his clientele was in West Pakistan. If, even after conjuring Pakistan into existence, Jinnah intended to spend six months of the year in his palatial Bombay residence, my father was not far behind in thinking, like so many of his fellow Lahoris, that Partition was a temporary inconvenience that would quickly resolve itself with everyone returning to their homes and resuming their age-old harmony.

My father's grocer of twenty years standing had his stall on Beedon Road running on one side of Laxmi Mansions. He told my father that what was happening in Lahore was *junoon* (a madness) that would soon pass. He, therefore, advised my father to place a big padlock on his front door and he, the grocer, would tell anyone who asked that 'Sankar sahib has gone away to Hindusthan'. He also offered to come to the rear door of the ground-floor apartment on the other side of the *aangan* (courtyard) and knock at around three in the morning with the day's supplies – and my father could pay later when normalcy was restored.

The grocer, like Jinnah and everyone else, had failed to reckon with the consequences of the Radcliffe Award, published on 17 August 1947, allotting Lahore to Pakistan though the city (if not the district) had a slight plurality of non-Muslims. Instantly, widespread anti-Hindu and anti-Sikh rioting broke out, resulting in a pogrom and genocide that denuded the city of virtually all its non-Muslim residents.

On that dreadful night of 17–18 August, when my father opened the courtyard door, the grocer pulled a knife on him. Appa hastily banged the door closed. I have always wondered whether the grocer did indeed mean to plunge the knife into Appa, or whether he was merely flashing the blade to prove his patriotism to whoever had spotted his midnight visits.

The next day, Appa called the Dalmias to send over a truck in which he packed what he could and set off on the half-hour journey to the Wagah–Attari border. This was perhaps the worst day of Partition fever. I deeply regret never having asked my father how he survived where thousands perished. But survive he did.

My father took refuge in his younger brother's flat on Delhi's Panchkuian Road. Later he told me the tale of how he had witnessed a thirteen-year-old Muslim boy begging for his life on Panchkuian Road, pleading, 'I'll say Ram, I'll say Krishna, but please spare me'; the butchers ruthlessly slashed his throat and left him dying on the pavement outside Appa's brother's flat. Partition was a nightmare that haunted Appa the rest of his life. In many ways, it is also the nightmare that has haunted my life and my politics.

Simla at Partition

Meanwhile, in Simla, where we were safe, I have the most vivid memory of a Sikh *jatha* (group) knocking on the door of our first-floor apartment at Three Bridges in Jacko (Jakhu) Hills. It must have been at around seven in the evening as there was a strict rule that I had to be in bed and asleep by 8 p.m. My mother opened the door, and half a dozen fierce-looking Sikhs strode into the hall demanding to know where the Muslims were. Amma said they had gone away to Pakistan. I, on the other hand, knew they were very much in the building – a whole family ranging from an aged grandmother to an infant child. One of them, a boy my age, was my favourite playmate.

I was about to say they were on the ground floor when a look in Amma's eyes that I had never seen before warned me to keep my mouth shut. I didn't speak. The Sikhs wandered around, smashed the outhouse and finally left. Next day, a body knifed to death was discovered on the hillside.

This memory – which has haunted me ever since – is remarkably close to the climax of Bapsi Sidhwa's searing novel, *Ice Candy Man* (though mine has a happier ending). It was many years later that I saw Deepa Mehta's deeply moving film, *1947*, based on the novel. There must have been hundreds of such incidents at the time – all underscoring the madness that gripped a subcontinent riven by communal hatred. Never, never, ever again.

I think the trauma of Partition aggravated Appa's long-festering ulcers. He had to be rushed to Madras for an operation and the whole family moved south for several months. I even had a brief spell in a Madras school before returning to Delhi at the end of 1947.

In Delhi, my brother, all of five, and I, just under seven, were taken to see Gandhiji at Birla House. My aunt, Dr Alankaram, was a close friend of Dr Sushila Nayyar, Mahatma Gandhi's personal physician. They had been students together at Lady Hardinge Medical College. The story goes that Mahatma Gandhi took the two of us in his arms and declared, '*Yeh mere aankhon ke chand aur suraj hain.*' (These are the moon and sun of my eyes.) I do not know if this is true. It sounds so good as to perhaps be apocryphal. But I was told the tale so often that perhaps this actually happened, and we have both grown with the Mahatma's blessings. Anyway, this is a bit of family lore to treasure.

What I am absolutely sure of is that on the evening of 30 January 1948, my brother and I were being walked by the family domestic help towards Birla House when we heard Gandhiji had been assassinated. The boy rushed us back home. There we found Amma bathed in tears, her hair all dishevelled, a picture of misery.

Appa goes abroad

Soon after the Mahatma's passing, my father embarked on his first journey abroad, spending three months in the UK and the US. He brought back a fascinating technological innovation – a 16-mm projector – along with a Laurel and Hardy film and a documentary on the building of the Boulder Dam in Colorado. This fascinated Jam and me. We must have seen 'Boulder Dam' at least a dozen times – we had no other reels to project.

On my father's return, he set about trying to find accommodation in a Delhi overflowing with refugees. There was just about nowhere to live – except with Members of the Constituent Assembly who were only occasional occupants of their government-allotted flats. Appa inveigled a Madras member,

O.V. Alagesan, to let us have a room in his apartment at 16-E, Ferozeshah Road – one room for six of us: father, mother and four children.

After a gap of nearly four years, my father was reunited with his family. But my mother saw that studies were impossible in this one-room set-up. Her attempts to put us into Modern School on Barakhamba Road backfired when we were sent for an admission test and the teacher got angry with us. My doting father declared he was not going to put us in a school where the teachers scolded his darling children. So we were left free to run around all day, play cricket and generally amuse ourselves, leavened by Sanskrit rituals taught us by Srinivasan, a young man who was articled to my father's company and later married my first cousin, Vishali. Their son, Venkataraman (Raja) now heads V. Sankar Aiyar & Co. from its Mumbai headquarters.

Amma watched all this with dismay. While she thought the priority was to get us into boarding school, my father wouldn't hear of it as he did not want to be separated from his boys. Amma had a college friend who had married the head of the Forest Research Institute (FRI) in Dehradun. Their son was among the most distinguished boys at the Doon School. So when my father flew out to Bombay on work, she literally kidnapped us and caught a bus to Dehradun.

It poured buckets of rain that day. The bus was a rattletrap that frequently broke down, and we smashed into a bullock cart. We got to Dehradun very late, very tired and terribly hungry. Finally, arriving bedraggled at FRI, we were helped out of our dripping clothes, fed and put to bed. Next day, bright and early, we were driven to school – and left to fend for ourselves.

Welham: 1949–1952

I was about ten days short of my eighth birthday and Jam was a few months over six. (Mukund, who joined us the following year, was not even five!) I found myself in Ambala House and Jam was accommodated in Bethany.

We were marched off separately to lunch. I was seated next to a boy with a topknot who asked me whether I played marbles. I confessed I did not. He offered to teach me. Beside myself with gratitude at having found a friend so quickly, I readily agreed.

After lunch, we repaired to the end of the garden that spread out before the dining room and went to the far end where Nater Prakash Singh scooped out a small hollow in the ground and asked if I had my marbles ready. I demurred, saying I did not have any marbles as I had not yet learnt the game. He rather grandly offered to loan me his marbles. Thus began the competition. Of course, I lost. He then said I owed him sixty marbles! I was horrified at the number but comforted myself with the thought that Amma would come to see us next day and I could get her to pay off my debt.

After a brief nap in my new house, I walked across to Jam at Bethany (for five- to six-year-olds). He startled me by saying we were at the wrong school; it wasn't Doon at all. Thoroughly alarmed, I asked him where he thought we were. He walked me to the gate and just outside was a board emblazoned 'WELHAM PREPARATORY SCHOOL' and below it the coda: 'FOR INDIAN BOYS'. I was stunned. My mother had dropped us at the wrong school and would never be able to find us again. And now where would I get sixty marbles to repay Nater? I spent my first night crying myself to sleep.

Next day, Amma arrived. I demanded to know why we had been put in the wrong school. Unfazed, she replied, 'Doon/Welham, what difference does that make?' I was appalled but also relieved and put to her my question about the sixty marbles. I don't remember her answer; I don't remember whether she got me the marbles; I don't remember whether I discharged my debt with honour; but Nater became a lifelong friend and I never played marbles again!

It did not take me long to adjust to a parent-less life. My initiation into the politics of protest began in my first term when I joined the rest of the class in objecting to our being made to sing 'My Bonnie lies over the ocean' (which was about Bonnie Prince Charlie of Scotland). Someone circulated a rumour that 'My Bonnie' meant 'My girl'. At eight, we wished to have nothing to do with girls and insisted on 'My Bonnie' being changed to 'My cricket bat lies over the ocean'! The teacher was compelled to fall in line with our amendment.

A highly dedicated band of English and Anglo-Indian women, along with one German Jewish refugee, made up the staff which built up the school under the inspiring but strict leadership of the remarkable Miss Hersille Oliphant: Miss Meisenheimer, Mrs Baron, Mrs Simon and Mrs Malik. They stayed on long after Independence saw most of their compatriots sailing home. They had made India their *karma bhoomi* (land of devoted duty). There were also a few young Indian teachers, of whom I remember best Mr Kurian and the physical training (PT) instructor, Mr Gaur, who gave me the appellation 'Cotton Wool Baby' because I was so terrible at PT and all other sports.

While I was all thumbs at games, and thus the object of derision of most of the boys, what saved my honour and gave me some social standing in the school was my ability to construct cricket stories out of my imagination and provide a running commentary. The stories usually had my classmate Mansur Ali Khan Pataudi, better known as 'Tiger' Pataudi, in a stellar role. He went on to become one of India's best-known and best-loved cricket captains. We shared the same dormitory with about a dozen others.

One of our dormitory mates was Preminder Maliah, whose claim to fame was that he had seen Kishore Sahu's Hindi version of *Hamlet*. After lights out, he would regale us with stories of Hamlet's friends calling out from the ramparts as the clock struck midnight: '*Arre, Aamlette, Aamlette, tere baap ka bhoot!*'[2] At which we would cower in our bedclothes shivering with fright until someone called for my imaginary cricket commentary.

One episode from the real cricket field remains etched in my memory. Tiger's father, the nawab of Pataudi, who had captained one of India's first cricket teams to tour England, visited his son at school and entertained us on the main field. Lined up on the embankment, we would call out for a four and sure enough the next ball would be smacked to the boundary. Then we would call for a six and the ball would soar into the sky and fall far beyond us. We were bewitched at this display of cricketing legerdemain. Tragically, just about a year later, the nawab suffered a heart attack on the polo ground and was dead before anyone could rush to help him.

I also fared well in writing 'compositions', as essay writing was known. When I visited the school more than half a century later, as chief guest for their Founder's Day celebration, the principal, Mrs Gunmeet Bindra, retrieved my first-ever piece to appear in print, in issue no. 12 of the *Welham School Magazine*.[3]

My youngest brother, Mukundan, was put into the school before he had quite celebrated his fifth birthday. Another boy of the same age had also

---

[2] The line is virtually untranslatable. '*Aamlette*' is Hindi for 'omelette'. This is what makes the Hindi rendition of 'Hamlet' so funny. And '*Tere baap ka bhoot*' only means 'Your father's ghost' but is idiomatically hilarious in Hindi. Scan the QR code on p. 43 to find out more.

[3] Reproduced on this book's website. Details can also be accessed by scanning the QR code.

been put into the school. Missing their mothers, the two of them would cry themselves to sleep in each other's arms. On hearing this, my mother moved to Dehradun and we found ourselves enjoying home-cooked food most weekends. My father too would drive up from Delhi from time to time. On one of these trips, he started back very early in the morning, around 4 a.m., fell asleep at the wheel and crashed into a tree. He was extraordinarily lucky not to have been killed on the spot.

My mother moved back to Delhi in 1951 because, by then, Mukund had been well drilled into school routine. Another factor behind her return was that at long last, the Dalmias, my father's principal clients, had allotted him a commodious apartment above their own offices in Scindia House.

Singular holidays

My father's practice was flourishing and so our holidays at home were often marked by novel experiences. One morning, he suddenly announced that all of us were to fly with him to Bombay. On landing, we were met by a liveried chauffeur and a luxury limousine. My father ignored the driver's overtures to get into the car and instead bundled us into a taxi, asking us where we would like to go. We were unanimous in suggesting Juhu Beach.

The taxi drove us there, but we were intrigued to find the limousine following us. We spent the entire day playing on the beach, with both the taxi and the limousine parked side by side in the shade. When the day's frolicking was done, we were again bundled into the taxi and driven to our usual place of stay in Bombay, Deepak Mahal on Marine Drive, with the limousine patiently shadowing us. On arrival, the taxi driver asked for his fare, which had ticked up to a humongous sum. My father directed the taxi driver to the chauffeur following in our wake and asked him to collect the fare from the chauffeur.

We later learnt this was my father's way of paying back Ramakrishna Dalmia for his insult in sending my father a cheque of Rs 500 for services rendered. Appa had contemptuously sent it back with a note attached on which three letters were scribbled: 'GTH' – Go to Hell! Terrified he might lose my father's irreplaceable advice and assistance on tax matters, Ramakrishna Dalmia had sent the limousine with the liveried chauffeur by way of a gesture of reconciliation. My father's telling revenge for

Ramakrishna Dalmia's act of lèse-majesté was to get him to pay, through his chauffeur, for this picnic.

Dalmia complied because he desperately needed my father's legendary professional skills. But they both came a cropper when the Bharat Life Insurance scandal broke the following year. I knew nothing of the details but my father found it prudent to sell his firm, V. Sankar Aiyar & Co., for a pittance to one of his partners, exit the company altogether and set up as an independent tax consultant. Dalmia went to jail. My father didn't.

The same winter, 1951, my father took the whole family on an Italian liner, the *Ugolino Vivaldi*, on a cruise to Ceylon (Sri Lanka). One of his clients, Pioneer Sports, couldn't remit their dues to my father in India due to the newly independent country's foreign exchange regulations. So, to liquidate his accumulations in Colombo, he took all of us on a quick five-day round of the island: Colombo–Peradeniya–Kandy–Nuwara Eliya–Ratnapura–Colombo, with my mother buying emeralds, sapphires and rubies as if they were marbles.

'Elections' at Welham

We returned to an India gearing up for the first general elections. I was utterly fascinated with the hoardings and posters; the jeeps roaring down the streets, loudspeakers blaring; the crowds that gathered around makeshift platforms and the orators who harangued them; and the colourful processions shouting slogans and singing patriotic songs. I determined that I would organize a mock election in my class at Welham.

All went well until the naughtiest boy, Anand Chakravarti, wrote up on the blackboard: 'Preetinder's Mom and Pop are Commies.' (Preetinder is now emeritus professor of chemistry at the Massachusetts Institute of Technology (MIT). A fistfight followed and the principal, Miss Oliphant, had to step in. The Welham School general elections were countermanded. Democracy at Welham was strangled at birth!

The seed of my lifelong infatuation with elections, win or lose, was laid by this first general election of December–January 1951–52. Through school, college and the Cambridge Union, and well into parliamentary and party elections in later life, if there was an election to be fought, I could not restrain myself from standing, and if I could not stand, avidly following every twist and turn.

My farewell present at the school was portentous. I was only the vice-captain of Ganges Company, but the captain could not be found when the principal announced that our company had won the games shield. So I was invited to stand in for him. It was the start of a lifetime of coming second and rarely first, yet gaining a reputation of being top of the class!

Doon: 1952–1958

I had done extremely badly in the Doon School entrance exam and got in only because Miss Oliphant persuaded Headmaster J.A.K. Martyn that I should be admitted. I was put in Eb/Eb, the lowest sections for both the arts and the maths/science sections. But after listening to me read about the Great Limpopo River from Kipling's *Just So Stories*, the class text, Martyn pushed me up to the 'a' section for the arts.

I never rose above 'b' for maths/science. One half of my brain just failed to develop. This did not faze me. One of my mother's favourite stories of her schooldays was of how she could never work out the time in which a train of such-and-such a length, travelling at so many yards per minute, would take to cross a fixed pole on the side of the railway track. She said she would be so busy conjuring up images of how the train looked, engine hooting, smoke billowing, and whether the sky was blue or overcast, and whether there were plains or hills in the background, that she never got around to solving the simple mathematical problem. I inherited from her my perfervid imagination and my inability to understand science or technology, or solve anything practical or mechanical.

All of us first-termers were lodged in a single dormitory in Holding House, under the benevolent guidance of S.P. Sahi and his French wife. One day, one of the boys hinted at the way we were conceived and the rest pounced on him, saying his parents may do things like that but ours didn't. The fracas ended when Housemaster Sahi intervened and gently explained what was what. I don't think any of us really understood!

If the first general election had fired my imagination, an event in my first term at Doon kept me hooked. We were told we had to gather in the assembly hall after dinner for a 'debate'. None of us eleven-year-olds knew what a debate was. I sat open-mouthed as the speakers took their turn, one by one, at the podium to support or oppose the motion 'This House believes in breaking bounds'. I was fascinated by the rationality of putting forward arguments and rebutting them, as against the fist fights with which arguments had hitherto, in my experience, been settled. I also loved the fact that brains were scoring over brawn.

P. Gopinath, a reputed intellectual much senior to me, who went on to a brilliant career as an international civil servant with the International Labour Organization (ILO), was the star. The cut and thrust of reasoned argument, laced with wit and repartee, has been an obsession with me ever since (throttled only now in my dotage by the inanity of TV debates of the Arnab Goswami kind).

In the next term, the spring term of 1953, my younger brother Jam joined us at Doon. He was not only academically unbeatable; he was also an avid and able sportsman. It took me a while to figure out that instead of being haplessly jealous of him, I would be better advised to simply make his achievements mine by taking pride in them. I have tried almost all my life to follow this golden rule but often failed. After all, how does one, as an elder brother, react when the geography teacher calls for silence in the school assembly to announce that he has awarded Swaminathan 51 out of 50 'because Swaminathan knows more geography than I do'? In comparison to him, I was an indifferent scholar and at sea when it came to any sport, I came into my own only in debating and to some small extent in acting on stage.

One morning, in April 1953, I was getting out of the boxing ring when I spotted a familiar figure waiting patiently. It was my father. He had unexpectedly come to Dehradun on work and had dropped in on the off chance of seeing me before he drove back to Delhi. The school schedule was so tight that I couldn't squeeze out more than ten minutes to spend with him. Little did I know I would never see him again.

Appa's air accident

One day, on the morning of 9 May, I was told to meet the headmaster in his office after assembly. He said I and my brothers (including Mukund, who was at Welham) were going to be escorted by the house captain, Chicky Ranganathan, in a taxi to Delhi for a 'religious ceremony'. Quite delighted at this sudden holiday, we hopped into the waiting taxi with sixteen-year-old Chicky in charge. He tried in vain to suggest that we might on arrival find something amiss. We were too excited to ask for more details.

I was, therefore, astonished to see an army of people sweep us up and swoosh us to our apartment on the third floor of Scindia House where my mother was sitting distraught on a white sheet. It took several minutes for me to gather that 'something amiss' related to my father, and still more time to comprehend that he had been killed in an air crash. It all became starkly clear when I was later led to the ground floor and saw his dead body lying motionless on an ice slab. As dusk fell, we were taken to Nigambodh Ghat where, as the eldest son, I was required to complete the rituals and light the pyre. That is when the horror of what had happened struck me with full force.

I was twelve and my father was no more. It now fell on me to play the role of the senior male. My first duty was to protect my mother. If she rose from her bed at night, I would follow her to ensure that she did not harm herself. My second duty was to my siblings. Jam seemed to have immediately comprehended our new situation but Mukund, at under eight, needed to be gently slipped into it. The most bewildered was my nine-year-old sister, Tara. She was the only one not in boarding school and my father adored her. I think the trauma affected her the most and has lasted a lifetime.

What I did not know was that in the two minutes it took the aeroplane to fall from the skies to the ground, we had gone from being of the family of a highly successful professional to being dead broke. During the Bharat Life Insurance scandal, my father had believed it prudent to rid himself of the ownership of the audit company that bore his name, knowing this would not deprive him of his personal brand name to continue in the profession. So, my mother learnt to her shock from S. Srikrishnan, the dazzlingly brilliant young man hand-picked by my father to head the firm, that apart from Rs 8,000 in my father's bank account, there was nothing else the family could access. We had no further stake in the firm and no other assets.

However, rummaging through his papers in his office, Amma came across a life insurance policy drawn on the London & Lancashire Insurance Co. that Appa had told no one about. It was for around Rs 3 lakh, a princely amount in those days, translating in today's money to about Rs 3 crore. Financially, we were saved. The fly in the ointment was that neither my mother nor my sister would be legally entitled to a penny of this, because they did not belong to the favoured gender under Hindu succession law (which was not reformed until three years later); so, us three boys were declared the inheritors but none of us was anywhere near adulthood. Accordingly, the sum was deposited with the Guardianship Court. Through our lawyer, the genial Sardar Bahadur Sahariya, the estate was put in the charge of my mother and, in return, we boys paid our mother a retainer to look after us!

Meanwhile, we were sent back to school to appear for our end-of-term exams and my mother moved south to stay at my father's ancestral village, Kargudi. She also put Tara into school at Kalakshetra, on the outskirts of Madras. Tara hated being pushed away like this, wondering why losing her adoring father should be compounded by putting her in a residential school thousands of kilometres away from her brothers. My mother relented two years later and brought her back to the bosom of the family, but I occasionally ran into taxi drivers in Madras who remembered the screaming, crying, struggling girl protesting at being dragged to Kalakshetra.

Day scholars at a boarding school

My mother decided she would move bag and baggage to Dehradun and make us day boarders at school. This was partly to save on expenses but mainly to keep the family together. Austerity was the leitmotif since what was available was unstintingly spent on maintaining the humongous expenses on our education. For Amma, education was the biggest asset and debt the evil to be avoided at all costs. Frugality came to her naturally and so for two summers running we had no fans in our flat. We severely restricted outings to restaurants or the cinema. We travelled third class. And we had no 'home clothes'. Our school uniforms served for us during our school holidays.

However, Alankaram *periamma*, who had been away in London when my father died, was an indulgent aunt. She brought back a very posh English bicycle loaded with fancy parts and accessories that was my one luxury through most of my adolescence. I also have a vivid memory of her husband, Uncle Mirza, buying me my first colour-crazy bush shirt. It was in Lucknow on 16 June 1957. I was sixteen and an ardent fan of Dev Anand, and he had worn just such a bush shirt in the hit film *CID*!

Careful readers might wonder from where 'Alankaram *periamma*'s husband' had cropped up. Had he not died six months after they were married, when she was but thirteen years old? Well, in the early 1950s, my aunt had been appointed medical superintendent of the Lady Lyall Hospital in Agra, where we had begun spending holidays with her. A certain Minhaj Ali Mirza, the superintending engineer of the state public works department stationed in Agra, would drop in occasionally.

We learnt from him that he had been sent on technical training to the US in mid-1947. There, he had fallen ill and was hospitalized during Partition. When he finally got back to India, he learnt to his horror that his wife had decamped with their children to Pakistan. He had no intention of migrating there and had thus been a grass widower for nearly a decade before his posting to Agra.

Both in their fifties and aching for companionship, they decided to get married. Uncle Mirza became a great favourite of ours. He was gentle, humorous, very fond of his wife and us, and respectful towards Amma. When we learnt that he was distantly related to the famous cinema playback singer Talat Mahmood, we started boasting to our friends about 'our cousin' Talat, though, as a matter of fact, we never met the singer!

My mother, however, was not happy, not because of Uncle Mirza's religion but because she construed the marriage as her elder sister's one-upmanship, flaunting her new status as a '*sumangali*' (married woman) over Amma's widowhood! But Uncle Mirza soon won Amma over by sheer charm and old-fashioned courteousness.

Amma after Appa

Although she would never have admitted this even to herself, my father's death had liberated my mother from what had been a terrible marriage. This is poignantly revealed in several letters from my aunt to their youngest brother, Pasupati, which my cousin, Kartik Pasupati, found and archived. A short passage should suffice. My aunt had just returned from the West to what she thought would be a family welcome. She was instead confronted with a family breakdown.

10 Feb 1950
Yesterday there was news from Delhi that Bhagyam, with 2 children, had left by a night plane for an unknown destination … When I got back late in the evening, there was a letter to me from Sam at Madras to say that Bhagyam had met him at Madras and that she was on the way to Kargudi. He mentions that she was very unhappy and that is all. Local news [is] that Sankar appeared to be worried about the differences of opinion between him and Bhagyam, and that both were thinking in terms of a possible legal separation. Now you know as much as I do about the drama that I have arrived to see.

16 Feb 1950
Matters are at sixes and sevens. It is difficult to apportion blame, but my reading is that both have been taking a line that is completely contrary to the other and neither is willing to admit being in the wrong. I have not seen or heard Bhagyam's version. It is impossible to forecast the events. I am just drifting – worrying and moping.

This is probably the reason why Mukund was put into boarding when he was not quite five. When my parents were together, verbal fights would break out at the least, or no, provocation. I was embarrassed and deeply ashamed because I thought such parental quarrels were unique to my family. And so I was immensely relieved when in conversation with school friends I discovered that volcanic contests between parents were not that uncommon.

I remember, even now with a shudder, being forced by Appa and Amma to choose between them. One morning, my father cheerfully asked whether Jam, Tara and I would like to accompany him on a night flight to Bombay and beyond. As a 'night flight' was so far missing from our list of adventures, we readily agreed to go with him.

But after Appa went to office, Amma, not to be outdone, told us that she was going to Mussoorie with Mukund, and if we wanted a treat at Hackman's restaurant, we should go with her. Jam and Tara quickly changed loyalties and I was left on my own with Appa. I cried buckets of bitter tears all through the four-hour night flight to Bombay. This despair was compounded when we proceeded further south. My fragile psychological condition was not much helped by my father mocking me to his peers as a 'cry baby'. It was the worst trip I have ever undertaken, the trauma intensifying after I heard of the wonderful time my siblings had in my mother's company.

There were many such episodes. But I think I have said enough to show how my father's passing away opened doors of opportunity for my mother. In fact, although she would never have said so even to herself, Amma was more content with life than ever. True, there were many financial hurdles to overcome as the single mother of four rather expensive children. But she was on her own, quite independent and entirely capable of taking her own decisions.

Moreover, she was quite the toast of Dehradun, which couldn't get over her driving all around town. There was, as far as I can remember, no other lady driver in the whole town. She was also a master at winning the confidence of anyone she thought would be helpful to her and, above all, her children. Such self-confidence in a woman living life on her own created an aura of awe around her. She was elected president of the newly formed Dakshin Bharat Sangh, beating my housemaster, K.N.P. Nair. Moreover, she had complete control over the four of us children and she thoroughly enjoyed that, her chief enemy being any teacher who did not praise her kids!

She also found immense spiritual comfort in Swami Sivananda. As a result, we children were often dragged to the ashram, much against our will. Jam and I hated it and the hypocrisy that surrounded the place, with the rich being favoured and the poor distanced. It drove us both to a lifelong scepticism about godmen and a distaste of anything that smacks of religion. My sister, on the other hand, was differently impacted. She did not quite follow Amma's example but found her solace in a different school of gurus. About Mukund, I frankly don't remember but I suspect he leaned towards his brothers. We also greatly resented having to attend the *bhajan mandali*s (collective hymn singing) Amma organized at home on Saturday evenings.

Notwithstanding this clash of beliefs, I must credit Amma for allowing freethinking in the family. We were never compelled to subscribe to her beliefs, or let her beliefs come in the way of arguments among ourselves. That is how we have become liberals and staunch secularists – albeit with different nuances. Amma enabled us to grow, in the most important sense of the term.

One of the happier consequences of all this ashram-going was a most enjoyable trek to Badrinath, along with a group of Sivananda *bhakt*s (devotees). Our party ranged in age from Mukund who was just turning ten, to an aunt of my mother who, I guess, was in her seventies. This, of course, meant long gaps opened up between the fast-moving younger lot and the slow-moving older lot. We took a creaky bus up to Pipalkoti and from there trekked in three stages – Joshimath, Govindghat, Hanuman Chatti – to Badrinath, our destination. Then Jam and I went one further stage to the edge of the Manas glacier, beyond the last inhabited village before the China border.

At Joshimath, we caught up with a team of Gentlemen Cadets from the Indian Military Academy. We got on famously. Much later that evening, long after darkness had fallen, my mother and her aunt arrived at the dak bungalow in Joshimath. One of the Gentlemen Cadets, Jamil Mohammed, ran up to her, calling out, 'Aunty, Aunty, the boys and Tara are with us.' My mother predicted that day that with his presence of mind, Jamil would go far, having unhesitatingly swept away her anxieties. She was right. Jamil headed the corps sent out to Batticaloa in Sri Lanka with the Indian Peace Keeping Force, among the few units to emerge unscathed from that ill-fated mission. He was serving with the rank of lieutenant general as GOC-in-C (general officer commanding-in-chief), Eastern Command, arguably in line for chief of army staff, when he was killed along with his wife in a bizarre helicopter accident at Haa in Bhutan. Many years later, I walked through the jungle to his memorial to lay a wreath in remembrance of a wonderful, ever-cheerful friend. I keep in touch with his son, Adil, a senior (now retired) army officer.

Life as day scholars

As is inevitable, I have lost the narrative thread. So, let me go back to our rehabilitation after my father's death. Much to our chagrin, the two of us, Jam and I, were taken out of boarding and converted into day scholars, as I have mentioned. My mother arranged to rent a flat on the other side of the *khud* from school, a steep decline from the road level to the dry riverbed of the Bindal and a steep incline from the riverbed to the road above.

We would cycle down the *khud* and across the dry Bindal riverbed at 6 a.m. to get to school in time for PT. The day would last at least twelve hours and often went on later because school society meetings, debates and play rehearsals would take place generally after dinner and we would cycle back home around ten at night through allegedly dangerous neighbourhoods, or '*chakku mohallah*s' (hovel of knives), although nothing untoward ever happened to us.

It was also the time I entered into my first – and last – commercial venture. I had seen an advertisement put out by the *Reader's Digest* seeking volunteers who would secure subscriptions. Subscriptions were at Rs 12 a year; I could retain Rs 5 and send the remaining Rs 7 to their US headquarters by international money order. (The going exchange rate was Rs 5 to the dollar; today (August 2023) it is over Rs 80 and falling!)

In 1954, India was still flush with sterling balances built up during World War II, and there were few exchange restrictions. All I needed to do to send the *Digest* their share of my take was to cycle to the Hathibarkala post office at the top of the road where we lived and send the remittance to Pleasantville, New York. My venture went well – until I ran out of family and friends to inveigle into buying the subscriptions. But, while it lasted, the venture was hugely profitable and great fun to undertake. The pin money contributed to the family expenses. That was small recompense for having crashed the family car into the gatepost while trying to learn to drive.

I was now over thirteen and getting into a difficult period of adolescence. I could not concentrate in class and often told little fibs to cover up my lack of application. Inevitably, this would lead to reprimands. My mother would invariably cushion these reprimands by blaming the teacher, not her son! But I had to shamefacedly confess to our English teacher, Mr Webb (who was from New Zealand) that in listing George Orwell's *Animal Farm* among the books I had read the previous week, I had blatantly lied. I was just showing off.

Yet, although it was long years before I got around to actually reading *Animal Farm*, it was in my very early teens that I started reading a lot and writing too. Our school library was well stocked and my father too had left behind a few very interesting, beautifully bound tomes. Books were the only distraction in the long afternoons we were forced to spend lying down quietly in the hot summer season. We read voraciously but much of it glorified Empire-building by a Britannia that ruled the waves. It was not the underlying politics of these tales but the breathless bravery of boys my age, or a little older, that got me avidly following their adventures.

My most vivid memory is of my siblings and I competitively reading the only copy we had of *Gone with the Wind*; it led to my waking early to get through a few pages before the family awoke and demanded equal time.

I also remember offering to bring my sister Tara back from her school, riding pillion on my famed English bicycle because if I got to her school early, I could resume reading *Gone with the Wind* without being disturbed until the gong went!

The only serious novels I remember reading are *How Green Was My Valley*, a heart-breaking tale of a poor family in a Welsh coal mining town; Kamala Markandaya's *Nectar in a Sieve*, another poignant story of a landless family struggling to survive a terrible famine; and Khushwant Singh's deeply moving *Train to Pakistan*, set in the ghastly time of Partition. I was, however, left cold by Mulk Raj Anand's celebrated *Coolie*, perhaps because of its arch attempts at translating Hindi abuses into archaic English for the benefit of an English-speaking audience (for example, 'Thou seducer of thy sister'!) Maybe, in my old age, I should give *Coolie* another chance.

It was an extraordinary band of teachers who stoked my love of letters: Headmaster Martyn himself, he of the Great Big Limpopo River; R.L. Holdsworth (Holdy), who peppered his teaching of Shakespeare with asides (such as wondering whether Laertes asking that Hamlet's body be carried to its 'untimely bier' meant a beer before 11!); Nolan, also from New Zealand, who introduced us to *The Bridge at San Luis Rey*; Dr S.D. Singh who made me read Conrad's *Lord Jim* (a novel I am still unable to comprehend); S.P. Sahi, whose evocation of Keats' 'Ode to the Nightingale' and Shelley's 'Ode to the West Wind' still reverberate in my head; and the gentle teacher from Ceylon, Vijay Hensman. Legends all.

My biggest regret is that we did not take our Hindi teachers, H.D. Bhatt and others, more seriously. Bhatt was a relatively well-known Hindi short-story writer. I enjoyed his short stories so much that I tried my hand at translating him into English. Unfortunately, the ethos in school was such that Hindi teachers were treated like the French teachers in the Billy Bunter stories. I think our entire generation was rendered unfit for independent India by being steeped far too deeply in English literature, with little Hindi and no Sanskrit. So we find ourselves today enduring the backlash of being trained for Tom Brown's Schooldays than for contemporary India!

I fear the school, despite its good intentions, really succeeded more in turning out excellent managers for British managing agencies in Calcutta and tea estates in Assam, than in rounding us off as good citizens of independent

India. But then, so many Doscos, as we call ourselves, have excelled in professions or vocations requiring the use of Indian languages that, perhaps, it is erroneous to generalize. Naveen Patnaik has repeatedly been elected chief minister of Odisha with hardly a word of Odia in his working vocabulary. And that's also the case with Amarinder Singh as chief minister in Punjab and Kamal Nath in the same post (albeit briefly) in Madhya Pradesh.

However, we were brought up and remained totally secular and free of religious prejudice. After all, our generation grew up under the shadow of Partition. Daily prayers in assembly had a lot to do with this. The songs were eclectic, ranging from the *doha*s (couplets or quatrians) of Sant Kabir to the stirring anthems of Allama Iqbal to the dulcet tones of Rabindra Sangeet, eschewing ritual or any one scripture. There were also poems we learnt by heart, such as thanking the Lord:

For hills to climb and hard work to do
For all skills of hand or eye
For music that lifts our hearts to Heaven
And for the handclasp of a friend

The school, thus, accustomed us to the 'Idea of India' as the inheritor of a broad, plural, multicultural, multilingual, multi-religious civilization.

I believe the school's prayer songs are among the finest collections of 'secular' prayers. A great deal of the credit for that must go to the British teachers who came out from Eton and Harrow, Westminster and Gordonstoun, even as it was becoming clear that the sun was setting on the Empire. They stayed on in Dehradun for the rest of their working lives, indeed some for the rest of their lives, to teach us to become modern Indian citizens, proud of our national heritage but completely eschewing racial prejudice and xenophobic nationalism. Most Doscos are paragons of a secular India.

Getting into trouble

By and large, I succeeded in avoiding getting into trouble. That is, until the prince of Patiala, Amarinder Singh, arrived in school. He had smuggled in Rs 100, a huge sum in that day, as illustrated by the fact that our authorized pocket money had risen from Rs 7 a month when I joined school to just Rs 12 a month when I left – and that too to be paid out by cheque, not in cash, so as to prevent us from breaking bounds!

On the eve of the mid-term break in October 1955, Amarinder handed over his hundred-rupee note to me, as I was a day scholar, asking me to buy him 'tuck' from Hamers, the local department store. Schoolboy's honour, I had to agree. I went to Hamers, ignored the astonished look on the face of the salesman at the quantities I was ordering, and succeeded in slipping the contraband goods into Amarinder's hands.

Relieved that I had run the gauntlet and not been caught red-handed, I was going about my daily grind when the housemaster, the formidable K.N.P. Nair, pounced on me and ordered me to report to him after lunch. Not quite knowing what was in store for me, I wandered into the dining room for lunch when the rumour came floating to my ears that Amarinder had laid out his illegal purchases on his bed and invited everyone to marvel at the mouth-watering treats he would be carrying to his mid-term camp. Word of Amarinder's public exhibition reached the ears of the housemaster, who then strode into the dormitory unannounced. My blood ran cold as I began to perceive the reason for my summons. Amarinder had apparently spilled the provenance of his haul to the ghastly Nair. When I went to him to receive my punishment, the man sadistically said he would let me know my punishment after I returned from the break – thereby making it the worst mid-term holiday I ever had.

In the event, I was given a yellow card – the only yellow card I ever received – a system of shaming the errant boy into mending his ways. Amarinder's escutcheon was stained with an almost perpetual red card, usually issued for such academic lapses as failing to do your homework. And yet, Amarinder has grown into one of our most distinguished Old Boys, having served several times as chief minister of Punjab, and emerged as a noted writer of military histories. Truly, as T.S. Eliot says in *Murder in the Cathedral*, 'our beginnings never know their ends'!

The yellow card did not stop me from accompanying Amarinder on a raid on the fruit trees of his father's estate just behind the school's Rose Bowl amphitheatre. We were not caught, and I salved my conscience by arguing to myself that as the orchard was Amarinder's family property, I could hardly be accused of robbery when he himself had led me into breaking off the delicious litchis and mangoes. (A Janus-faced argument, no doubt, but perhaps that is the moral moment when I embarked on my political career!)

A political awakening

My political awakening happened the following year when I had just turned fifteen. Nasser's nationalization of the Suez Canal, and the Anglo-French-Israeli invasion of Egypt that followed, was the moment of awakening. I followed as best as I could the unfolding of events and became passionately anti-colonial.

This was also when my first Letter to the Editor got published in the *Times of India*. Egypt, in retaliation for the invasion, had closed down shipping through the canal for British, French and, of course, Israeli vessels. This had led to London and Paris kicking up a huge ruckus. I argued in my letter that Britain had closed the Suez waterway to German shipping in the world war – and so who were they to protest Egypt shutting the canal to enemy shipping?

I also became achingly aware that privilege, not merit, determined one's position in society. The school was chock-a-block with the scions of the richest and most powerful. Yet, it was evident that they were being rewarded by destiny for birth, and not really any merit. Yet, it was also true that within the school compound no distinctions of birth or wealth were credited. For example, no one gave a toss that the prime minister's grandson, Rajiv Gandhi, had joined school (in my third year). Without being made explicit, it was ingrained in us that while we were all equal within the school's walls, we were, in some ineffable way, superior to others brought up beyond those walls. This contributed greatly to the sense of arrogance of which all of us were accused.

By the time I left school at seventeen for the wide, wide world, I had become emotionally a dyed-in-the-wool Red. I see now that this was not the consequence of reading Marx before I understood expressions like 'immiserization of the proletariat' but sheer envy at so many of my schoolmates being certain of inherited wealth and position while others, like me, would have to struggle to make the grade. I thus became a very vocal advocate of Revolution even before I appeared for my final school-leaving exam. But at that time I sincerely believed there had to be a better way of organizing society than the inhuman inequality that surrounded one. That is a basic principle that has always influenced my thinking on specifics. It has made me a 'utopian socialist' in the most pejorative sense of Marx's vocabulary.

Thoughts of a career

Now, there arose the question of a career towards which to orient my higher education. Before my father's accident, I had wanted very much to join the air force, principally because I wanted to see other countries. After the accident, the air force was ruled out, but what was the alternative? That is when I came across an article by R.D. Sathe, who was just about the first Dosco to join the freshly minted Indian Foreign Service (IFS) after having seen out World War II as a Madras Sapper.

Sathe's first post after Independence was as consul general to Kashgar, in China's Sinkiang (now called Xinjiang) province. But the following year, in 1948, Kashgar got cut off from our embassy in Chungking by Mao's revolutionaries with all contact between western and eastern China sealed off as Mao beat back Chiang Kai-shek to Taiwan; not only did all communication between the embassy and the consulate cease, the consulate general was also deprived of funds to meet their daily requirements. Sathe innovated a system of buying provisions from Kashmiri traders to whom they would hand over *hundi*s (letters of credit), which the Ministry of External Affairs (MEA) honoured when the traders returned to Kashmir. (When I tried to engage Sathe's accountant on the subject twenty years later, he shook his head in horror and exclaimed Audit were still chasing him to explain why he had ordered two tins of ghee when one might have sufficed!)

When the posting ended, Sathe decided the only safe and reliable way of returning to India in the midst of the Chinese People's Revolution was by trekking from Kashgar to Kashmir. His account of that journey was published in the school's first alumni journal, *Chandbagh*.[4] The travelogue is filled with

[4] The travelogue has been retrieved from the archives and may be seen on this book's website by scanning the QR code on p. 43.

names like Depsang and Shyok river with which all of us have now become familiar as hotspots on the Ladakh frontier with China.

I was transported by this account. If this was life in the foreign service, that is what I wished to be part of. I never wavered in that aspiration despite discovering that long treks are not really part of life in the IFS.

I had gone on a real-life trek to conquer Bakria at 12,480 feet during my last school mid-term holiday in early April 1959 but sadly didn't manage to scale it. We were defeated by rain, sleet, hail and snow:

> Bakria loomed tantalizingly close and the stiffest part of the climb was over. A short walk along the final ridge, a slight climb of 100 ft and we would be on top. But the rain god had different ideas. No sooner had we gone a few more yards than it came down with all the force it could muster.[5]

When we returned to Dehradun from Bakria, I heard at Kwality restaurant, where we were treating ourselves to a final repast, that the Senior Cambridge results were out. We quickly finished our meal and rushed to school. I stayed well away from the noticeboard, in an attempt to fend off what I was sure would be bad tidings. I had scraped through to a first, but my score was abysmal, placing me almost at the bottom of the first-class rankings. But I had crossed the threshold into admission to St Stephen's College, Delhi University.

I applied for a BA Hons in political science because our history teacher, K.B. Sinha, had invited me to deliver my first-ever lecture to the History Society on any subject of my choice. I chose the Naga problem, in part because it was then a hot topic of public discussion but mainly because I had been horrified by the tales of wanton cruelty that my friends at the Indian Military Academy recounted of their first posting as second lieutenants in Nagaland.

It was also in that final term that R.L. Holdsworth, the acting headmaster in Martyn's temporary absence, was persuaded to let us bring out a students' newsletter, *The Suppressed Echo*. Holdy also sportingly agreed to write an introductory piece for the inaugural edition:

---

[5] I wrote up the story of the trek from a retrieved copy of the Doon School *Weekly*. Interested readers will find extended extracts by scanning the QR code on p. 43.

> I know all the authors personally and I know that they have not an atom of malice between them. I hope, therefore, that the censor will be merciful to their early efforts. They are the 'bright young things' of the Doon School. They are not equally expert. The authority on the impressive subject of 'The Freedom of the Press' has never read John Stuart Mill [that was me!].

But as soon as Martyn returned, he put a stop to the venture. He thought our efforts were not laudable, but 'nonsense': school discipline would be subverted.

My solitary school achievement

It was in the same month that I scored the only distinction of my school days: winning the Bakhle Memorial Essay Prize on the subject 'Many men owe the grandeur of their lives to their tremendous difficulties'. I gave the examples of Napoleon at Waterloo; the assassination of Abraham Lincoln; Marie Antoinette and Sir Walter Raleigh; and Robert Scott, arguing that it was only because Wilberforce and Amundsen did not face 'tremendous difficulties' that they did not become household names like these more famous others. I ended: 'Who are we to disturb the beatitudes of historians by the platitudes of philosophers?'[6]

I don't know whether my achievement was underscored or undermined by my younger brother Swaminathan winning the Bakhle Memorial Literature Prize at the same time. After all, he also won the Marker cups for every science subject – physics, chemistry, maths – and, in addition, was something of a star on the playing field. I reminded myself of the promise I had made to myself years earlier, when I saw him race ahead in the cross-country run, that I had either to spend my life envying him or make his victories my own by boasting he was my younger brother. I never succeeded in reacting consistently.

There were, however, two small segments of the extracurricular life in which I could claim a higher place than Jam. One was debating – in both English and Hindi. I became the school debating captain and that stood me in good stead when I went on to St Stephen's, the Cambridge Union and, much

---

6 Reproduced in extenso on this book's website. Readers can also scan the QR code on p. 43.

later, four terms in Parliament. Jam has won his spurs as India's most widely read and, arguably, most influential columnist in economic and business and, sometimes, political affairs. I was also more successful than him in making friends. My friends usually became his friends.

The stage was the other venue where Jam yielded to me. In my last term at school, Deelip Surve, the most dominant personality of our year, played the title role in James Elroy Flecker's *Hassan,* a popular school play as it required a cast of thousands and, therefore, every boy, however hopeless, could be found at least a walk-on role.

The play was made into something of a musical by our music teacher, Mr Deshpande, putting some of Flecker's exquisite poetry to (mostly) lusty Indian music. Hassan, the hero, is a kind of chorus, present on the stage throughout and commenting on the follies of men and monarchs. While Surve played Hassan, I was selected for the role of Rafi, King of the Beggars, who is planning a proletarian revolt against the caliph, Harun al-Rashid (quite in keeping with my evolving political thought!)

The play begins with Rafi being caught and brought in chains before the sultan. Opposite me was Wajahat Habibullah in the role of Rafi's sweetheart, Pervaneh. It was mortifying to proclaim to Wajahat, in front of 350 adolescent boys who could find sexual innuendo in a peanut, 'I would drown Baghdad in blood to kiss your lips again!' The reviewer said, 'Mani, as the King of the Beggars, managed to be dashing, pathetic and heroic in turns.'

It was taken for granted that the Gombar Trophy for best actor would be given to Surve. However, my English teacher and first housemaster, S.P. Sahi, said he had just come from a meeting at which the award was discussed. Apparently, it was generally agreed that I most deserved the trophy, but the final decision was to award it to Surve because otherwise 'it would break his heart'. I accepted the blow but wondered, *What about my little heart?*

Doon School: An assessment

This is, perhaps, the appropriate juncture to assess the experience of school, the positives and the negatives. First, the minuses. Adolescence is a terribly difficult time. And to have to cope with it without the reassurance of a familiar home and friendly parents is challenge enough. Add the army of tyrannical school captains, house captains, prefects and monitors, and one gets an insight into why so many in boarding school are burdened by cowering loneliness. With that mix the agony of those like me who were hopeless at sports, in a stifling atmosphere where brawn was certainly celebrated over brain. And, overlaying it all, the oppressive absence of girls just when all kinds of hormones have started sloshing around one's system!

Then why is it that while most alumni agree that we had 'a rotten time of it', we have such sweet memories, so much nostalgia, so much pride in being Doscos? First, I would credit the outstanding teachers, especially eccentrics like Holdy and the stern headmaster who knew each of us by name and carefully watched over our nurturing; second, lessons in the dignity of labour at Tunwala village and on the campus; third, the assiduous but subtle cultivation of a sense of community that gives us our well-deserved notoriety for snobbishness and conceit but also the self-confidence to take on the world. But most important was the morning assembly where an eclectic collection of non-denominational prayers and songs ranging from Kabir and Allama Iqbal through Rabindranath Tagore and others gave us a lifelong moral compass, an enduring sense of India's diversity and the imperative, therefore, of a broad, inclusive secular, compassionate outlook.[7]

My final plea was (and remains) to make the school co-educational, but, alas, it stagnates, six decades and more after I left, a unisex, Victorian relic!

End of school

After school ended in June 1958, we went up as a family to Mussoorie where a lawyer friend of my mother's (a fraud, as we soon learnt to our huge cost) had found us a small house to live in free for a month. It was to be our first family holiday without any fringes of religion and ritual. It lasted but a few hours. For the lawyer and his client arrived that evening in pouring rain and told us to vacate immediately.

---

[7] The book's website https://www.maverickmemoirs.com/ has two Founder's Day addresses – by the renowned poet Vikram Seth and myself. They show that even though the two of us experienced school in very different ways, our final assessment was remarkably similar. Rudrangshu Mukherjee published both speeches in his second edition of *The Great Speeches of Modern India* (Random House India, 2011). Details are also available by scanning the QR code on p. 43.

My mother and I set out in a thunderstorm to find alternative accommodation. I was taken aback, as we crossed the gate of the posh Savoy hotel to hear her say, 'Let's go in here.' How could we possibly afford that hotel? I had not taken into account my mother's expertise in such matters. At the reception, our clothes dripping, my mother persuaded the receptionist that this was an emergency and whatever the house rules, he must accommodate all five of us in a single room as that was all we could afford.

Having thus smuggled in her brood, she took us to the fearfully elegant dining hall, admonishing us to restrain ourselves to whatever was cheapest in the vegetarian section of the menu. Once seated, she looked around and embarrassed me by rushing up to one of the other diners with a cry of joy. My embarrassment abated when it turned out that the lady and her husband had been friends of the family in Lahore and had continued to prosper after Partition.

Their son, Kuldip Narang, became very warm and friendly after he discovered that I too was waiting, like him, for the interview call from St Stephen's. Once it came, he insisted that I accompany him in his car to Delhi and stay with him in his impressive bungalow on Cavalry Lane on the other side from the college. Unfortunately, I was so belligerent in voicing my socialist convictions that I found myself in frequent arguments with his father. One of these stormy sessions led to my arriving late for the interview.

St Stephen's: 1958–1961

I was made to wait on a bench in the corridor near the bursar's office when Professor Balbir Singh, one of the famed college eccentrics, bustled in to tell me that I had applied for a BA Hons in political science, but they did not have that subject in the college. 'What,' I asked, somewhat insouciantly, 'do you have?' 'Economics,' he replied without taking umbrage. 'I'll take that,' I said.

Any Stephanian reading this today will find the story incredible. These days you have to score over a hundred per cent in your school-leaving exams to even begin to be considered by the college for Eco Hons. In my day, the pedigree of your school mattered more.

I made the grade but wondered how, given that I had scored but a low first in my Senior Cambridge exam. Many years on, Balbir told me that my 'excellent reputation' had preceded me. I never learnt who was the unknown patron who recommended me so strongly.

Class of '61

St Stephen's was a lyrical experience. It is now over six decades since my stint there. Rather than attempt to restore the atmosphere of those days with my fading memory, I base most of my reminiscences of St Stephen's on an essay I wrote for the centenary issue of the college magazine, *The Stephanian*, in 1981.[8] Here are some edited excerpts (with some of the juiciest bits deleted!):

The Class of '61

My first ragging: Chandrashekhar (Shekhar) Dasgupta bearing down on me, 'Do you believe in democracy?' Actually, I didn't but didn't dare say so; so, I squeaked a tiny 'Yes' and watched him thunder on about how it was all a bourgeois fraud.

Dasgupta and Mazumdar (old Muzzy) fed me with the *China Development Review* until I learnt to recite (cooked up) rice production figures with the reverence my ancestors brought to bear on *shloka*s [religious verses]. Even today l remain convinced that Karl Marx pronounced, 'A spectre is haunting Europe . . .' in a definitively Bengali accent.

For a more sober underpinning in political economy, I turned to Nand Kishore Singh (or Pseud Psingh, as his crueller friends called him). His pockets bulging with mimeographs filched from the Planning Commission, a copy of *Encounter* – the definitive symbol of being an intellectual – tucked under his arm, he took me through the paces and gave me large dinners at the Khyber [restaurant] in exchange for worshipful silence.

And, above all, Deepak Lal, frightfully twee but with a giant brain: to match wits with him was like taking a knife to a grinding abrasive. A poor man's Wittgenstein.

---

[8] Those interested, particularly Stephanians of my generation, are invited to read the unabridged article on this book's website by scanning the QR code on p. 43.

There were the endless arguments. We really thought it all mattered, we really believed we could change the world: all that was needed was to understand it.

But it was not all philosophy and politics. There was literature too. I was bowled over by Lawrence Durrell's *Justine* and his translations of the Greek poet Cavafy's poems, 'The City' and 'God Abandons Antony'.[9] Eliot caught our imagination: Prufrock and his coffee spoons; the woman in 'Gerontion' 'poking the peevish gutter'.

There was that wonderful word 'remembrances' picked up from a D.H. Lawrence poem learnt for the Wright Memorial Elocution contest. I won the top prize and wanted to buy Cheiro's *Palmistry for All*. Scandalized, Dr Ghosh summoned me to the staff room and said I was not to be frivolous but purchase something improving. I remained adamant. At which Dr Ghosh glanced furtively around, stuck out his palm and asked if I would read it!

Then there were the debates. My favourite memory is of a pixie from Indraprastha College who saw fit to start reciting Gray's 'Elegy Written in a Country Churchyard' where the entire hall recited along with her the rather hackneyed lines:

Full many a gem of purest ray serene
The dark unfathom'd caves of ocean bear:
Full many a flower is born to blush unseen,
And waste its sweetness on the desert air.

Well, for decades she's been a member of Parliament and one of the most influential members of my party. So the last laugh is on us!

Another cherished memory: Shekhar Dasgupta and I went to Aligarh to debate the subject 'In the opinion of this House, Man should go to the moon'. Speaking against the motion I opened with a line Shekhar suggested: 'Mr President, sir, after having enjoyed the hospitality of your university, I believe Man should not go to the moon: he should come instead to Aligarh!'

---

9 For those interested, the two poems and Durrell's glittering aphorisms are included in this book's website. Scan the QR code on p. 43 to know more.

That led to cat calls; whistling; pandemonium; four-anna coins being thrown on stage; flying kisses. Of course, we won the cup hands down. Twenty years later, I was posted to Karachi. The phone rang and a hesitant voice asked, 'Sir, excuse me, sir, but are you the Mr Aiyar who came to a debate in Aligarh in 1959?'

Another memory. Chirpy (Yogesh Chandra) and I set off to the annual declamation contest at the Military Academy in Dehra Dun. We spotted the two prettiest girls (from Lady Irwin). He snuggled up to one of the girls. On the other side of the aisle, I snuggled up to the other. Fourteen years later, one cold January day in 1973, that one became my wife.

The St Stephen's elections to the college Union revealed both the gory world of chicanery and the glorious world of uncompromising integrity. A day or two after I first joined college, terrified at each monster who descended like an Assyrian wolf to rag me, I was relieved that this giant – Vinod Dikshit – was only asking most politely for my vote that I promised him mine immediately and wholeheartedly. A few days later, along came the rival candidate, Ravi Dayal (Bonzo) with his wonderfully persuasive charm. I crossed the floor. My defection was deservedly punished – Vinod Dikshit won by a mile. In fact, no one I ever supported ever won an election.

And, oh, yes, we did go in for classes occasionally. Dear old Doc Ghosh on Five-Year Plans: 'The Five-Year Plan is a plan for five years. *Samjhe na*?' (Understood?)

There was Thangaraj, whose extraordinary accent, combining Boston with Basavanagudi, tended to make one's mind wander from the Japanese economic history he taught straight out of Lenin: 'Imperialism is the last stage of capitalism.' And Kurian (later economic adviser to the Namboodiripad government in Kerala and a member of the Rajya Sabha) who taught me much of my economics and penned the most eloquent testimonials, about which my tutor at Cambridge rasped, 'Good testimonials, yes, but why must the man write them on pink toilet paper?' Our head of department was Professor N.C. Ray who was so upset when I stole away a first from under the nose of his favourite student that he refused to congratulate me.

But the last thing we cared for were our studies. Life, real life, meant only one thing – girls. Those were the days when we devoted our energies and attention to that pinnacle of all sexual achievement: the purchase of two cups of coffee!

Another incident and I am through. A bosom friend, the notorious Vinod

Suri, got into trouble with a fellow Stephanian called Chaudhry. Chaudhry hired someone to drive past the two of us on a scooter and slap us hard. By the time we returned to college, we found ourselves college heroes, especially among the college toughs who threatened to bash up Chaudhry when he came to college next day. This threat was carried to Chaudhry.

Next morning, as I was at my very early morning study session, a shadow fell across my table. A human gorilla entered, thumping his chest and saying, 'I, Kapoor, Sabzi Mandi. If a hair of Chaudhry's head is touched, you'll pay for it.' I protested, 'Look, I have nothing to do with the revenge that the college *dada*s (toughs) are seeking.' But, insisted Kapoor, would I at least apologize to Chaudhry? Despite the obvious physical danger of refusing, I replied, 'No, I just don't like the man.' Kapoor responded, 'I don't either. So let's shake hands. And any time you want someone beaten or killed, just let me know, Kapoor *dada*, Sabzi Mandi.' Happily, I have had no occasion to take him up on that gracious offer!

There were six of us lying in the sun one December afternoon. Someone asked, '*Yaar* (a common Hindi expression for "friend"), after you leave college what do you want to do?' Five of us answered, 'Join the foreign service.' And all five of us are now in the foreign service.

Which tells us all we need to know about what is right with St Stephen's – and what is wrong with the country. A random selection of five, competing with several hundred thousand others, and all five of us emerging successful: it shows how narrow is the economic and social base in India. It also shows how narrow are the horizons of our ambitions.

In a parliamentary democracy, bureaucrats only run things; it is the politicians who rule. But there are virtually no Stephanians in politics. By keeping out of the fray, we have perhaps ensured that we will neither dangle from the hangman's noose nor be shot at dawn – but do we risk going down in history as The Group that strangled itself in red tape?[10]

That was forty years ago. Alas, we have moved into an age where virtually no Stephanian even appears for the civil services exam and politics remains as bereft as ever of Stephanians. The ethos of the college has also changed.

---

[10] The reference to 'The Group' is from the title of a famous novel by Mary McCarthy on a group of women in a US college. More on my rip-roaring years at St Stephen's is available at this book's website, which can be accessed by scanning the QR code on p. 43.

In September 1960, at the start of my third year in college, I went to the flea-bitten Capri cinema in Dehradun to watch *The Bachelor of Hearts*, about a young German undergraduate at Cambridge. Emerging intoxicated with the incredible beauty of the university but, more so, with its apparent bevy of nubile young women, I became determined to get to Cambridge after my own graduation.

During the Christmas break, I bought myself a sheaf of aerogrammes and assiduously wrote to every college at Cambridge and Oxford that I had heard of, seeking admission. Several of these colleges did not even exist! And most did not care to reply. Of those that did, all but two said they had no place. The two that did not reject me outright were both at Cambridge, Caius (pronounced, in the meaningless way the English have, as 'Keys') and Trinity Hall. They both stipulated that I might write to them again if I got a first in my upcoming BA Hons exam.

A first?! What an impossible ask from someone as casual about academics as I was. Nevertheless, either I would lose the Cambridge houries or I had to get a first. And so, I buckled down to it, even forgoing my daily shave to save time. I gave up all debating and acting, but I did make the occasional contribution to the undergraduates' satirical journal, *Kooler Talk*, that lasted for several decades after we left. Asked to write a reminiscence for *KT* on its silver jubilee, I began: '*KT* was founded by Sarwar Lateef, Peter Philip and Montek Singh Ahluwalia. And if you've spotted that they were a Muslim, a Christian and a Sikh, you are no Stephanian.'

I devoted myself to preparing to follow in the footsteps of *The Bachelor of Hearts*. I also discovered a personal eccentricity. I could not keep my eyes open after dinner, but I could wake up early. So, while the others were raising Cain, I would go to bed, and while the world slept, I would wake at 4 or 5 a.m. and devote myself to revising my lecture notes and reading recommended texts.

Moreover, I invented a way of summarizing arguments in favour of any proposition with an acronym formed by the key letters of the arguments. I did the same with the arguments against. So about a dozen letters, easily learnt by rote, took care of all that could 'be carried in one small head'.

I also discovered that to keep a clear head I had to give myself over to pleasant distractions like P.G. Wodehouse in the hours just before the exams.

This meant that as we walked to the exam hall, my tense companions would be struggling with last-minute mugging while I would be bursting into little peals of laughter as zero hour approached. This, I later learnt, had a most demoralizing effect on the competition. I, on the other hand, felt on top of the subject as I took on each of the eight papers. I particularly enjoyed rising to the challenge of the essay topic, 'The Concept of the Margin', on which I poured out the distilled essence of what I had learnt of the 'dismal science'.

There was only one moment of profound anxiety. I remembered after I had handed in one paper that I had forgotten to enter my roll number. To my intense alarm, the invigilator would not return my answer paper for me to do so. Fortunately, he relented. I heaved a sigh of relief. I had done well, I felt, but would I get the coveted first?

A Calcutta interlude

My final exams over, I took myself off to Calcutta for my first adult holiday. My college friend, Vinod Suri, had landed himself a job with the Imperial Tobacco Company, which paid him the enormous salary of Rs 2,000 a month, besides a huge flat in tony Middleton Row, just behind posh Park Street. He promised a good time for all at his expense. He was as good as his word and we went around the cinemas, tea rooms, restaurants and bars. The song of the season was: 'I've kissed some girls of Naples, I've kissed them in Paree/But the ladies of Calcutta do something to me.'

As for the return journey to Delhi, Suri said the travel department of his company would take care of the booking as he himself would be travelling with me in the same train – albeit by first class AC. Typical of him, he did not disclose to me that the travel desk had told him they could make bookings only for close female relatives of ITC executives. So he had casually told them he needed the booking for his sister.[11]

When we fetched up at the station, I was horrified to find that I had been booked into the ladies' compartment under the name of 'Miss Suri'. There was

[11] For other tales of Vinod Suri, the most disreputable friend I've had, please see this book's website by scanning the QR code on p. 43.

no alternative to getting in and braving it out. The other ladies, of course, kept looking at me askance and whispering among themselves. The train lurched forward and picked up speed. The conductor fetched up and demanded to know what I was doing in the reserved ladies' section. The ladies around were agog with the expectation of an unfolding scandal. I decided that whipping up indignation was my only way out. Raising my voice, I said, 'My mother is German and has given me the German name Mitz. You bloody railway-wallahs always spell it as "Miss". Find me another seat and I'll move. But this is all your fault, not mine!' The conductor retreated. The mood altered and cheering broke out.

The ladies loudly insisted I could remain as the fault was entirely that of these useless railway officials. It was one of my pleasantest journeys, with the ladies sharing with me the delectable eatables they had brought on board. I discovered the lady next to me, Romola Ray, a teacher at Loreto College, Calcutta, was going to London that autumn for further studies, and as I was hoping to also go to England, that made for a strong bond as the train chugged its thirty-six-hour way to Delhi.

In early June 1961, soon after I returned to our home in Dehradun from my holiday in Calcutta, the results were published. Jam was staying in Delhi with a cousin, who kept shouting on the phone that I had 'passed', drowning out Jam's voice excitedly saying I had not only 'passed' but got a first and stood first in the university, way ahead of the only other person – Eliamma Mathew of Miranda House – to score a first.

I could barely believe what I heard. But I jumped on my bicycle – the 'English luxury' – and caught up with the *tonga* (horse-driven carriage) in which my mother was trotting along to the market to give her the good news. Now all that remained was to inform Caius and Trinity Hall that it was time for them to fulfil their end of the bargain. Caius replied that they had pledged the seat to another Indian student (they hadn't). Then, on 12 July 1961, Trinity Hall wrote in to say that they were ready to take me. I floated on a cloud.

The best available sailing was Anchor Lines' SS *Cilicia* but on being contacted they said they only had single accommodation cabins left; my mother, in a spirit of 'in for a penny, in for a pound', decreed that her eldest would sail in style, and I found myself all of a twitter getting foreign exchange sanction for £600 a year, a passport and visas for Karachi, Aden and Egypt, which were our ports of call. I also received a £5 gift from my aunt along with a cheque for a similar amount that I was to encash at her bank in Chelsea. In addition, I had a letter of introduction from a family friend, Dewan Harish Chand, a renowned homoeopath, to his sister in the accounts department of our High Commission in London. This was to prove the most valuable of the gifts I was carrying.

But first I had to visit St Stephen's to collect my kudos. Sarwar led the applause in the dining hall when I entered. But when I got to Doc Ghosh, he shook his head in disbelief and said, '*Tujhe kaise yeh first mila? Tum toh ladkiyon ke peechhe Coffee House bhagte the!*' (How on earth did you get this first? You used to run after the girls in the Coffee House!) But he, nevertheless, had the grace to congratulate me in a somewhat bewildered manner.

It was worse when I reached out to my head of department, Dr N.C. Ray. 'You didn't deserve it,' he thundered. 'Arun (Shourie) should have got it, not you.' He then turned his back on me, spurning my proffered hand.

I wrote about this twenty years later in the centenary issue of *The Stephanian*. When I visited the college on Founder's Day, Dr Ray was fuming. 'You have insulted me,' he charged.

'How, sir,' I innocently asked, 'have I insulted you?'

'You said I did not shake your hand when you got your first.'

'You didn't,' I smoothly replied, 'but here it is' – and received my due twenty years late!

And so ended my sojourn at St Stephen's – an unforgettable learning experience where I made many lifelong friends, but, alas, no girlfriends. That, inshallah, would happen in Cambridge!

See detailed footnotes and endnotes by scanning the QR code above.

2

Cambridge

1961–1963

Sailing to England

My mother and I went by train to Bombay. I boarded SS *Cilicia* and found myself standing next to an utterly subdued character. I had been introduced to him and his parents on the dock. He had merely nodded his head in a distant manner. As the ship shuddered and set sail, the figures waving farewell to us from the shore grew smaller and smaller. Suddenly a voice demanded, 'Do you think the bastards can see us?' 'I don't think so,' I replied. At which he casually pulled out a pack of cigarettes from some hiding place and, lighting one up, invited me to a drink at the bar. I got the impression that he didn't emerge from the bar until we docked at Liverpool. But before you laugh, note that he went to become one of the most well-known advertising executives in India!

Barely had we had lunch (from an incomprehensible 'continental' menu) when the ship began to lurch and heave. I took to my bunk until we reached Karachi some thirty-six hours later. Thereafter, either the sea got calmer or we had discovered our sea legs, but I certainly enjoyed the journey to Aden more. By the time we got to Suez, we were all seasoned sailors.

Some of us took the tour to the pyramids, where my most vivid memory is of being put on a pair of camels called Whisky and Soda. We then headed to Port Said and caught up with our fellow passengers at a sleazy nightclub, where the principal dancer was the spitting image of Jacqueline Kennedy.

Somebody – I rather think it was I – made the mistake of saying so a little too loudly, and a hulking American seaman rolled up at our table threateningly: 'You're talking about our First Lady.' We apologized, cut and ran.

On board were two friends from St Stephen's, Hindal Tyabji and Jitendra Daulet Singh, and my classmate from Doon, Harprit Singh Sandhu – who was going further, to the US. I also made friends with an East Pakistani, Huq Chowdhury, who gave me a glimpse into the concerns of the Bangladeshis that were to boil over in the years to come.

A lot of time was spent hanging out with a young thing from Kenya, Kokila. There was a Sindhi lady from Bombay who said I could make some pin money by writing about my adventures in Cambridge in her magazine. And there was a Dr Prem and his British wife, settled in England for many years, who were returning home after their annual vacation in India. The steward who was busy organizing passenger concerts, had some fun at Kokila's expense: as she spiritedly sang the 1950s' hit song 'I've got a lovely bunch of coconuts', he interjected, 'Here, have a banana.'

I spent a lot of time writing my diary (alas, since lost). My big find in the ship's library was the autobiography of a leading English lawyer and later judge, Gerald Sparrow, *Not Wisely but Too Well*. He had not only graduated from Trinity Hall but also become president of the Cambridge Union, my own overarching ambition!

As we arrived at the placid lake they call the Mediterranean Sea, the daily news bulletin circulated on board informed us that Dag Hammarskjöld, the Swedish secretary-general of the United Nations (UN), had been killed in a freak accident when his plane crashed in the Congo. It made for heated discussion among us.

The more leftist-inclined like me trotted out theories that the Americans must have been behind it, as they had connived in Moïse Tshombe murdering Patrice Lumumba to capture mineral-rich Katanga, practically owned by Belgian conglomerate Union Minière, in which the Americans had huge investments. Others insisted it was just an accident.

We stopped at Gibraltar in the middle of the night, so my first glimpse of Europe was of Portugal from the sea; we docked at Liverpool at dusk on a grey, damp October evening. Next day, we disembarked after twenty-one days at sea, with me hanging on to a pack of two hundred Churchman's cigarettes that it was de rigeur to buy duty-free. It was on the ship that I had fallen to peer pressure and started smoking. I promised myself I would stop as soon as these two hundred fags were over, but it took fourteen years to shake the habit.

Exploring London

I took the train to London, worrying all the way, since I had been warned that there were no coolies in London. Happily, I found a porter to haul my steel trunk into the taxi. I was then driven, still nervous, to the Indian Students' Union on Fitzroy Square, and met the warden, a man with the extraordinary name of Dr Schwarz Malaiperuman.

Next day, I went to the High Commission's accounts department on Jermyn Street armed with my letter of introduction from Dewan Harish Chand to his sister, a charming lady who invited me to dinner saying I should meet her son, Jagdish Krishan Kumar, who would be going up to St John's, Cambridge, with me. Krishan and I hit it off immediately and became lifelong friends. That is why I described Harish's letter as the most precious gift I carried to England.

There still being a couple of days to go before my date with destiny at Cambridge, I idled the hours away at India House, where I ran into R.K. Narayan and rather stupidly said, 'You're very famous,' to which he mildly replied, 'Really?' I also met up with Mohan Singh of All India Radio and we went together to see *My Fair Lady* at the Drury Lane theatre. I just loved it. I still do. I also dropped in on an acquaintance at the Tamil section of the BBC in Bush House, who offered to help me render into Tamil brief accounts of life at Cambridge that he would then have me record for broadcast on the BBC's Tamil service. He said he would pay me £5 per programme – an enormous and quite unlooked-for bonus.

After hopping on the bus to King's Road, Chelsea, to find the bank at which I was to encash my aunt's cheque, I walked myself to exhaustion on that long street before I reached the right branch. The manager saw the signature and remarked, 'Oh! The Indian lady with the platinum blonde hair! I remember her well. Do give her my regards.' And I walked out £5 the richer.

Deepak Lal, my *ami de coeur* (bosom buddy) from school and St Stephen's, returned from his favourite occupation of gazing at stained glass in the cathedrals of Italy and invited me to join him and his friends at the New Punjab restaurant on Goodge Street. I found it easily because we had been brought up on a diet of Monopoly, and I was familiar with key place names in London!

Deepak squired me round the cinemas and theatres of what we had been taught was the greatest city in the world. We watched the Italian new wave films *La Dolce Vita* and *L'Avventura,* which I barely comprehended, and a matinée of Albert Finney in *Luther*, of which I understood even less, before he saw me off to Cambridge at Liverpool Street station. Later, he wrote long letters explaining the import of what he had shown me, thus beginning the process of 'civilizing' this small-town hick, me. I stopped even trying to acquire culture after gaping uncomprehendingly through two long hours of *Last Year in Marienbad.*

Cambridge at first sight

At Cambridge, the cab dropped me off at the Porter's Lodge at Trinity Hall in a tiny alley tucked behind Caius. I was much relieved when the porter said he would have my luggage taken to my rooms on B staircase but before I went there would I please drop in on the senior tutor who was waiting for me.

The genial Graham Storey beamed a warm welcome and bade me sit down. I thought I had better score some brownie points immediately to get off to a good start and so, referring to the principal of St Stephen's who had spent the previous year at the Hall, said, 'Mr Rajpal sends his regards.'

'Who?' said Storey.

I then remembered the man had changed his name when he returned to India.

'Sorry, I meant Mr Ramsden. He's changed his name.'

'Well,' responded Storey, 'I do hope you give a better account of yourself than he did.'

There fizzled out my brownie point.

I found my way to my staircase. It didn't take long to unpack my meagre belongings after which I fumbled my way down to the Front Court. There were two subcontinentals standing there looking a little forlorn. We introduced ourselves. One was Jamshed Hamid. The other was Khurshid Kasuri, exquisitely turned out in a beautifully cut three-piece suit and an expensive overcoat. A bond was created when I said I was born in Lahore, Khurshid's hometown. Many, many years later – fifty at least – Khurshid was to confide in me that the reason he had walked up to greet me was that he had never before met a Hindu! He had picked, I told him sourly, a rather poor example. A gong sounded and we filed into 'hall' together (Cambridge jargon for 'dinner'). As I worked my way through a tasteless piece of unspiced meat and boiled vegetables, little did I know that my first meal in Cambridge was in the distinguished company of the man who was to become the best foreign minister Pakistan has ever had!

Next morning, there hove into my presence the bedder. 'I'm Mrs Strangward,' she announced, 'and they put overseas gentlemen on B staircase because I'm very good with overseas gentlemen.' I froze. Mrs Strangward disapproved of everything. She also scolded like a schoolmarm while she efficiently dusted and swept, tidied things up and made our beds (hence, 'bedder'). Some months later, she burst into my rooms saying, 'Mr Hamid is dead.' I rushed around to Jamshed's rooms and found him lying perfectly still. Alarmed, I tentatively picked up the *razai* (duvet) that covered his face. An eye, just one, opened and in a hoarse whisper he asked, '*Chudail chali gayi hai kya?*' (Has the witch gone?) Actually, Mrs Strangward meant well and hid a kindly heart behind a prickly mien. A real rough diamond.

My first few weeks were lonely. The young Englishman is reserved and shy. My first British friend was a Methodist, Sean Monahan, whose mother had adopted a boy of Indian origin. That emboldened him to reach out to me. Through him, I met others, but the group that attached itself to me was a set of devout Christians who kindly took me to see the Ely Cathedral, but soon realized their interests weren't mine.

Sean was keen on taking me to the Sunday service, but I made a bargain. I would accompany him to church only if he accompanied me to the Marxist Society. We went to his church where the sermon was on the biblical text 'Strait is the gate and narrow the path that leads to Heaven.' Sean looked quite shamefaced as we emerged from the service. He kept his part of the bargain and we went together to the next meeting of the Marxist Society where the speaker waxed eloquent on the patent lie that there was total freedom of worship in the Soviet Union. This in the forum named after the philosopher who had proclaimed 'Religion is the opium of the masses'! It was my turn to emerge shamefaced.

I also found that in deference to some strange Christian tribal belief, only fish was served in hall on Fridays. I took one look at the trout that was placed before me and blanched; its beady eye was reproachful and I just could not bring myself to slice it. I left the table hungry and went to find Krishan. He suggested we sate ourselves at an Indian restaurant. There was one quite close to his college and it had a fixed menu at 6 shillings. Affordable – just about!

I tried out my little Urdu on the waiter. He looked bewildered. I later discovered why the waiter couldn't understand my feeble attempts at Urdu: almost all 'Indian' restaurants in England (at the time) were set up and run by Sylhetis from East Pakistan who proudly spoke only Sylheti besides a few words of pidgin English. It was a discovery West Pakistanis were also making – and they would pay the price ten years later.

Krishan and I decided to meet at one of these restaurants every Friday. Occasionally, Krishan, who had been brought up in England and spoke English like a native, would bring along a friend. These included Richard Kuper from South Africa who hated the apartheid regime and had no desire to return to the land of his birth; a Buddhist vegetarian, Stephen Broido, who spent a great deal of his time in meditation; a brilliant art historian, Tim Clark; a public school communist, Jim Hinton, whose privileged past had instilled in him, as in George Orwell, a hatred for the class to which he belonged; and Tim Lankester, who was sharing digs with Krishan (Cambridge jargon for lodgings outside college) and who would later head the London School of Oriental and African Studies and be the Master of Corpus Christi College in Oxford besides working for a spell in Delhi with the World Bank. Of course, he was knighted.

Cambridge Union

Much of my time was spent at the Union. I joined the snaking queue to attend the traditional opening debate of the Michaelmas (pronounced, in that bizarre English way, as 'Mikkelmas') term – 'This House has no confidence in Her Majesty's Government' – and barely managed to squeeze into the chamber. I was transfixed. The level of the arguments and the rapier wit on display were superior by far to anything at Delhi University. I so wanted to make my debut that from my far corner (standing room only) I kept raising my hand to catch the president's eye but was lucky not to be called as I knew nothing of British politics.

But I persistently attended both the formal Tuesday debates, where there would be distinguished politicians or commentators, and the more informal Thursday debates just among the undergraduates. It exposed me to the Union and the Union – which was quick to spot regulars – to me.

I was the only leftist to speak in favour of allowing the Cambridge University Conservative Association (CUCA) to hire the Union chamber to listen to Oswald Mosley, the British Blackshirt fascist. My point was the same as Voltaire's. Free speech required us to give the floor to opinions we hated.

I participated in several debates and got sufficiently known to the aficionados to file my candidature for the Standing Committee at the end of my first term. I was not elected but was well ahead of others in their first or second year. The Marxist Brian Pollitt, son of Britain's Stalin, Harry Pollitt, who was the toast of the Union, assured me that I was bound to get elected by the end of the academic year.

The end-of-term elections of the office bearers to the Union were shaping up to be the most controversial since the Oxford Union debate in 1933, the year Hitler came to power. Then, the House had resoundingly voted for the motion 'This House will in no circumstances fight for its King and country' – a result, it was popularly claimed, that led to Hitler concluding that Britain would not go to war against Germany. The widespread interest generated in the outcome of this Cambridge election reverberated well beyond the closed confines of the Union.

An American, Barry Augenbraun, was pitted for the post of president against the incumbent vice president (VP), Brian Pollitt of King's College. Brian was standing on an avowedly communist platform. Tensions ran high as the Cold War had a few months ago reached its freezing point with the building of the Berlin Wall and President Kennedy declaring, '*Ich bin ein Berliner*' (I too am a Berliner) – although it was wickedly whispered that in idiomatic German his words meant 'I am a hamburger'!

In the UN Security Council, Khrushchev had taken on the West, stunning his audience with the claim 'We shall bury you', which the Pollitt camp indicated might be the first subject taken up for debate in a Pollitt-run Union. There was an unprecedented turnout. The counting took place in an atmosphere of rising suspense, with the two candidates racing neck and neck until it was announced the American had won – and Western capitalism was saved.

Within hours, Pollitt had written to the proctors alleging sharp practice on the part of Augenbraun. He was able to establish the American had sat in the buttery of his college, St John's, facing the Union building, and signed a number of chits for mugs of beer on his account; consequently, there was a disproportionate rise in the number of St John's voters casting their ballots in the last half-hour before the polls closed.

The proctors set up a select committee of six of the Union's senior office bearers, including four life members, dons and distinguished public figures who were senior members of the university. (At Cambridge, you never 'leave' the university; you continue as a member of the university even after graduation, whatever else you may do.) The select committee unanimously held that Augenbraun was, indeed, guilty of breaching the Union's laws and invalidated the declared result, besides barring him from standing for elections for at least three terms. This judgement was received glumly by right-wingers of the Michael Howard variety. Michael, now Baron Howard, later became leader of the Conservative Opposition and has always challenged the decision of the proctors' committee, in my view quite mistakenly.

Then Pollitt proved how English he was. He decided not to contest again and put off his bid until the end of the Easter term the following year. It had been a most stirring photo finish and I was proud to be counted among his men. John Gummer, a Tory, became president and later a minister under Thatcher.

Brian Pollitt's closest friend was Rahul Khushwant Singh, also at King's. Rahul was president of the Cambridge India Society. Once, he got Kingsley Martin, renowned editor of the *New Statesman*, to address the Society. Getting him as a speaker was quite a feat as Martin was something of a hero for us since his socialist news magazine had staunchly supported independence for India. The following day, I was wending my way to an early morning lecture and was astonished to see an unmistakable head of white hair bobbing along King's Parade in the freezing cold. I caught up with Martin and asked what he was doing so early in the morning. With a twinkle in his eye, he replied,

'I'm always up early when I visit Cambridge, to come here and watch the blue knees of the girls cycling in from Girton flash past me!'

Rahul's pièce de resistance was bringing Peter Sellers to the India Society. It caused a wave well beyond the small Indian student community. The demand for tickets was so great that Rahul had to hire the debating chamber of the Union to seat everyone who wanted to attend. The financial intake was enough to entirely retire the outstanding debt accumulated by the Society over the years.

Peter Sellers began by saying he would not be making a speech but would answer questions. The first – and, as it turned out, the only question – to be asked was whether after playing a prudish Indian doctor in *The Millionairess* with Sophia Loren, he would play a lecherous one in another film. Sellers kept the gathering in splits for the best part of an hour, recounting one hilarious episode after another, putting on an astonishing variety of accents and vouchsafing the professional secret that Sophia Loren knew no English and had to be coached every few minutes to learn her lines by rote.

Supervisors (tutors) and other mentors

As Trinity Hall had no economists among its Fellows, and I was the only undergraduate reading economics, I was found a director of studies in distant Churchill College, then a collection of prefab huts on the outskirts of the university. I had to get to Churchill, on cycle or on foot, in the biting cold that overtook us by Guy Fawkes Day (5 November).

My supervisor for economic theory, the main paper, was the most colourful Dr Frank Hahn. Hahn had this patronizing habit of calling me and my supervision partner, the New Zealand Shell scholar John (Jock) Milne, 'children'. Hahn was a martinet, unsparing in his criticism, often asking Milne and me how we had been let into Cambridge in the first place. When he set me to read a Canadian economist, Harry Johnson on 'Reciprocal Tariff Curves', I was thrilled at having, I thought, fully understood the argument. I put down what I had learnt and arrived expectantly for the supervision. 'What makes you think,' Hahn began, 'that you are any less bright than a fat, cigar-chewing Canadian?' He had unerringly spotted that I had swallowed Johnson whole without applying my mind or my critical faculties. I realized how inadequate had been the learning by rote and mnemonics that had served me well at

St Stephen's, but I was far too occupied with climbing the greasy pole at the Union to mend my academic ways.

On one occasion, I walked into Hahn's study wearing my school Old Boys' blazer. He looked up disapprovingly and, pointing to the badge on my breast pocket, asked censoriously, 'What … is that?' I proudly replied, 'That, sir, is the Lamp of Knowledge.' Quick as a flash came his retort: 'A pity they didn't light it while you were at school.'

Milne and I somehow survived. In the second term, Hahn started suggesting that perhaps Jock and I could be saved after all. Then, in the third term, he set the cat among the pigeons saying, 'One of you will get a first.' Milne and I argued over that in the corridor after that supervision, Jock maintaining that Hahn was referring to me and I insisting he must have meant Milne. In the event, both of us got a 2.1 (an upper second) and moved on to our second and final year.

Hahn was most amused when I asked whether he could arrange supervisions for me with Maurice Dobb, the most well-known communist don at Cambridge (and rumoured, perhaps quite falsely, to have recruited in the 1930s the notorious Cambridge Five). My problem was that my meagre allowance would not permit me to pay for supernumerary supervisions. Hahn offered to find out.

Hahn was as good as his word. I received a brief message dropped at the Porter's Lodge from Professor Maurice Dobb inviting me to his rooms at six one evening. I fetched up to be sternly told that 'Supervisions are to be paid for'; he added, more gently, 'But if you would like to come around for a sherry any Thursday evening around six, you would be more than welcome.' I was in the august presence of the great author of *Soviet Economic Development Since 1917* that had thrilled me at St Stephen's. And here I was going to be seeing him every week. Far better, I thought, than attending futile meetings of the Marxist Society.

But it proved progressively more disappointing. When I asked him about the people of Hungary rising against the Soviet annexation of their country, Dobb blandly replied, 'A socialist country cannot, by definition, be imperialist.' Then, hoping to hear him rebut Ken Berrill's argument that Marx was wrong in attributing the laying of the railways in India to promoting Manchester's commercial interests, I got the impression that Dobb seemed not to have read

Marx's writings on India; he sounded even more floored than I was at Berrill turning Marx on his head and arguing that the timeline of the expansion of the railway network clearly indicated that it was aimed at containing any future armed uprising like 1857. The commercial houses had merely taken advantage of the new infrastructure.

After a while, Dobb remarked that these sherry evenings were going nowhere, and we might as well terminate them. I readily agreed. It was quite a revelation to find that academic gods too can have feet of clay. On the other hand, seeing the high academic regard in which Dobb was held at Cambridge for over fifty years, I have to grant that he probably found my understanding of Marx and the Soviet model of development too shallow to waste more time on me.

There was a young Indian academic, a great favourite of Maurice Dobb's and the only one for whom Hahn seemed to have any respect, Amartya Sen. He had just started teaching at the university after having won a Prize Fellowship and being made a senior scholar for an outstanding critique of Mahatma Gandhi's advocacy of the spinning wheel as the road to economic liberation, *Choice of Techniques*. As the most junior member of the economics faculty, Sen's lecture slot was scheduled at 9 a.m. when most undergraduates were unwilling to venture out into the freezing cold. Nevertheless, his lectures were the most crowded. His exposition of the 'Prisoner's Dilemma', the foundation of welfare economics, was particularly celebrated. Amartya Sen deservedly went on to win the Nobel Prize for economics (in 1998).

He and his wife, Nabaneeta, lived in a small flat on Trinity Street, around the corner from my college. We became friends and I often visited their home. Nabaneeta was effervescent, warm and hospitable, and a noted poet in her mother tongue, Bengali. Sen was more reserved but tolerantly amused with my naïve leftism, my recitation of snatches of T.S. Eliot, my adoration of Lawrence Durrell's *Justine* and my passionate pursuit of politics at the Union. They made a lovely couple, but the marriage did not last long. I did not think it my business to enquire why, but I always regretted the break-up. I maintained my friendship with Nabaneeta until she passed away in 2019.

With Amartya, the boat got a little rocked when, nearly a half-century later, he found himself unable to accept my suggestion that the key to solving the problems of health, education, poverty and social justice – to which he had so successfully drawn the world's attention – lay in entrusting the critical last-mile delivery of public goods and services to democratically elected, effectively empowered institutions of local self-government, the panchayats and nagarpalikas. I was deeply disappointed that one I so admired, and whose endorsement, as a Nobel laureate, would have been invaluable, should find little merit in what, I was convinced, was the only way to combine sound economics with sound administration.

For sociology, I was put in the supervisory care of another Churchill don, Michael Young. There could not have been a happier choice. We hit it off very well. It was only later that I learnt he had drafted the Labour Party manifesto that led to Attlee's upset victory over Churchill in the 1945 election after World War II. He was also something of a pioneer in sociology, a subject that Oxbridge in the early 1960s tended to look down upon as a jargon-filled American fad, rather than a serious academic discipline.

Michael Young went on to establish sociology as a respectable academic discipline and a useful tool for the making of sound policy. He was later knighted and raised to the peerage as Baron Young of Darlington. After I had handed in a couple of essays, he remarked with a twinkle in his eye that I seemed to be both a Marxist and a Freudian!

Short visits to Europe and London

Apart from immersing myself in the Union, I also tried my hand at acting. The Experimental Theatre Group of the university had announced rehearsals for roles in Shakespeare's *Twelfth Night*. I was only given a tiny role in the opening scene but the troupe went to Switzerland and France and I clambered aboard at a nominal price. I thus got to see the Continent for the first time through my acting 'skills' even if I made no impression on the theatrical scene at Cambridge. I also made several friends, at least two of whom – Sam Dastoor, an Indian, and Miriam Margolyes – went on to distinguished careers on the London stage and repertory.

I returned from my theatrical adventure to the coldest winter in Britain in seventy-five years. My lodging in London was a students' hostel called Academy House. Everybody would leave for work or their colleges and I had to find the sixpence required to keep the gas going for half an hour.

The six pennies would add up in quite a short while to a not inconsiderable fortune. So I would go to a nearby restaurant that allowed me to linger for up to three hours during which I would read a book and treat myself to a hot but meagre lunch.

I saw a lot of Krishan in London. We were invited by a common Hall friend, Andrew Medlicott, to dinner with his father, a former national and conservative member of Parliament (MP) who had resigned the Tory whip in 1956 as one of the 'Suez rebels' opposing Anthony Eden's conniving with France and Israel to invade Nasser's Egypt. Addressing the father, Krishan said, 'Sir Frank … isn't it?' And the beatific smile that lit up our host's face showed me I had missed a trick! The conversation turned to the uses and abuses of television, and I railed against the medium. Sir Frank was, therefore, most amused, when after dinner, I was transfixed watching Daphne du Maurier's *Rebecca* unfolding on the screen!

News came in that the Indian army had liberated Goa. I was very upset that, in violation of the tenets of non-violence, we had sent in our army to liberate the last colonial enclave. Krishan took me along to see his brother-in-law, the fiery communist Boltu Sengupta, who patiently played out for my benefit all the arguments that justified the armed incursion. I remained only partially converted but enough to mount a robust defence in one of the university publications against the most absurd argument of them all, that Britain had to take up the cudgels for the Portuguese because they were 'our oldest ally', harking back to Elizabethan times when the Spanish Armada was held back by Drake with the help of the Portuguese.

I returned to Cambridge for Christmas lunch, as my senior tutor had invited me to his country home to listen to the solemn ritual of the Queen's Christmas broadcast before tucking into turkey with all the trimmings.

Cambridge grows familiar

By my second term, I had begun to feel more at home. I had made a number of friends at Trinity Hall, principal among them being James Fulcher and Richard Brown, who introduced me to the joys of pub crawling and climbing over the walls to get in or out of the college without being spotted by the porter.

I also started being invited to 'bird and bottle' parties, which meant that you brought along something to drink (the 'bottle') and a lady companion (the 'bird') as the ratio of men to women at the university, excluding au pair girls at the language schools in town, was about 8:1. The place to go fishing for the latter was the International Centre on Trinity Street.

The university's spanking new Marshall Library had been inaugurated and was a well-heated refuge from the cold. I would spend all my afternoons there, occasionally preparing for my supervisions (Cambridge-speak for 'tutorials') and for speeches at the Union, but most often to devour *Marxism Today*, a journal that fed my native anti-Americanism with all the tales of American iniquities around the world. Perhaps because Cuba had cocked its snook so tellingly at the US at the Bay of Pigs recently, I absorbed much about US excesses in Latin America, becoming something of an encyclopaedia on Cuba's Batista, Jimenez of Venezuela, Stroessner of Paraguay and miscellaneous other tyrants, paragons all of unmitigated political vice.

The Marshall Library tea room was an excellent place to make friends, among whom I counted Amiya Bagchi, a voluble Calcutta communist; Amit Bhaduri, a well-informed leftist economist; and Bimal Jalan, destined to become a highly regarded governor of the Reserve Bank of India. It was also there that my friendship grew with Norman Lamont, now Baron Lamont of Lerwick, a future chancellor of the exchequer with whom I often crossed swords at the Union as he was a dyed-in-the-wool Tory.

There was also the impish Christie Davies, a brilliant sociologist, who specialized in the sociology of ethnic jokes, and had a way with the working class and a special affection for Gujarati entrepreneurs. He once memorably remarked, 'I get on with Indians because they, like the Welsh, are on the fringes of society.' He famously interrupted a pompous reactionary speaker at the Union who was railing about tiny countries having the same vote as the ones with large populations with the innocent observation, 'I think, sir, I see a Chink in your argument!' It brought the house down.

Seeking romance

On the romantic front there was little progress. I had scanned *Varsity* to find a public dance to go to my first Saturday after coming up. It was easy enough to get there but much more difficult to actually build up the courage to ask an unknown girl for a dance. So I stood nervously on the edges of the dance floor watching others boldly walk up to girls they didn't know and ask them to take a turn on the floor.

After a long while, I took the plunge. The young woman was courtesy itself. Dances were limited to three minutes, the time it took to play a 45 rpm record. Our three minutes over, she demurely said, 'Thank you very much,' and I escorted her back to her place where, within minutes, someone else asked her and she went whirling off. There was a Pakistani standing next to me who had taken an amused view of my valiant initiative. '*Waqt kyon zaya karte ho, yaar?*' he asked. '*Woh toh chalegi nahin!*' (Why are you wasting your time, my friend? That one won't work!) There and then I learnt that there are uses to Indo-Pak collaboration!

On my very last evening in Cambridge, two years later, I crashed a party and there, sitting on a couch right in my line of vision, was the same young woman. She smiled and said, 'I've been following your career with interest.' I was no longer the diffident undergraduate of my first dance. I swept her up in my arms and told her that as she was the first girl I had danced with in Cambridge, she would also be the last. An extraordinary coincidence that I would not have believed if it hadn't happened to me!

A Scandinavian adventure

I stood again for the Union's executive committee at the end of the second Lent term and found, as predicted by Brian Pollitt, that I had risen several rungs on the ladder even if I was not elected. The incoming president for the Easter term, Michael Howard, put me down for a 'paper speech' in a Thursday debate for the Easter term, which meant my name would be on the order paper. It was acknowledgement that I was 'up and coming'.

Pleased at my progress, I took myself off during the Easter vacation on a hitchhiking trip to Germany, Denmark and Sweden. I called it my 'Academy House vac' because a Danish student I had made friends with at Academy House invited me to stay with his family in his village of Kastager on Lolland, an island wedged between the main peninsula and Hans Christian Andersen's town of Odense. It was Nona Handoo, an Indian girl I had met on the eve of taking the boat to England, who had told me about Academy House being inexpensive lodgings for indigent students; she had also offered to introduce me to her Swedish friend in Gothenburg, Jane Kjellström, who, she assured me, would be happy to show me around her city. I decided to include Gothenburg in my holiday itinerary.

As a practised cross-Channel voyager, having twice done the crossing with the Cambridge Experimental Theatre Group, I went across a third time and took a student's concessional ticket for a train to Hamburg. There, I was met by a distant cousin, Saras (Saraswati), and her German fiancé, Armand Müller, who clicked his heels and very formally shook hands. (Years later, I visited them in their Dusseldorf home and learnt that Saras's mother was with them but lying very ill. I was accompanied by an Indian Christian girl whom the mother quite wrongly took to be my desired wife. She also knew that my mother would strenuously object to the tie-up. I shall never forget her injunction, 'Marry her,' she ordered me, 'even if your mother objects – because the Indian mind is like its geography: the further south you go, the narrower it becomes!' Alas, she passed away the following week.)

Saras and Armand took me home for the night and next morning put me on the ferry to Denmark. At the car bay I spotted a gentleman who seemed to be travelling solo. I collared him and asked if I could hitch a lift with him once we got to the other side. He looked doubtful but nodded. Throughout the crossing, I kept an eye on him so that I would not miss him when we docked. When we arrived at the Danish end, he signalled that I should wait for him outside the gate. I was much relieved when he stopped and asked me to get in.

We drove for a while in silence, then to get the conversation going I asked if he had ever been to India. He relaxed and said he had been with Rohtas Industries in Bihar. I remarked that that was an interesting coincidence as my late father had been the auditor and income tax adviser to the Sahu Jains who were the owners. 'Oh, you're V. Sankar Aiyar's son!' he exclaimed, much to my amazement. He had known my father well and had been very upset when the air crash happened. He gently added, 'It is only because you are from India that I gave you a lift. Otherwise, you never know who you're taking and what might happen on the way.' He was going to Copenhagen and I had to get off midway to find my way to Lolland. He dropped me off at the turning and sped on his way, wishing me good luck.

A couple of lifts and a ferry crossing later, I fetched up at the Kastager farm. They were most hospitable, proud of their exotic guest and very keen to make me as comfortable and at home as they could. The only problem was that none of the family spoke any English. We settled down, however, to sign language. I discovered that my friend's father, who had never been anywhere outside Denmark, had one abiding passion. He loved atlases and a huge globe adorned his drawing room. His favourite pastime was to work out impossibly complicated journeys, such as travelling from Lolland to Casablanca, then on to Buenos Aires and, rounding Tierra del Fuego, crossing the Pacific to go past Samoa and on across the oceans back to Kastager. He then joyously traced these fantasy journeys on charts. In real life, the only journey he ever made was from his farm to the nearby town. He was understandably proud of having once gone all the way to Copenhagen!

After a couple of days with this pleasant family, I started hitchhiking and making ferry crossings to reach my 19-shillings-a-day hotel in the Danish capital. An Indian was a rarity (then, no longer now) and I got lifts easily because the Danes were curious without being inquisitive. Within a day, I left behind Helsingör (Hamlet's Elsinore) and Helsingborg on the Swedish coast and fetched up at Jane's place. She had made arrangements for me to stay at a Salvation Army hostel, dirt cheap but clean and tidy. I spent the days wandering around town and satisfying my hunger pangs with a single hot dog, eaten with plenty of gherkins and French fries, to half-fill my stomach.

When Jane (pronounced 'Yone') found that it was my twenty-first birthday on 10 April, she insisted on getting me a present. I tentatively asked if as my birthday present she could put through a call for me to my mother and was delighted when she readily agreed. She booked the call and asked me to reach her home at 6 p.m. sharp. The phone rang and we heard the operator forwarding the call through exchanges in Frankfurt, Istanbul, Tehran and Delhi, but then the connection to the Sivananda Ashram snapped, and we were left disappointed. But I really appreciated her having taken so much trouble.

She had invited a friend of hers, an Egyptian Copt, to join us for dinner and then sent us off to enjoy Gothenburg's nightlife. We preferred a park bench and talked politics until late in the evening. I returned to my hostel knowing I had to make an early start next morning to hitch across the vast and virtually empty breadth of Sweden to Stockholm.

I was in luck. Within minutes, I got my first lift out of town in a truck that drove me some 70 kilometres to the vicinity of Vänersborg, where the truck driver was turning off the highway towards a small town called Skåra (pronounced Skora). I got out there as I was heading to Stockholm. It was getting cold and I wrapped myself as cosily as I could in my duffel coat. Trucks and cars were few and far between. None stopped. Then, to my horror, it started to snow. Needing to find shelter, I entered a roadside bookshop. The storekeeper was very kind and let me wait till the snow let up. Outside the falling snow started assuming blizzard proportions. Lunchtime came and the proprietor said he was going to his home at the back of the shop. But he gave me gratis a bar of chocolate and, pushing a bunch of girlie magazines towards me, said I was not to worry. He was not going to push me out into the snowstorm.

Then, as dusk was falling, the snow let up and I returned to my place on the edge of the highway. Again, cars and other vehicles were few and far between. I had to find shelter before it grew dark. There seemed to be no alternative to trudging into Skåra. The pavement was treacherously, even dangerously, slippery, with my feet creating puddles. I felt weary in body and spirit, comforting myself with thoughts of a hot mug of tea and a grilled sandwich, which was all I could afford, when, suddenly, a great big Volvo drew up beside me and the driver called out, asking me in English whether he could drop me somewhere. He pointed with his thumb to the rear seat and I gratefully slid in. He asked me where to, and I was just recounting my saga about journeying to Stockholm when a female voice from the front seat chirped up, 'Let's take him there.' I had not spotted the woman earlier as she was bundled up next to the driver.

We stopped off at a bank in the nearby town of Skövde and she went in to draw some money. So, I asked the driver, Karl, who she was. He said her name was Maria and she was the only daughter of a Gothenburg shipping magnate. 'And you?' I asked. 'I'm her paid chauffeur.' Mischievously, I said, 'Only her chauffeur?' He confessed. 'Well, also her lover when she is in the mood.' Maria returned, stuffing a wad of banknotes into her bag, and we were off.

I fell asleep in the back seat. I don't know how long we drove. But when Karl shook me awake, we were in a dense forest. He gave me a frankfurter (with gherkins and French fries!). As I munched on the lifesaver, they chatted among themselves very amiably in Swedish before falling into each other's arms. I left them to it and went back to sleep. I was again shaken awake. I don't know how much later.

'Look at Maria,' Karl said. 'She's having an epileptic fit. I must take her back to Gothenburg.' 'Where are we?' I asked. 'And what time is it?' 'Skåra,' he replied, 'where we picked you up. It's three in the morning. I've arranged a room in a motel for you and here is some money to take a train back to Gothenburg. But I must get her home immediately.' And with that, he drove off. It had been an extraordinary start to my twenty-first year!

Campaign for Nuclear Disarmament

I arrived back in London in time for the last leg of the annual anti-nuclear weapons Aldermaston march from Hyde Park to Trafalgar Square. Along with a group of leftist Cambridge friends, we walked the short distance singing:

> We shall not, we shall not be moved. (Repeat)
> Just like a tree planted by the water
> We shall not be moved.

It was a heady experience. I have never since deviated from my position that nuclear weapons are evil and must be abolished. The march ended and I went for dinner at a modest Indian restaurant, proudly flashing my Campaign for Nuclear Disarmament (CND) badge. This attracted the attention of an East African Indian, Praful Patel, who went on to a distinguished leadership position in the British Indian diaspora.

Next morning, I hopped on to the pillion of the motorcycle of a Royal Air Force officer returning to his base outside Cambridge. When we stopped on the way and I took off my duffel coat, he took a horrified look at the CND badge and said, 'If I knew you were one of those, I'd have never picked you up!' We agreed to disagree, and he did not drop me off until we entered the university town by Trumpington Road. He drove off waving me a cheery goodbye. Journey's end!

My third term and elections to the Union Executive Committee

By my third (Easter) term, it was obvious that I had to prioritize working for my civil services exam. I had picked two papers despite not knowing anything about the subjects – International Law and British Constitutional History – because friends had advised that these were 'scoring' papers.

There were only six months to go for the competitive exams and I had to revise my notes for the two economics papers (higher and lower) and the Indian history paper, as also stuff my head with general knowledge, especially scientific and technical stuff. My father's tome that I had lugged to Cambridge, *How It Works and How It's Done*, circa the early 1950s, proved invaluable. I also had to be a regular at the Union if I wanted to be elected to the executive committee at the end-of-term elections. Juggling all these kept me fully occupied.

The weather was gorgeous, and the city was familiar by then. I had made lots of friends and was brimming with self-confidence. I never learnt to punt but others were willing to 'pole' me up the river as I particularly wanted to visit Grantchester at 'ten to three' to see if there was 'honey still for tea'.

It slowly dawned on me that I had never before felt as much at home as I did at Cambridge. But the realization came with another shock revelation – that I had been brought up to become a coconut Englishman, brown on the outside and white within. It made me fiercely nationalistic and determined to bone up on all the Indian history, culture, civilization and heritage I had not been taught.

Term was ending and Prelims (the end-of-year exams) were on the horizon. I did not particularly study for them, partly because of Hahn's assessment that 'one of you will get a first' and partly because the upcoming exam appeared to be a repeat of my BA Hons exam that I had passed with flying colours at Delhi University. More to the point, I reckoned, were the Union elections.

There was a most dramatic development. On the eve of Pollitt's (final) exams, a group of right-wing toughs broke into his bedroom at King's and so badly roughed him up that they broke his wrist and he had to get an amanuensis to write his answers. The university was scandalized and, unsurprisingly, the vote, when it came, was overwhelmingly in his support.

The executive committee elected was the most leftist that Cambridge had seen in years. I was among them. The national press was so galvanized by the event that, for the first time ever, I found my name in the *Times*. My moment of glory was, however, dimmed by my being described as a 'Pakistani radical'. It undermined my faith forever in the accuracy of media reporting!

The long summer vac

It was in the long vacation following the Union elections that I had my Damascene moment. I had picked up second-hand from outside Heffers Bookshop, where books on discount were displayed, *To the Four Winds*, the autobiography of Clare Sheridan, a well-known sculptor and a cousin of Winston Churchill's. She spent nearly three years in Moscow (1919–22) and got to meet every major Russian leader of the period from Lenin to Trotsky to Zinoviev, Bukharin, Dzerzhinsky and many others (but not Stalin).

Her favourite was clearly Leon Trotsky, who invites her to tea. She describes the elegant silverware, the dainty teacups, the spotless napkins and the delectable cucumber sandwiches. She gushes, 'Comrade Trotsky, I just don't believe the terrible stories they tell about you.' At which Trotsky pulls out a pistol and, putting it to her temple, says, 'If I thought you could harm the Revolution one whit, I would shoot you here on the spot.' Then, returning the pistol to his pocket, he smoothly continues, 'But as you do not count, do have another sandwich.' I froze. When I couldn't face up to even a dead trout staring at me with its beady eye, where was I going to lead a revolution? I could not mix Gandhi with Marx!

As the long vacation (June–October) was upon us, it not only meant we had to find our own lodgings and pay market rent but also that we had to fend for ourselves for food. My annual allowance was too meagre to allow anything filling. My solution was to remain in bed until midday to stave off hunger and survive on baked beans and bread for brunch.

A cheerful Sri Lankan, Hemal Pieris, shared my St Clement's Gardens digs. I loved talking Ceylon politics with him. It was all 'Aunty Sirimavo' and 'Uncle Felix'! Besides, he was an excellent cook and occasionally served up the most delicious Sri Lankan dishes – provided you could take their heavy spice and chilli content. A number of 'overseas' students with nowhere to go were also hanging about the university, as were the au pair girls and language students at the International Centre. We also did the unthinkable: bridge the yawning gap between 'town' and 'gown'. One of the town men was a graphic artist, Charles, who promised to make up a mock *Time* magazine cover with me on it. That never happened but we became good friends. Sally Johnson from one of the women's colleges moved in and brightened our company. She introduced me to her friends, Anne McDougall and Rosalind Crabtree. The four of us became something of a 'gang'.

A few Hall friends also came back for extra tuition. I have a vivid memory of a true Cambridge moment. One warm afternoon in August, I walked into the Junior Combination Room to find my friend James Fulcher sprawled in front of the unlit fireplace. He looked up at me, the picture of misery, and whispered, 'Mani, I'm disintegrating within.'

In September, I decided to accompany my newfound 'town' friend, Charles, on a trip to Gothenberg. We stayed in the same Salvation Army hostel that Jane had found for me the previous spring. But as it was now getting cold, and the hostel did not provide bedding, we found a newspaper vendor nearby who offered to provide us with unsold papers at the end of his working day. We gratefully accepted the offer and took turns wrapping the newspapers around each other to sleep in cosy warmth. From Gothenburg, I took the train to Oslo, where a friend, Brit, found me accommodation in a youth hostel. My civil services exam was coming up in a month's time. So, I would go every morning to the Oslo Bibliotek on Drammensvei to try to do some studying. I must be the only IFS officer to have prepared for the exam in a Norwegian library!

Jam arrives

After the break in Sweden and Norway, I went to London to receive my brother Jam who had been admitted to Magdalene, Oxford. I arrived at the Indian Students' Union where, when I asked about Jam's whereabouts, everyone giggled and pointed to the betting shop down the road. And, yes, there he was, having spent his three weeks on the SS *Cilicia* boning up on the current form of racehorses. In the last twenty-four hours, he had already raked in a small fortune. How could I object?

However, a month later, he fetched up at Cambridge saying he had lost his entire annual allowance doubling his bet every time his horses lost. Inevitably, his money ran out. I offered him tea, sympathy and a token contribution, which he gratefully accepted, and said he would be working in a mortuary over the Christmas vacation because they were the ones who paid the highest daily wage.

Unbelievably, he recouped all his losses, then lost them all over again! He was rescued only by my mother prevailing on a relative at the Reserve Bank of India to find a way of sending him an additional grant of £600. He thus had three years at Oxford, one more than most of us 'senior students' enjoyed. But his interest in speculation paid off when he started, later in life, playing the stock market and has now become much, much richer than in my wildest dreams – or his!

Meanwhile, I had busied myself preparing for my first formal speech in the Union proposing the motion 'The Liberal revival is ridiculous'. This was the outcome of a by-election at Orpington that had brought in a Liberal MP, a party that was variously described as a dying or dead duck. The opposition to the motion was led by Jeremy Thorpe, the rising star of the Liberals. I thundered my extreme left line with such unbridled oratorical passion that one of the speakers said disparagingly I sounded like Keir Hardie in a cloth cap (the miner who is a Labour icon)!

It may seem strange that Pollitt was organizing debates on the 'Liberal revival' when the major issues of the time were the Cuban crisis and the India–China war, which broke out later that month (October 1962). But at the time no one was even mildly surprised because there was no hint in the public domain that these crises were coming to a boil.

Civil services exam

Even as the Chinese forces descended from the Thagla Ridge to the Namka Chu, the civil services exam started. There was an exam centre at India House for the convenience of candidates appearing from the UK (one flew in from the US too). The inconvenience imposed on us, however, was that the exam began in London at 5 a.m. to match the Indian opening time of 10.30 a.m. Rahul Khushwant Singh, who was taking the exam with me, suggested that we doss down at the YMCA on Great Russell Street, from where India House was a short walk down.

There was a life-saving transport cafe open at that unearthly hour where we could have a cup of tea. We arrived at the venue, a little tense and somewhat nervous, and I was bewildered to learn that a telegram had arrived for me c/o the High Commission of India. Opening it, I found that it was from Muzzy, the St Stephen's wit and communist, who was rather incongruously doing his chartered accountancy in a pinstriped suit in the city. The telegram read: 'Good wishes for all success in the Chinese Administrative Service exams. Muzzy.'

Good lord! I crushed the telegram and stuffed it in my pocket and went into the exam hall, laughing but concerned that one of the High Commission staff might have surreptitiously read it!

Over the next ten days or so, trips to London became routine. Fortunately, most of the optional papers were held at a more civilized hour and I could take the 19-shilling day-return ticket from Cambridge to Liverpool Street and back. The downside was that half a dozen day trips began adding up soon to a pretty penny and I was back to hot dogs (with gherkins and French fries) for lunch.

The General Knowledge paper went well when I chanced my hand by attributing to refrigeration the same process of cooling as air conditioning, which I had learnt by heart from my father's tome. That turned out to be right! The English essay was a cinch, as were the Economics papers. The International Law paper ended up being child's play because the crammer I had brought to England had correctly foretold many of the questions actually posed.

The Indian History paper was doubtful because while I had gone with a vengeance into the administrative and economic problems of the Slave Kings, I could not remember when the Slave dynasty ended, and the next dynasty took over! The examiner was kind and allowed that the more important thing was that I seemed to have a sound understanding of the administrative and economic problems of mediaeval sultans!

It was the British Constitutional History paper that really troubled me because in my school and undergraduate days I had read little history, no British history, and no constitutional history at all of Britain or any other country. I was entirely dependent on David Lindsay Keir's *The British Constitution* and the cram pamphlets.

So, the evening before the exam, I asked my friends Krishan and Tim Clark to finish dinner at 'first hall' served at 7 p.m. and then await me in Krishan's rooms at St John's. Both were brilliant historians (a youthful promise they have long fulfilled) but not in agreement over Krishan's anarchist views of the evolution of Britain and its Constitution. Well past midnight, they fielded the 'probable' questions I had selected from the crammer and went into a splendid polemic and forensic display of their rival interpretations of key developments in the history of Britain's Constitution-making. I was enthralled.

Next day, I confidently confronted the question paper and, drawing extensively on my one-evening tutorial with Krishan and Tim, handed in my paper. But sanguine as I was, I little expected to score a staggering 75 per cent – an excellent illustration of what even a few hours of quality education can achieve!

'Golden October turned to sombre November' (Eliot). Cambridge was agog with the Cuban missile crisis, and the Indian student community (there were no Chinese students then, more's the pity) with the Chinese army making mincemeat of our troops. That drama played out until the Chinese unilaterally announced the withdrawal of their forces on 22 November 1962 after almost reaching the Brahmaputra.

This led to the surprising conversion of even Amiya Bagchi from his communist convictions (he has since reverted). For my part, I could not whip up the righteous indignation that came so easily to most of my countrymen. I also found myself unable to definitively answer the question posed by Jim Hinton, the King's College Marxist, as to whether the average Tibetan, and generations of Tibetans to come, would really prefer to remain with authoritarian, theological and feudal Lama rule, or prefer the modernization and development the Chinese occupation would inevitably bring (although levels of authoritarianism would remain the same).

As for Cuba, Pollitt did schedule a scintillating special debate that left most of us leftists feeling that there was little to choose between Kennedy and Dulles/Joe McCarthy. The India–China debate was left over to the following Lent term with the Canadian, Ian Binney, in the chair.

My best speech at the Union

Our high commissioner in London, Mohammed Currim Chagla, had been invited to the debate. It turned out to be my star performance. The motion was 'Non-alignment is sanctimonious rubbish'. I spoke for the opposition after Chagla and tore into the proposers of the motion. Turning my face to the wall and then swirling around, my gown flying around me, I looked straight at the very right-wing guest speaker for the motion and said, 'We could always join the other side,' then walked up to him almost eyeball to eyeball to thunder, 'And how would you like that?' It brought the house down. I ended with the fervent plea, 'For God's sake, leave us alone.' We defeated the motion hands down. It led to Norman Lamont remarking that I was 'by miles the best speaker of our generation'[1] – a Cambridge Union generation that included six senior ministers in John Major's government!

Ian Binney then pitted me and Norman against each other on the motion 'Israel is a dream at the Arabs' expense'. As neither of us knew much of the subject, we found ourselves sitting opposite each other in the Marshall Library, reading alternately the same articles and counter-articles in *The Spectator* by Arab and Zionist experts. I made the mistake of leaving the library before Norman and so he had a counterargument ready that I had not read and used to great effect in the debate that followed.

I missed a point when my long-standing rival, the extremely rude and bumptious Chris Mason, queried me on what I had to say about Nasser's threat to drive the Jews into the sea. It only occurred to me later that I should have replied, 'The hon'ble gentleman will recall that the last time the Jews were driven into the sea, the waves parted!' On second thoughts, though, perhaps it was just as well I didn't, as I lived around the corner from the local synagogue.

I certainly lost (temporarily) the friendship of several Jews, notable among them being David Kleeman of Trinity Hall, but it did lead to a lifelong interest in the Palestine question. And I did win a point, for the first and only time, with my supervisor, Frank Hahn, when, after reading a report in *Varsity* about the debate, he exploded, 'What nonsense you speak.' He added, 'And I'm not saying that because I'm Jewish.' I merely raised a quizzical eyebrow – and that silenced him!

The debate consolidated my lifelong friendship with Norman Lamont. It was he who stood by me as proposer for my next elevation in the Union. We all knew that Simon Rocksborough-Smith was unbeatable and that I would easily defeat the obstreperous Chris Mason. Norman tentatively put me down for secretary when he found Simon had been put down for VP. When Simon and Mason found I was down for secretary, Simon withdrew his name and put down Mason for VP. Promptly, Norman withdrew my name for secretary and restored my candidature for VP. This farce was repeated several times over the last hour of nomination.

---

[1] Stephen Parkinson, *Arena of Ambition*, Icon Books, London, 2009, p. 158.

I then made a huge political mistake. Finding that nominations would close in five minutes, with Simon down for VP and me for secretary, Norman and I decided this was it and walked out of the building without waiting for Simon and Mason to also leave. At literally the last minute, Simon withdrew his name and put down Mason for VP. Neither Norman nor I were on the spot to counter this skulduggery. In the event, Mason became VP, and I, secretary under the presidency of Ken Clarke (later, a frequent secretary of state and the most honoured veteran of the House of Commons). He put me down in the order papers to open for the motion 'American overseas policy has not contributed to world peace'. I let myself go!

I make it to the IFS

Meanwhile, I learnt that I had passed the written exam for the IFS and had to fly to India for the interview, then return to Cambridge for my final tripos exams. When the results were announced, I thought I had stood eighth in the all-India rankings, but then discovered that Vinod Kumar Chandnarain Khanna was not two persons but one – V.K.C. Khanna – and so found myself promoted to seventh position.

But I was only fifth in the IFS, which many contemporary service officers will find astonishing because the Indian Revenue Service has overtaken all other services as the preferred alternative (presumably for the take it promises!). I actually met a young IFS probationer a couple of years ago who replied 'six hundred', when I asked him what his rank was, and then went on to complain that he did not want the IFS at all but the Union Public Service Commission had threatened him that if he did not accept the IFS, they would downgrade him to a Class II service!

I subsequently found that almost the majority of those selected for the IFS in my year were born in Pakistan, where their parents had left behind much of their property. This made for greater flexibility in choosing diplomacy as a career because there were no family businesses left to induce them to stay in India. A curious outcome of Partition.

Aiming for the presidency

I flew back targeting the presidency of the Union rather than any academic distinction in my tripos. Since the vast majority of the Union's presidents had made it only in their fourth year at Cambridge, it was pretty audacious of me to make the bid at the end of my second academic year. Yet, with Chris Mason as my principal challenger, I thought I would make it quite easily. Then, unexpectedly, Oliver Weaver declared his candidacy. I was not unduly fazed thinking that two right-wing candidates would divide the Tory vote and I could slip in.

I had reckoned without the notorious 'CUCA crocodile' of the Cambridge University Conservative Association that ensured the participation in the vote of a number of die-hard Tories who had no interest in the Union other than defeating left-wing candidates. Some seventeen years later, I learnt that I had my own nano 'crocodile' – the tiny Indian vote mobilized by Rajiv Gandhi, whom I barely knew. He had gone among the Indian students and urged, 'There's an Indian standing for president and the least you guys can do is to go to the Union and vote for him!' So, as Rajiv began his political life canvassing for me, it is only appropriate that I should end mine canvassing for him!

Voting was by single transferable vote. I lost the first round by five votes. That losing margin rose to twelve in the second round when the second preference votes for Mason, who had been eliminated at the end of the first round, were counted. One factor contributing to my defeat was *Varsity* running a headline on the day of the election that raised the key question: 'Commuting President?' It pointed out that as I had passed into the Indian diplomatic service, I was planning to take a probationary assignment in the London High Commission and, as a life member of the Union, commute between my desk job and the Union during my presidency, should I win. This doubtless lost me a few votes – but the difference between victory and defeat was only a few votes!

There remained my final tripos exam. As my IFS results had already been announced, there was nothing particular to be gained by doing well. Also, without doing much work the previous year, I had quite comfortably obtained an upper second. I thought I could do the same again.

Everything went relatively well until I went in for the Money, Banking and International Trade paper. In the middle of writing the paper, my mind suddenly went blank. Writer's block or a nervous breakdown? I did not know which. I was aware that if one failed even a single paper, one would be failed for the entire degree. Believing the worst, I was walking back disconsolately from the Marshall Library when, on Silver Street, I found my supervisor for the subject, Aubrey Silberston of St John's, walking towards me. He asked how I had fared.

'I am afraid, sir,' I replied, 'I've failed.'

'Oh, they can't fail you,' he replied breezily and walked on.

In the event, I got a lower second (what was colloquially called a 2.2). I decided that Silberston must have fiddled the result in my favour.

I did not get the opportunity of checking out with Silberston until half a century later. When, in 2010, Trinity Hall did me the honour of electing me an Honorary Fellow, the Master, Martin Daunton, hosted a lunch for me and asked me to suggest the guest list. I asked for Aubrey Silberston. Silberston accepted the lunch invitation and I wrote asking him whether I could meet him earlier in the morning at around 11 a.m. He arrived before me and, although neither of us really recognized the other, we were soon seated and after some polite conversation and the ordering of coffee, I asked him the question that had been troubling me for fifty years: had he fiddled with my results? If not, why had he said to me, 'They can't fail you?'

Silberston was indignant. He said Nicholas Kaldor (a famed economics don of Hungarian origin at King's) might have done something like that but he just wouldn't. He remembered neither me nor our Silver Street encounter but could assure me that I must have genuinely passed and deservedly obtained my degree. A weight rolled off my conscience.

I had also asked the alumni office whether they could fix a meeting for me with my principal supervisor, Dr Frank Hahn, who I had heard was in poor health. They received an inimitable Hahn response: 'Please tell Mr Aiyar to check the obituary column in the *Times*, and if he does not find my name in it, he is welcome to tea at 4.30 p.m.!' I was received most cordially by him and his wife, Dorothy. Not much later, I read a report that he had passed away.

Term over, I went off on a final vacation to Norway. And there received a telegram from the MEA reading: 'Regret to inform you that you have been rejected from all services.' I immediately realized it was my commie image that had caught up with me. I was already booked on a boat sailing down the Oslo fjord to Newcastle. It should have been the climax of a great holiday.

Instead, I could barely take in the incredible beauty of the hills on either side of the fjord.

From Newcastle, I caught a train that dropped me off at Cambridge. The only person I needed to see was Graham Storey, my very sympathetic and concerned senior tutor. He was most supportive, assuring me the college would back me to the hilt in my coming struggle for justice and a career.

See detailed footnotes and endnotes by scanning the QR code above.

3

Towards a Life in Diplomacy

Getting in

I returned to India on the morning of 15 July 1963. That very evening, I found myself with the president of India in his large bedroom at Rashtrapati Bhavan. He lay in his four-poster bed, propped up against a wall of fluffy pillows to receive his personal guests. His son, the well-known historian, Dr S. Gopal, was in attendance.

My mother, with characteristic chutzpah, had leveraged her connection with Dr Sarvepalli Radhakrishnan dating back to the early 1930s, when she was his paying guest at the Andhra University vice chancellor's palatial residence in Visakhapatnam. She had got on famously with Gopal, who was then a little boy, and the call had been arranged through him.

Dr Radhakrishnan brushed away my stuttering explanations to focus on the nub of the issue. 'Did you,' he said, 'join the Communist Party in Britain?' I replied I could not have because I was not a British citizen. And, of course, as the Indian Intelligence Bureau (IB) well knew, I had not joined the Communist Party in India. In that case, remarked the president, how could I be kept out after passing the exam so convincingly? He then went on to elaborate that he had been in the chair in the Rajya Sabha when Prime Minister Nehru had assured the house that a member of the civil services was as entitled as any other Indian citizen to his political preferences and vote for any party of his choice but could not be a member of any political party, not even the ruling

Congress. That, emphasized the president, was the government's policy and my case had to be decided on that basis. He turned to Gopal and instructed him, 'Please ask Lal Bahadur to see me.' Lal Bahadur Shastri was then the home minister.

We took our leave. A few days later, Gopal rang me to say that the home minister had been 'given a wigging by Father' and I could expect to hear the good news within the next few days. Instead, under what was known as the 'Kamaraj Plan', Lal Bahadur Shastri was among the ministers dropped from the cabinet to take up 'party work'. At that moment, I felt the battle was lost.

My mother was convinced that I was being called a 'Markist' – she never could pronounce the 'x' in Marx – because I lounged around in jeans. Her silver bullet was to go to Laffan's in Connaught Circus so I could get myself outfitted in a raw silk jacket and well-tailored trousers. This was hot and uncomfortable in an age when air conditioning was rare. So, I carried the jacket by its hook on my shoulder, the pocket stuffed with the only tie that I owned (a bourgeois pretension that, in principle, I rejected!) and she provided the clean white ironed shirt to go with it.

Thus accoutred, I went to see the senior officer at the MEA, Special Secretary (Administration) Rajeshwar Dayal. He received me like a long-lost brother. His opening words were, 'I married the daughter of the richest industrialist in Uttar Pradesh – and that has made me a communist for life.' He added, 'At Oxford, I always had a pink card standing on my mantelpiece. What they've done to you is nonsense. I will speak to the prime minister about your case and get him to correct this injustice.' I could not have asked for a better advocate. But nothing happened.

Meanwhile, my mother found us paid accommodation with another MP, Savitri Nigam. She took me to see Shastri's successor as home minister, Gulzarilal Nanda. There, I was ushered into a large room where a small figure was hunched up behind a humongous desk. I recognized him only because I was an avid follower of the cartoons in *Shankar's Weekly*. The new home minister frowned, listened with a marked lack of patience to my pathetic pleas, then abruptly dismissed me. I thought that was the end of the road.

So, I started looking for alternative avenues of employment through two Doon School Old Boys who had achieved high distinction: George Verghese of the *Times of India* and Aamir Ali of the ILO in Geneva. They were both very kind but of little practical help. My despair deepened.

Over the years, listening to whispers in the corridors, and with the external affairs minister minister, Pranab Mukherjee, instructing Foreign Secretary Shivshankar Menon to allow me a peek into my personal file (when I was serving as a cabinet minister in 2008), I was able to piece together what then happened. The IB were adamant that they would not revisit their finding that I was a dyed-in-the-wool Red, and as it was only months since the Chinese had taken us on, all were agreed that it would be dangerous to induct me into a sensitive government career. On the other hand, some others were equally adamant on my being taken in. Among the latter were the deputy high commissioner in London, Kewal Singh, who had made enquiries with both MI5 and Scotland Yard, and found both had nothing on me. The high commissioner, M.C. Chagla, also strongly opposed the decision to keep me out, enquiring whether we were to follow the American example of looking for Reds under the bed. Acting on the president's instructions, the very senior ICS officer Subimal Dutt was beavering away on my behalf. And from Cambridge poured in letter after letter of support from the dons who had taught me and the college Fellows who had known me. One who did not know me but was most supportive was the master of my college, Sir Ivor Jenkins, who, by rotation, happened also to be the vice chancellor of the university. I think Nehru would have been most impressed with Sir Ivor's argument that it was terribly wrong to have taken so life-changing a decision about 'one of our men' without consulting the college. To no one do I owe more than Rajeshwar Dayal, who widely and convincingly canvassed for me.

I, of course, knew nothing of this then. I was consumed by a sense of angst. In a mood of weary despair, I went to see my school classmate, Arvind Pande, who was returning to Christ's College, Cambridge, after the long summer vacation. He said his father's friend, Special Secretary (Home) L.P. Singh, had dined with them the previous evening and, on learning that Arvind and I had been at school and Cambridge together, wondered why I had not been to see him. I told Arvind that as I did not belong to a bureaucrat's family, I was not well versed in the protocol; if the legendary special secretary wanted to meet me, why did he not just order me to come and see him?

While I was in the middle of explaining this, Arvind's father, B.D. Pande, came home. He was among the country's brightest civil servants, and destined to become cabinet secretary and governor of Punjab during Operation Blue Star. At the time of my first meeting with him (October 1962), he held the key job of gold controller. He peremptorily ordered me to call on L.P. Singh at eleven the next morning in his office in North Block.

Dressed like a mannequin in my raw silk jacket and tie, I arrived well on time and was taken to a small room with a massive desk, sitting behind which was a giant of a man, the famed L.P. Singh, cigar in mouth, dominating the room (and everybody in it). With a downward sweep of his cigar, he motioned me in some irritation to 'Sit down, sit down'. I did. He began, 'You are not a prisoner in the dock. I just want to ask you a few questions.' I nodded. The questions started. I fielded them as best I could but found myself suddenly in the middle of a heated argument with the special secretary (home) over the true meaning of democracy.

Just that morning, the papers had said that Harold Macmillan in England had been succeeded as prime minister by a belted fourteenth earl, Lord Home (pronounced 'Hume') who was still to divest himself of his ermine and get elected to the House of Commons. Did he call that 'democracy'? Warming to the subject, I referred to President Gamal Abdel Nasser of Egypt. Everyone called him a dictator, I said, but if he held an open election in his country an overwhelming majority would vote for him as he was an Arab icon.

L.P. Singh listened to me with unwonted patience but riposted that the only time he had ever been abroad was to the United States, and, on his way back, he had halted overnight in Cairo. That night Nasser had rounded up the leaders of the Coptic community and had them all either exiled, thrown into prison or shot dead. Did I call that democracy?

At that point, I went berserk. I reminded the special secretary that he had begun by telling me that I was not to regard myself as a prisoner in the dock, but I was being denied three privileges to which a prisoner was entitled. What, asked the domineering L.P. Singh, were those three privileges?

First, I said, the prisoner in the dock is assumed innocent until proved guilty. I was being asked to prove my innocence. Second, I said, picking up steam, a prisoner in the dock is told what the charges against him are; I had no idea what was the evidence the intelligence authorities had gathered against me. Third, I went on more angrily, a prisoner in the dock is provided an attorney if he cannot afford one himself; I was not even being allowed to call my witnesses. Exhausted at my own temerity, I slumped back in my seat. The special secretary pulled the cigar out of his mouth and barked, 'Aiyar, you're in. Now out.' And I walked out wearing the haze of smoke from his cigar like a halo!

It took another two weeks for Home Minister Gulzarilal Nanda to overrule his officers. He noted that he had seen me and talked to me at some length. It seemed to him that although I had pursued an intellectual association with Marxism, he had no reason to disbelieve that I had never been a member of the Communist Party, let alone an active worker. He therefore recommended to the prime minister (who was also the external affairs minister) that there remained no justification to debar me from government service.

Nehru entirely endorsed this, adding that he too had heard good reports of me. Thus, under Prime Minister Nehru's personal signature, I crossed my personal Rubicon on 24 October 1963. It had been worth the trauma I had undergone to become the first IFS officer – since the initial formation of the IFS back in 1946–47 – to be admitted to the service under Jawaharlal Nehru's own hand!

I was astonished at this outstanding example of how an obscure aspirant could be given such a patient hearing by so many from the highest ranks of the civil service and from the president to senior ministers. Not even a year had passed since the India–China armed conflict of October–November 1962. With the defection of Kim Philby, the Vassall affair and the Profumo scandal that rocked Great Britain in the first half of 1963, there could not have been a more opportune moment to hunt for alleged communists to prevent them from infiltrating government service. But here were statesmen and senior civil servants (excluding intelligence chiefs) more than willing to revisit their initial negative reactions to ensure that injustice was not visited on even one young citizen without adequate, proven cause. India under Nehru was truly a democracy. Alas, that democracy is disappearing even as I write these words.

Many decades later, when I was at the Prime Minister's Office (PMO), I became friendly with IB chief, M.K. Narayanan. He volunteered the information that it was he who was my case officer in IB and added, with an air of regret, that every time he thought he had me by the short hairs, yet another VIP missive would land on his table and he would have to start writing his negative recommendation all over again. When immediately after I left the service I asked him whether he would show me the papers indicting me, he replied proudly that, as a conscientious intelligence officer, he had shredded the papers. Many decades later, when staying with him in Raj Bhavan, Kolkata, in 2009, where he was serving as governor of West Bengal after a decade as the national security adviser, I asked him whether he had got his information from the BIS. He nodded. At which, I told him BIS stood for British Information Service; UK's intelligence agencies were Scotland Yard and MI5/MI6. So, had I been charged on the basis of newspaper reports? He did not answer.

The last word, however, remained with my dear friend, Shekhar Dasgupta, as so often in my life: 'They found you were a Marxist – but of the Groucho variety!'

At the academy

I junked my raw silk jacket, threw away my tie and fetched up at the Lal Bahadur Shastri National Academy of Administration in Mussoorie. Deepak Lal had driven his roommate, a police probationer, quite mad with the Western classical music he played; one sonata for shaving, another for dressing and an entire symphony for getting into his pyjamas at night. The policeman vacated with relief, and I moved in.

As many as a quarter of that year's Indian Administrative Service (IAS)/IFS intake were from St Stephen's. So, we soon formed a cabal, much, I suspect, to the annoyance of the others. But in which other grouping would I have found a Shankar Menon to greet me with the cry 'You've returned from Cambridge a parody of yourself!' Deepak got all of us busy with rehearsals of Brecht's *The Caucasian Chalk Circle*. It was like being back to our antics at college.

The director of the academy excused me from all exams as I had joined the course so late. So I found myself with plenty of time to laze around in the winter sun. I spent an inordinate amount of time unsuccessfully attempting to engage the interest of the most attractive girl in the batch, to the puzzlement of the other women who just could not understand what made this one so special!

I was asked to choose a foreign language to learn – any language, the ministry specified, other than French which had already been allotted to five others. So I chose Swahili. The ministry gave me French!

The one exam I had to take to be confirmed in the service was the Hindi paper. Rumour had it that the only way to pass Hindi was to worm oneself into the good books of the Hindi teacher, Joshi. In the previous batch, Gopi was said to have passed his compulsory Hindi exam by walking up to Joshi shaking his head in sorrow and muttering, 'Subramaniam, poor Subramaniam, dead, sir, dead.' Bewildered, Joshi asked, 'But who is he and how did he die?' Gopi dolefully replied, 'You failed him, sir, in Hindi, so he was not confirmed – and now Subramaniam has killed himself.' Gopi was then passed – with flying colours, so that Joshi would not have two suicides on his conscience! (Probably rank fiction but it served its purpose!)

I, therefore, was determined I would use my many spare hours cultivating Joshi, who welcomed the cringing attention bestowed on him. The standard ploy was to humbly go up to him and whisper, 'Sir, please tell me, should I get married or not?' Joshi would invariably reply, '*Aap wife se shaadi karna chahte ho, ya dharmapatni se?*' (Do you want to marry a 'wife' or a 'dharmapatni' – a traditional bride?) Looking suitably bewildered, you would ask him to explain the difference. '*Wife*,' he would reply, '*woh hoti hai jo Mall Road par apne pati se aage chalti hai, khatak, khatak. Dharmapatni woh jo ki jaanti hai ki apne pati ke peeche chalna chahiye aur idhar udhar nahi dekhna chahiye!*' (A 'wife' is one who walks ahead of her husband on Mall Road, swaying her hips and going clip clop on her high heels. 'Dharmapatni' is she who walks respectfully behind her husband and does not look around her here and there!)

Joshi's one grudge was that no university had accepted him as a lecturer, which was why he ended up in this dump of an academy. I was, therefore, delighted to find that among the themes listed for the Hindi essay paper was '*Bharat ke Vishwavidyalaya*' (India's Universities). I jumped at the opportunity and penned my opening lines, '*Bharat mei tihattar vishwavidyalaya hain. Inki jagah tihattar gaushale hote toh kuch antar nahin padta.*' (There are seventy-three universities in India. If instead there had been seventy-three cow pens, it would have made no difference.) I am not sure Joshi read more than those two lines to give me the highest marks for this scandalous essay!

The oral interview in Hindi was conducted by a historian who, for reasons that will become clear, must remain anonymous. He had written a book in English emblazoned with the legend on the cover: 'Foreword by K.M. Panikkar.' The flyleaf said the author had been at Oxford. To ingratiate myself with the examiner, I decided to read it. The foreword said, in effect, that the book was rubbish – but it was true that it was a foreword and it was also true that it was written by Panikkar!

I went in and the first question the interviewer asked was whether indeed I had studied at Cambridge. I confirmed that. He then embarked on a long discourse – in English – on his days at Oxford. I listened politely. The interview then ended – and I was astonished to find myself at the top of the list! One compulsory paper to be confirmed in the service over. There was still the hurdle of accounts to be accomplished. And the compulsory foreign language paper.

Although I had been exempted from attending any classes, I was included in a 'syndicate' to collectively write on 'The Private Sector in India'. The group chose me to make the presentation. When I reached the point in the paper which argued that the key to private sector development was 'enterprise' and that Kerala was way behind Punjab because Kerala was way behind in entrepreneurship, a minor storm broke out.

Someone in the rear of the hall started shouting that I was insulting Malayalis by suggesting that Sardarjis should invade Kerala to get the economy going. There were counter-shouts from some Sikh probationers, one of whom never failed to mention the Battle of Jamrud. When order was restored, I found that the rumpus had been kicked up by Krishna Kumar, IAS – whose son married my daughter forty-three years later!

Krishna won his spurs as the collector of Ernakulam who so successfully mobilized huge crowds to attend vasectomy camps that he was specially invited by the UN to address the first UN Population Conference in Bucharest in 1970. When Suneet and I got married in 1973, we travelled to Ernakulam on our honeymoon and Krishna invited us to dinner. His wife, Usha, was hugely pregnant. Perhaps I am the first father-in-law in history to have first met his son-in-law while he was still in the womb!

Krishna was also the first in our batch to resign from government service to pursue an alternative career in politics. He was repeatedly elected to the Lok Sabha from the Kollam constituency and for ten years served as minister of state in a series of portfolios in a series of central governments. Like me, he now languishes in the political doldrums.

Two major international incidents and one domestic tragedy occurred in that month of November 1963 which marked my entry into the service. On 2 November, Ngo Dinh Diem was murdered – I still believe at the instance of, or at least with the connivance of, John F. Kennedy. A few weeks later, Kennedy himself was shot in Dallas. Then, news came in of five top Indian generals having been killed in a helicopter accident in the vicinity of Poonch, Jammu. The generals included Tibbu's father, General Daulat Singh, one of the few army commanders to have distinguished himself in 1962. It cast a pall on the probationers.

The final event at the academy involved the IFS probationers meeting the director, S.K. Datta. It was the first time we were gathering together as the Chosen Ones. The director began by saying that he had never known what exactly the IFS did, but he had been told that diplomats had to attend a lot of cocktail parties. It was essential that we should not make fools of ourselves. So, the only advice he had to give us was to drink a spoonful of olive oil before going to cocktail parties. Class dismissed. No one else taught us anything more useful!

We left soon after on our Bharat Darshan. Our first stop was Delhi where we were taken to see Yamini Krishnamurthy dance. I was overwhelmed watching Yamini glide across the stage as if she were skimming over it. The impression she left was so strong that I named my second daughter after her. That month-long heritage tour left an indelible impression on my mind, as I expect it did on the others. We had all, of course, heard of India's historical wonders but apart perhaps from the Taj Mahal and Lal Qila, few among us had actually experienced the ancient glories of our land.

I had shocked myself at Cambridge by the self-discovery that I felt so much at home in England because, consciously or otherwise, Doon School had brought me up to be a good little Englishman. Now I was discovering all that we had accomplished when the English were still wandering around in bearskins. I am sure neither Mahatma Gandhi nor Gurudev Rabindranath Tagore would have approved of such narrow nationalism, but I confess to a kind of epiphany at what I still needed to learn of my own country and its civilization. Fortunately, I and all my colleagues had long retired from the service before strident, bigoted nationalism became the clarion call of Modi's India.

I think the biggest revelation was the temple at Ellora, built by anonymous hands over centuries, carving an entire rock from top to bottom, knowing the work would not be finished in their lifetime and leaving not their names but their work to celebrate their art. I first bought A.L. Basham's *The Wonder that Was India* and then Jawaharlal Nehru's *The Discovery of India* to give some intellectual heft to my incipient patriotic fervour. I also started catching up on the meaning and sense of Tagore's poem that we had all learnt by rote at school: 'Where the mind is without fear and the head is held high . . .'

We travelled down south and, after visiting the grand Chola-era Brihadeeswara Kovil in Thanjavur, I took Deepak and Chukku (Arundhati Ghose) to experience village life in my nearby ancestral home in Kargudi. In the train on our way back to Madras, the dinner halt was at Mayiladuthurai junction, which would become my parliamentary constituency three decades hence. At Madras, we went our separate ways to our district training posts: Deepak to Dharwad; Karnataka, Chukku to Jabalpur, Madhya Pradesh; and I to Rajkot, Gujarat.

Training – of all kinds

At Rajkot station, I was met by Meghnath, who informed me that he was the *chaprasi* (peon) attached to me for the duration of my three-month stay. He did nothing but accompany me on foot to the collectorate and back, spending most of his time contentedly lazing around. I learnt the invaluable lesson that a district officer could not do a spot of work without the assurance of dozens of low-paid employees hanging around him, doing nothing but bolstering the officer's public image and personal ego.

At the office, the collector, R.B. Shukla, was friendliness personified. The only trouble was he hadn't a clue what to do with me. I spent my time staring down the curious, but not one paper passed by my desk, and I could not understand a word of the Gujarati language in which conversations were conducted with the locals, as no one was translating anything for my benefit. For the first few days, I had no one to converse with but Meghnath. Obviously, 'district training' had been conceived without anyone having a clue as to what to do in 'the antres vast and deserts idle' with a probationer who was dreaming not of the gutters of Rajkot but of the Eiffel Tower. It was all *jugaad*, on-the-spot improvisation.

Collector Shukla then hit on the bright idea of substituting me for him on the subject of 'India's Foreign Policy' for a lecture he had been invited to deliver to the Lions Club of Dhoraji, a small town in Rajkot district. My first oration on foreign policy after becoming a certified member of the IFS was to a puzzled bunch of small-time traders in a little-known mofussil town located in the middle of the jaw that juts into the Arabian Sea. But they did seem to appreciate the speech (or whatever they understood) and enthusiastically embraced me afterwards with cries of 'Manibhai Shankarbhai'.

I was later sent for my 'taluka training' for a week to Morvi (now spelt Morbi). The mamlatdar seated me at a desk in his own room but once again there was nothing to do until an agitated group of farmers barged into the office and complained bitterly about something in the local dialect, gawking at me all the while. The mamlatdar looked anxiously at me and, taking courage in both hands as it were, said the delegation had heard that there was a 'foreigner' in town who was visiting Patel villages but not Ahir ones. To avert a caste clash, I offered on the spot to visit their Ahir village, if they wished, the same evening.

I was received royally and then seated on the ground before a 'plate' made of large, dried leaves stitched together. On that plate was then heaped a mountain of *gur* (jaggery) festooned with a sprinkling of sugar, on top of which was drizzled a generous helping of ghee. The whole village gathered around. I still think that was the moment at which my rendezvous with diabetes began. I somehow swallowed enough of this concoction to be able to decently stop. I was then served a coarse cereal (bajra or jowar) chapatti and the most chilli-hot vegetables; I could barely put any on my tongue without tears streaming down my cheek.

The mamlatdar thought this historic (if fiery!) evening should be appropriately celebrated with a meetha paan. We stopped at a roadside stall in Morvi town and the mamlatdar ordered paans. The shopkeeper and the mamlatdar conversed in Gujarati. I only caught the word 'IFS', and heard the shopkeeper say, in some awe, 'Indian Forest Service?' When he was disabused of that, he asked the mamlatdar to tell me that I may be 'educated' but he was 'rich' – a Deng Xiaoping in the making! Another useful bit of 'training' to fit into the jigsaw puzzle of my district exile.

The mamlatdar, having been reassured that I was an 'okay' kind of guy, invited me to dinner with his family prior to taking me to see a film in the local cinema. I went along to his home but found him dallying over starting the meal while the clock ticked towards the time of the screening. I pointed this out and was astonished at his answer: 'Do you think they'll dare start the film without me?' Sure enough, when we eventually fetched up at the cinema, the projection had not started out of deference to the mamlatdar. That is the power of the local administration. It was an important lesson for an IFS probationer to learn.

That week a young man of about my age dropped by my office, introducing himself as the heir apparent to the Morvi throne. To put what that meant into perspective, he informed me that the minute he was born his father had applied a drop of champagne to his tongue – and he had just gone on from there! One night after I had returned to Rajkot, he suddenly appeared at my door in the circuit house with the strange request that I leave the door open while he seated himself facing the open door. We had idly conversed for half an hour when a car suddenly drove up at breakneck speed and the prince of Morvi dashed out of the room with a quick 'Thanks, goodbye'. It was only next morning that I learnt what the mystery was about.

I ran into the rajkumar next morning. He looked mighty pleased with himself. He and his companions had driven all over the district through the night to persuade Congress candidates (with adequate 'incentives') to switch parties and become Swatantra Party candidates in the upcoming panchayat elections. They thus captured the majority of the panchayats and the district council. Politics in the raw! Tragically, a few years later, the Morvi dam burst and most of the fiefdom of the heir apparent was drowned. The prince himself passed away, as he inevitably would, of cirrhosis of the liver.

More 'training' came when I asked permission to visit my IAS batchmates who were in Junagadh on the south-western edge of the Saurashtra peninsula doing their training in 'community development'. The collector kindly arranged for me to be driven to Keshod by the mamlatdar of that taluka. After dropping me off on the highway, the mamlatdar hung around until he managed to flag down a truck bound for Junagadh. I got in next to the driver and found to my relief that he spoke some Hindi. After driving silently for a while, the driver very politely and deferentially asked if I would answer a question that was troubling him. I assented and he earnestly enquired, 'I am told the white men have left India. Tell me, is it really true that the English have left India?'

Saurashtra, which in colonial times, was known as Kathiawar, was a congeries of some one hundred princely *jagirs*, tiny but autonomous, requiring the presence of very few British administrators. As a result, their absence was not much noticed. By the time we reached Junagadh, the truck driver had been given his first lesson in contemporary Indian history – but I learnt more about contemporary Kathiawar/Saurashtra from his question than anything he picked up from me.

Perhaps the most useful, long-term lesson I learnt there was from the commissioner of Rajkot division, S. Gangopadhyaya, a dour and apparently humourless Bengali *bhadralok* (distinguished gentleman), who asked me to accompany him on a tour of Kutch. The scenery was spectacular as we crossed the wastes of the Little Rann and suddenly found ourselves in the sylvan oasis of Bhuj, the district capital. But before quite reaching Bhuj, the commissioner stopped at a village to conduct a *jamabandi*, a bureaucratic ritual to check on revenue collections but most often used to listen to and redress, if possible, grievances, collective or individual.

So, after the formalities were completed, Commissioner Gangopadhyaya asked whether the gathered villagers had anything to tell him about other matters. At first, there was an embarrassed silence, then one person spoke up. He heaped praises on the mamlatdar. He was followed by several others in the same vein. It seemed no one had any grievance to take up with such a senior officer as the commissioner of the division. The meeting broke up. We returned to our vehicle.

The commissioner volcanically burst upon the mamlatdar, giving him a vicious dressing down. I was puzzled but said nothing until we were well on our way. I then hesitantly asked, 'Sir, everyone in the village was so full of praise for the man, why were you so angry with him?' Gangopadhyaya patiently explained, 'In Gujarat, even if everyone says they are satisfied, there will be someone who complains that the price of sugar is too high. No one did. So I knew the mamlatdar was a tyrannical fellow who had threatened them with punishment if any of them dared complain about anything to the commissioner. That's why I had to pull him up.'

Another very important lesson came two days later, after a fascinating tour of Kutch, when, after recrossing the Little Rann of Kutch, we stopped at a small tea shop. By then I thought I had got to know the stern commissioner sufficiently well to pierce his hauteur and reserve. So I said to him, 'Sir, you obviously don't care for any of this "*bandobast*" (pomp and show) arranged to receive you.' The commissioner nodded. 'In that case,' I continued, 'why do you permit it?' Quick as a flash came the commissioner's riposte that has reverberated in my ears for half a century: 'Aiyar, modesty is a virtue. There is no need to flaunt it!'

During this time, I got another kind of training from Ranjit Chib, my outrageous friend from St Stephen's and Cambridge. He had joined the Tata Administrative Service and been posted to their chemical factory in Mithapur on the edge of nowhere in the north-west corner of the Saurashtra peninsula. Seriously deprived of his daily peg (or should I say vat?) by Gujarat's stringent prohibition laws, Ranjit had taken to making his own wine. To this end, he had bought a cartload of grapes and filled his bathtub with them. House rules required all guests to spend half an hour every day stamping on the grapes to squeeze the juice out and get the resultant mess to start fermenting. I did my daily quota. The last thing I expected to learn on my district training in India's most abstemious state was how to become a human wine press!

That puts me in mind of my encounter in the circuit house with Jane Something-or-the-Other, the US consul who was covering Gujarat from Bombay. Over dinner, she whispered, 'Would you like a drink?' I nodded. 'In that case,' she said, 'just wrap a bottle of soda in a towel and come up to my room. They'll all be thinking we're up to the other thing and we can just quietly have a nightcap!' I should perhaps have, then and there, penned my first DIY book: 'How to Live with Prohibition – and Learn to Love It!'

In between these episodes, I sat for hours in my room wondering how to endure more weeks of this gnawing boredom. Reading Upamanyu Chatterjee's novel, *English, August*, about an IAS probationer, Agastya, posted to a remote district in central India, I relived the paralysing ennui. My only forms of relief were reading and rereading Ian Fleming's James Bond masterpiece, *Goldfinger*, and writing long letters to friends and family.

I also got thoroughly sick of the thali in the dining hall, which I had to eat all the time because all the other items on the menu were way beyond my measly salary of Rs 440 a month. But the thrice-daily ritual of traipsing morosely to the dining hall was enlivened by the occasional visits of the MP for Rajkot, Minoo Masani. He had been elected in the sensational by-elections to five parliamentary constituencies that followed the disastrous India–China war of 1962 and marked the end of the Nehru era. I had attended Masani's splendid talks at St Stephen's where he had destroyed the student politicians' pathetic attempts at defending cooperative farming.

In the dining hall, I listened eagerly to Masani although my views were way to the left of his. If only Masani had stuck to the Gandhian path on which he had embarked under the tutelage of the Mahatma when he was an idealistic young man in the early 1930s, he may have become one of our best ministers. Instead, he chose to become Rajaji's faithful number two and simply faded away from the political scene.

The agonizing trial of 'district training' ended in a hundred days and I, thanking the Lord (or whoever was responsible) for not having been forced into the IAS, moved to the next phase of training in the state capital, Ahmedabad (Gandhinagar was then under construction). On the train there, I discovered that Meghnath had accomplished his primary purpose in serving as my *chaprasi*. Every single currency note had been whacked from my wallet on the eve of my departure. My last lesson: money is fungible and cannot, therefore, be traced!

In Ahmedabad – a dead loss of a city then – there were distractions, such as reading Gandhiji's amazing concluding statement in 1922 in the very courtroom where he was tried for sedition, located in the State Guest House. In it he had pleaded to be given the strictest penalty provided by law because he had knowingly and deliberately broken the Sedition Law which he considered unjust. (The enduring irony is that we still have this colonial Sedition Law, and are still grossly misusing it, seventy-five years into Independence.)

Apart from these private self-taught lessons in history, once again, no one seemed to know what to do with me on my ten-day secondment.

One task was formally calling on the state's home minister, Hitendra Desai, who made a profound impression on me but then disappeared by joining Morarjibhai in the political wilderness; another person I met was a very young Verghese Kurien, brimming with enthusiasm over his milk cooperative in Anand, south of Ahmedabad. His highest ambition at the time was to make a cheese called Amul to rival Kraft. His venture has long vaulted that modest goal.

Another memory that remains vividly with me is meeting the home secretary, an ICS man, Mr Dalal, who sneered at me for opting for the IFS.

'You should have joined the IAS,' he admonished me and went on to explain why: 'When I was driving to office this morning, I saw that a portion of the cement railing on a bridge had crumbled. I ordered it to be repaired – and by the time I return home, it will have been. That,' he ended triumphantly, 'is the power of the domestic civil service.'

As I was leaving the secretariat in the evening, a car pulled up beside me. It was the home secretary. 'Get in,' he ordered in the usual gruff manner of the ICS, 'I'll drop you at the State Guest House.' Gratefully, I clambered in beside him. As we arrived at the bridge he had referred to in the morning, he was all anticipation and I was in a parallel state of mind and spirit. But when we reached the broken railing, it was still broken and forlorn. I was never prouder of having chosen diplomacy over the IAS!

The Delhi stint

The ordeal ended. The train that took me home stopped a little outside Delhi, and I jumped out for a minute to – literally – kiss the soil of liberation. In the capital, we were assigned to Accounts (and most of us wished district training had never ended). We were saved when our solitary lady batchmate, Chukku, burst into tears before A.N. Rao, the principal officer concerned, and begged him to let her have the questions. When he did, she pleaded, 'What is the use of knowing the questions? Please also give me the answers.' Poor Rao did – and all of us passed Accounts.

The next training was Cyphers, in a dungeon located below ground level in the basement of South Block. As we emerged one midday at lunchtime, Pandit Jawaharlal Nehru himself stepped out of the lift. On seeing us, he asked his aide, '*Yeh bachche kaun hain?*' (Who are these children?) It was my only encounter with a man I have admired all my life. He was dead a few days later.

Each of us by then had been assigned a territorial desk. I got East Pakistan. When the news came of the great man's passing, the desk officer – a fussy old promotee officer – insisted (I thought quite rightly) that as Nehru had said '*Aaraam haraam hai*' (Resting is a sin), we should continue working. But a message arrived saying all offices must be closed as a mark of respect to the departed soul.

At the funeral procession the next morning, I was standing in the milling crowd outside Teen Murti House waiting with a heavy heart for the cortège to pass when I heard someone asking me, '*Sunne mei aaya hai, sahib, ki Vyjayanthimala bhi aayengi. Kya sach hai?*' (I am told, sir, that [super star] Vyjayanthimala is also going to be in the procession. Is that true?) I felt sick to the stomach. The cortège passed and all of us had a last glimpse of the greatest prime minister India ever had or is likely to have. An age had ended.

We were then moved to Sapru House to, at long last, learn something of the profession we had opted for: foreign policy. The director of studies was Manohar Lal Sondhi who had quit the IFS immediately after his probationary posting in east Europe. He had seen the horrors of communist occupation and felt he could not work for a foreign policy that condoned Soviet colonialism.

The very best lecture we heard, in my opinion, was Sisir Gupta on Pakistan. He began with the striking line 'India's central foreign policy dilemma is that we are caught between a Pakistan, with a hundred million people, which is "obsessed with its smallness" and an Indonesia, with a hundred million people, which is "obsessed with its largeness" (under Soekarno, who had just then pressed for the Indian Ocean to be renamed the 'Indonesian Ocean').

We also had an excellent teacher of American history and politics in Professor Venkataraman. By then I had been told that my first posting would be to Brussels, headquarters of what was then called the European Common Market. Professor Girija Mukherjee lectured us on European integration – but in three months of weekly classes, he never got beyond Charlemagne!

In the afternoons, we were free to go to the library and work on our two obligatory theses. I chose to write on Vietnam, little knowing it would be invaluable preparation for my posting to Hanoi, and Algeria, which was then in the turbulent aftermath of independence. My Vietnam paper is long lost – a pity – but I still have my paper on Algeria, largely because I gave it to Peter Cella, a New Yorker somewhat older than us, who was in the same French class at the Université Libre de Bruxelles. He took it back to America with him by mistake to his apartment on East 33rd Street and First Avenue. Some forty years later, on retirement, Peter moved from his legal career to the West Side and discovered it among his personal effects. So I am hanging on to it as a kind of family heirloom.

Evenings were spent mostly at La Bohème, although all we could afford was a nimbu pani, which we stretched beyond endurance for hours on end.

It resulted in an introverted threesome – Deepak, Chukku and I. We pooled in and bought a second-hand 1950 Austin A40. We shared the monthly petrol bill, and although we were never stingy on its use, the amount never exceeded Rs 200 a month! As I was the only one who knew how to drive, the car effectively became mine and so it fell to me to attend to its frequent repairs at the garage in Karol Bagh from where we had picked up the vehicle, *Chalti ka Naam Gaadi* (the name of a famous Hindi film which means, 'That which moves is a vehicle').

Inevitably, this rather incestuous relationship, that excluded virtually everyone else, resulted in our friendship breaking down and it was not until years later that Deepak and I made up, largely at Deepak's initiative. Thereafter we remained lifelong friends, all three of us.

See detailed footnotes and endnotes by scanning the QR code above.

4

Sprouting in Brussels

1964–1968

A really fun first posting

By November 1964, we had all departed to our respective destinations: Chukku to learn German in Vienna; me to Brussels to learn French; and Deepak to Oxford to complete his MPhil before proceeding to Tokyo to learn Japanese.

Accompanying me to Brussels was K.P. Balakrishnan (Bala). He had a higher ranking, having stood third in our batch as against the more modest fifth position I had secured. That occasioned a piece of skulduggery on my part that still brings a blush of shame to my cheeks. He was to be designated third secretary (I) and I was to be third secretary (II). I suggested, with all the innocence that I could command, that it might facilitate understanding if we were to be designated by the initial of our surnames. This was readily accepted – and I became TS (A) while poor Bala was relegated to TS (B)!

On the very afternoon of our arrival, we were asked to report within the hour to an officers' meeting with Ambassador K.B. Lall at the chancery in the Square du Bois, an aristocratic townhouse overlooking the leafy Bois de la Cambre, where another occupant was Peter Townsend, Princess Margaret's fiancé. Lall doubled as our representative at the General Agreement on Tariffs and Trade (GATT) and the United Nations Conference on Trade and Development (UNCTAD) in Geneva, where he spent most of the week, returning only to meet his Brussels staff on the weekend. I remember that first encounter with Ambassador Lall quite clearly because he made such an impression.

That day, Belgian TV showed a group of Gorkha soldiers with the UN Peacekeeping Force mowing down a Belgian family fleeing Katanga, the secessionist province in the former Belgian Congo. Having debated threadbare the line to take, and having assigned responsibility for combating the negative fallout of that on India's image in the press and the foreign office, the ambassador turned with equal enthusiasm to matters of somewhat lesser import. Such as discussing ways of encouraging Belgian schoolchildren to participate in the *Shankar's Weekly*'s art competition, and which Indian magazines we should keep in the waiting room where Belgian visitors awaited their visas. I was mesmerized by the man's unflagging energy to deal with the deadly serious and the utterly trivial, and the equal attention paid to all issues.

I was detailed to accompany the ambassador on a visit to Luxembourg to find a distinguished local to preside over the proposed India–Luxembourg Friendship Society. We found one in the person of an eminent medical practitioner, Dr Pierre Worré, the father of the defence minister's daughter-in-law. After the visit I prepared a set of minutes that came in for high praise. This led to my being put in virtually autonomous charge of nurturing our relationship, as the world's 'largest democracy', with what was undoubtedly the world's 'smallest democracy'! I was thus launched into a career of taking notes and following up. (Postscript: Half a century later, half the Luxembourg economy, constituted by the Arcelor steel mills, would be bought up by Lakshmi Mittal, a seasoned entrepreneur of Indian origin!)

The meeting ended with arrangements made for Bala and me to be driven to Rotterdam to avail of the Christmas sales to buy ourselves overcoats worthy of our newfound status as professional diplomats. We were driven there and back by Jayant Patel, a cotton textiles importer who had chosen Brussels as his European base largely because his brother-in-law, Vinay Verma of the IFS, had been posted to Brussels. Jayant's wife, Mira (Aster), was at the Sorbonne working on her thesis, 'Henri Bergson and Aurobindo Ghosh'. It was the start of one of my warmest friendships that ended only when Jayant passed away in Auroville some fifty years later. Mira remains a close friend.

Our first encounter with cocktails, a vital component of diplomatic lives, came within a week of our arrival, with an invitation in French to cocktails at the residence of First Secretary A.N.D. (Sheel) Haksar. The French word he used was *assister* which Bala and I took to mean that we were required to assist with serving the drinks and cleaning up the glassware. It was a relief to discover that *assister* in French meant 'attend'. We were honoured guests.

Early on, Bala and I were deputed to visit a school in Ghent that was celebrating their 'India Days'. We were to give a talk each. The highlight was my meeting with one of the teachers, Maurits Coppieters, who was a founder-member of the Volksunie party, a gathering of Flemish activists who had raised the flag of linguistic insurrection against the domination of a French-speaking elite that not only looked down on the Flamands but also considered them collaborators in the German occupation during the war. (Some of them indeed were, but less for Nazi sympathies than out of indignation at their domination by the French-speaking Belgians. Sounds familiar to south Indian ears – and both Bala and I were south Indians.) I learnt more about Belgium that morning than the poor children did about India. Coppieters went on to win a seat in the Belgian parliament and ever after remained a valuable source of information on what the Flemish half (or more than half!) were thinking.

Another task was visiting a merchant ship in Antwerp where the Indian crew had mutinied against their British officers. We gathered both sides on deck. In high indignation, one of the Indian *lashkar*s (seamen) shouted in uncertain English, 'First mate call me black bastard. I not black. I not bastard!' The first mate indignantly spluttered that he had never said so, but his expression betrayed his guilt. It soon became clear that there was no real quarrel, but the lonely seamen were looking for a shoulder to cry on – and the embassy had sent down two! As many of the seamen were from Kerala, it was left to Bala to shoulder the burden of comforting them in Malayalam while I admonished the captain to keep racism for shore leave. The mutiny was quelled, and we were invited to the captain's table for a somewhat liquid reconciliation lunch. An early lesson in conflict resolution.

The pièce de resistance was, however, the discovery of an enterprising Belgian lady who had opened a general goods store on the quay, calling it Nani ki Dukan – Grandma's Shop – because many of the ships' crews were from the subcontinent. She ran a brisk business on the strength of just this name without ever having visited India!

Our mornings were taken up with French classes at the Institut Audio-

Visuel at the Université Libre de Bruxelles: the 'Free University of Brussels' – 'Free' standing for freedom from religious affiliation. Our teacher was a young woman, Mme Anne Detry. She began by reading in English an introduction to her course that ended with the startling confession 'I do not understand what I have just read out. I speak only French!'

It turned out that we were the very first class to be enrolled and that the course had been designed to allow us to learn the language as a child does; we were, therefore, banned from even attempting to read French newspapers or to try speaking French outside the classroom. We were a truly motley crowd comprising Germans, Italians, Spaniards, Latin Americans, a Cuban lady, a young Japanese hippie girl (who slept through most of the classes, exhausted by dancing through the night), a Turk and a Syrian from Aleppo, besides the inevitable quota of Americans. We were reduced to communicating with each other at break time in gestures, or, in violation of the rules, in pidgin French.

One of the Americans, Peter Cella, kept trying to engage the Cuban in conversation because he felt guilty at what his country was doing to her country. But either because she was shy or because she felt her English was inadequate or, most likely, because it would be regarded as 'politically incorrect', she just would not reciprocate. Peter made a lasting contribution to our diplomatic training: as an expert in wines, his family being vintners, he taught us which wine went with what food for us to order from the United Bonded Stores. The Turk, the Syrian and the two Indians (us) constituted a Third World grouping. It was all great fun.

Presiding over us was a Belgian linguistic psychologist, Josianne Hamers, who confided to me that Bala and I were picking up the language faster than everyone else because both of us knew three languages already (English, Hindi and Tamil/Malayalam) and so absorbing a fourth language came easily. This was not so for the unilinguists – the Americans were at the bottom of the class.

Midway through the course, which came with some very fancy audio equipment through which we could both listen into each other as well as get instruction from the teacher, we came to the word '*même*' meaning 'even'. The sentence was, '*Je parle le français, l'anglais et même le japonais*' ('I speak French, English and even Japanese', the emphasis being on '*même*'). The Japanese girl was sleeping it off as usual, murmuring the sentence in a dull monotone, not emphasizing '*même*' and so not getting the essence of the exercise. I suggested the practice sentence be amended to read, '*Je parle le japonnias, l'anglais et même le français.*' She immediately got it – to wild applause from the rest of the gang.

The course ended in three months by which time we had reached only Lesson 8: – '*Kathrine a dix ans aujourdhui*' (Catherine is ten years old today). The sentence is a defining moment for anyone making a transition from English to French for:

- It teaches one to guard against 'false friends': Although Kathrine and Catherine look the same, the pronunciation is markedly different; in French, it goes 'KAATH-reen'; in English, 'Cath-rin';
- In English, 'is' precedes age; in French *a*, which means 'has', precedes the number of years;
- '*dix ans*' is pronounced 'deezon' – a crucial phonetic link where a word that ends in a consonant and is followed by a word that begins with a vowel are run into each other to '*fait le liaison*'; and
- Three sounds in the last word meaning 'today' do not exist in English: '*au*', '*ou*', '*hui*'.

Once we had got that sentence right, Mme Detry decreed that our foundations in French had been well and truly laid – and we could proceed to Molière! Instead, more wisely, I moved to Alphonse Daudet's *Lettres de mon Moulin* (Letters from My Windmill) under the guidance of Josianne, who agreed to teach me to read and write French. So effective was Anne Detry's method that more than half a century later, and without any regular practice, I can still carry on a conversation with the required panache – which matters more in French than vocabulary or grammar! Remember Professor Higgins in *My Fair Lady* remarking, 'The French don't care what they do actually, as long as they pronounce it properly'?

A few months later, I passed the ministry's compulsory foreign language exam and was confirmed in the IFS. It was the only departmental exam I had honestly passed!

That year, 1965, was filled with much excitement. There was the India–Pakistan conflict in April 1965 in the Rann of Kutch, followed in September by war in Kashmir, and across the India–Pakistan land border. Bala and I were asked to get the Indian perspective out in the Belgian press. I succeeded in writing an article in French (with considerable help from Elisabeth and

Viviane of our Belgian staff) that was carried in the leading French-language newspaper, *Le Soir*.

An unexpected bonus came when I went to call on a photojournalist, Jan Poelaerts, for a particularly vicious and uninformed article on Muslims in India, fed to him by the Pakistan embassy, when our new prime minister fielded Dr Zakir Husain for president. Seeing my indignation, he started showing me photographs of his girlfriend in the nude -- and the Pak embassy were left wondering what changed Poelaerts from a dedicated friend into a Pak baiter.

I also learnt a valuable lesson in diplomatic etiquette from my Pakistani counterpart, Ahmad Kamal, and his wife, who showed me how to maintain a friendly and equable mien even when our countries were at war. It was a lesson I have lived with but, alas, often only observed in the breach. I subsequently met a lot of Pakistani (and Bangladeshi) diplomats and reflected that they were so able that if it had not been for Partition, I might never have made it, in competition with them, to a career in diplomacy.

We third and second secretaries made up a merry band. Apart from our regular once-a-week lunches, we would often gather for parties in each other's homes that lasted all night or continued in a local nightclub *L'Interdit* (The Forbidden), where the commissionaire, dressed resplendently in epaulettes and glittering gold braid, habitually greeted me with a cry of '*Excellence*' (because only ambassadors were exempt from paying an entrance fee at the door). When I passed this on to my ambassador, he sourly remarked, 'I now know why my reputation is being ruined.'

That apart, I made numerous friendships. Among them was a Japanese, Mitsuhei Murata, with whom I am still in regular correspondence, and a Nigerian, Bayo Akinyemi, who had been at St Stephen's but before my time, and his colleague, Bandela Olagun. Also, Ahmed Sidky, an Egyptian, who eventually made it to ambassador in Rome and his Lebanese friend of whom he would say, 'If you ask a Lebanese what two plus two equals, his reply would be, "It depends on whether you are buying or selling!"' There was Grace Armah from Ghana, whom I took to the Senegalese Ballet. She threw me in the interval by querying, 'So you wanted to look before you touched?' Another very close companion was Guillermo Fernandes of Ecuador and Paul Dempsey of Ireland (who ended his career as ambassador to India). There was, above all, Jeremy Kinsman of Canada who has remained a lifelong friend and, before retirement, served as Canada's consul general in New York, ambassador in Moscow, Brussels, The Hague and Rome, and high commissioner in London. But, closest of all was Bryan Gould, a New Zealand-born British diplomat, whose one-line suggestion for resolving the Kashmir issue was to set up a cricket team with five Pakistanis, five Indians and a Kashmiri captain, then take on the world!

I loved Bryan's story of drafting a speech for his ambassador who had served in Brussels as a third secretary before the war. The ambassador began his 1965 speech by remarking that when he was a third secretary, he had to write all of his ambassador's speeches, but now everything was different, and he had been obliged to prepare his own. He then proceeded, insouciantly, to read out what Bryan had written! That neatly summed up the existential reality of third secretaries worldwide through history.

Bryan left the foreign service to return to academia in Oxford, where he very kindly looked after my youngest brother, Mukundan. He moved into politics, became MP for Southampton Test and Dagenham, and rose to be Michael Foot's right hand (or would 'left hand' perhaps be the more appropriate description?). He then quit politics to return to his native New Zealand; I have had the good fortune of meeting him and his wife, Gillian, there.

There was also no end of Belgian pals who knew little English and thus helped to hone my French. My best friend among them was Romain de Porter with his endless trove of off-colour jokes that he loved to hear me translate into English for those who failed to get the point in the original version. He had a great friend, an Egyptian who knew no French but would walk up to unknown women in the Roi d'Espagne beer hall whispering, 'Fooky-fooky' – and was astonishingly successful!

Talking to the Belgian staff at the embassy who helped with newspaper and magazine translations gave a great fillip to my grasp of a new language. And my work brought me in touch with numerous officials and journalists, several of whom barely knew any English. I also learnt a number of catchy French songs, principally those of Françoise Hardy ('Tous les garçons et les filles de mon age') and Patricia Clarke ('C'est ma chanson') that I occasionally hum to myself. And the simple but deeply moving poems of Maurice Carême.

Luxembourg became a major arena of my activity where I was tasked to set up the India–Luxembourg Friendship Society (and used the opportunity to visit a nightclub where the performer could simultaneously rotate the tassels on her nipples in opposite directions!). None of the members knew anything about India beyond a vague notion that all Indians (whom they called 'Hindous', despite correction) were highly spiritual (despite the living example before them!).

It was decided by the end of 1965 that we had collected enough members and generated enough interest to inaugurate the Amities (Friendship Society). Ambassador Lall suggested we write to the President's Secretariat for a message and I arranged for it to be printed in a box on the front page of the leading newspaper of the city, the *Luxemburger Wort*.

The condition was that I should deliver the text to them the previous day by 4 p.m., so that they could translate and print it. Noon came in Brussels, but there was still no message. I needed at least three hours to drive to Luxembourg. I went into the ambassador's room in something of a panic to tell him no message had come. The ambassador quietly remarked that it had. I was taken aback: 'Where? Where is it, sir?' His reply was classic K.B. Lall: '*Tum likho na!*' (Why don't you write it?)

I was horrified. I was being asked to forge a message from our head of state! Ambassador KB gently explained, 'After all, it is only a *babu* (a lowly official) like you who is going to write it in Delhi. So why not in Brussels?' I rushed out of the room, grabbed a pen – and wrote the greatest piece of prose that was ever put out in the name of that great stylist of the English language, Dr S. Radhakrishnan. I took it back to Lall who read it carefully and then paid the highest compliment in his lexicon: '*Khoob, bahut khoob*' (Good, very good).

I rushed off to Luxembourg where I arrived breathless but triumphant. I had made it just in time. The next day, I walked to the nearest kiosk and ordered myself ten copies of the *Wort*, for there on the front page, as promised, was our president's message to the people of Luxembourg. I then wandered into Luxembourg's only department store to pick up a few geegaws for the inauguration. A salesgirl came up to me to say there was a call for me from Brussels. It was First Secretary Haksar on the line, sounding very alarmed. 'The real message has come!' he exclaimed, and added, 'That's the trouble with you and the ambassador – always trying to beat the system.'

My world collapsed around me. I had just succeeded in getting past the communist tag to get into the IFS – and here I was complicit in felony, against the president of India, no less. I called the ambassador who listened, paused and then reprimanded me: '*Tum kuch samajhte nahin ho.* [You don't understand anything.] The president is so keen on friendship with Luxembourg that he has sent two messages; the first is the one you have had printed on the front page in a language no one in India understands, and the second that I will read out at this evening's inauguration!'

It was not, however, quite as easy getting out of the next imbroglio into which Ambassador Lall landed me. A rather dishevelled young Indian called on him with a Belgian girl in tow – a countess, she claimed, no less – and explained that he had stowed away on a ship from Bombay that docked at Antwerp. He had stolen out of the ship, met this young countess and was now looking for a job – any job. The ambassador, who was a sucker for a sob story, sent him to me to find him employment with the Brussels office of Air India or any of the parastatals – the Cashew Nuts Board, the Tea Council – which had opened their offices in the city.

All declined, so I, who was looking for a *chaprasi*, asked him whether he would consent to doing such a humble job. He promptly agreed and I prevailed on admin to take him on. I was most satisfied with his work and delighted at having pleased both my boss and met my office requirements. Then, one day at lunchtime, there was a huge rumpus. The man had seen our India-based security guard misbehaving with one of our Belgian staff, Jacqueline, and intervened. This had led to fisticuffs in which my man had been clearly worsted and had then run off, leaving no trace.

I was ordered by the irate head of chancery, who loathed both the ambassador and me, to ring the lady chief of the Foreigners' Police. She rang me back after a while to say that they had been to the man's one-room dump in a dilapidated section of town and discovered two passports – both Pakistani! So, I had been responsible for employing a Pakistani in the Indian embassy – and that too within two months of our going to war with them! The end loomed. I don't quite know how, but KB somehow succeeded in getting both of us off the hook.

Another major area of my activity was the Belgo-Indian Friendship Society whose leading light was Mme Cliquet, a large and boisterous blonde, followed by André van Lysbeth, a devotee of Swami Sivananda (in whose ashram my mother spent an inordinate amount of time). Van Lysbeth's yoga institute was a smash hit long before our current prime minister made organizing International Yoga Day the chief task and responsibility for Indian missions abroad. About twenty of their members, Indophiles all, along with Kesterlin, the secretary general of the mayor's office, were most excited about a fortnight's visit to India in January 1966 that they were planning. From all reports, they had a rip-roaring time in India. Alas, the Air India aircraft in which the delegation was travelling back from India crashed on the Mont Blanc outside Geneva – and all of them perished. (Dr Homi Bhabha died in the same crash.)

For some reason that I am unable still to fathom, I blamed myself for the accident, having been so involved in the preparations for the visit. I needed to find solace – and found it quite unexpectedly in Huy in the Ardennes, which I had to visit for a function organized by the Nobel Laureate Father Pire's Peace Institute, dedicated to the memory of Mahatma Gandhi on the anniversary of his martyrdom, 30 January 1966. There was something about Father Pire and his surroundings that radiated peace, tranquillity and comfort for my stricken soul. I returned to Brussels whole and psychologically stabilized.

I also came to know a large number of Indian artists of various disciplines. The sculptor, Amarnath Sahgal, actually moved into my small one-bedroom apartment and settled himself for a month or more on my drawing room sofa while attempting to organize exhibitions for himself in different European countries.

Amarnath was followed by Kekoo Ghandy of the Chemould Gallery who had brought a number of paintings by then little-known Indian artists for the Edinburgh Art Festival and contacted me to explore the possibilities for exhibitions in Belgium and Luxembourg. I arranged a dinner for him to introduce these works and artists to a number of culture editors and art critics. The flight from London arrived late, so Kekoo enquired whether in view of the advanced hour he might come straight to my flat from the airport and spend the rest of the night there. I readily agreed – not realizing that three months later, he would still be there!

The compensation was that he introduced me to many of these artists, some of whom – like S.H. Raza and F.N. Souza – went on to command huge prices. They were willing to let me have an artwork or two for a minimal price to thank me for help rendered but I was in too impecunious a financial state to afford even the drastic cut-prices on offer; had I had the required amount then, I would be a millionaire several times over by now!

We also had concerts by Ravi Shankar and Alla Rakha in several places – Liège, Ghent, Brussels – besides Luxembourg. This was the height of the India fervour that gripped European youth in the wake of the Beatles visiting India to learn meditation at Maharishi Mahesh Yogi's ashram – a moment in cultural history symbolized by the ad that read, 'You don't have to be a Hindoo to play the sitar'!

The enthusiastic organizer of the concerts was a young man who headed the Jeunesses Musicales (Youth Music Lovers Society). Unfortunately, he tripped up at Ravi Shankar's inaugural concert in Liège when he remarked that the second half of the concert had been 'brilliant'; Ravi Shankar turned on him furiously and spat, 'What was wrong with the first half?'

I was accompanied to the Luxembourg concert, which was the first event organized by the newly founded India–Luxembourg Friendship Society, by the young and (at the time) relatively little-known danseuse, Sonal Mansingh, who had married my IFS batchmate and was glad of the opportunity to showcase her art to European audiences. When the applause for a Ravi Shankar–Alla Rakha *jugalbandi* (duet) reached a climax and the thousand-strong audience burst into transports of appreciation at their wizardry, I whispered to Sonal that both were outstanding. She turned up her nose and whispered back, 'Just watch when I perform tomorrow!'

Next evening, she was as good as her word. She left an audience that had never before seen a Bharatanatyam or Odissi performance breathless with her magic. I shared in the encomiums as her orchestra – for she was accompanied only on a tape recorder that I operated! It was a sensational evening.

When we got Sonal back to Brussels, Jayant Patel and I took her to a nightclub where I invited her on to the dance floor. She demurred, saying she did not know how. So, I swept her up and taught her the foxtrot: one-two-three-four! Ever since, I've tried to get her to call me 'Maître', the master who taught her ballroom dancing!

We also had a Gandhian, Govindan Ramachandran, who had a mass of unkempt white hair over a swarthy countenance (a bit like V.K. Krishna Menon) and came alive on the stage with his mesmerizing rhetoric about the Mahatma's legacy. He never remembered the subject on which he was supposed to speak and would ask me sotto voce what his subject was just as he rose to go to the podium. His words then flowed without pause in a flood of well-constructed thoughts and sentences that held the audience spellbound. It was truly an exceptional experience to listen to him night after night as we travelled together all over Belgium.

I returned when I could to economics. I wrote a paper on the 'GATT Long Term Arrangement on Cotton Textiles' that received the ambassador's approbation, in token of which he asked me to study and critique a paper by the Economist Intelligence Unit on 'Aid Weariness'. We ourselves seemed wearied of aid, of receiving aid or constantly asking for it, largely from Western sources. That led me to another diplomatic milestone. I was to accompany R. Venkataraman, minister (economic), to a meeting about aid from Belgium for the Kalpakkam nuclear power plant. At the last moment, Venkataraman fell ill; so I had to proceed on my own. On returning, I sent off my first-ever telegram in cypher.

Eventually, Western reluctance to help resulted in the Soviet Union stepping in and I was with Prime Minister Rajiv Gandhi when he visited the Kalpakkam plant to switch on nuclear electricity transmission in December 1985, twenty-one long years after my first juvenile involvement with the project. The transmission of power failed next day; that, however, is another story!

Bhoothalingam chosen to replace Ambassador Lall

Towards the middle of 1966, KB was transferred to India. A renowned ICS civil servant, S. Bhoothalingam was to replace him. I was more than a little apprehensive because the ambassador-designate had the reputation of being a martinet. The new ambassador's luggage arrived. But he didn't.

I never quite understood the details, but a scandal had been built up around Bhoothalingam's role as steel secretary by a group of left-wing Congress parliamentarians led by Chandra Shekhar and Mohan Dharia. The charges were never proved but, as recounted in Bhoothalingam's memoirs,[1] the rumours had the curious consequence of the Belgian royal palace withdrawing their

[1] S. Bhoothalingam, *Reflections on an Era: Memoirs of a Civil Servant*, Affiliated East-West Press, Chennai, 1993.

agrément because they did not want a 'tainted' ambassador accredited to His Majesty the King of the Belgians! As Bhoothalingam remarks, this was rich coming from the descendants of King Leopold who had robbed the Congo blind!

We were asked to ship the luggage back to Delhi. Another ICS officer, T. Swaminathan, arrived in Bhoothalingam's stead. I had a remote connection with him in that his younger son, universally known as 'Conky', had been at school with me.

The new ambassador lacked KB's flamboyance (and heartily disliked his predecessor as well). However, he was undoubtedly able. Indeed, his ability was such that he was cabinet secretary when the East Pakistan/Bangladesh crisis erupted five years later. Ironically, K.B. Lall was the principal defence secretary alongside Swaminathan. They put aside their personal differences to give India its most spectacular military victory.

K.B. Lall lost none of his tongue-in-the-cheek wit in the midst of all the tensions. Asked by the press whether he apprehended a pincer attack by China across the Himalaya, he drily replied, 'I think we may assume that both sides are praying for snow!'

Soon after Ambassador Swaminathan's arrival, I was granted home leave to visit my aunt, Alankaram *periamma*, whose health had deteriorated alarmingly after she had been diagnosed with cancer. Tragically, she died a few days after I took leave of her in her Bombay hospital.

My 'soul force' car

Before leaving for Delhi, I abandoned the disgraceful Volkswagen in which I had met with an accident on the very day I bought it second-hand from a departing colleague. As I had not had time to get it insured, I could not afford to repair the damaged right-hand door and so had to clamber into the driver's seat from the other side, having secured the damaged door with a rope! (The brakes were also a problem; so I christened it the 'Gandhi car' for it could be halted only by soul force.)

Its replacement was Jayant's Fiat in which we had travelled all over Europe. I thought I would pay for it with the Belgian francs I thought I would be earning during my home leave. As it turned out, pay during home leave was in rupees, so when I returned, I had a car but no Belgian francs with which to pay for it. Jayant accompanied me to the Westminster Bank, and the bank manager offered to convert my overdraft into a loan.

I was unbounded in my gratitude that so simple a method had been found to get me off the hook. It was Jayant who pointed out that there was absolutely no need for me to feel beholden to the bank manager because that man was going to make money in interest out of the loan. I had so little business sense, I had not realized that.

Mahatma Gandhi's centenary

My return to Brussels coincided with a major change in my focus of work. I was put in charge of organizing the centenary celebrations in Belgium of Mahatma Gandhi's birth. Her Majesty the Queen of the Belgians kindly consented to grace the inauguration with her presence. The Belgians are such avid royalists that this alone ensured that the eyes of all Belgium would be upon us and we could retrieve our name as a peace-loving nation, erasing (or, at any rate, moderating) memories of Indian peacekeepers firing at fleeing Belgian families in the Congo, and India and Pakistan going to war twice the previous year for reasons incomprehensible to the average Belgian.

My counterpart was the genial and enthusiastic Jean-Paul Baugniet. He was innocent of all English and, thus, a useful flintstone on which to hone my French. Things were moving along swimmingly when in October 1967, just as I was getting into the staff car to leave for a meeting with Baugniet, a messenger rushed up to say that I was required urgently by the ambassador.

Ambassador Swaminathan held a piece of paper and, shaking his head sadly, announced that my transfer orders had come; I was under orders to return to headquarters immediately. He went on to explain that he had received intimation of this sometime earlier and had been in correspondence with the foreign secretary (FS), Rajeshwar Dayal (my old patron), to delay my departure till the Gandhi centenary was launched the following year. But a letter from the FS had just arrived saying that was not possible and I should return to Delhi without delay. Then, rather sentimentally, Ambassador Swaminathan said he really couldn't press the matter further as he and I were both Tamilian Brahmins and it would look as if he were advocating my case for parochial reasons.

I took it on the chin and, as I returned to my waiting staff car, one of our assistants, M.B. Tuli, asked if he could take a ride with me. I readily consented, and as we swung out of the gates of the Square du Bois, I told him of my transfer orders. He asked the driver to stop, went out of the car to examine the car's number plate, checked the number of kilometres on the speedometer, asked me for my date of birth, looked at the time on his watch, rechecked the date on which we were having our conversation, made some rapid-fire calculations in his mind and confidently announced that I would not be leaving Belgium on transfer till 16 October the following year, 1969. I protested that this was nonsense. Tuli remained adamant, maintaining that he was a numerologist and his calculations had never proved wrong.

Astonishingly, within a few days, Delhi changed its mind and said I could stay in Brussels till the Gandhi centenary the following year. Tuli had been proved right, but what of his prediction that I would stay till 16 October? The Gandhi centenary was to fall on Wednesday, 2 October 1969, and the weekly Air India flight would transit through Brussels the following Wednesday, 9 October. That was the day I would have to fly out. Tuli was unfazed. His calculations had shown my date of departure as 16 October – and it would be on 16 October that I would fly out. In the event, the Air India flight on Wednesday, 9 October, was cancelled – and I flew out the next Wednesday, 16 October!

This defies all rationality. But imagine the jolt I got when years later Indira Gandhi was assassinated and in a panel of astrologists and numerologists, M.B. Tuli – who on retirement had set himself up as a professional numerologist – proved to have been the most accurate in his prediction of her demise. Of course, the code of astrologers and their ilk does not permit disclosure of the specifics of death. Their forecasts on this subject are, therefore, always couched in ambiguities; but it appeared that Tuli had got the details right.

I remain an atheist and put Tuli's predictions down to coincidence, but I also remain unconvinced that all this is just mumbo-jumbo. In despair, I cling to the belief that there must be some rational explanation that science will one day uncover.

Interlude with my youngest brother

My youngest brother, Mukundan, had obtained a scholarship to intern at London's famous King's College Hospital and visited me in Brussels. Two of my Cambridge friends, Christie Davies and Krishan Kumar, came over from England and the four of us set out in my car on a most enjoyable tour that took us to the Black Forest, with a night in glorious Tübingen; then on to Winterthur in Switzerland on one of the most beautiful drives I have ever been; past Luzern and Lausanne to Geneva, where Mukund was particularly keen on seeing the flower clock (no accounting for tastes); then via Besançon to Paris.

Somewhere along the way, Christie whispered to me that Mukund was going rather a lot to the bathroom and he had once followed him to find the basin awash in vomit. I dismissed this as the result of Mukund not being used to the twists and turns of the mountain roads. I did not realize this was the first alarm signal that should have had me sitting up and finding out what was wrong.

Next, we were in Paris, at a very fancy apartment in the 16th arrondissement where we were to spend a couple of nights courtesy a friend. Mukund asked her to accompany him on a walk 'under the bridges of Paris'. There he told her that he was very upset that his girlfriend at Delhi's AIIMS hospital was not responding to his letters and had perhaps decided to ditch him for someone else. Our friend told me of Mukund's disclosure but I thought no more of it.

1968: An eventful year

Meanwhile, 1968 turned out to be one of the most news-filled years in world history. It was the year of the Tet Offensive that starkly showed how the war in Vietnam was being taken to higher and higher levels of tragic absurdity. The most powerful nation in the world was battering a guerrilla movement launched defiantly by one of the poorest, most wretched countries on earth. And all the bombs rained on North Vietnam were failing to shake the determination of Ho Chi Minh and his comrades to not give an inch.

In America itself, the war had become so unpopular that students were taking to the streets chanting, 'Hey, Hey, Hey, LBJ! How many kids did you kill today?' Internal turmoil was so rife that Lyndon Johnson had to withdraw from contesting the presidential election. The Democratic Convention in Chicago became a pitched street fight between the 'pigs' (police) and the people. Martin Luther King was assassinated. Los Angeles' largely Black suburb of Watts burned. Students at the University of Kent campus were shot dead. It was the year of the 'flower children'. Hatred and unbridled love jostled against each other. For me, Leonard Cohen's songs summed up the mood and yearnings of an entire generation.

Nearer me, the rebellion of the students and workers in Paris broke out the day after May Day. Student revolutionaries like Daniel Cohn-Bendit, a German Jew, later MP, and Paul Berenger, later to be prime minister of Mauritius, became household names. The Bible of the movement was the booklet *'Les Murs ont la Parole'* (The walls have the floor), filled with witty graffiti: 'Freedom will come when the last capitalist is hanged by the entrails of the last bureaucrat'; '*Soyez réaliste, demandez l'impossible*' (Be a realist, demand the impossible); '*Il est interdit d'interdire*' (It is forbidden to forbid); 'Run comrade, run, the old world is coming up right behind you.'

Persuading myself that as I was not accredited to France and there could be no real objection to my joining the student revolutionaries at the barricades, I got Jayant to drive us both to Paris. There we met up with his wife, Mira, who, being a student at the Sorbonne, knew all about where to take us. We fetched up in the auditorium of the university: it seemed to be the centre of the universe. Mira then took us to the Théâtre d'Odéon in the Latin Quarter, another major theatre of the revolt. She remembers me jumping on to the stage and thundering at the audience. I have but a faint memory of this youthful excess. The novelty of the revolution soon wore off.

In August 1968, the modern dance genius Maurice Béjart, founder of the Ballet du XXe Siècle (Twentieth Century Ballet), whom I had encouraged to visit India to see our dance forms for himself, became a good friend and invited me to the 'world premiere' in Avignon of the ballet *Shakti* that he had conceived after his visit to India. It gave me the opportunity to see how the student–worker revolt had spread to other parts of France. There was a roundabout in the centre of the city that the students had 'captured'. I listened to several impassioned speeches about 'liberty', 'oppression', 'exploitation'.

Then a genuine worker mounted the platform. His grandfather, he said, had to work twelve months a year without any vacation; his father was given a week off in the year; he himself was entitled to a month's leave along with the *treizium* (thirteenth-month wages) being paid: the bonus of an extra month's wages to pay for his holiday. What 'exploitation' were these kids talking about? That for me ended the revolution.

See detailed footnotes and endnotes by scanning the QR code above.

5

At War in Vietnam
Hanoi: 1968 (November)–1969 (July)

Nixon v/s Ho Chi Minh
India's CG v/s His Consul

A potentially exciting posting

I was, however, destined to see a real revolution from up close. Instead of transferring me to Delhi, the ministry decided to send me as consul to Hanoi. (How my security clearance had swung like a pendulum to post me to an avowedly communist country was a mystery never explained to me!) I was to work under K.S. Shelvankar, a political appointee of the prime minister, who had been closely associated in London with V.K. Krishna Menon during the freedom struggle; in 1943 he had written a devastating critique of the economic consequences of British rule in India. The Hanoi posting seemed quite an exciting prospect for me.

My departure from Brussels was imminent. The Mahatma's centenary celebrations were launched with due pomp and ceremony. There were many tearful farewells. I had thoroughly enjoyed my first posting; made a horde of friends of all nationalities; travelled all over Belgium and Luxembourg; journeyed extensively in the countries surrounding Belgium and Luxembourg; learnt a new language with a measure of competence; and been introduced to a profession I was thrilled at having chosen.

I stopped off in Delhi for a few days on my way to my next posting. There I learnt that Mukund had attempted, on his return from Europe, to cut his wrist and was only fortuitously saved from bleeding to death by the mother of the AIIMS psychiatrist whom he was seeing. I tried to get him to tell me more, but he refused to elaborate. No, it was not the girl who had abandoned him as he had already found a substitute in another fellow student, Sujata. Instead, he explained, what had humiliated him was being defeated in a student election by a cretin whose slogan was 'Time and Tide Wait for No Man. Vote for Sahni!'

However, he had come third in the final exams at AIIMS and won the Rhodes Scholarship for admission to Oxford. He said he was astonished at that because on arriving for the dinner with previous Rhodes scholars who selected the new scholars by talking to the candidates over dinner, he had spotted Girish Karnad, the playwright, who was a friend of mine, and asked him, 'I say, what do these bastards ask?' and Karnad had solemnly replied, 'I can't tell you because I am one of the bastards.' Mukund thought that was the end of the Rhodes road for him. Instead, he was chosen! He sounded too upbeat for me to worry any further.

Preparing for Hanoi

I went to meet T.N. Kaul who was marking time as secretary (East) before moving up to foreign secretary. He asked me whether I knew why I had been selected to go to Hanoi. I breezily replied, 'To assist the consul general who does not belong to the service, sir.' Kaul put me in my place with a curt 'No, young man, to learn from him'.

I was also told I was to escort Mrs Mary Shelvankar who was following her husband, who had arrived at his post a few weeks earlier. She was a large, voluptuous blonde, extroverted, affectionate and full of good humour. 'When I enter the pub in my village at home in Scotland,' she revealed to me early in our journey, 'someone always calls out, "Here comes Mary, bringing in the milk!"' That seemed to augur well; if she was such fun, surely her husband would be similar.

We landed in Bangkok where US military aircraft were lined up exactly as described in Mary McCarthy's *Vietnam* on which I was boning up. The streets were full of huge American GIs with tiny Thai girls hanging on to their arms. I did not know whom to feel sorry for: the girls or these gigantic GIs, many of whom would be dead or grievously wounded fighting for their lives against 'Charlie', the opprobrious name given by the Americans to their Vietnamese challengers.

Thanks to Mary, we had dinner with Ambassador K.R. Narayanan at the Baan Thai in Bangkok, a most elegant restaurant set in the most beautiful garden I had ever entered. Then Mary, with me trotting along, took an overnight train to the Laos border. Dawn was just lighting up the sky with a gorgeous, orange-coloured sun rising over the broad bosom of the magnificent Mekong river; exotic, scenically stunning, the fresh morning air filled with birdsong. We crossed by ferry and were met on the other side by the embassy chauffeur who drove us to Vientiane along, we were told, the only tarred road in Laos.

A couple of days later, we fetched up at the airport to catch the weekly courier flight of the ICSC (International Commission for Supervision and Control) that the 1954 'peace' accords had set up for each of the three Indo-China countries: Cambodia, Laos and the two halves of Vietnam – the main office in merry Saigon and a subsidiary bureau in sombre Hanoi. India was the chair; the other two members were Canada and Poland.

Lyndon Johnson's bombing halt

While waiting for the flight to land that evening of 2 November 1968, I switched on my transistor radio and heard the announcement of President Johnson's decision to halt US bombing over all of North Vietnam. I thought there would be celebrations galore and dancing on the streets when we landed in Hanoi. Instead, all was dark, few were on the streets, and it seemed nothing had changed.

I began my new assignment next morning by comparing the English and French versions of Ho Chi Minh's reaction to the bombing halt. Word for word, the statement read the same in both versions except that one sentence in the French version, which had come out later, was underlined. I concluded that the underlining was significant as it seemed to have been done after due reflection. In English, the sentence read: 'We shall fight on till we have swept the last aggressor from our soil.' The import of that one sentence was slowly unveiled over the next several months.

I was put up in the rather spare and forbidding Hotel Bien Hoa. Trying to order dinner, I found my daily allowance would not go further than breakfast. I now understood why my predecessor, Ranjit Sethi, had insisted on staying with Shelvankar for the few weeks they had served together. I survived by joining the mess run by the junior officials and moving into a modest spare suite in the building next to the chancery that housed all the staff.

The consul general himself turned out to be the polar opposite of his wife. Tetchy and touchy, he attempted to imitate his '*beau ideal*', V.K. Krishna Menon, but had neither Menon's overweening self-confidence nor his overwhelming personality.

He was also deeply upset that the North Vietnamese were not willing to put up with the Government of India playing ducks and drakes with them by accrediting to their capital a consul general with the personal rank of 'ambassador'. This was in order to avoid the full force of the US Battle Act descending on our bellies to cut us off from US PL-480 food aid on which we were pathetically dependent for national survival. At the same time, we were signalling to Hanoi – wink, wink – that we regarded them as the real representative of the Vietnamese people even if we could not openly say so. The North Vietnamese were fighting a war for independence against the greatest military force on earth and would not waste their time and energy appeasing a consular crow pretending to be an ambassadorial peacock. So, they would not grant him the honorific of 'Excellency' nor allow him a CD number plate for his car. As far as they were concerned, India had not accorded them diplomatic recognition and established only consular relations. They were not ready to play games with us behind the veil.

They were also unimpressed with Shelvankar carrying a 'personal letter' from Prime Minister Indira Gandhi to Ho Chi Minh. Denying Shelvankar an audience with the legendary leader of the revolution, their foreign office asked the consul general to leave the letter with the head of their Asia department. Shelvankar had, quite simply, been conned by the mandarins of our foreign ministry. All this should have been settled with the North Vietnamese before sending him out.

No wonder his innate surliness burst into view. And just like Krishna

Menon was wont to do, Shelvankar decided to take out his frustration on his deputy: me. So, while the Americans and the Vietnamese fought their minor battle on the Killing Fields of the South, the major war in the North was fought between the consul general and me!

The battle was, however, postponed by a month owing to Shelvankar being summoned to a meeting in New Delhi of genuine Indian ambassadors to South East Asia. After cautioning me that in his absence, I was to use the designation 'chargé d'affaires' and not 'acting consul general' to underline his ambassadorial status, the Shelvankars went off and for a whole month peace reigned on both the US bombing front and at the consulate.

Hanoi reveals its hand

Meanwhile, negotiations had been proposed at the Hotel Majestic in Paris between the Saigon government and the US, on the one side, and the Hanoi government, on the other. Hanoi was holding out for the National Liberation Front (political arm of the Viet Cong) to also be included. Viewing all this from afar – as India was not involved – I was intrigued to receive a call from their foreign office summoning the 'acting consul general' to a meeting with the head of the Asia department. We returned a formal reply saying the 'chargé d'affaires' would be honoured to attend. The protocol officer welcomed me as the acting consul general of India; the head of the Asia department did the same. They wanted to make it clear as spring water at the source that they did not regard the unfortunate Shelvankar as an 'ambassador'.

What followed was even more intriguing. The head of the Asia department said they regarded India as a trustworthy partner in international affairs and as a country that genuinely had the interest of the Vietnamese people at heart. Therefore, he had been instructed to share with me their views on how the Paris negotiations should proceed. He said that if the fighting were stopped in the South and the National Liberation Front were recognized, the North, for its part, was willing to see a representative coalition government being formed in the South, and to postpone reunification to an indeterminate future.

I staggered out, wondering why their negotiating strategy was being revealed to a junior officer (I was only twenty-seven years old). They could have awaited the consul general's return as no parleys had yet started at the

Hotel Majestic. What was the hurry? The only rational argument I could come up with was that this was a hangover from the Geneva Conference of 1954. There, the French prime minister, Pierre Mendès-France, had remarked there were ten participants – nine at the conference table and one outside (India – Krishna Menon). Menon's role, in what were effectively 'proximity talks' between the Viet Minh and the US, had been crucial to the outcome of that conference. Hanoi was perhaps under the impression that India might still be able to resume its mediatory role by 'being present' in Paris. To the best of my knowledge, on discovering that there was no such Indian interlocutor available, they never disclosed any such information to us again.

I reported back to Delhi – sitting with the cypher assistant in a stuffy, locked room – so that there could be no question of any unauthorized person listening in. I needn't have bothered. My cypher telegram was not even acknowledged. It was addressed only to Shelvankar. He either pocketed it – or even chewed it up!

Reflections on the war

While Shelvankar was away, I had the British vice consul, a stripling of some twenty years, over for dinner. The Democratic Republic of Vietnam's (DRVN) treatment of the Brits was even more cavalier than their treatment of Shelvankar. Whitehall had dispatched Her Britannic Majesty's envoy, Mr Philo, to Hanoi without either according diplomatic recognition to the DRVN, or even having a consular agreement with them. Therefore, the receiving government called Mr Philo's office – you've guessed it! – 'Mr Philo's office', denying him and his staff any diplomatic or consular privileges.

The vice consul arrived and the conversation turned to the Ho Chi Minh Trail that literally began outside our chancery. Dozens of Vietnamese cycled past every few minutes, their cycles laden with bamboo poles on which they balanced their pots and pans, the spare changes of clothing they were allowed, and essential or supplementary food supplies and prophylactic medicines, all the way through the trail in Laos, or through underground tunnels a thousand kilometres or more, to fight the Americans and the South Vietnamese army, the Army of the Republic of Vietnam (ARVN) in the south. En route they faced deadly, disabling Agent Orange attacks in the forests.

When I expressed admiration for them, the vice consul reminded me that an American U-2 could cross the whole of Vietnam in ten minutes at a height of 60,000 feet and take photographs; they could even spot the saucer on which his coffee cup was balanced and the photographs would show the pattern on the saucer better than I could see with my naked eye. How on earth could these guys on bicycles defeat American might? I have been looking for the vice consul ever after to rub it in that it was the 'guys on bicycles' who won!

A routine work life

My work as the head of chancery (HoC) was incredibly routine. Most of the time, I was initialling notes verbale saying:

> The Consulate General of India presents its compliments to the Ministry of Foreign Affairs of the Government of the Democratic Republic of Vietnam and requests the honourable Ministry to please supply the following:
>
> i. v kilo chicken
> ii. w kilo mutton (goat's meat)
> iii. x kilo potatoes
> iv. y kilo onions
> v. z kilo peas
>
> The Consulate General of India avails itself of this opportunity to renew to the Ministry of Foreign Affairs the assurances of its highest consideration.

As we were required to indent all our supplies from the foreign office, I could really see no reason for my other major task as HoC – signing the monthly price returns the ministry insisted on to determine our foreign allowance. When I was presented my first returns for November 1968, I baulked at signing it as clearly the figures were all fudged. The accountant and the other officials convened a council of war and sent Ganapati, an assistant, whom they had shrewdly identified as my favourite, to persuade me to see good sense.

Ganapati patiently explained that a previous consul general had made use of the regular and invariable morning and afternoon aerial bombings by the Americans to gather the staff together in the consulate's bomb shelter, which was the reinforced basement of the chancery. While the bombs continued to rain over the city, the consul general would while away the long, boring hours waiting for the 'all clear' to sound by picking up his pen and diligently filling out the price returns himself. His argument was that the IA&AS – Indian Audit and Accounts Service (otherwise known as the Indian Aiyars and Aiyangars Service) – was so full of Madrasi Brahmins that none of these cowards would dare visit war-torn Vietnam to check for themselves.

Ganapati agreed that the figures were all fictional but if we altered them to reflect the reality, the same Madrasi Brahmins would enquire how prices had so suddenly and drastically fallen. We senior officers could save ourselves, but what would become of the poor officials who were only obeying orders? So, to save the junior officials from a fate worse than death, would I please agree to sign the returns? I consented – but on condition that we would freeze the price returns for the whole of the following year. I still await recognition from the Vietnamese authorities for having so dramatically arrested inflation.

Two rather pleasant rewards followed from my maiden visit to the head of the Asia department. One, half a dozen Vietnamese officers were given permission to attend a luncheon organized by me to discuss the outside possibility of cooperation between our two countries in cultural matters. The discussion came to nothing but when I asked them to sign the visitors' book, I found that the last time any Vietnamese official or politician had visited the consulate was six years earlier, on 26 October 1962 at the outbreak of the India–China war when K.R. Narayanan was the consul general. So just the acceptance of this invitation was something of a diplomatic breakthrough.

The other was that the consulate was permitted to take a one-day holiday in Halong Bay. It is now a renowned tourist resort, but back in the dark days of 1968 it was a strangely neglected spot, with nothing to see or do except watch cute little Vietnamese children playing '*Ba mee của tôi*' – shooting down fantasy American aircraft!

We, nevertheless, had a welcome break. Our usual mode of entertaining ourselves was to go all together to Gia Long airport to collect the diplomatic bag which arrived by the ICSC courier once a week on Fridays. This had all the elements of tension and suspense of an Agatha Christie play. For, after we had spotted the silver streak in the clear blue sky heralding the arrival of the plane over Hanoi, a Vietnamese official, sadly shaking his head, would lugubriously inform us, 'Velly bad weather, velly bad … no plane landing.' This was to signal their disapproval of something the ICSC had said or done. With sinking hearts, we would watch aghast as the plane turned around in the air and headed south, dashing all prospects – for another whole week – of seeing (or sending) mail from home, Indian newspapers or correspondence with the MEA. Indeed, there was no guarantee that the Hanoi authorities would allow the ICSC plane to land the following Friday, or any given Friday into an indefinite future.

This situation led to my being tangled in the coils of complicated correspondence with the ministry on an already knotty issue: a refund they were seeking for the private use of the staff car. First, I had to figure out how did I, a mere probationer, ever secure access to a staff car for private use? After long cogitation I remembered that one day, on exiting from the ministry, we had tried to start our 1950 Austin-40 and found the car would not move. One of the staff car drivers lounging in the vicinity had come by to help us and announced there was no petrol in the car. He offered to drive down to the nearby petrol station in his staff car and bring us a gallon of the life-saving fuel in a can. We had gratefully accepted the offer; the driver returned, and off we went on our merry way, little knowing that the mills of the ministry, like the mills of God, may grind slowly but they grind exceedingly small. I must have signed some staff car book that the driver had held out to me. I couldn't remember, but there was my signature in black and white. There was no denying it. I was liable to pay the exacting sum of Rs 1.25 for 'private use of staff car'.

My guilt established, I asked the accountant to deduct the sum from my pay bill and informed the ministry. Some weeks later I received the ministry's stern reprimand that deductions like these were not permitted from the pay bill; I had to pay by cheque. I replied that I had left my State Bank of India chequebook in Delhi as I thought I would have no use for it in war-ravaged Vietnam. The ministry asserted that the location of my chequebook was none of their business. I had to issue the cheque.

Inevitably, it was several weeks before the chequebook was traced and sent to me from Delhi by my brother. I eventually received it thanks to the grace of Ho Chi Minh's government who took time off from fighting the Americans to give permission for the ICSC plane to land. Then, with the accountant as my witness, I signed and issued a cheque in favour of the Government of India for the princely sum of one rupee and, not to forget, twenty-five paise.

That over, there were the unavoidable delays in actually getting the diplomatic bag carrying the cheque on board the ICSC aircraft for delivery via Saigon to New Delhi. My ordeal – and the ministry's – was finally over. The loss of interest must have exceeded the entire sum of the cheque!

A visit to Hong Kong via China's Cultural Revolution

On one of the few flights that was allowed to land came authorization from the ministry to buy furniture for the chancery and, more importantly, the consul general's residence. I tried to entrust the chore to my staff, but they were wary of undertaking a task for which they were not equipped and nervous of incurring the consul general's wrath if he were displeased with their purchases. They unanimously asked me to go to Hong Kong for a few days and buy the needful there.

Perhaps too readily for my own good, I fell in with this suggestion and booked myself by China Travels to visit Hong Kong to get this much-needed requirement. I flew to Nanning, with the *People's Daily* being read out in Chinese over the Tannoy for the duration of the flight. It was the height of the Cultural Revolution.

At Nanning, the passengers and I had our passports stamped and then caught a domestic flight to Canton (now known as Guangzong). At the Canton hotel, I picked up a souvenir, Mao's *Little Red Book*, that I have carefully preserved on my shelves for half a century. Then I found that China Travels had made a boo-boo. They had failed to book me, like all other foreigners, on the 'foreigners' train'. So, I was hastily bundled into a passenger train that stopped at every station and took six hours to reach the border at Shamchun (now called Shenzen), an industrial metropolis today, but then a small and undistinguished town. All the way, the loudspeaker was on, thundering out editorials from various official publications, but it wasn't too bad. The Chinese train staff plied me with hot green tea, most welcome, while I leaned back and watched the Young Pioneers dancing with the Red Book in their hands throughout the brief stops we made at every wayside station. It was an educative introduction to China in the throes of Mao Tse-tung Thought.

I wrapped up my work in Hong Kong within a couple of days and headed back to Hanoi. On the Kowloon ferry, I overheard someone saying that all flights over China had been grounded because something very significant had happened: the Chinese had exploded their first H-bomb! So I was prepared for an extended stay in Canton but was not prepared for the guide I had hired twisting himself towards the back seat to ask what I thought of the 'great peace-loving act of the Chinese people'. I retorted, 'What peace-loving act?' and he smoothly provided the rejoinder, 'Exploding the hydrogen bomb!'

We, however, struck up a friendship as he drove me around the city regaling me with tales of Chiang Kai-shek having fed communists live into engines to make his trains run. Our camaraderie had grown so great that by the time we reached Canton airport for the flight back to Nanning and Hanoi, and were sitting out the delay watching a mournful traditional Chinese ballet, I made so bold as to ask him sotto voce if he was married. His eyes twinkled as he confirmed he was. I asked him if his wife was with him in Canton. He sighed that she had been sent to a faraway farm for retraining and that they could meet only twice a year, once when he got a week off to visit her, and the second time when she got a week off to visit him. I was glad to be born an Indian.

My return to Hanoi was full of drama. Owing to my having been held up in Canton for 'reasons beyond my control', that is, the Chinese H-bomb, I arrived in Hanoi after the Shelvankars had returned, bringing my mother with them. It was clear that Shelvankar was most put out at having had to cope with my mother (although Mary had taken it in her stride quite cheerfully). What had upset him even more was that on visiting the Vietnamese foreign office on his return he had been told that the acting consul general had met the head of the Asia department. Why had I not objected to their not referring to me as the 'chargé d'affaires'?

He was even more irritated when he further heard that in his absence, we had not only traipsed off to Halong Bay (he had been refused permission to go there) but that I had also hosted a lunch for Vietnamese officials (who never accepted his invitations). And, as for my visiting Hong Kong, he alleged he had not been shown my message informing him of the reasons why I was going. When he further learnt that the Vietnamese foreign ministry was organizing a Christmas dinner-dance for junior consular and diplomatic officers, but not for ambassadors/consuls general, his cup of woe overflowed.

Mary, Mary, quite contrary

Shelvankar's ire was not confined to me. He had incessant rows with Mary, who would then fetch up tearfully at my apartment to seek a shoulder – mine – to cry on.

One morning, she had peeped over the staircase in their house and seen a Chinese-looking gentleman sitting in the drawing room downstairs with her husband. So she thought this was the opportune moment to show off a magnificent gown she had had made from a flowing Chinese silk dress that her father had picked up (looted?) when he was sent to China to quell the Boxer Rebellion. She put it on and swayed down the staircase calling out to her husband's guest that her gown was Chinese.

How was she to know that he was the Mongolian ambassador deputed by the Soviet bloc to explain to the Indian consul general the nature of the fighting that had broken out between the Soviet Union and China across the Ussuri river? The Mongolian ambassador had smiled politely. But after he had taken his leave, Shelvankar had let loose, shouting that Mary's dressing in a Chinese gown, and pointedly drawing the visiting ambassador's attention to it, would have given the ambassador the impression that India was on the Chinese side in the fighting!

Mary arrived at my home, her eyes brimming with tears. Referring to a hit film of the time, *Tea and Sympathy*, which tells the tale of a headmaster's wife falling in love with one of her husband's students, she said I was not to mistake her intentions but she had to see me for only I would understand the hell she was undergoing in this godforsaken place. I heard her out, offered what sympathy (and tea!) I could and saw her out when she was more in control of herself. I don't think that endeared me to my boss.

In his own envious eyes, Shelvankar caught up with my achievement over Halong Bay, when he got permission to visit the Perfumed Caves. Mary insisted that Amma and I accompany them. We set out in the car. After a long journey that involved trekking up and down a hillside after being transported by a rowboat, we were all out of sorts when we returned.

Mary had brought along a hamper. But Shelvankar insisted there was no need to stop and picnic as he would like to get home for dinner. The quarrel continued as we drove back to Hanoi. Mary abruptly asked us if we were hungry. Amma and I both confessed we were. So she ordered Hung, the chauffeur, to stop. Shelvankar, to prove his point, remained in the car while Mary brought out a most welcome thermos flask of really hot sweet tea, loads of sandwiches and a packet of biscuits. We devoured it, while her Krishna remained adamantly ensconced and foul-tempered in his seat. Our repast over, we drove on and I thought that was the end of it.

Grave consequences of a picnic

How mistaken I was! Next day, I was summoned to the consul general's presence. He was furious. 'You ate my biscuits,' he muttered, adding, 'without my permission.' I stuttered, 'But, sir, Mrs Shelvankar gave them to me.' He then devised the strangest punishment ever inflicted.

He had already ordered me to send drafts of anything I sent the ministry to him for approval, most of which were routine acknowledgements and other HoC trivia. (He clearly had as little to do as the rest of the consulate!) Referring to that, he demanded to know, 'But how am I to know that what I approve is what you actually send?' He then struck his final blow: 'From now on, you must show me the final typed letters before signature.'

It was the last straw. I broke down. I walked to the nearby Petit Lac in the centre of the city, found myself a wooden bench and cried my heart out. In later years, when I revisited Hanoi with the external affairs minister and later still with the prime minister, I would force other members of the delegation to pay their obeisance to that wooden bench. But on my last visit in 2000, I found the wooden bench had been dismantled to make way for a steel replacement. So my dream of seeing that wooden bench converted into a memorial to my sorrow – like the one for Mahatma Gandhi at Pietermaritzburg station in South Africa – will, alas, remain unrealized!

Notwithstanding their constant *tu tu main main* (petty internecine quarrels), Mary was really quite fond of her husband and very proud of him. Her pride was greatest over Krishna Shelvankar's friendship with the renowned American writer Henry Miller. But she had clearly not read Henry Miller's most famous book, his semi-autobiographical *Tropic of Cancer* in which there is an outrageous sequence where Krishna (mentioned by name) is taken to a Paris bordello and does something so disgraceful that it doesn't bear repetition.

So, since every pulchritudinous adolescent of my generation has read that passage (even if he had not read anything else by Miller), I have, for years, been able to dine out on this story!

Miscellaneous jobs

By way of work, I read all I could about the history of Vietnam and the wars they had fought against the Chinese, the Japanese, the French and now the Americans to regain their independence. 'Nothing,' as Ho Chi Minh's most famous and much-repeated slogan affirmed, 'is more precious than Liberty and Independence': '*Không có gì quý hơn, độc lập tự do.*'

I wrote some fanciful dispatches about how we could trade with Vietnam in non-ferrous metals once the never-ending war ended (if ever) and what areas of cultural cooperation might be envisaged. I assiduously studied the turgid language of the *Vietnam News* daily bulletin that their ministry sent cyclostyled in English and French to all missions.

The Paris peace talks got under way. They were held every week on Thursday. I discovered I could predict whether the DRVN would take a hard line or be accommodating on the following Thursday by studying the *Vietnam News*. I counted the number of times the expression 'We shall fight on until the last aggressor is swept from our soil' was repeated in the bulletin over Friday to Wednesday. The cut-off point was three. If it was repeated less than three times, the North Vietnamese would show some flexibility; if they repeated it more than three times, it signalled a hardening of their stand. I don't know whether this bit of trivia was noticed by the US negotiators.

Vietnamese acquaintances

The only Vietnamese we met informally were our local staff. My favourite was Vinh, who was my age. He had never known peace; I had never known war. As an only child, he had been exempted from the draft but, in return, he had to do the job assigned to him, which was to be a sweeper at our consulate. Highly intelligent, well educated and very talented, he would spend much of the day – after completing his sweeper duties – tracing the strip cartoon 'Phantom' from the *Illustrated Weekly of India,* and filling in the balloons with Vietnamese translations of the English dialogue. The 'cell' in our consulate, comprising the Vietnamese staff, convened in a self-examination session and poor Vinh was reprimanded for poisoning the minds of his colleagues with such subversive bourgeois rubbish.

The 'cell' was also where our cook-cum-maid took her complaint when Amma screamed at her over some minor misdemeanour – par for the course in benighted India, but just not on in the workers' paradise of Ho's North Vietnam. On the maid's behalf, a delegation of the 'cell' met the consul general to register their objection to such misbehaviour. I was impressed at the workers' solidarity on display; at the same time, my already low stock with the consul general plummeted even further!

In addition to their salaries, Vietnamese staff also received, from their authorities, coupons to dine at street-side food stalls, go to the cinema and visit Vietnamese operas, which were a popular form of entertainment. My mother and I were deeply touched when Vinh and his girlfriend invited us to the opera, sharing these precious coupons.

Another interesting interlocutor was Du, the official translator assigned to us by the Vietnam authorities. I had begun to know him when I decided to take up Vietnamese as my second foreign language. But that came to an ignominious end for I could make no sense of the tonal distinctions that are characteristic of the language (which is why the script requires so many diacritical signs: for instance, 'ban' could mean 'busy' or 'pig' depending on whether you raised or lowered the pitch in speech!)

Although our lessons came to naught, Du (pronounced 'zu') and I would walk together to official meetings, less because the staff car was not always available and more because out in the open, there was no way our voices could be picked up. I would engage Du in free and frank conversation, trying to get the native perspective of the political situation and the nature of Vietnamese society under the pressure of war.

Du's replies were thoughtful but tended to toe the official line, largely, I think, because he believed in the line himself. This in itself was significant because it reflected the general trust in the leadership. That is what gave ballast to all the hardships they were put to in the interests of independence. I tried to shake him by saying that individual human rights would never be handed back to the people even after the war ended, nor would prosperity come their way even if peace and reunion were achieved. He demurred, his favourite retort being, 'After the war...'

I was proved right on my first assertion and hopelessly wrong on my second. Indeed, on my last visit to Vietnam in 2000, the prosperity of Hanoi was mind-boggling, but even more mind-boggling was the complete absence of any animosity towards the United States. They had simply moved on – a lesson we in India have never learnt.

To return to my sojourn in Hanoi ... During the Tết festival celebrated in February 1969, not only were all the streets decked and specially lit up but all the doors of private homes were flung open. My mother and I, wandering around wonderstruck, were invited in by the beautifully attired women of various households to share a snack and a few broken but heart-warming words of greeting. I was staggered to see girls, normally dressed in white shirts and black trousers, suddenly filling the streets in their exquisite silk *áo dàis*.

As the government became more confident that the bombing had really been halted, they opened a restaurant for foreigners, one day of the week, Thursdays. It had only one item on the menu: ice cream. A Moroccan and an Algerian, both defectors from the French Foreign Legion after the drubbing the French received at Dien Bien Phu, provided the only conversation on a single, invariable subject: how awful Hanoi had become since girls from New Caledonia stopped coming to the University of Hanoi (which made me yearn for a posting to New Caledonia!)

The only other entertainment was invitations from the North Korean embassy to attend film screenings dominated by the podgy Kim Il-sung walking on to the stage applauding himself. I should also mention the screening of *The Bliss of Mrs Blossom* at the Canadian mission, the one time I laughed continuously for ninety minutes in dreary Hanoi.

The termination of my posting

To get away from the stifling atmosphere, I thought I would apply for home leave. When the application form was brought before me, I found there was a query asking whether I wished to be posted back on the completion of leave. I ticked the NO box. Shelvankar was overjoyed.

My leave and transfer to headquarters were sanctioned together. I had spent only nine months in North Vietnam. That made me sad, but the end of my private war was a relief. Fortunately before I went, the DRVN government organized an official function to which even junior consuls were invited: it was my sole opportunity to see Ho Chi Minh in person – albeit from a distant corner of the auditorium. Two months later, he was dead.

My mother and I flew to Vientiane by an ICSC flight that was actually allowed to land and take off from Hanoi on schedule. After a few days there, we went on to Bangkok and I was tasked to visit the embassy to ascertain where I could find my mother untainted vegetarian food.

The head of chancery was a gregarious, generous, open-hearted gentleman called P.N. Sharma, who said the best place for such food was his home. He also tipped me off that the gossip was that as punishment for my performance in Hanoi, I was scheduled for the lowly post of US (PC – Personnel 'C' category); with my office in the barracks behind South Block, I would be required to deal with postings, transfers and the personal problems of clerks and assistants. So, the ghost of Shelvankar was to haunt me even in Delhi for the next three years.

We became extremely friendly with PN's wife, Sushma, and their four children – Roonie, Anita, Veeni and Poochi – in the couple of days we were there. I had arranged a quick trip by train down the Malay Peninsula, after which we were to come back to Bangkok – staying with the Sharmas, as PN insisted – to catch the Air India flight home. Amma and I got off the train at Fort Butterworth and caught the ferry to Georgetown, Penang. In Penang, we found ourselves clean but modest accommodation in a hotel called the White House and I quickly discovered that the best place to meet my mother's exacting dietary requirements were the free vegetarian meals served in Buddhist monasteries.

The main news story was the Americans landing a man on the moon. With my usual technological illiteracy, I wondered what public purpose was being served by the feat. It has taken me decades to discover that without it, this book would have had to be written in longhand (and would, therefore, have been shorter!). After a few days of lazing around on beaches and taking a dip or two in the water, we were ready for the next stage of the journey. I noticed that my mother had slowed down and was not her brisk self.

We took a shared taxi to Kuala Lumpur and stayed with my predecessor in

Brussels (who was my best friend Jayant Patel's brother-in-law, Vinay Varma). Anti-Indian riots had swept through the city and I considered cancelling that leg of the trip after Penang. But Amma insisted on pressing on since her main objective was to visit the Malay rubber plantation in the vicinity of Kuala Lumpur where her guru, Swami Sivananda, had worked as a doctor in the first quarter of the century. Amma managed to see all she wanted but her stamina was giving out. So, she decided to go to Singapore to catch the Air India flight to Madras instead of returning with me to Bangkok.

Before I returned to Bangkok, I repaid Vinay's hospitality by advising him to include the phrase 'without regard to my personal safety' in filing a report to headquarters on the riots when he had driven around some of the worst-affected parts of town (albeit from the safety of his diplomatic vehicle). I told him to add the words 'cut that out' after the phrase so that Vinay could reply, if charged with empty boastfulness, 'But I told the PA to cut that out.' In the event, not only was he not reprimanded but actually received a congratulatory posting to Washington, DC.

Back to the Sharmas

Meanwhile, to return to the second leg of my Bangkok adventure. The train journey back was without incident. On arrival though, I learnt that Ambassador K.B. Lall, now commerce secretary, would be reaching Bangkok for a meeting of ECAFE (UN Economic Commission for Asia and the Far East; now renamed Economic and Social Commission for Asia and the Pacific: ESCAP). I postponed my departure just to meet him and inform him of the fate worse than death that was awaiting me in Delhi. I later found that he had indeed leaned on the FS to try me out in the newly constituted Economic Division of the MEA, which did turn out to be my next posting.

My host, P.N. Sharma, was in seventh heaven because he had accomplished the near-impossible task of getting the ambassador's dining hall air-conditioned well in time for a grand dinner planned for Independence Day. The ambassador played out a kind of dress rehearsal by holding a dinner, toasts and all, in honour of P.N. Sharma. The next morning, PN, proud as a peacock, woke me to bid me goodbye before leaving for the chancery. Later that morning, he suffered a massive heart attack. By the evening, he was gone.

I once again postponed my departure, convinced that my place was by the side of the suddenly deprived family. I eventually stayed on a week and grew very close to all of them.

Early one morning, just as dawn was lighting up the sky, I accompanied Roonie to the Bangkok river to mingle – quite illegally – PN's ashes in the waters of the river. When they got back to Delhi, I helped them settle in. It was the least I could do. Sushma was remarkably gutsy and ready to take on the world. She later made a career with All India Radio.

See detailed footnotes and endnotes by scanning the QR code above.

6

Headquarters

1969–1973

A relatively quiet beginning

Everyone in the MEA, beginning with the joint secretary, Kunwar Ram Pratap Singh, had been warned that I was a 'most difficult' officer. They were startled to find that there was nothing 'difficult' about me.

In quick succession, I had two directors. Inderjit Singh Chadha, a physicist by academic training, had an eye for spotting error and zeroing in on it, and lavishing praise where this was the right thing to do, and L.N. Rangarajan, also a physicist with an even more incisive mind; he too was generous, the sign of self-confidence. Only those who know their own worth can really afford to share words of encouragement about their juniors and subordinates.

Physicists are self-confident and hard-working because they are the ones who have stood at the top of their class from nursery up. Since they think in mathematical formulae, they tend to express themselves subtly, shortly, succinctly, without gathering the wool typical of the humanities mind. I was lucky to find these two officers who became mentors when I was at an impressionable age. I needed such officers to complement me because half my brain – the science half – was either dead or had never been alive.

Meanwhile, N.K. Singh (NK to everyone) – my old friend from college and now the trade policy expert in the commerce ministry – and I resumed our friendly competition. Secretary K.B. Lall tasked NK and me with jointly preparing a paper on establishing appropriate criteria for identifying the 'Least Developed Countries'. This was holding up matters at the UN Second Committee discussing the coming Second UN Development Decade. Raúl Prebisch, the Brazilian president of the second session of UNCTAD, had dismissed the First UN Development Decade as a 'Development Decade without a Development Strategy'. This was the context in which NK and I received our instructions, but where there was a prize to be collected (approbation, in this case) NK was not one to share it. Without informing me, he finalized his paper unilaterally and handed it in. By the time I got my act together, I knew I had been beaten to the final post. We were summoned to The Presence together.

KB was at his commanding and confusing best. He handed back our papers and asked us both to rewrite them. Bewildered as to where we had gone wrong, we asked which points we were to revise. 'How would I know?' came KB's instant response, 'I have read neither. But what makes either of you think your first effort is the best one? And,' he added, dismissing us, 'this time come back with a joint paper!'

I found myself rather more often in Udyog Bhawan than in South Block. In the MEA, there was almost no one with any knowledge of, or interest in, matters economic or commercial. The IFS was embarrassingly ignorant of anything to do with the Wealth of Nations. KB's meetings were, in any case, much more fun to attend. He loved 'mind-forming' exercises, as a kind of step-by-step teach-in. On one occasion, I was literally startled out of my seat by a remark one of our senior secretaries made at a meeting of a galaxy of secretaries. Seeing that I was about to intervene, KB sharply reprimanded me, '*Tum chup raho*. [Keep your mouth shut.] Mr Kaul's mind is beginning to tick. Let it tick awhile!'

I received a visit from Vinay a few weeks later, in transit from Kuala Lumpur to DC. Furtively, he asked whether he might spend the day in my room in Shastri Bhawan. I expansively invited him to certainly do so – but whom was he running from? 'FS,' he replied. 'Why?' I enquired. '*Arre yaar*,[1] my transfer to Washington is somebody's mistake and if they find I am in town, my transfer order can still be cancelled. So I'll spend the day in the safety of your room,

[1] Meaning 'Oh! My friend' – a commonly used Hindi expression among friends.

leave early for the airport and hide in the airport bookshop, then board the flight, and no one will be able to pull me out of it till I get to the US!'

My first international conferences

In April 1970, for the first time in my life, I represented India at an international conference as part of the Indian delegation to the annual meeting of the UN's ECAFE. I found the experience exhilarating, educative and entertaining. Soon, I had my second outing – to the World Food Congress at Amsterdam. I spent most of my time cultivating the thousands of youth delegates from around the world. I had NK to thank for this. It was his father, the agriculture secretary, who arranged my inclusion. In the middle of the conference, our agriculture minister, Jagjivan Ram, was summoned back to become the new *raksha mantri* (defence minister). Amma quipped, '*Jai jawan, jai kisan!*'[2]

Mukund joined me there from Oxford. We went together to see a pornographic film. Amsterdam was emerging as the world's sex tourism capital (with Bangkok snapping at its heels). So it seemed an appropriate thing to do. But after we'd been in the cinema for about fifteen minutes, Mukund remarked, 'Let's leave, *yaar*. This is too much like rounds in hospital!' We took a boat ride instead, on Amsterdam's canals.

Jam's and Tara's weddings

Meanwhile, our family life was getting complicated. Jam, keen to get married to his girlfriend Gitanjali, was compelled by my mother to postpone his wedding by six months to give him time to 'cool his ardour', as she colourfully put it. The needless delay only stoked his determination to marry Gitanjali. Very attractive, she was a painter of talent like Jam himself. It was ridiculous Amma should behave in such a fashion, insisting she wanted only a south Indian Brahmin bride for her son.

At the wedding in March 1970, Amma misbehaved with everybody, treating Gitanjali's mother like dirt. This doomed the marriage from the start.

---

2 Meaning 'Victory to the Farmer! Victory to the Soldier' – an expression of Prime Minister Lal Bahadur Shastri's, made popular during the 1965 war with Pakistan.

The wedding over, having succeeded in strewing the maximum amount of unhappiness on the maximum number of people, Amma's focus moved to Tara, who had just returned from a year in Denmark. Unlike the boys, she was ready for an arranged marriage. At this point, there occurred another of those astrological coincidences that have arrived, metronome-like, in my life.

The story goes back to 1952 when my father did the *kumbabhishekam* (inaugural ritual) of a Ganesh temple he had built on Baba Kharak Singh Marg (then Irwin Road). At the time, this was Delhi's first south Indian shrine. The ceremony was conducted by the well-known savant Anantarama Dikshitar. He had told my mother that Tara was under the cloud of a 'cat curse'. Someone in the family had killed a cat and the cat had pronounced a curse on my poor innocent eight-year-old sister that she would not be married until the appropriate rituals (*prayaschit*) had been carried out.

My mother could not, for the life of her, have tolerated a dead cat in her pristine vegetarian premises. Now, faced with the reality of her twenty-six-year-old daughter gently growing into spinsterhood, my mother's memory went into overdrive. She recalled that when my father had still been alive, a small kitten had slipped into the house. Amma had put out a saucer of milk for the kitten and we had left the house for our usual family outing in the evening at the Boat Club at India Gate. When we got home, my father had brusquely said he had thrown the kitten out of our third-floor window on to the very busy street below. It now occurred to her that my father might well have been telling the truth and the poor animal might indeed have come under the wheel of a passing vehicle.

So Amma started looking for a way to repeal the 'cat curse'. She was informed that the only way was to have the stories of nine mythological weddings recited over nine nights. She was also told one Shri Nagabhushan specialized in these ritual recitations. She sought him out. He readily agreed but enquired whether he might bring along a friend who was deeply interested in listening to these sagas. My mother welcomed him into the home.

Nagabhushan's friend noticed Tara playing hostess and, learning that she was unmarried, asked whether he might suggest his son, Captain Ramkumar of the merchant marine, as a possible bridegroom. Thus, the 'cat curse' ended in the middle of the ritual *prayaschit*! The wedding took place the following month. Never underestimate the occult, however much it might offend the norms of reason.

An amusing incident occurred on the eve of the wedding. Someone we had never seen dropped in, saying he felt it his duty to shower his blessings and a wedding present on his friend Sankar's daughter, as he owed all the prosperity in his life to the bride's father. We were told my father and he had jointly fought an income tax case. The case was won but the client had no money to pay them. So he offered them a plot of land each in his village. My father refused the plot saying 'he could not live among the jackals'. He asked his partner to keep both plots. The village, it turned out, was called Malcha. Over the next few years, Malcha Marg became one of the most expensive addresses in Delhi. The ex-partner dropped off the wedding gift and hurriedly took his leave before we got around to asking for our plot back. A good thing too – for we inherited no family property and have thus remained a united family which, with property in contention, would probably not have been possible.

Moving to another ministry

On my return to Delhi from Amsterdam, rumours started circulating that my status had changed from 'pariah' to 'much desired'. I was being sought to replace S.V. Purushottam as special assistant to Dinesh Singh, the external affairs minister. Dinesh Singh was a member of Indira Gandhi's 'inner circle' – the famed 'kitchen cabinet' – who had fallen from grace and was likely to be dropped from his post shortly. Although Dinesh had never met me, it was reiterated by virtually everyone he asked that I should be that replacement.

I had just started getting involved with Ambassador Syed Shahabuddin in Venezuela on the fascinating subject of Indian technical expertise in what was then a major river basin development project – of the Orinoco basin. So, I was able to return my regrets through many of the grapevines that proliferate in South Block.

Meanwhile, Dinesh was moved out of the MEA and named minister of industrial development and internal trade. His secretary was T. Swaminathan, my former boss from Brussels, who immediately brought my name back into play for private secretary. Dinesh then consulted his favourite officer, K.B. Lall, with whose help Dinesh had presided over the UNCTAD conference in Delhi on the Second UN Development Decade in 1968. Lall also suggested my name. I think that more or less put the lid on the decision. Instead of dallying at lower levels, Dinesh went straight for the jugular and asked his successor, Foreign Minister Swaran Singh, for me by name, saying the MEA had plenty of officers to spare. Swaran Singh, who had barely heard of me, promptly agreed.

This time, it was the FS himself, Shelvankar's friend and sponsor, who called saying he knew I was reluctant but when the minister issued orders, his orders were to be obeyed, not challenged. What made me finally agree to join Dinesh was his assistant, Jain, dropping in to enquire whether there was anything they could do for my assured comfort. I asked very tentatively if I might have an air conditioner. Jain's jaw dropped. One air conditioner? I could have a fleet of them if I wanted! After all, I was the minister's man.

And, thus, on 4 September 1970, I moved from the MEA to the private secretary's small, spare and extremely cool room in Udyog Bhawan. My first visit was to the minister. He was in conference with his senior officers. When it was my turn to speak, I muttered only the words, 'Tata House, sir, 55-T.' He had not even known we had been to the same school. It sealed an association that lasted over the next three decades, through good times and bad, times of turbulence and times of triumph.

The minister's special assistant was J.P. Singh, a genial IAS officer and my senior by a couple of years. His mouth was always a massive red stain, a result of red betel juice in the day and red wine at night. He and I worked out the division of labour. We agreed that the best arrangement would be for files up to the licensing stage to come to him, and files after the licensing stage to go through me for other permits such as technology clearance and capital goods.

Dinesh loathed the system, saying he was running the ministry for the 'retardation of industrial development'! I would generally meet him in his magnificent study after dinner, and over a convivial scotch and soda (only for me, he was a teetotaller by preference) we would go through the files with me orally explaining what appeared to be inadequately explained. This, of course, meant more delays as Dinesh in his extraordinarily neat hand posed questions that needed clarification. He never wrote an assertive note.

This practice of writing notes on files made for the hilarious if apocryphal story of the chief minister of a state who had been promised a large sum of money for his approval of a file. He signed 'Approved'. The payment was slow in coming. So the minister sent for the file and wrote 'Not' before 'approved'. Alarmed, the industrialist coughed up. At which the file was sent around a third time and amended to read 'Note approved'!

Deaths in the family

The evening of the day I moved to the new ministry, I received the very sad news of my favourite Uncle Mirza passing away. My mother and I rushed to the Old Delhi railway station and boarded the overnight train to Lucknow. When we went to the head of the Ramakrishna Mission to enquire where we might take a last glance and say our last farewell, we were shocked to be told that they had already burnt the body and were anxious only that we should not contest the will.

Thereby hangs a sordid story. Back in 1966, Alankaram *periamma* had retired from service, while Uncle Mirza had been promoted to chief engineer, public works department. They used their life's savings to purchase two adjacent buildings at the junction of Asoka Road and the Mall, a prime location in the heart of Lucknow's Civil Lines. They had barely settled in when she was found to be afflicted with galloping cancer. She had but months to live.

They had been most sincerely and wholeheartedly involved in the establishment of the massive Ramakrishna Mission hospital in Lucknow. Mirza Uncle had provided his services gratis to engineer the complex; Alankaram *periamma* was to be the first medical superintendent. The twin residential bungalows were to be handed over to the Mission, after their passing away, for use as a VIP guest house.

My aunt lasted till January 1967. That gave me time to meet her one last time in Bombay where she was under treatment at the Tata Cancer Institute. She had led an extremely worthy life and deserved to live out the rest of her days, post retirement, in comfort. Yet here she was wasting away with cancer of the lungs.

Once she passed on, Uncle Mirza did not have the heart to live on in the same house. So, he soon made arrangements to move out and into a small guest room at the ashram. This was not incompatible with his undoubted spiritual piety. He was a very broad-minded Muslim in the best Lakhnawi tradition. In under a year of his own retirement in 1969, he too was found to be suffering cancer of the lungs.

The Ramakrishna Mission would be inheriting the entire valuable property. But the monks at the ashram were concerned that the cup might get dashed from their avaricious lips. Hence, the refusal to wait for a gathering to give Uncle Mirza a family funeral.

I was stunned at the boorishness on display. We said our silent goodbyes to one of the most decent human beings it has been my privilege to know and love. It only strengthened my prejudice against 'holy men', which had started with the shenanigans at the Sivananda Ashram and was finally confirmed in the Ramakrishna Mission, Lucknow.

Enter Suneet

Among my tasks was to draft the minister's speeches and prepare the tour programmes, as well as accompany him. This last I particularly enjoyed. One such trip was to Madras, Trichy and Madurai. On the return journey, I was requested by a Madras businessman of some eminence to exchange seats with him. As my seat was next to the minister's, I quizzically raised my eyebrows and Dinesh indicated I could accept the request.

I swapped seats and found myself in the same row as a young European lady diplomat. She enquired whether the gentleman I was accompanying was, indeed, the minister, and we began a conversation. I had been invited by an IFS colleague to what in those old-fashioned days was called a B&B (bottle and bird, as explained earlier) party. The bottle was easy enough but I was still in search of a 'bird'. It appeared one had landed on my lap. So I asked her, and she readily agreed. We agreed that I would pick her up and go together. On the dot, she descended and suggested we go to some other party. As my colleague was one of my closest friends, I was more than a little put out. We compromised. We would first go to my party, and then to hers.

It was in this somewhat distrait mood that we arrived at the party, and I looked across the room to see Suneet standing there. I had met Suneet first at an elocution contest at the Indian Military Academy, Dehradun. She was then all of sixteen and I was eighteen. She was representing her college, Lady Irwin, and I mine, St Stephen's. We had sat next to each other at the contest, and because I lived in Dehradun, I was able to invite her, her teammate, their teacher and my fellow competitor, Yogesh ('Chirpy') Chandra, to drive with me to Mussoorie to spend the day there before getting on the train for Delhi. We had had a thoroughly enjoyable time, returned third class to Old Delhi railway station and said our sleepy goodbyes early next morning.

I had not really seen much of her since, but we had remained distantly in touch over the past twelve years since we shared a number of friends. As the producer at All India Radio's External Services, her favourite voice for her general news services programme was my brother Mukund's. And Gitanjali, whom my brother Jam married, was her best friend. That evening was a revelation. Picnics and other events followed, and it was not long before it was established that we were an 'item'.

Suneet was preparing to go abroad for a three-month course of training in TV at Glasgow. To a confirmed bachelor like me – as I thought of myself – there seemed little danger in investing more in the relationship. I was to visit Kabul. Rather casually, I asked her what I could get her from there. 'A carpet,' she said in an offhand manner. I had no idea about carpets. So it came as a shock to discover what carpets of even the meanest size cost. Eventually, I walked into the carpet shop at the hotel nonchalantly, picked up one of the pocket-size squares on display and asked if I could buy it. The shopkeeper seemed insulted. He said these were samples and not for sale. Thus ended my first attempt at wooing!

A second hurdle came up when I asked her for her phone number. 'Look it up in the book,' was her response. I did. Her mother's name was Mrs Vir Singh. So, I first went down the Vs. No luck. Then I tried the Singhs. There were hundreds of them. I went down the list more than once. Still, no luck. I was wondering how to effect a breakthrough when one of those extraordinary coincidences of my life occurred yet again.

My steno had gone on leave and the establishment sent me a temporary replacement. He heard me making anxious enquiries about Suneet's phone number from common friends – and hesitantly intervened to say that his regular job was none other than as steno to Mrs Vir Singh! I should look up her number under T for Teji – her first name. I rang the number and struck gold. Suneet was amazed that I had located it.

We were now deep into the elections of early 1971. Dinesh asked me to join him in his constituency of Kalakankar, near Allahabad. I went with some reluctance because it meant time off wooing. But once I got to Kalakankar, it turned out to be a rich and different experience. I accompanied the minister on several of his campaign tours, generally in the last vehicle of the car-cade.

One day we arrived for lunch at a feudal lord's sprawling home. I was the last to emerge as I was at the tail end. There seemed to be unusual excitement in the air. It seemed someone had spread the rumour that I was a Brahmin from Rameswaram. So the assembled villagers were even keener on having '*darshan*' (a scared viewing) of me than of the candidate and receiving my blessings. As I advanced towards the welcoming horde, I called out, 'No, I am not a Brahmin from Rameswaram but a Mussalman from Lahore.' The crowd dispersed, disappointed.

I returned from Kalakankar just in time for Gitanjali's birthday party at which I knew Suneet would be among the prominent invitees. I found myself getting in deeper than I had intended. Suneet had her own priorities, though, the topmost being to complete the endless formalities required to proceed abroad. One day, she walked unannounced into my office to ask for my help to contact someone in the finance ministry.

I still can't explain what happened to me. As she was ushered into my office, I started having palpitations and shivering uncontrollably. That had never happened earlier or subsequently. It took me a while to get myself under control, contact the person she needed and ensure that her work was done. The memory of that afternoon abides. Perhaps this is called 'falling in love'.

Then Suneet flew out and I resumed my usual, somewhat aimless existence. The election results were announced. Mrs Indira Gandhi had won an overwhelming victory against a combined Opposition. The margin of her victory was over two-thirds. I was thrilled. Then came the blow. Dinesh was dropped from her line-up of ministers. Although it was eighteen years before he returned to the cabinet, I was a welcome guest in his home all along, so much so that when he was eventually inducted into government, Suneet and I were the only invitees, other than his family, to the celebratory dinner he held.

Over these years, Dinesh introduced me to a galaxy of political leaders – ranging from his best friend Piloo Mody, to Chandra Shekhar and Nath Pai and Madhu Limaye (an astonishingly disproportionate number of Congress dissidents and MPs of the Opposition, but then those were the days of real democracy, when political opponents were opponents, not enemies).

Back to the Economic Division

I returned to my old job at the Economic Division and was soon immersed in work related to the Second UN Development Decade. There was also a flurry around Nixon's decision to delink the US dollar from the gold standard. Since I was expected to join the delegation to the UNCTAD conference in Peru, I was also able to wangle a place on the delegation to the UN General Assembly.

Meanwhile, Suneet returned from Glasgow. We resumed seeing each other and it was clear that, barring anything unforeseen, we would soon be tying the knot. This provoked tension between my mother and sister, on one side, and me, on the other. I decided I should not get married until I had my transfer orders as otherwise my mother would make life impossible.

Suneet, of course, resented the delay but could do little about it as I had not in fact promised any wedding bells. My departure for New York came around in mid-September. She was very sweet about it and even gave me a list of singles' bars I could visit in New York if I was lonely.

At the UN

The UN was a revelatory experience. I felt I had found my metier. Foreign Secretary Tikki Kaul had been on the flight from Delhi with me and was somewhat put out to find that I, a mere undersecretary, had been included in the delegation. It was not until the preliminary non-aligned conference reached the economic paragraphs of the draft declaration that I came into my own. The FS looked startled as I confidently piloted a long list of amendments to the draft text of the economic section, explaining the logic behind each of the proposed amendments. I obviously knew my subject. It was unusual for an IFS officer of that time to be steeped in economic diplomacy and Tikki Kaul belonged to a generation that regarded economic diplomacy as somehow not quite worthy of the profession. I had made the grade.

Although Peru never happened, I was encouraged to stay on in New York for some three months and sent to the annual International Monetary Fund–World Bank conference in Washington, DC. A resolution I drafted advocating a UN Committee for Development Planning – to ensure that the Second Development Decade was indeed a development decade with a development strategy (unlike the first one) – secured a staggering one hundred and thirty co-sponsors. I don't think a single member state, other than the US and the Europeans, baulked at this. The entire Third World backed my initiative. This involved individually canvassing each delegate and moderating opposition to abstaining, rather than voting against. The Committee for Development Planning was on the way to being constituted. In the course of this exercise – my first in multilateral diplomacy – I made a number of lifelong friends, most particularly the bilingual delegate of Burkina Faso (Upper Volta), Hamar Diallo, who went on to become his country's foreign minister.

While I was attending to mundane matters like development, a storm was brewing over Bangladesh. Bangla members started peeling off from the Pakistan UN mission. In the end, the fort was manned by just two diplomats, Agha Shahi, the permanent representative, and Munir Akram, his only remaining deputy, after the bright Bengalis walked out. I became quite close to Munir, one of the few IFS officers to do so, largely because I admired him for what I regarded as a splendid rearguard action in what was clearly a losing diplomatic battle.

Indira Gandhi passed through New York to her star-crossed meeting with Nixon and Kissinger. She had booked two tickets for the Andrew Lloyd Weber musical sensation of the season, *Jesus Christ, Superstar*. At the last moment, she decided not to go in view of objections from the Christian community of Kerala. As I was the only officer not officially involved in her visit, I was offered the two tickets, front row centre. I have never visited the theatre in greater style!

The Bangladesh War

All good things must come to an end. My visit to New York came to a close towards the end of November and I flew to London to see Mukund, at the time in Oxford on his Rhodes Scholarship. He persuaded his scout to act as butler at a most elegant dinner he hosted for me in his rooms at Trinity. There was another couple invited. They brought the news that war had broken out between India and Pakistan and that 'the Taj Mahal had been bombed'. The latter was, happily, untrue; it was 'the city of the Taj', specifically Agra cantonment, that had been attacked.

The next day, I arrived to chaos at Heathrow. No one knew whether flights to India would be taking off. Then came the news that one flight would be going to Bombay. I decided to chance it and was really lucky to find an instant connection from Bombay to Delhi.

The Second Development Decade was forgotten as we readied for war. Windows had to be taped. Street lights were switched off or dimmed. Cars moved around without headlights. Rumour had it that the Pakistanis intended to target Ramakrishnapuram so as to rid the Hindus of their two favourite gods in one go!

We sat glued to the TV and the newspapers. It was a while before it became clear that the Pakistan army did not stand a chance. At the very moment the surrender was being signed in Dacca (Dhaka) I was asked by Joint Secretary Ram Sathe to accompany him to a meeting in the Planning Commission with Professor Sukhomoy Chakravarty and Dr Ashok Mitra to organize relief supplies for the newly liberated country.

Indira Gandhi wanted no excuses from the Bangladeshi refugees to linger on in India. My job was to take minutes, write them up and get them transmitted to the participants as early as possible the next morning. It was high-pressure work and suited me to a T. I soon became the ministry's sole repository of what was to be done for relief supplies, carrying in my head the full list of supplies, the quantities, and sources to monitor what was being done and what more needed to be done.

The mission in Dhaka was a home for me in itself because most of my IFS friends – Arundhati Ghose (Chukku), Shekhar Dasgupta, Sati Lambah and, above all, Mani Dixit – were posted there. It was the most well-staffed, high-profile mission we ever set up: truly, the cream of the cream. Arjun Sengupta later joined as minister (economic) in the Mission and thus became my counterpart in Dacca to the role I was playing in Delhi as the sole officer on the Bangladesh Economic Division desk (which went by the somewhat amusing acronym, BED!). We have never before or since had such an outstanding group of officers posted in one mission.

Trips to Dhaka

It fell to me to escort the first trade delegation to Dhaka within a month of Bangladesh's liberation. As our delegation disembarked, Dixit came up to me and wickedly whispered, 'Remember, the slogan of your delegation is "*Amar sona, tomar Bangla*!"' – our gold, your Bengal – a cheeky play on the Bangladesh national anthem.

The Indian army was very much in evidence. At breakfast one morning, I saw Sydney Scharnberg, the *New York Times* correspondent who had done more than anyone else to bring the tragedy of the East Pakistan pogrom to the world's attention. I went up to him. He said, 'You guys are losing the plot. All your army people are claiming they won the war. They give little or no credit to the Mukti Bahini. This is going to cost you in the end.' The prediction came true. After Mujib and his family were brutally massacred in 1975, General Zia-ur Rahman, one of the first senior Pakistani officers to raise his rifle in revolt, took Bangladesh down an anti-India path that did neither nation any good. Arrogance extracts a huge price, a lesson we never seem to learn with our neighbours.

I returned to Delhi but was soon back in Dhaka, thumbing rides in army helicopters. One of these took us to the Hardinge Bridge, the railway bridge the Indian army engineers had repaired in almost no time – something of an engineering miracle. The following day, Mujib was to inaugurate this key infrastructure. The railway authorities said they wanted to do a trial run to check whether all was well. The railways were looking for volunteers to undertake the trial run. Dixit said that as I was the most junior officer present, I was the most dispensable. And, so, he was nominating me to stand at the fender while the train engine made its experimental crossing. Urged on by the other officers, I swallowed my apprehensions and took my place at the fender. My heart was in my mouth. One look at the fast-flowing Padma river made it clear what was in store if anything went wrong! We crossed without incident and I, carefree now, agreed to ride back on the engine over the bridge.

It was on this trip to Dhaka, or one soon after, that the ambassador to Bangladesh, the formidable and forbidding Subimal Dutt, invited me to tea at his home. My colleagues were outraged. They wanted to know why such courtesies were being shown to the most junior of officers. I traipsed along and had a most pleasant conversation that bridged the many decades between us. It was only many years later, when I learnt of his role in facilitating my entry into the IFS, that I realized why he had wanted to meet me. He had been tasked by the *rashtrapati* (the president of India) to ensure that I was taken into the IFS and was naturally curious to know who I was and how I had fared.

My principal mission was to try to adjust the quantities of different relief supplies to stay within the ambit of the Rs 25 crore sanctioned. I succeeded in bringing negotiations to a satisfactory close. On my return, Sukhomoy was beside himself with satisfaction. He took it upon himself to assure the cabinet secretary that I had sorted out all problems and he need not hunt around for an additional sanction.

That was when Subimal Dutt struck. His voice was like a cold dagger slicing through the air when he interjected, 'Undertakings between undersecretaries do not constitute agreements between governments.' That put the lid on it. Additional funds were sanctioned, and I was able to inform my Bangladesh counterpart, Enam Choudhury, that our discussions stood null and void as our government had decided to find the money to undertake the supplies promised. It was a most useful lesson in how to confront tricky issues.

Another major adventure involved restarting the Chhatak cement factory. This factory was conceived in the 1930s when Partition was generally regarded as a mad idea. The limestone came from Cherrapunji (in today's Meghalaya) by aerial cable to the low-lying Chhatak factory where it was converted into cement – the only cement factory in East Bengal. Partition drew the border between the two countries immediately below the aerial ropeway. So, what was limestone from a captive quarry suddenly became international trade! For the first eighteen years after the vivisection of India, that made no material difference. But after the 1965 Indo-Pakistan war, all supplies from Cherrapunji were politically prohibited and the east's dependence on cement supplies from the west only grew. This was an intolerable burden; so the restoration of the aerial ropeway became a major requirement after liberation.

Within six months of Bangladesh's independence, I escorted a delegation from the factory to Shillong and, after initial discussions with the Assam authorities (Meghalaya was still to be formed), we wended our way down to Dawki on the northern border of Bangladesh. From there, we made our way to Sylhet and then, in a most romantic boat ride, to the factory itself. Limestone supplies were soon resumed. I would regard that as my single most significant contribution to the resurrection of Bangladesh.

I had also contacted Rehman Sobhan, the Bangladesh economist who had been in the forefront of the nation's liberation struggle, and suggested setting up a Joint Study Group on jute. It was proposed that we might nominate an Indian economist who had been at Cambridge around the same time as Sobhan. This individual was then serving as a modest economic adviser in the Indian commerce ministry. His name was Dr Manmohan Singh.

I sat up over a weekend to write up the brief for the delegation. The brief was not complete until Sunday morning and I could see no way of getting it across to the economic adviser except by delivering it myself to his home in Model Town on the other side of Delhi University. I cheerfully drove to the neighbourhood and located a house with a plaque bearing his name. I entered the compound. There were some children playing on the lawn. I asked if this was Manmohan Singh's residence. On being assured it was, but Singh was out, I handed over my sealed envelope marked 'Top Secret' and drove away.

It was only during our transit halt in Calcutta (Kolkata) next morning that I had the opportunity of asking our economic adviser whether he had had the opportunity of glancing through the brief. With a pained expression (that I was to become familiar with over the years) he shook his head and said he was totally unprepared because no papers had reached him. I realized with a shock that the envelope had been delivered to the wrong Manmohan! Coaching the real Manmohan proved the easier task. I did so by giving him a copy of the brief.

The meeting in Dhaka between the two old friends, both of whom had worked on jute in their academic exertions, was quite a reunion. Some preliminary progress was made and it seemed a road had been opened to cooperation in the one sector in which India and Bangladesh were the dominant world producers: Bangladesh in raw jute and India in manufactured jute products.

When we returned to Delhi, my immediate boss, Peter Sinai, said our most important task was to retrieve the 'Top Secret' brief. We breakfasted together and then set out for Model Town. When we got to the house where I had deposited the sealed envelope, an old, white-bearded man came out looking extremely puzzled and careworn. He said someone had come on Sunday and given his grandchildren this envelope marked 'Top Secret'. He was terrified an attempt was being made to involve him in some political conspiracy. He handed over the envelope as if he were getting rid of a scorpion and thanked us for relieving him of this terrible burden. Peter and I returned triumphant.

One final episode from my Bangladesh days. D.P. Dhar, then chairman of Policy Planning, was visiting Dhaka while I was there. We had idly talked over breakfast about what I was doing, but I didn't realize I would soon be filling a lacuna in his Bangladesh team. When he called that evening on the minister of transport, Captain Mansur Ali, one of Mujib's most trusted lieutenants, I went along for the ride. In the room, Captain Mansur upset the balance by sending for an aide. DP, not to be outdone, also called for 'Narayanaswamy' to be sent in. His staff did not know whom he was referring to until someone decided that the matter under discussion being economic, 'Narayanaswamy' must mean me! Thereafter, the mission nicknamed me 'Narayanaswamy', but DP eventually got the name right.

He also seems to have decided that he needed me on call until the post-liberation scenario had stabilized. On the flight to Chandigarh in July 1972 for the Simla conference with Bhutto, he heard that I had been transferred to Addis Ababa. So he threw a tantrum, insisting that poor Swaran Singh must cancel my transfer orders on the spot if he, DP, were to proceed to Simla. In these circumstances, I suddenly found myself in Delhi indefinitely.

Marriage

That was somewhat inconvenient for me personally. I had come to the conclusion that the only way of ensuring my marriage would survive my mother was by getting out of Delhi as soon as we were married. Now that I was to remain for an unspecified period, I had to make alternative plans.

I decided I should in principle settle my future and let destiny take the course it would. I remember vaguely muttering something to Suneet about getting married while we were at a garbage pit near Lodhi Gardens. But it was a proposal so wrapped in ambiguity that, for years after, Suneet would shake me awake and demand to know why I hadn't proposed to her. As the garbage pit is my witness, I swore I had. (I thought I had – and went home from the garbage pit to ask myself whether I had known what I was doing. I asked myself the question in the mirror, and the answer the mirror returned was that I had decided in full consciousness, and there really was nothing I wanted more dearly.)

Suneet and I went to the Ganesh temple my father had built to discuss wedding arrangements. Imagine my shock at learning from the head priest that they were only allowed to officiate at Brahmin weddings – and Suneet, far from being a Brahmin, was not even a Hindu. The temple priest offered to find me what Graham Greene has called a 'whisky priest', but I was so angry I refused to compromise and we decided on a civil wedding under the Special Marriage Act, 1954.

So, in August 1972 I made arrangements with a lawyer to meet us at the Tees Hazari courts and get the banns published. Mukund also sent me a power of attorney from Oxford to act on his behalf to arrange his wedding with Sujata at about the same time. That way, he would have to visit India only once for both weddings. Suneet and I fetched up at the courts. The lawyer handed me a curious form to fill. It asked all the key questions in the past tense: When were we married? Where? Did we have any offspring? I realized to my horror that the idiot had given me a divorce form to fill, not a wedding notice!

Anyway, after the formalities were over, we celebrated with lunch at my favourite restaurant from my college days: the Khyber at Kashmere Gate. Sujata also joined us. The die was cast and there was now no looking back – nor the least desire to do so.

As the month of *Margayi* (mid-December to mid-January) is considered inauspicious in Tamil Nadu, we decided that Mukund's wedding should be scheduled before *Margayi* set in and ours as soon as the month ended, with the great Tamil festival of Pongal, on 14 January. Mukund and Sujata were married without ado, largely because the head of AIIMS had warned my mother not to thwart Mukund in any matter. However, Amma (and my sister Tara) were making such a nuisance of themselves over my tying the knot with a non-Brahmin non-Hindu that I begged them not to attend my wedding and spoil the atmosphere as they had succeeded in doing at Jam's wedding.

I thought I had secured their agreement. But at the formal engagement the Sunday before our wedding, Amma suddenly turned up. My poor mother-in-law-to-be was sent into a tizzy trying to make Amma feel welcome, but my mother's purpose was, of course, nefarious. She suddenly got up and strode off proclaiming that she had come to her eldest son's wedding and instead found herself at a funeral because 'among us' – a favourite phrase of hers – the head is covered only on occasions of mourning. And here I was with my hair covered with a handkerchief in deference to Sikh custom. I was infuriated and the rest of the week was spent in a futile effort to stop her from attending the wedding and throwing another tantrum.

To go to court on my wedding day seemed a bit too much, so I requested the deputy commissioner (DC) of Delhi, a friend, to depute the subdivisional magistrate, South Delhi, as the officer to officiate at both Mukund's wedding and mine. He turned up at Mukund's wedding dressed in hideous checked trousers and quite ruined all the wedding photographs! So, I got my friend, the DC, to kindly transfer for one day his most elegant lady officer, Additional District Magistrate Vinita Singh, from North to South Delhi – and she stole the show!

I had been most impressed with Kahlil Gibran's advice to brides and bridegrooms on how they should allow 'spaces between them' so as to not impede the partner's growth. I asked Mukund, who had a wonderful speaking voice, to read the poem out at the wedding, but, at the last moment, he could not find a copy of *The Prophet*. So, you can imagine my joy when decades later, my daughter, Yamini, came up to ask whether I could read the same passage at her wedding!

My next post abroad

My posting to Addis having been cancelled, the MEA decided to post me to the Permanent Mission of India (PMI) to the UN at Geneva. Suneet and I were thrilled to go. But then I heard that Principal Defence Secretary K.B. Lall, my previous boss from Brussels whom I had grown to admire more and more, was returning to Brussels as the head of our mission to the European Economic Community (EEC, predecessor of today's European Union).

I went to Avtar Singh, secretary in charge of administration, and told him that I much appreciated the ministry having posted me to PMI, Geneva. But could that posting be shifted to Brussels as K.B. Lall was going there as ambassador? We had not only had an excellent relationship earlier but Dr Lall had virtually acted as my 'boss' in the Economic Division as well.

Avtar Singh reprimanded me that IFS officers could only have a 'boss' in the MEA but he appreciated the significance of what I was asking for and ensured I was duly accommodated. It was just about the best wedding present I could have asked for.

Honeymoon

But there was still the honeymoon. I had made bold to suggest an itinerary that took me all over the country, acquainting myself with the principal export hubs from India to west Europe. The joint secretary (administration), Surendra Singh Alirajpur, the genial tribal princeling who had let me have Hyderabad House for my wedding reception, was only too ready to oblige.

Neither of us realized that the ambitious programme of travel I suggested would cost a bomb and there were limits to what could be spent on 'Bharat darshan'. Most of India's exports to Europe and the UK came from the most salubrious tourist resorts – Jaipur for handicrafts; Udaipur for emeralds and jewellery; Bombay for most everything; Goa for ore; Cochin (Kochi) for coir; Madras for leather; Hyderabad for tobacco. Alirajpur sanctioned this odyssey without checking on the expense.

It was only when we returned that he found he had far exceeded his authority. So he promptly made some changes in leave allocation: I had apparently been 'on duty' for the duration of the honeymoon and would now be on leave pending my departure for Brussels. But KB had begun preparing for his new assignment and wanted me to help him. So I ended being on duty during my honeymoon, and on leave as I dealt with KB's usual volley of demands for research.

Preparing for negotiations

We had to negotiate our way through the thicket of the EEC's hideous rules and regulations to save India's exports to our most important destination – the UK – under what was called the Joint Declaration of Intent (JDI). The JDI pledged the EEC and the UK to taking special measures to safeguard the interests of the South Asian members of the Commonwealth who were otherwise set to lose their privileged, decades-old access to Britain. Fortunately, the many papers KB made me churn out proved invaluable in readying myself for the task ahead, but hugely annoyed my bride who wanted to know why I was leaving the task of getting ready for Brussels almost entirely to her.

Finally, in mid-May we left for Brussels via Cairo. There was plenty to do by way of sightseeing, but I had so exhausted myself finishing KB's 'homework' I was left quite unable to keep my eyes open for the scheduled visit to the pyramids and the Sphinx during night-time. Suneet didn't forgive me for this until I succeeded years later in having her accompany me on a trip to Egypt and we finally went to the pyramids and the Sphinx at night. It was spectacular. I also bought myself my favorite t-shirt that read: 'A camel can go without a drink for a fortnight. I can't!'

See detailed footnotes and endnotes by scanning the QR code above.

7

Brussels Redux

1973–1976

Settling back in

While I quickly discovered that this posting as first secretary in the Indian Mission to the EEC, was completely different from my previous one as third/ second secretary in our embassy to Belgium and Luxembourg, my French had fortunately not deserted me and much of Brussels city was familiar. Initially, my attention was focused on getting a villa to live in, preferably in the cherry blossom district (commune) of Boitsfort. We found such a villa and, by some deft negotiation, succeeded in bringing the basic rent within my allotment. It was a joy to move into our first married home. We bought our first car – a Morris Marina that we got cheap because Britain was trying to break into the European market and was throwing discounts around like confetti – and slowly brought in furniture to make the home inhabitable.

It was not long after that the embassy doctor, Dr Schuind, informed us that we might expect our first child in May the following year. Suneet and I remained in silent communion in the car as we digested this transformational moment. Suranya arrived as scheduled and without complication. She was a beautiful and friendly child, completely trusting in the goodwill of the world. When, therefore, she was taken for her inoculations, she was smiling gaily at the doctor who suddenly pricked her. While she inevitably howled in pain, her main emotion was not so much pain as betrayal. The paediatrician, Dr Desirée, was a gentle lady and soon won back Suranya's confidence.

My mother-in-law had contacted the Guild of Service in Madras and, through her friend, the well-known social worker, Mary Clubwala Jadhav, had found a young woman, barely eighteen, to look after her granddaughter. Nagamma seamlessly melded into our family and soon became more of an elder sister for Suranya than a babysitter. She called us both by the Tamil names of 'sister' and 'father' and was to remain a steadfast companion for all of us.

Negotiating our way

On the work front in Brussels, we found the EEC had a somewhat off-hand way of dealing with India. They were bewitched by the prospects in China which had just become legitimized by Nixon and Kissinger visiting Mao. The ACP – Africa, Caribbean, Pacific – was their preferred sphere of influence. India was barely in the picture, the EEC's very colonial view being much influenced by India having been a British colony (much as most of the ACP had been European colonies); therefore, they believed the future of the subcontinent was the business of the UK, rather than the EEC.

KB was having none of this. He arrogantly rejected the draft Commercial Cooperation Agreement (CCA) that landed on his desk. He decided to respond by filing before the EEC a series of 'mind-forming' papers with the aim of educating the Europeans on why India mattered. They replied, more than a little irritated, that they were not interested in the larger picture; they just wanted to settle the commercial aspects of the relationship early through the draft CCA.

K.B. Lall stalled them. He brought up Article I of the Treaty of Rome, 1957, that had led to the formation of the European Common Market which was now the EEC (before becoming the present EU). That article provided the foundational principle that only 'democratic' countries could qualify for membership of the European Common Market. Ambassador Lall wanted to know which of the countries the EEC was negotiating with could qualify for membership of the Community – whereas India obviously could if we had been in Europe. It was the only card that we could play to trip up their star-struck Napoleonic vision of the People's Republic they had scorned over the past quarter-century.

Unfortunately, KB was not backed as he should have been by the Government of India. MEA thought this none of their business. And the commerce ministry did not have the imagination to see that unless the political parameters were defined, there was no way we could build a forward-looking economic relationship with Europe. Moreover, Y.T. Shah, who had taken over as commerce secretary, loathed K.B. Lall (largely because he had to endure many slights and jibes from Lall's manner of speech). This led to endless tension between the ambassador and his nominal masters in Delhi.

The EEC's commissioner for external relations was Sir Christopher Soames. As the British ambassador to France, he had negotiated the UK out of the de Gaulle impasse, after de Gaulle called an international press conference at the Élysée and appeared before the world media to growl 'Non' into the cameras, as his one-word statement on whether he would rescind his veto on UK's entry into the Common Market. The general then went on to ask in apparent bewilderment, 'But why all this fuss? I only said Britain is an island and the US is not in Europe!' Brexit has only borne out de Gaulle's perceptive view that Britain is, or aspires to be, a world power and does not understand what it means to be 'European'. (It also reflects the British view, held more widely than is acknowledged, that 'Wogs begin at Calais'.)

But de Gaulle had been eased out after the 1968 students' and workers' revolt and the French no longer had the backbone to stand up to the Brits. Soames had seen a historic opportunity and persuaded de Gaulle's successors to relent. Ambassador Lall, on the other hand, was bent on changing the rules. He would not give way on the question of India being described as 'a democracy' in the CCA before clause-by-clause negotiation of the text. The Europeans had a Cartesian way of compartmentalizing politics from economics in their dealings. Lall would not accept this as it militated against India's future interests.

Meanwhile, other complications arose. The JDI, as conceived in 1971, was jointly applicable to the three independent, sovereign countries of South Asia that belonged to the Commonwealth: India, Pakistan and newly named Sri Lanka (earlier Ceylon). But the JDI was adopted in 1971 and here we were in 1973 in a completely different setting. For one, we were now four countries with the addition of Bangladesh. For another, India and Bangladesh did not have diplomatic relations with Pakistan. Only Sri Lanka had diplomatic relations with Bangladesh, India and Pakistan. But the Europeans, for their part, refused to deal with us individually, insisting their mandate was to deal with us collectively.

Therefore, Mohsin of Bangladesh, Tariq of Pakistan, Samaranayakke of Sri Lanka and I started meeting clandestinely at the Sri Lankan mission to see what our common problems were and what mechanisms, including GSP (GATT's General System of Preferences), there were for solutions. Unfortunately, the GSP applied in principle only to manufactured goods, not commodities in which we specialized. Apart from jute and coir, there was a clear common interest only in cotton textiles, but the Europeans were reluctant to talk about this outside the framework of GATT's long-term arrangement (LTA) for cotton textiles. That meant there was virtually nothing we could talk about with the EEC on these most important segments of our trade – at least in Brussels.

We also found that many unprocessed items, where we were dominant global producers – such as sugar, basmati rice, flue-cured Virginia (FCV) tobacco, cashew nuts, mangoes and ethnic foodstuff – and carpets were stuck on the theology of whether handcrafted and non-manufactured agricultural goods could be covered under the GSP. I found myself often being deputed to Geneva to see what solutions were available under GATT or UNCTAD.

Jute was regarded as separate from other textiles and accepted as important to Bangladesh, though not to quite that extent to India. However, the Europeans were adamant that they would first negotiate with Bangladesh and only then offer the agreed terms to India. The Bangladesh ambassador was, however, a poet and a freedom fighter, quite innocent of economics. He, like everyone else, was in awe of KB and told his deputy, Mohsin, with whom I had previously worked, that he should leave it to the Indians to determine what was in Bangladesh's best interests. So, Mohsin received the EEC draft and passed it on to me to suggest suitable amendments. He then offered these amendments to the EEC, thus subverting their best-laid plans.

Then there occurred a change of government in London and the incoming Labour Party promised to 'renegotiate' the terms on which the UK had joined the EEC. KB saw this as a golden opportunity to push India's interests. These fell into five principal categories: Indian ethnic foods; FCV tobacco; cattle feed;

coir products; and carpets below a certain level of knots per square centimetre. We started a campaign alleging that the India-born immigrant community was being discriminated against in the UK by being asked to pay customs duty on products that were not indigenously produced in Europe, nor, specifically, the UK. Moreover, there was no reason why Europe should discriminate against our FCV tobacco in favour of the more expensive American producers and traders who had secured duty-free access to the European market. As for carpets, we argued that ours were not like Iranian carpets but had a lower number of knots per square centimetre and, therefore, needed to be treated differently.

The Commission was also invoking fears of aflatoxin against Indian peanuts, both for human consumption and as an essential ingredient for cattle feed. We fought a rearguard action against such transparent misuse of non-tariff barriers. We came up with the in-house joke: 'Let the peanut farmer, Jimmy Carter, become US President and he'll settle these Europeans!'

Hand-knotted carpets, on which depended the livelihood of millions of Indians, in locations ranging from Mirzapur to Kashmir, were qualitatively different from Europe's manufactured carpets. There was clear consumer preference for hand-made carpets. On the other hand, Persian carpets, with a much higher number of knots per square centimetre, constituted the top end of the market. We fought for a distinction to be made between the lower segment (ours) and the upper segment (Iran's). We eventually prevailed.

On FCV tobacco, the fiercest opposition came from an Italian expert in the Italian Permanent Mission to the EEC, del Gizzo, who was out to protect the Italian tobacco lobby that grew an inferior kind of tobacco that was, in fact, non-competing with Indian or American FCV tobacco. I visited Rome, and found that del Gizzo was a misguided lone rocket. I, therefore, concentrated (and succeeded) in bringing del Gizzo around. In this, I was grateful to my British counterpart, John de Fonblanque, for his moral and practical support.

We then came up against another obstacle: German phytosanitary regulations. So, I accompanied an Indian tobacco delegation to Hamburg. We were taken to the nearby port of Bremerhaven and watched a demonstration of their cigarette-smoking machine. It was mesmerizing: different coloured pencils traced different poisons emitted as the machine smoked its way through a cigarette. It was enough to decide me. I had been a heavy smoker since my

Cambridge days. Clearly, I should not be doing to my lungs what the machine was showing. I decided to end my habit as soon as I could.

An opportunity came a few weeks later when we went home on leave. On the way, we stopped with Sati Lambah at Rome, from where we took a train to Naples. I found I had left my cigarettes behind at Sati's and took that as a sign from above that I must abandon the practice – now or never. There was a policeman who attached himself to us as we reached Naples, saying that amongst the most dangerous places in the city was the railway station plaza and so he would accompany us as we found ourselves a hotel room. He offered me what turned out to be my last cigarette as we waited for Suneet to check out our hotel room. She soon returned, quite satisfied with the arrangement. I squashed out the half-finished cigarette and never touched the weed again. Ironically, Germany has since overtaken the UK as the principal world importer of our Virginia tobacco!

Family news

In May 1974, I received a very disturbing rebuke from Tara. She wrote to enquire why we had not rushed to Oxford to help Sujata cope with Mukund's fresh attempt at killing himself. The AIIMS director, Dr Wig, had told us after Mukund's first attempt at cutting his wrist, that if Mukund was allowed to do what he wanted to do, we could hope for the best (although of course there were no guarantees); this was why my mother had not put up any opposition when he married a Christian. This last incident was a blow to all our expectations.

I rushed across the Channel. But Mukund, even as he played a most hospitable host, refused to disclose what had caused him so much anguish. Sujata was equally reticent. There was no one else I could turn to. We were to pay a heavy price for the couple keeping their secrets to themselves.

Just about six months later, another tragedy struck. My sister Tara's eldest son, Varadu, who had just turned four, had gone for his first day at school with a friend who was his age. His mother invited Tara to lunch. When they got there, Varadu entered the kitchen and Tara attempted to drive him out. Unfamiliar with the geography of the flat, he ran out of the rear door of the kitchen – instead of returning to the adjacent dining room – and tumbled down a cast-iron staircase for three floors. He was no longer breathing when Tara reached him. Fortunately, Mukund was in India at the time and managed to reach Calcutta but Tara was understandably inconsolable. It was a shattering tragedy for her and the family.

Mukund returned to Oxford the following month to complete his doctorate in endocrinology, and he was looking forward to returning to India to start work at the new St John's medical college and hospital in Bangalore. But an American endocrinologist, who had seen his work, insisted on him moving instead to Richmond, Virginia. Mukund resisted but as Sujata's study still had to be financed, he eventually succumbed to Richmond's blandishments. He hated Richmond despite his boss being more than kind to him because something was tugging him back home. So he spent an unhappy year in America while his peers were urging him to not be so foolish as to return to India when the pickings were so rich in the US for both Sujata and him.

However, to escape the claustrophobia that seemed to envelop him in Richmond, he accepted an offer from Arthur Yen, professor of endocrinology, to join his major research project at the University of California in San Diego. Mukund went, knowing little about how he would fare, academically or socially in California, but it was clear that he felt lonely as Sujata had got herself a job in Richmond and a lot of their earnings were wasted on flying from the east coast to the west coast for weekend visits that gave them little pleasure and much grief.

Negotiations continue

Meanwhile, in Brussels, the Commission saw no European interest being adversely affected by the import from India of our lentils, our spices, our flavourings, but it wondered what the Latin equivalents for the Indian terms were. This led to hours in our library, with the very efficient Mrs Mukherjee, a German survivor of the war, opening dozens of botanical books, laying them out and patiently working through as many Latin botanical names as we could find. I could not have done it without the indefatigable Frau Mukherjee. I then took all these terms to the European official dealing with tariff lines and we were soon able to provide Latin coherence to an Indian menu. The Commission unbent and we secured continuing duty-free entry for the typically Indian condiments that eventually found their way into continental kitchens. Indian cuisine, of course, had already become part of the UK's everyday diet.

Coir posed another particular problem. An important Indian export item, it had little indigenous competition in Europe except for one small factory in Rotterdam. Ambassador Lall argued that it was ridiculous to harm a large community of coir manufacturers when no tangible European interest was involved. His patient persuasion of the British permanent representative, Sir Michael Paliser, began paying dividends. Soames and his lot were establishing British credentials by sticking to the letter of the law, which provided that the Common External Tariff (CET) would apply to all imports into the Community (including the UK) except those explicitly on an exempted list. Paliser quietly ensured that Whitehall appeased India by demonstrating they would make an exception with coir.

On the morning of the visit of the Indian commerce minister, D.P. Chattopadhyaya, my ambassador instructed me to call on Soames' *chef de cabinet*, David Hannay (now Lord Hannay), to inform him that the British had agreed to press for exemption from the CET for coir. Extremely distressed, he shouted, 'The Best of British luck to them,' but I came away confident we had scored one over Soames.

Chattopadhyaya arrived (accompanied by my old friend N.K. Singh) and we took the delegation to Berlaymont Palace, the EEC headquarters. There, Soames asked the minister to meet him separately. He complained to a bewildered Chattopadhyaya that only one person stood in the way of friendly relations between the EEC and India: Ambassador K.B. Lall.

Lall took immediate revenge by informing Soames that Britain had agreed to exempt coir from the application of the CET. Furious, Soames called in Hannay, demanding to know if the UK was in fact modifying the strict terms of the treaty under which the UK had been admitted. Hannay somewhat shamefacedly confessed that, yes, that was the case; moreover the other commissioners had accepted that the exemption was justified as compatible with the terms of the Treaty of Accession.

The ambassador quietly registered this victory over Soames – and more importantly, this victory over the fundamentalist market mullahs of the Commission. We left Soames in some doubt over whether he should be gloating over his rebuke to Ambassador Lall through the minister, or be crestfallen since Lall had put one over Soames.

But Commerce Secretary P.C. Alexander did not back Lall on 'democracy' and cravenly allowed the CCA to go through without fundamental change. He also displayed no understanding of the importance of our 'ethnic foods' argument, which was also opening the road towards a resolution of other complicated issues, such as FCV tobacco and carpets.

The Emergency

A month or two later, my phone rang in the morning. It was Mrs Lall on the line. She told me an 'Emergency' had been declared in India, adding she was trying to get hold of her husband who was on one of his trips around the EEC and Geneva. She also mentioned some of the Indian political leaders under arrest. I could not believe my ears.

I rushed to the office and rang Hamid Ansari, our information counsellor, and said Mrs Lall seemed to be out of her mind. He quietly advised me to come to his office and see the teleprinter message. I had to now believe my eyes. From being the world's largest democracy, we had slipped into becoming one of the world's worst dictatorships. The list of those arrested and being chased was a who's who of our most important politicians.

As the ambassador was away, I had accepted the invitation to a diplomatic reception that evening (I think it was the Philippines National Day). When I reached there, the first person I saw was my EEC counterpart, Hansen. As he came up to me, he rather brutally remarked that it was just as well the Commission had not accepted Ambassador Lall's demand for the inclusion of 'democracy' as a description of India, else the CCA we had just signed would today be in tatters. What could I do but look away? We had lost more than the CCA; we had lost everything.

A month into the Emergency, the Indian prime minister decided to depute a parliamentary delegation to visit their European counterparts in the European parliament. There was, indeed, a pending invitation to do so but no one expected to receive the delegation during the holiday period, July–August. I was on a driving holiday with my wife and one-year-old Suranya through the Rhine and Danube valleys to Nuremberg, Prague, Budapest and Vienna when a message arrived summoning me back to Brussels post-haste.

The delegation comprised the deputy speaker, G.G. Swell of Meghalaya; Dinesh Singh, my earlier boss; Vayalar Revi, a fiery young socialist from Kerala; and the veteran MP, N.K.P. Salve. On learning that I was the son of a chartered accountant like him, Salve reprimanded me saying I should have followed in my father's footsteps and earned more in a day than the government was paying me for the whole year!

Vayalar Revi was shy, a little out of place but friendly. Dinesh was genial, expansive and frank, amusedly listening to the stock phrases the others in the delegation were using to justify the Emergency: 'liberty turning to license'. He whispered to me that the delegation had no interest in the EEC and had only been sent to keep potential troublemakers out of Delhi when Parliament was convened for its first meeting after the Emergency declaration. Swell was pompous but unbent when we were listening to evensong in the magnificent Strasbourg Cathedral. Taking advantage of the noise, he revealed that he had been asked to lead the delegation only because the prime minister was doubtful of his loyalty to her being higher than his loyalty to the Constitution. The Lok Sabha officer accompanying them warned me not to pay for anything as the team were given ample allowances and would fail to repay me if they so much as borrowed a franc from me!

Visit to India

An essential component of the CCA, as seen by the EEC, was the technical assistance the Europeans were to offer as part of their efforts at import promotion of Indian goods. We were not particularly enthused as we could not quite see how they could help in this. India had all the know-how and technical expertise to promote its own exports; what was a challenge for us were the constraints of policy that no foreigner could overcome on our behalf. Nevertheless, when the Commission chose leather and leather goods as the first practical step towards implementing their view of the CCA, we readily agreed; by that time we had an understanding of the potential of the Europe market, hitherto something of a closed market for leather and leather goods.

I was deputed to accompany a team of shoe manufacturers to India where Prem Seth of the State Trading Corporation played host. The team largely consisted of somewhat boorish shoe merchants who loved to complain. '*C'est*

Belge de rosspeter': it is Belgian to complain, said one of the more difficult ones. The visit was not, therefore, a very happy public relations exercise (especially because our very early morning departures meant the Europeans were sleep deprived) but I did make friends with some of the British members and one German whose only complaint was that they were making the visit 'five years too early' – by which time, he said, we would catch up with Europe's main leather supplier, Spain. That was a prescient view: India has now replaced Spain as the Community's principal supplier of leather and some leather goods. There was also a very friendly Belgian whose principal interest, however, was in adopting an Indian child. Michael Drury, the wry Irishman at the Commission, summed it all up when he told us at the review meeting that he understood the awful accommodation in Kanpur at a Hotel called the Republican had made 'monarchists' of the dispirited members of the delegation!

After the delegates left India, I went on a long visit to coastal Andhra Pradesh to buttress our arguments about FCV tobacco. It was extraordinary to see the women workers in colourful saris fluttering up the road to reach the tobacco-processing factories. It was an object lesson on how to train essentially agricultural workers as industrial workers.

Drafting the European parliament's 'Opinion' on the CCA

On returning to Brussels, I received a call from an Italian officer in the European parliament's secretariat in Luxembourg asking me to visit their offices to take a preliminary look at the draft 'Opinion' that he had to submit through the appropriate committee to the European parliament. I was happy to oblige. He showed me the draft. Bad English was its least fault; it said nothing of substance. I asked whether I might take the liberty of drafting an alternative text. He was only too relieved.

I sat down at a typewriter and banged out a few paragraphs that brought in everything we had lost in the negotiation, including a special stress on India being a democracy that would have qualified for EEC membership had we been geographically in Europe; explaining that the current Emergency was 'temporary'; and dealing with substantive outstanding issues of carpets, FCV tobacco, etc. To give a final punch on the nose to Soames, the draft congratulated the Commission on having extended duty-free treatment to coir imports from India.

The Italian official was beside himself with gratitude. He asked me to visit the European parliament's bureau in Brussels the following Wednesday to meet the chairman of his committee, a French député (member of the European parliament), and get the draft past him.

I rushed back to Brussels and, with a sense of some achievement, took my draft in to the ambassador. For the second time in my career, he paid me his highest compliment: '*Khoob, bahut khoob.*'(Good, very good.) I reached the European Bureau's Brussels office – and waited and waited and waited. The Italian came in to say the proceedings in the conference room were getting heated and he was looking for an appropriate break to bring his chairman out to meet me. But came the lunch hour and all my waiting was proving futile. The Italian advised me to have my lunch and return at 3 p.m. by when he would have persuaded his chairman to come out and meet me. Despondently, I made my way to the chancery and reported to the ambassador on the morning's disappointing developments. He remained his usual calm and collected self and said I only needed a few minutes with the French député.

Bucked up, I returned to the bureau at the appointed time. There was no one in sight. The Italian then emerged and, looking rather downcast, said the chairman was very sorry, but his meeting was stretching indefinitely and, as he had to be in Paris that evening, he would be taking the Trans-Europe Express (TEE) – Europe's poshest train – to Paris immediately after the meeting. I could leave the matter in his official's hands. The draft 'Opinion' had to be filed by the weekend.

I returned to the chancery totally despondent. The entire episode had been an exercise in futility. Entering the ambassador's room disconsolately, I launched into my sorry tale, ending with: 'And he will be taking the TEE to Paris this evening.' Ambassador Lall quietly said, 'And so will you.' I sat up in astonishment. 'Yes,' Lall continued, 'so will you. Now get yourself to the station – and all the best.'

I rushed to the Brussels Midi station and arrived well in time to take my seat in the very elegant lounge reserved for TEE passengers. The député arrived and couldn't believe his eyes seeing me there. '*Que faites-vous ici?*' (What are you doing here?) he demanded to know.

'*Je vais à Paris. Et vous?*' (I am going to Paris. And you?)

Gruffly he confirmed, '*Oui, moi aussi.*' (Yes, me too.)

And walked off. It was not an auspicious beginning, but I had all of three hours in which to tackle him on the train. It arrived. We boarded. It was a vestibule train. I waited until the journey was well under way, then walked down the corridor and found him.

'*Pas maintenant. Après le thé*' (Not now. After our tea.), he said.

I was content and returned to my cabin.

After an hour, I set out again. This time, he motioned me to sit down and bluntly asked, '*Qu'est-ce qu'il y en a pour moi?*' (What's in it for me?)

I then proved myself a true *shaagird* (pupil) of K.B. Lall. Without any authorization, I replied confidently, '*Vous êtes notre invité au prochain Jour de la République.*' (You are invited as our guest to the next Republic Day.)

He was not yet done. '*Et mes amis?*' (And my friends?), he asked, pointing to his companions.

On the principle of being hanged for a sheep as for a lamb, I replied, '*Eux aussi, ils sont invites.*' (They too are invited.)

That did it. '*D'accord*' (Okay), he said, and cleared my draft unseen.

Eventually, I neither followed up my oral invitation nor did the French député press me. I think he was just teasing me.

And that is how the 'Opinion' of the European parliament on the CCA came to be written but not before I further annoyed Soames by visiting Strasbourg when the Opinion came up for debate and provided written and oral speaking points to participants! Soames complained to Lall about my being in parliament and influencing the proceedings. But Lall told him I was only doing my duty.

Final days in Europe

Soon after, my transfer orders as Commercial Counsellor and Deputy Chief of Mission to Baghdad arrived. We took a continental tour beginning with a visit to some of the most scenic spots in the Ardennes before going on to Geneva, Chamonix and the Mont Blanc; then, through the Mont Blanc tunnel to a small village in the Aosta Valley, followed by Florence, Rome, Pompeii, Naples and Amalfi/Positano and Sorrento; then on to Belgrade via Dubrovnik;

from there to Athens and Mykonos; and, finally, Istanbul, before arriving in Baghdad. I enjoyed the trip but Suneet did not as she was over six months' pregnant with our second daughter, Yamini.

See detailed footnotes and endnotes by scanning the QR code above.

8

Baghdad

1976–1978

Settling in

On arrival in Iraq we visited the vegetable market directly from the airport to stock up before heading for our guest house. At the entrance to the market there were a number of gibbets on which were mounted sheep's heads – our stomachs churned at the gruesome sight. Sheep heads' soup was a favourite appetizer in Iraqi cuisine. It was reminiscent of what we had been taught at our rather colourful classes on medieval Indian history by Amin sahib at St Stephen's who had told us about the Delhi Sultanate's Balban displaying the heads of defeated rebels on gibbets for his son. It was a warning of the fate that awaited the son if he were to defy his father after he took over as the new governor of Bengal.

Another shock awaited us as we entered the guest house. Nagamma, who had reached Baghdad a few hours before we got in from Istanbul, was full of stories about what was showing on Iraqi TV channels. The screen displayed the bodies of 'Syrian traitors' loyal to the rival faction of the Syrian Ba'athists led by the legendary Michel Aflaque. The bodies were still swinging on the gallows and had been put on exhibition for more or less the same reasons that inspired Balban. The Iraqi Ba'athists regarded this as appropriate for family viewing!

An immediate concern was finding a good gynaecologist for Suneet. We also needed to find a house and eventually found exactly what we wanted on the other side of the Qanat-al Jaish (Army Canal). This was a bit like a diplomat in Delhi finding accommodation in Model Town! But as our chancery was located at the Baghdad equivalent of Chandni Chowk, it was not that eccentric a choice.

Our chancery's history was intertwined with Iraq's history of repeated revolutions since they overthrew the monarchy in 1958. An Iraqi businessman, Ahmed Chalabi, had gone with the advance party to Turkey, where King Feisal was due to make a state visit, and was there when the revolution occurred on the eve of the king's departure. Had he returned, he would doubtless have been executed, as were so many others connected with the royal family. He waited abroad till Bush invaded Iraq in 2003 and then came back as an American puppet head of government. While in exile, Chalabi asked his friend, the Indian ambassador, I.S. Chopra, to take over his estate that included his residence and a guest house. The guest house became our chancery. The army chief who had led the coup was a horse-riding, polo-playing companion of our ambassador and, therefore, readily agreed to this arrangement. Chalabi was paid his increasingly nominal rent in Turkey.

Our other priority – and most colleagues felt it should be the first – was hunting for a really commodious deep freezer. This was because all wholesale and retail, especially of foreign foodstuff, was in the hands of state distribution outlets and so reached the markets in bulk only from time to arbitrary time. As soon as something special arrived, the women would be on the phone to their friends informing them what was newly available. This would lead to mobs rushing to these outlets and forming serpentine queues to stock as much as their freezers allowed – as God (and perhaps not even He) knew when replenishments would arrive.

Thus, my mother-in-law was totally distracted from attending to Yamini's birth when she arrived because Golden Delight apples from France had just hit the stores. She and Nagamma, armed with the largest available bags, muscled their way into the queues to procure enough apples to satisfy Eve!

Yamini, my second daughter, was born just after midnight on 9 December. She and I bonded because of the colic that afflicted her as an infant. Listening to Eliot's *Murder in the Cathedral* and the songs of the greatest minstrel of the twentieth century, Leonard Cohen, I would place her stomach down on my lap and thump her back till she sighed with relief. Yamini's elder sister,

Suranya, started school at the Indian School in Baghdad but was there only for a few months because we were transferred soon after she was admitted.

Working out an alternative strategy

As for work, on arrival, I was given a note in a sealed envelope penned by my predecessor. It directed me to use the enclosed key to open the top right drawer of my desk. In the drawer was a list of persons to be contacted who could tell me who to bribe and how much, for securing orders with the state-owned trading and industrial companies. I was horrified. I had not joined the IFS to become a middleman or a businessman's pimp. In high dudgeon, I marched in to see Ambassador Romesh Bhandari. He listened to me patiently and advised me to tear up the list.

I asked him to kindly brief me on our long-term vision for India–Iraq relations. He smilingly replied that Iraq was ruled as a district of the Bombay Presidency in the 1920s during the period of the British Mandate. Our long-term objective was to restore that position!

Put firmly in my place for my pompous self-righteousness, I shredded the note and decided to find an alternative strategy for restoring our exports to Iraq. The oil-producing countries had become staggeringly rich in 1974 immediately after the 1973 meeting of the Organization of the Petroleum Exporting Countries (OPEC). The meeting was held in the aftermath of the crushing defeat the Egyptians (and other Arabs) had suffered in the Yom Kippur War with Israel. The OPEC powers then decided on raising petroleum prices to what they saw as a 'reasonable' or 'market' level. Suddenly, a huge number of very rich Gulf countries, including Iraq, burst upon the global stage. In consequence, our exports to the Gulf generally, but Iraq in particular, had boomed in 1974, only to collapse in 1975. I had been selected for Baghdad to find out why and what to do about it.

To my mind, this was the inevitable consequence of giving bribes to secure orders, then short-changing the customer with inferior stuff and losing their patronage. Many of our top companies had got involved in disputes with Iraqi state entities. I could see that my main task would be to disentangle these controversies that the Indian exporters were seeking to cover up. They were calling the state-owned Rafidain Bank the 'Ruffian Bank' for refusing to let them encash their bank guarantees without the approval of the state enterprises they had left dissatisfied. I have never forgotten the reply I got from one leading Indian refrigeration company for the mess they had made of air conditioning at the top-rated hotel in Basra. The owner sent me a one-line handwritten reply: 'If only you knew...'

Patiently, state enterprise by state enterprise, Satyabrata Pal, one of the brightest officers ever recruited into the IFS (later, one of the most sensible and balanced ambassadors ever sent to Islamabad) and I dealt with the issue. Accompanied by Amin, an Arabic-speaking emigrant from Hyderabad who had been locally recruited into the commercial section, we visited each state enterprise in turn. We wanted to assuage their feelings and to get them to work out a compromise.

The Iraqis eventually agreed to do so when they found our sympathies lay with the cheated importer, not necessarily with the Indian exporter. One of the biggest issues that we resolved was between Bharat Steel Tubes (BST) and the Iraqis when we discovered that the BST's seamless pipes were leaking and far from 'seamless' because an Indian exporter had picked up discards from the BST factory and passed them off as BST's own!

India's State Trading Corporation had formed its own consortium of exporters to meet the sudden surge in Iraqi demand. The complications were hideous. We eventually got all of these exporters to effect compromises but not before my already low regard for Indian private enterprise had plummeted further. The one exporter who never visited the embassy because he could handle all his problems – and there were obviously not too many – was the representative of a small firm called Reliance Textiles. I was not surprised at their subsequent rise – and rise, and rise.

An unexpected but welcome consequence of all these treks was to discover the extent to which women were participants in key positions in Iraq: a lady headed the State Organization for Industrial Housing; another was the principal legal adviser in another state enterprise; a third was the chief engineer; and the gentle Samira held with great panache her position as purchase manager in the Iraqi Cement Company. Driving past the Mustansariya University on my way home from office, I would be greeted by the sight of boys and girls, not one of the latter wearing a veil, sitting around together as if they were at the Sorbonne! This liberation of women and the equality granted them at the workplace, as well as Saddam's exemplary secularism in keeping Sunni–Shia relations in harmony and extending full civic rights to the Armenian Christian minority were, in my opinion, some of his greatest achievements.

But there was no excuse for the arbitrary violence of the state on which the dictatorship was based. There was the daily spectacle of drivers being pulled out of their cars and beaten to a pulp by the traffic police. Gruesome stories of torture in the White House on the main Sa'adoun Street, the former US embassy, were endlessly recounted. We heard the tragic tale of a top economist at the planning ministry being arrested on emerging from the lift after he had gone down to meet a foreigner to whom he had given an appointment the day before he received a government circular ordering all civil servants to secure prior permission to meet with foreigners. His body was returned to his family for burial to show that under torture, he had maintained his innocence.

Between my Yugoslav counterpart and me, there was an ongoing argument over whether the Iraqis most favoured India or Yugoslavia. According to him it was obviously India, as the chairman of the Iraq–India Joint Commission was none other than Saddam's most powerful minister, the minister in Saddam's personal office. I said, no, it was obviously Yugoslavia as their chairman was the minister of planning who handed out all the juicy contracts. Our argument was settled when Saddam had both ministers executed together on 5 August 1979!

An impossible boss

Unfortunately – perhaps tragically – for me, Romesh Bhandari was transferred to Delhi before 1976 ended, and was replaced by an asthmatic and, therefore, cantankerous, eccentric, highly mixed-up man, Ambassador Dilip S. Kamtekar, who took a more or less instantaneous dislike to me.

He told me later that it started with my apparently whistling tunelessly under my breath while accompanying him to his presentation of credentials, and it was compounded by other incidents. Such as when, at a dinner in his house, the chief guest's wife reached for a bowl of nuts across a wide, circular brass table. Both Kamtekar and I tried to pick up the bowl for her but Kamtekar was quicker on the draw. He complained that I had made him do something beneath his dignity when it was clearly my duty as the more junior official to have reached the bowl first!

What broke the camel's back was thc annual Baghdad Trade Fair. Ambassador Bhandari had repeatedly succeeded in getting the best located pavilion at the entrance, and the other missions had complained to the Iraqi foreign ministry about the favouritism shown to India. The Iraqis invited me to the fair grounds to check other alternatives they were offering. I was quite pleased with the pavilion the Iraqis offered and agreed to its being allotted.

On returning to the office, I rushed to Kamtekar to tell him of our triumph, only to have him look increasingly sceptical and insulted; he believed Delhi would think his predecessor had got the better deal. To explain the advantages of the pavilion we had been allotted, I picked up a pencil from his desk and drew a sketch on a pad also picked up from his table. The fact that I had borrowed a pencil and notepad from his table without seeking his permission was the last straw!

Notwithstanding this act of lèse majesté, our presentation at the fair was by common consent a great success. Kamtekar had to suffer the mortification of finding me called to the podium to receive from Saddam Hussein himself the prize for the best pavilion. It left him even more upset at me.

To deal with such an impossible man, I had the help of a brilliant young man, Talmiz Ahmed of the 1974 batch, who arrived to replace Satyabrata Pal in early 1977. It was the beginning of a lifelong friendship. He was not only a buffer against Kamtekar's excesses, but joined in our new strategies to win Indian business with insight and enthusiasm. The best way was to stoop to conquer: to apologize saying mea culpa and then moving to further lucrative orders instead of getting stuck in arguments over the earlier order.

To our mea culpa approach to commodity (merchandise) exports, we added a new line of picking up tenders for small construction projects and persuading Indian companies to submit their bids. Then, Amin, under the direct supervision of Talmiz and me, would passionately promote these Indian bids to the Iraqi state enterprises.

Within about a year (1977 to end 1978) the projects bagged by us soared from just two to sixteen projects and in value from Rs 11 crore to Rs 175 crore. At the same time, by sorting out disputes dating back to the boom years, we were able to increase merchandise exports from India to Iraq by 300–400 per cent between my arrival in October 1976 and my departure in December 1978. Should I have hidden my light under his bushel to please Kamtekar?

Eventually, by focusing on commodities (merchandise) exports and construction contracts, the commercial section, after my departure, first under Talmiz Ahmed and later Rajen Abhyankar, succeeded in getting the lucrative contract for the prestigious Council of Ministers' building, a consultancy for the Indian Railway Construction Company for a key railway project, and the invitation to Indian firms to build all the railway stations along a key new railroad, besides numerous other minor and major construction contracts. By the time the Iraq–Iran war ended the bonanza, India had emerged as the country of choice for partnering European and other firms in securing contracts, or subcontracts, for nearly $100 million worth of construction projects.

Jealous rather than pleased at the success his commercial section was having, Kamtekar decided to keep to himself the mega project of the Baghdad–Hsaiba railway line, which was to transport potash from the western desert to a fertilizer factory in Baghdad. Our principal competitors were Brazil. Kamtekar had set his heart on winning the Government of India's kudos for landing the project. He, therefore, decided to play the cards close to his chest to beat the Brazilians, trusting principally to Saddam's much-vaunted admiration for Indira Gandhi (the man had even organized a rally in Baghdad in support of the Emergency!)

The Brazilians, however, breasted the victor's tape when Kamtekar, confident of winning the huge contract on political grounds, did not permit the head of the Indian delegation to seek Delhi's approval to offer a last-minute discount. Brazil clinched the contract principally because our cabinet tied the negotiating team to too restrictive a brief. Ambassador Kamtekar, in a message from the FS, was most unfairly held personally responsible by Prime Minister Morarji Desai, for this 'failure'. (It was just as well we lost the bid because the Iraqis never paid the Brazilians.) Needless to say, Kamtekar took out his frustration on me!

I was so disturbed by the turbulence in my relationship with Ambassador Kamtekar that within months of his replacing Ambassador Bhandari, I wrote to Kamtekar on 5 March 1977:

> ... because of your evident lack of confidence and trust in me and your frequent irritability at my presence, it would perhaps be in our mutual interest if I

> were to be transferred out of Baghdad as soon as possible … I recognize, of course, that in making this request for an urgent transfer, I am putting my own prospects in serious jeopardy … I appreciate that I will have to bear the consequences of this request.

There was no reply, but I suspect this had some effect on what followed.

For, in the following month, April 1977, I was informed personally by Foreign Secretary Jagat Mehta that I had been promoted to the Selection Grade of the IFS. But the letter of congratulations carried a sting in its tail. I was reprimanded for my 'intellectual arrogance' that was allegedly 'impeding the collective effort' and ordered to 'moderate my behaviour'. Although I accepted that I 'had been on occasion impatient and petulant' and offered to reform myself, I really did not know what I was to reform. After my performance at my next post, Jagat Mehta seemed to have revised his opinion and even claimed that it was he and he alone who had been responsible for my selection! So, perhaps the 'reprimand' was only for the record.

My suspicion that the reprimand was the result of Kamtekar's inexplicable malevolence was confirmed when several years later the ministry sent me for review his comments on me and my performance for calendar year 1977:

> His main problem is tactlessness, too good an opinion of himself and an obstinate disposition which yields only reluctantly to discipline … He has had to be warned about indiscreet remarks made in the hearing of outsiders about Indian firms … It has not been easy to inspire cooperation and less self-assertive and self-opinionated behaviour … He would have to make serious efforts to correct his innate flamboyance, self-assertion, and excessive enthusiasm about matters to which he gives a high priority in order to avoid indiscretion in work and public relations … I would have liked to see more maturity at this stage of his career.

And his report for 1978 was even more damning. 'Loquacious and verbose in expression … Intellectually alive but self-opinionated and superficial … Tends to be over-confident, superficial and is carried away by enthusiasm.' Phew!

This was countered by a single line from Ambassador Lall's comment to the ministry: 'deserves accelerated promotion.' My patron saint in the foreign service, Ram Sathe had become the foreign secretary. He set up a one-man enquiry under Ambassador Bhandari who took little time in examining these reports and my rejoinder to recommend that Kamtekar's assessments be expunged, a recommendation the FS was only too happy to accept.

Congenial company/Likeable locals

As for the Iraqis I met socially, several factors made for the exceptionally warm relations we enjoyed notwithstanding the ever-present fear of the state. For one, the excellent political context in which we met and worked made entry and exit from Iraqi offices very easy and smooth for us.

In what I regard as the most courageous thing I saw any Iraqi do, the almost square-shaped lady of the house immediately opposite our home braved state surveillance to cross the road and walk through our gate to warn Suneet, who had just delivered our second baby and was trying to lose weight, that if she continued to grow any thinner, she ran the risk of my abandoning her. Iraqis prefer their women with plenty of armour plating!

My fellow diplomats were very friendly, in particular the Japanese, the Yugoslavs, the Belgians, the Bangladeshis and the Sri Lankans. One or two of the Americans were friendly as well. (The Americans worked out of a section of the Swiss embassy – talk of the tail wagging the dog!) The large community of Indian technical experts, the Indian Air Force and army officers, and some Indian business executives provided good company. There was also a sprinkling of long-resident Indian expatriates. Unfortunately, we discovered the Alwiyah Club too late in our stay to make much use of it although the club remains etched in my memory as the site where we first heard Boney M singing 'Daddy Cool', which became a family favourite.

Indeed, so warm were Iraqi feelings for Indira Gandhi that when she was defeated in the 1977 elections, many Iraqis wore black armbands to signify that they were in mourning. I had an appointment that evening with one of the best-educated and most sophisticated Iraqis I met, the head of their management school, with whom the Administrative Staff College, Hyderabad, was engaged in working out a cooperation agreement. When I walked into his office and accepted the obligatory hospitality of jeeb chai (highly sweetened tea) served in Turkish glass teacups, the managing director sighed and got the conversation going with the comment, 'Madam Gandhi *khalaas*' ('finished', an Arabic word that had long entered Hindustani).

I was personally so thrilled the Emergency had ended and its perpetrators defeated that I could only agree, breezily, 'Yes, Madam Gandhi *khalaas*.'

To which came the wholly unexpected retort: 'Shouldn't do this to a woman.'

'Shouldn't do what to a woman?' I asked.

'*Khalaas*,' he said, showing his finger slicing his throat.

I hastened to assure him, 'No, no, no, Madam Gandhi not *khalaas*.'

Intrigued, he queried, 'Madam Gandhi *khalaas*, not *khalaas*?' He went on, 'In our country revolution means a *ruba* (quarter) of the population is killed, *ruba* is imprisoned, *ruba* is sent into exile – and we rule over the remaining *ruba*!'

I comforted him that such was not the practice in India! And that Indira Gandhi was very much alive and would soon be active in Opposition politics.

George Fernandes visits

We received our first ministerial visit in October 1977 after the new Janata Party government took over: George Fernandes, minister for industry. He was accompanied by a number of journalists, including the star of his generation, M.J. Akbar. I met Akbar on the evening of his arrival at Satyabrata's place. In sycophantic admiration, I gushed to him that his piece in *Sunday* magazine on the riots in Varanasi was excellent. Sourly, he wanted to know what was wrong with his other pieces.

It was not until we rode together in the same car to Babylon next day that Akbar began to unbend. He was only twenty-six years old, but his celebrity status had clearly gone to his head. I invited him home to lunch the next day and supplied him with a steady stream of my speciality, daiquiris. I learnt the invaluable lesson – because Akbar was to loom large in my life well after that first meeting – that the way to Akbar's heart was through his throat. That sealed our friendship and we remained friends until he betrayed himself by joining the Bharatiya Janata Party (BJP).

The ambassador hosted a dinner for the minister the evening I found myself dining at Satyabrata's with M.J. Akbar. Kamtekar and George Fernandes could not get on with each other. George found the ambassador humourless and obsessed with minor matters of protocol while Kamtekar, I suspect, found George to be more flippant and informal than he liked his ministers to be. I also think the ambassador's mask slipped and his admiration for Indira Gandhi was revealed.

There was no danger of this happening with me. So, on finding that George dreaded the prospect of having to spend another evening with Kamtekar, I enquired whether we could take him and his delegation to a rather risqué nightclub. He instantly agreed. On the way there, we got engaged in deep discussion on why, even if he disliked Indira Gandhi so much, he was also against a man I greatly admired, Jawaharlal Nehru. George was more than willing to discuss the issue without pulling rank or getting annoyed. We found ourselves a small table in a corner at which to continue our animated conversation while two Filipino lesbians on the stage cavorted and gyrated. It was altogether a most pleasant evening and laid the ground for a friendship that took the two of us through the troughs and swells of life over the next thirty years.

Najaf/Karbala

One of the more unusual tasks the embassy was required to perform was administering a trust that had been set up in the 1930s by the Shia Nawab of Rampur to financially assist Indian Shias who had settled in the Shia holy towns of Karbala and Najaf on the Euphrates river. I went along for some of the relief distribution functions, accompanied by our Arabic translator, Azmi. It was terribly hot with temperatures hovering around 100°F as we met the head of the Indian Shia community, Maulana Osama, in Najaf and distributed the grants.

The highlight of these visits was a magnificent Hyderabadi banquet laid on by Osama, which we slept off on the way back to Baghdad. I noticed that notwithstanding the searing heat, Azmi had not drunk any water. So, I queried him. 'Take water from Shia hands?' he exploded. 'Never! They know I am not one of them and would have spit in the glass before offering it to me.' That was the Shia–Sunni gap Saddam was bridging and that has been completely destroyed ever since the US and its 'coalition of the willing' embarked on the 'liberation' of Iraq.

Mukund, my youngest brother, departs

In March 1978, I received a letter from my brother Mukund in San Diego that I read beside a bridge on the fast-flowing Tigris. In that letter, he told me he had again fallen victim to one of his fits of depression and his psychiatrist had advised him to hospitalize himself before embarking on a course of lithium therapy. As a medical man of rare ability himself, Mukundan saw that this could lead to a lifelong addiction and, quoting T.S. Eliot, he said he did not want to be 'a pair of ragged claws scuttling across the floors of silent seas'.

I never heard from him again. A few days later, I was given a telegram from the joint secretary, West Asia and North Africa, Vinod Grover, conveying the tragic information that Mukundan had been discovered dead in his apartment, with an empty bottle of barbiturates at his side. I rushed back to India to look after my mother who was strangely composed. Jam, who was much more visibly upset, quoted Keats from 'Ode to the Nightingale': 'To cease upon the midnight with no pain.' Had I not sometimes felt like that? He was a little taken aback when I replied I had never felt that way.

We completed the various rituals, which included throwing handfuls of rice into the sacrificial fire, and I fancifully wondered whether when these saplings had been transplanted, they knew that Destiny had written on the rice grains that Mukundan would last only till the paddy ripened?

Mukund was truly a Renaissance man, as steeped in science as he was in the humanities. He was the one who introduced me to E.H. Carr's famed lectures, 'What Is History?' And was instrumental in introducing me to many of Eliot's poems. It was to him that my friends and I would turn for sunshine when moods of depression clouded over us. Indeed, my friend and IFS colleague Chukku called him our 'Sunshine Boy'. He was not only my youngest brother; he was also my closest friend. I miss him very much.

Why he took his life has ever remained a mystery. His psychiatrist in San Diego – who agreed, after some hesitation, to correspond with me – described Mukund's mental illness as 'psychotic' and endogenous to him and not the consequence of outside (exogenous) factors. Certainly, his first attempt at cutting his veins pre-dated his meeting Sujata. Who then knows why? Sorrow at this huge loss still throbs within my being.

Amma decided to come to Baghdad with me and stayed with us for about three or four months, during which time I took her to a picturesque tourist village in the Kurdish mountains beyond Sulaymaniyah to distract us. It was of little use. I was overcome by guilt at what I could have done to have brought peace to Mukundan. But Amma was not going to needlessly hold his death on her conscience. That gave her an inner strength while I writhed with sleepless nights haunted by his memory.

Salvation came in an entirely unexpected way. Within four months, my sister-in-law, Sujata, married Richard Buck, the American friend Mukundan had brought from Oxford for Jam's wedding. I was relieved. I felt that if this was Sujata's way of dealing with the loneliness and bewilderment she must have been experiencing in distant America, it was, by far, the best way out. My sister, however, remains suspicious that Sujata was in some way responsible for the tragedy.

Tenth anniversary of the Ba'ath Revolution

In July 1978, the Iraqi Ba'ath Party celebrated the tenth anniversary of its revolution. The Indian agriculture minister, Sardar Surjit Singh Barnala, was our principal delegate. He was accompanied by my batchmate, Arun Abhyankar, who was rumoured to have a serious drinking problem.

We were in competition with a Pakistani firm to secure a major land reclamation project at Khalis, a site about a hundred kilometres north of Baghdad. I asked Barnala whether I might organize an official visit by him to Khalis (without mischievously adding that it would be the nearest he would get to Khalistan!). He readily agreed and we set out in the blistering sun for this destination.

When the time came for the delegation to return to India, Arun Abhyankar refused to change from the towel around his waist into travelling clothes or quit his room. He had gone back to the bottle. Barnala left without him and I went to his hotel room and persuaded him with great difficulty to move to my home and then go over to the ambassador's. Tragically, Arun subsequently drowned in his bathtub while in an advanced state of alcoholic intoxication, leaving behind a lovely, long-suffering wife and a beautiful daughter.

The Ayatollah and Saddam

The Ayatollah's revolution was gathering momentum in Iran. I was astonished when, in October 1978, with the overthrow of the *ancien régime* imminent, Princess Ashrafi, the Shah's somewhat notorious sister, was accorded a state welcome in Baghdad. I had imagined Saddam would be delighted at the prospect of a republican regime but found he dreaded a revolution engineered by Shia clerics.

The reasons became apparent: Saddam was deeply apprehensive of a Shia 'double Cannae', where the revolution in Iran might incite the Shia majority to Saddam's rear on the Euphrates to rise against Sunni rule and rouse the Shia tribes who inhabited the marshes in the delta at the confluence of the two rivers that gave Mesopotamia (Land Between Two Rivers) its classical name. If they joined hands with their co-religionists in Iran, they might be able to squeeze the Sunni community into handing over their country to Shia clerics. The Americans were aware of this and decided to exact their vengeance on Khomeini by encouraging Saddam to take on the Iranians.

Saddam, for his part, thought the Arab-speaking Iranians in the area of Khorramshahr opposite Basra would join their fellow Arabic-speaking Iraqi Sunnis in providing an opening for a full-fledged Iraqi invasion of Iran. The US encouraged Saddam to run a counter-revolution leading to a bloody war in which thousands (or millions?) of very young boys were killed. It ended Iraq's years of peace, tranquillity and prosperity. Later, the Americans discarded Saddam after his invasion of the 'eighteenth wilaya' – Kuwait – and subjected his regime to sanctions so severe that, over the next decade, these killed an estimated half million Iraqi infants.

I always considered Saddam to have wrought the miracle of balancing his Shia and Sunni populations, but the combination of the Ayatollah's successful revolution and the American invasion of Iraq in 1990 broke the bonds Saddam was attempting to forge between the two communities.

My term in Baghdad ends

At the end of two years in Baghdad, my transfer orders to Karachi arrived. When my stay in Iraq ended, I was as relieved as Kamtekar must have been. But of course I could not go without a final reprimand.

I had decided to throw a 'champagne breakfast' for my farewell. My Iraqi friends turned up in unexpectedly large numbers. As our guests departed, the ambassador, whose scowl never left him, pulled me aside and sternly asked, 'You know what "champagne" means, don't you?'

'Yes,' I replied, 'celebration.'

'So you are telling the Iraqis that you are celebrating your departure from their country.'

I couldn't believe such a thought could occur to any but the most perverted mind. Kamtekar was the possessor of such a mind.

See detailed footnotes and endnotes by scanning the QR code above.

9

'This Is an Enemy Country, Right?'

Karachi, Pakistan 1978 (December)–1982 (January)

Karachi on the horizon

I was on a brief family holiday in London in the summer of 1975 when the idea of seeking a posting in Karachi first came to my mind – although the Karachi office had remained virtually shut since the '65 war and definitely shut at the start of the '71 war. Speculating about future postings is a civil service disease. We were in the garden of a foreign service colleague and my old college friend Chandrashekhar (Shekhar) Dasgupta pointed out that besides the importance of Pakistan, there was a grand residence and a beach cottage at Hawkes' Bay in Karachi attached to the post. Most excitingly, I would be the Boss, my own titular boss being a thousand miles away in Islamabad.

But as no agreement had been reached with Pakistan on reopening the Karachi office, I found myself heading out to Baghdad in October 1976. In March 1977, Indira Gandhi was comprehensively defeated, the Emergency I hated had ended, and Morarji Desai took over as prime minister. He appointed Atal Behari Vajpayee the foreign minister. I was deeply disappointed, for I thought Vajpayee, as an RSS man, would base his Pakistan policy on the deep-running anti-Muslim prejudices of the saffron brotherhood to which he belonged. Instead, to my delight, he promoted a most constructive approach to Pakistan.

Then, on a late October evening in 1978, I turned on the radio and was stunned to hear that the government had decided to open our consulate general in Karachi, and that too almost immediately. I had been in Baghdad only two years and that meant at least a year more in Iraq. Someone else would get the posting on which I had placed my hopes and my heart. Imagine, therefore, my delight on receiving a telegram about a fortnight later announcing my selection for Karachi! I was to immediately report for a briefing to Delhi and prepare to leave for Pakistan.

Initial experiences

At about 1 p.m. on 14 December 1978, I landed at Karachi airport. I was slightly taken aback to be introduced to a Pakistani called Mubarak Shah who was in the small welcome party. He said he had been expressly sent to invite me to the home of his boss, Abdus Samad, chairman of Premier Tobacco Company, who was originally from Madras. I said I could not possibly go there directly from the airport but would make my way soon after settling in. Mubarak Shah insisted on accompanying us to Hindustan Court where I would be staying until they got India Lodge, the official residence, ready.

I went straight to my new office at India House. This was a soaring four-storey building with numerous rooms but totally dilapidated. It had been utterly neglected, like all our vast properties in Karachi, since 1965 when the capital was moved to Islamabad and war had broken out. My team – comprising two clerks temporarily deputed from our embassy in Islamabad – and I huddled into a small room with one telephone between us, while workers swarmed over the premises.

The phone rang. It was from the office of the deputy commissioner of Sukkur. At the other end was an unfortunate liaison officer escorting a Hindu sadhu who, at L.K. Advani's pleading, had been permitted by the Pakistan authorities to return to Sadh Bela, near Sukkur, to provide spiritual succour to the relatively large community of Hindus who remained in Upper Sind. The poor man stammered that he had a terrible problem on his hands that only I could solve. I hesitantly asked what the trouble was. He cried out that the Muslim *mureed*s (followers/devotees) of the Hindu saint were insisting that they meet the visiting Hindu priest to secure his blessings. Would I

Amma and Appa
S. Bhagyalakshmi (1910–88) V. Sankar Aiyar (1907–53)
Lahore, 1940

Dr S. Alankaram (1906–66),
my mother's elder sister
Lucknow, 1960

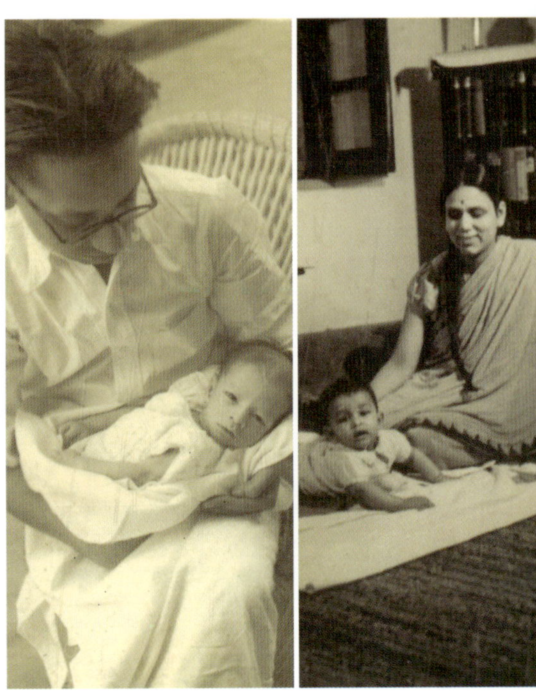

In Appa's arms and as a crawling baby
Lahore, 1941

Me with my favourite toy that led to my being nicknamed Sher Khan
Lahore, 1942

Tara, me and Jam with Mukund leaning in front
Lucknow, 1957

Seated on the extreme left as secretary of the Union*
Cambridge Union, 1963

Standing extreme right with my IFS colleagues*
Mussoorie, 1963

* To know more about the eminent personalities in these photographs scan the QR code on page xii.

Suneet and I, pronounced man and wife

New Delhi, 14 January 1973

Collecting papers as the conference spokesman at the NAM Summit

New Delhi, 1983

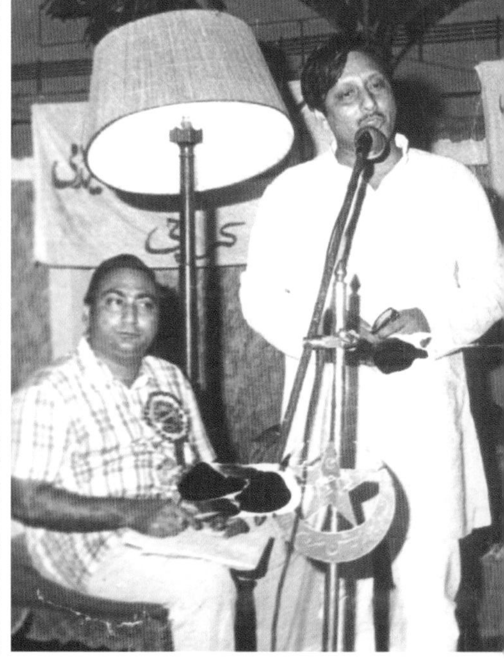

Addressing Pak Hind Prem Sabha

Karachi, 1979

Receiving a Sindhi delegation led by the Hyderabad mayor to protest the riots sparked by the Moradabad Eidgah firing
Karachi, 1980

Receiving the first minister of Sind Rasool Baksh Talpur at India Lodge
Karachi, 1981

PM Rajiv Gandhi and I, as joint secretary to the PM, in discussion
Patiala, 1985

Rajiv Gandhi and Sonia Gandhi, with me in tow, on a rural tour
Madhya Pradesh, 1985

PM Rajiv Gandhi and Sonia Gandhi being welcomed at my ancestral village
Kargudi, Thanjavur district, 1987

PM Rajiv Gandhi and I, at a press conference
Calcutta, 1989

PM Rajiv Gandhi and I, in a helicopter in Ladakh en route the remote avalanche-hit Zanskar Valley, laughing at a joke by Farooq Abdullah (not in the picture)
Ladakh, 1989

First election campaign with my family. My youngest daughter Sana is seen with me in the jeep.
Mayiladuthurai, Tamil Nadu, 1991

Campaigning with Suneet (back to the camera) in one of the seven elections I fought, three of which I won
Mayiladuthurai, Tamil Nadu, 1996

please give him permission to let them do so? I could barely believe that this was going to be my first task as consul general. Somewhat grandiloquently, I granted the permission.

It was my first – and lasting – lesson in how gaping was (and is) the abyss between the stereotype of Pakistan and Pakistanis that most Indians carry in their heads, and the ground reality. It was also the first lesson I learnt in how much the ordinary Pakistani (particularly the immigrant, the *muhajir*) identifies with us. That alone explains the liaison officer bypassing proper diplomatic channels and directly communicating with the representative of a 'foreign power'. This would never have happened with the Brits or the Americans, nor even with the Iranians or the Chinese. I was seen as indistinguishable from the local bureaucracy, largely because I looked like them and was passably fluent in their everyday language: Hindustani, not formal Persianized Urdu. This lesson was to be dinned into my head over and over in the next three years.

I finally gave in to Mubarak Shah's desperate pleas for me to accompany him to Abdus Samad's home. I had learnt that Samad was one of Pakistan's more prominent industrialists, running his Premier Tobacco Company in competition with Pakistan Tobacco (the front for the former Imperial Tobacco Company that in India had changed its name to India Tobacco Company and then to ITC). So I was not surprised by the immensely long circular drive up to his magnificent mansion.

Samad was at the door to receive me and escorted me down a long corridor that had a number of young men lined up to my left and an equal number of young women lined up to my right. As he went through the introductions, I found that they were all his sons and daughters-in-law, or his daughters and sons-in-law. What struck me was that all the Karachi siblings were married to spouses from Madras. So the first thing I said to Samad as we seated ourselves was, 'But why have you married all your children to Indians?' His astounding response was, 'Because I am an Indian!'

Before I could quite digest his reply, he went on to explain that he had been seventeen or eighteen years old at Partition. His father's Hindu agent in Sukkur, who ran the marketing of their beedi and chewing tobacco manufacturing units in Tamil Nadu, had 'fled to Indore'. His father, therefore, asked Samad to proceed immediately to take over the retailing at the Sukkur end. He had done so and was quite happy as he could frequently visit his family in Madras.

But, in September 1949, in retaliation for Pakistan not having devalued its rupee along with India after the pound sterling was devalued vis-à-vis the US dollar, India banned almost all trade with Pakistan. Samad was thus left with nothing to do and decided, with his family's consent, to pack up and come home. He applied to the Indian High Commission for the issue of an Indian passport and became extremely worried when the High Commission informed him that as, in the meantime, he had become a Pakistani citizen and acquired a Pakistani passport, the Government of India would refuse to let him change sides. Samad informed his family who were among the strongest financial supporters of the Congress in Madras province. This led to Kamaraj and other Madras Congress leaders calling on Nehru in Delhi and 'saying that if Samad was not an Indian, neither are we'. Nehru apparently calmed down the irate Madras Congress leaders with the assurance that he would find a way around this.

Sure enough, a little while later, Samad heard from the High Commission that his case had been cleared and he could visit the consular officer to collect his Indian passport. But when the Pakistan government came to hear of this, their finance ministry drew up an indictment of the company's tax returns and imposed such heavy penalties on Samad that they would drive his family firm bankrupt. The authorities quietly let him know that if he declined the Indian offer of a passport, an accommodation on tax matters would be reached.

At this point, Samad said, he could think of only one man who could save him: 'An Aiyar,' he said, 'like you.' Partition had yet not affected the professional classes. And so, this Indian income tax adviser flew into Karachi fairly frequently to handle Samad's cases. But, complained Samad, as soon as news of the man's arrival reached the ears of the tax department, the IT officers would descend on the Indian expert with their files to get his opinion on cases they were finding difficult and Samad would find his problem bypassed.

Nevertheless, he persisted. Then, he said, he opened the papers one morning to find that this Aiyar had been killed in an air accident.

'You're talking of my father,' I interjected.

Samad sat up, shook his head sadly and said, 'I should have guessed. He was V. Sankar Aiyar and you are Mani Shankar Aiyar. On that day,' he went on, 'I knew I would have to remain a Pakistani because there was no one else to save me.' He wiped a tear from his eye.

In this way I discovered that through his untimely death, my father contributed a millionaire to Pakistan.

Visas, the ultimate diplomatic weapon

Everyone wanted to know when we were going to open the visa office. That was impossible until we had inhabitable offices to work out of, and an adequate complement of staff with at least rudimentary housing. Delhi was most receptive to my requests for additional staff backed by a most supportive ambassador in Islamabad, Katyayani Shankar Bajpai. But however much our contractors hurried, repairs to the office and residences were going to take at least a couple of months.

That led to my first fifteen minutes of fame. The Lahore High Court had pronounced ex-Prime Minister Zulfikar Ali Bhutto guilty of murder within days of my reaching Pakistan. The Supreme Court was next in line. When, in early February 1979 it finally confirmed the death sentence, it was, of course, the lead story in all newspapers. And, in the widely circulated *Sun* newspaper, the second lead on the right-hand front page boomed, 'Visa Office to open shortly: Aiyar'.

I finally received a brace of consuls (and later two more) and some 125 clerical staff to cope with the huge load of visa applications expected. When it was announced that the visa office would be inaugurated in early March, nearly a thousand visa seekers (some estimated the crowd at five thousand) formed concentric circles around the consulate and patiently waited day and night to collect their visa application forms. I went among the throng trying to persuade them that now that the office had opened, they could disperse and come back another day. They wouldn't budge. They said they had not seen their folks in India for thirteen long years, missing births, marriages, illnesses, deaths and festivals, and as they did not know when our visa office would be suddenly closed, as so often in the past, they were determined to wait until their turn came, even if this were to take days.

Then I saw an old woman sobbing on the side. I asked her what the matter was. It seemed she had waited in line for two days and nights and then had to go to the nearby cantonment railway station to relieve herself, and on return found her place taken and was being bullied to stand at the end of the snaking queue.

That did it. I announced every visa application form would carry a rubber-stamped date, based on the capacity of my staff to handle the workload, and if the visa seekers came to the office between nine and ten on the morning of the given date to hand in their completed forms, they could return between four and five in the evening to collect their stamped passports. To begin with, there was considerable scepticism but as we were able to steadily prove our claim, news began to spread that the consulate's word could be trusted. This was to generate unprecedented goodwill.

I also learnt an important lesson in simplifying procedures and getting rid of red tape. My principal security guard, Kutty, fetched up in my office one afternoon, before the visa office had formally opened. He begged me to see a visa applicant who was tearing his hair and beating his breast wailing that he must be given a visa immediately to visit India to see his ailing mother. Would I make an exception and please receive this man?

I asked Kutty to show the man in. He arrived clutching a telegram that he laid before me on the table. After glancing at it, I sternly demanded to know from where he had got the telegram. Offended, the man asked where did I think he had got it from. From the telegraph office, of course! I asked him to repeat who was ill. He sobbed and replied that his mother was on her deathbed.

'In that case,' I said, 'why does this telegram say "Father serious"?' He grabbed the telegram, sucking his tears back into his eye duct, and swore barely audibly, 'That bastard Hindu!' I let that abuse sink in and persisted, 'I'll give you the visa if you tell me who gave you this telegram.' He said there was a Pakistani Hindu visa tout outside the gates, who was selling these fake telegrams at Rs 50 a telegram. 'I told him my mother was ill and the scoundrel has given me the wrong telegram saying "Father serious."'

After checking the Black Book that listed all those to whom the issue of visas was forbidden, I had a visa issued to the man, then arranged for the 'Hindu' visa tout to be removed from the premises, also instituting an enquiry into how he had gotten into business. I learnt that 'proof' in terms of a letter or cable, backed by a sworn affidavit, was required before consideration could be given to issue an out-of-turn visa. This provided the loophole to our visa entrepreneur to launch his business, especially as our Hindu clerks were keen to listen to a fellow Hindu's recommendation.

I changed the system to dispense with telegrams and affidavits. I said KE (for Karachi Emergency) visas would be issued to anyone who asked but the visa would have to be utilized within a week (rather than the three months usually given); they could visit only one place (against the normal three); and they would not be entitled to another visa for at least a year after they had been issued this one. Later, bowing to social realities, where the elite felt slighted to have to wait in queue even if only for a few minutes, I also introduced the KV (for Karachi VIP) visa which the recipient received from one of the consuls or me while sipping a cup of tea.

It took over a year for the home ministry in Delhi to discover these innovations. I was reprimanded for unauthorized changes but my ambassador in Islamabad, Shankar Bajpai, smoothed the ruffled feathers of the irate home secretary, got me off the hook and let me get on with it.

By the end of my term, we had issued over 3 lakh visas and not a single case of misuse had been reported. The visa has been an immensely effective way of positively influencing Pakistani public opinion. Yet, the chief strategic use to which it has been put is to ban or restrict the issue of visas to ordinary Pakistanis to display our disapproval of what the Pakistan government, or its 'deep state', is doing.

The simple truth is that terrorists do not apply for visas. Nor do smugglers. We target quite the wrong audience when we wield the visa as a weapon of revenge.

Facing demonstrations

I had another instructive experience in June, about six months after we opened the consulate. I was at a lunch at the Beach Luxury Hotel in honour of an Indian Oil Corporation delegation. My administrative assistant, Shirur, came on the line to say that our consulate was under siege; a few of the attackers had even broken into India House and were assaulting our staff.

I called my wife, Suneet, who, ever practical, calmly counselled me to not tell Aurangzeb, my Pakistani driver, why I was leaving the lunch so precipitately, instructed him to take the flag off the car and get Shirur to await me by a gate that was usually kept closed so I could let myself in. I did as I was told and soon found myself on the field of battle – for that is what it was.

Fortunately, the local deputy superintendent of police (DSP), Martin D'Souza, had been informed of the attack and succeeded in driving out the attackers. I asked him whether he knew who the ringleaders were. He said he did. I asked him to get about six of them to come up to my room and explain their grievances. This, of course, was quite in violation of the usual protocol that requires protesters to be restrained at a safe distance from the premises of a foreign diplomatic mission. Martin agreed.

I seated the ringleaders and ordered a round of coffee, then asked them to tell me what was troubling them. It seemed there had been a communal riot in West Bengal and they had come from Karachi University to ask me to tell our government that this violence against innocent Muslims was unacceptable to them. I wanted to give each of them the opportunity to vent their grievances and so started a round robin. The fourth speaker startlingly introduced himself as 'Rajiv' and, saying that he was a medical student, asked why we troubled Muslims in India so much when he, a Hindu, had never faced any difficulty in Pakistan.

I was rescued from having to answer by the insistent ringing of the telephone. It was Martin. In a strained voice, he said, 'Sir, can you please bring the boys down? The others are getting restive and saying their leaders are being entertained to coffee by the consul general.' I said they were, indeed, but I would rush them down to prove they were no quislings. By then, the crowd had been cleared and my last view of them was one enraged young man clutching the railing of the locked gates while leaping up and down, yelling, 'Morarji, *kutta*, Morarji, *kutta*' (Morarji, dog, Morarji, dog). I sighed and turned away wondering whether I should join him!

This set the tone to cope with other protest demonstrations to follow. This lot never returned. Occasionally, I would run into a smile on a young face I didn't recognize and wonder if it belonged to one of those who had challenged me that afternoon.

Making friends

Ambassador Bajpai had been posted as first secretary (political) in the Karachi High Commission in the run-up to the 1965 war. He had made an army of friends, who were dragooned into getting me inducted as a member of the Sind Club. They were also tasked by Bajpai to introduce me to as wide a circle as they could. This led to a dinner invitation to the home of one of his friends, Zafar Hasan. I was sitting next to a rather taciturn individual with whom I thought I should strike up a conversation. So I asked him the obvious but completely banal question: had he been to India? 'Yes,' he said shortly.

To get him to open up a bit, I went on, 'Oh, I see. Where did you go?'

'Meerut,' he replied gruffly.

I persisted, 'And for how long?'

'Three years,' he responded.

And then it dawned on me that he had been a prisoner of war!

Seeing the stricken expression of embarrassment on my face, he unbent and asked whether my wife and I would care to join him and his wife for dinner at the Sind Club the next day. And then added that they had an excellent bottle of port laid down in the cellar but I would have to sign for it (though of course he would be paying for the bottle)! This was because, under General Zia-ul-Haq's puritanical rule, Muslims, even Muslim diplomats, had been forbidden from using the bar.

The evening's surprises did not end there. I had sent my driver on other duties, so Zafar assured me he would have us dropped home. I clambered into a car driven by someone who introduced himself as Brigadier (Retd) 'Jimmy' Akhtar Aziz.

In the course of conversation as he drove us, Jimmy said he had served in the Lahore sector in one of the most bitter engagements of the 1965 war. Fiddling with his wireless, he came across the Indian commander deploying his troops. Recognizing the voice as that of Kapoor, one of his course mates at the Indian Military Academy, he cut into the wavelength and exclaimed, '*Arre,* Kapoor, Jimmy here. I beat you at everything in the academy and I'll beat you again tomorrow.' Kapoor apparently responded with a hearty laugh. And this they called war?

After we returned from the dinner, Suneet turned and asked me, 'This is supposed to be an enemy country, right?' It was a question that haunted me through my three years in Karachi and continues to haunt me. Is Pakistan an 'enemy' country?

Using the tip given me by Poncho, the friend who had taken us to dinner and a glass of port at the club, I made a habit of fetching up at the bar of the Sind Club at around noon and, in my capacity as the sole Hindu diplomat in the consular corps, standing rounds of drinks to anyone who asked (and many who felt too shy). Thus, I found the number of my acquaintances leaping in geometric progression.

They, in turn, began inviting me home. Considering that this was Zia's Pakistan, I was amazed at the freedom with which they spoke of people and politics (not to mention the lashings of Scotch whisky that were consumed). Zafar had been at St Stephen's with Zia and would regale the company with tales of the '*namazi*'[1] turning out in '*achkan-churidar*'[2] for his classes and generally being mocked by his fellow Stephanians for his obsession with OTC (Officers Training Corps – this was during World War II). I laughed along with the others but secretly wondered when the police would descend on Zafar for his levity. They never did. And soon, I acquired from my Pakistani friends a stock of 'Zia jokes' (many quite unprintable!). No one patriotically objected to these when I dined out on them.

This was not the first dictatorship in which I had served. I had spent a year in Hanoi under Ho Chi Minh, then two in Baghdad under Saddam Hussein. But there was no resemblance between the pursed lips and terrified demeanour of the Vietnamese and the Iraqis with their vicious police compared to the easy-going, laid-back attitude in Zia's autocracy. I often used to say to my Pakistani friends, 'Yours is an inefficient dictatorship and we run an inefficient democracy. So, the net level of freedom is about the same in the two countries!' This quip, however, had few takers!

Indian friends, and colleagues serving in Islamabad would ask how I coped with being followed everywhere. I would patiently explain: 'I never let on that I know I am being followed. I take only one precaution. Before slipping into bed, I raise the cover to check whether it really is my wife or an intelligence guy in drag!'

I have often thought that the single greatest beneficiary of Zia's dictatorship was none other than me. For after Zia had hanged Bhutto, he closed down

[1] One who prays five times a day as stipulated in Islamic practice.

[2] A long coat and tight, leg-hugging pyjamas; formal dress.

the National Assembly, and the politicians and journalists started flocking to Karachi: it was not only about as far as they could get from Zia, but also relaxed and comfortable to live in, with little danger of being hauled up for free and frank private conversations.

The protocol was also well understood. As we seated ourselves, the host would invariably ask, 'Tea or coffee?' A trolley would be wheeled in, and one's eyes and then one's tongue feasted on the most delectable fried shrimps and crabs, pakodas and samosas. The trolley was wheeled away and brought back laden with sandwiches and vol-au-vents and other Western offerings. Just as one's stomach was beginning to protest, out went the trolley again and returned with tandoori chicken and kababs that melted in the mouth. Once again, the trolley would be wheeled out and brought back overflowing with cakes and pastries and gulab jamun and kheer. Finally, and invariably, the host would turn and apologize, 'Sorry, I forgot, tea or coffee?'

In such a congenial atmosphere, with no time constraints, the dialogue would unfold, the host, in particular, needing little encouragement to get his hopes and fears, his remembrances and reminiscences, off his chest.

At the other end of the social spectrum, far removed from the rarefied English-speaking, whisky-guzzling Sind Club, was the Pak Hind Prem Sabha, set up just weeks before I reached Karachi. It was a wholly Urdu-speaking middle-class *muhajir*[3] outfit, dressed for the most part in *achkan*s and *sherwani*s,[4] muttering the Dilli/Lakhnawi '*Aadab*' in greeting rather than the '*As-salaam-alaikum*'[5] Zia was attempting to standardize. Many of their wives and daughters were in *burqa* or *hijab*.[6]

The Sabha comprised poets and poetasters, litterateurs and other wordsmiths, journalists from Urdu-medium and English-medium journals, a sprinkling of retired civil servants and army officers, all united by deep

[3] Literally those who have performed the 'hajj' – the pilgrimage to Mecca (Makkah). In this context, a name given to themselves by Indians who had migrated to the 'new Medina' of Pakistan.

[4] Traditional long coats, generally worn to indicate Muslim identity but popularized in independent India as a formal national dress.

[5] Respectful salutations, the second translated as 'Peace be upon you', generally used by Muslims of the subcontinent but also widely used by others.

[6] *Burqa*: full face cover; *hijab*: covers the head but not the face.

nostalgia for the India they had left behind. In fact, it was all I could do to avoid smirking when I heard them talking of filthy little towns like Amroha and Sambal as if they were recalling Paris in the spring or Tokyo in the season of cherry blossoms.

The Sabha was where I had my first exposure to Urdu poetry, little of which I understood, yet much of which I thoroughly enjoyed. These get-togethers would be followed by delectable buffets of what was called '*Dilliwallah khana*'.[7] My speeches delivered in my wholly inadequate Hindustani (splattered with Urdu words and expressions I was acquiring) were considered 'cute' and resonant of the linguistic milieu the audience had left behind. Their content gelled with the remembered familiarity of the Ganga–Jamni *tehzeeb*[8] (an expression I learnt from them) of the India they quit for the 'Medina' in which they dwelled with an abiding resentment of the restrictions placed on them by sanctimonious clerics and the authoritarian military.

Journalists

I also cultivated, as diplomats are wont to do, the press corps. This was greatly facilitated by the National Day receptions of one consulate or the other. Zia rule, of course, did not apply at these heathen gatherings. One only had to wend one's way to the bar to meet all the journalists. (Although I would not countenance any third country interfering in India–Pakistan affairs, I would make an exception for the waters of Scotland, as these are the most effective in lubricating any Indo-Pak conversation!)

A permanent fixture at these receptions was Ahmed Chhapra, the president of the Karachi Press Club. His boast, made in all earnestness, was that his club was the only islet of democracy left in the ocean of military dictatorship. He himself was repeatedly elected, in free and fair elections. One of the highlights of his leadership was the invitation extended to the renowned revolutionary Pakistan poet, Faiz Ahmed Faiz, to recite his verses. That was where Faiz himself recited his immortal '*Hum Dekhenge*' (We shall see!), as dramatic a

---

[7] Delhi food.

[8] Culture: *Ganga–Jamni* refers to the parallel flow and ultimate confluence of north India's two main rivers, from where they mostly hailed.

challenge as has ever been thrown at tyrants everywhere. The audience went ecstatic, with the police firmly kept out of the club by order of President Ahmed Chhapra, the 'only elected president in Pakistan' as he loved to claim!

This merry band of journalists was not only critical of military rule; they also filled me in on the excesses of Bhutto's 'democracy'. It was these journalists who provided contacts with the local Urdu press, far more widely read and influential than news and commentary in English, and much more steeped in the ideology of Pakistan than *Dawn* or *Morning News.*

Nawa-i-Waqt, however, spewed poison and *Jasarat*, the organ of the Jama'at-e-Islami, was not far behind. I did what I could, at a personal level, to vault over their visceral dislike of me as an Indian. With the editor of *Jasarat*, I think I succeeded; with *Nawa-i-Waqt,* I failed miserably. Towards the end of my stay, *Jasarat* carried a news item attributed to MENA (Middle East News Agency), which reported what was then little known: that differences had cropped up in Prime Minister Indira Gandhi's household between her and her recently widowed daughter-in-law, Maneka. Alongside this news item, *Jasarat* ran an editorial saying this illustrated the ghastly way in which young Hindu widows were treated.

I called the editor to fix an appointment with him. He immediately invited me over. On reaching his cabin, I said I did not want to talk to him alone but with all his staff present. Intrigued, he obliged. Once everyone had gathered, I made a little speech. I said Jawaharlal Nehru had been born a Hindu and so had his wife, Kamala. But their daughter, Indira, had married a Parsi, and of their two sons, one, Rajiv, was married to a Christian, and the other, Sanjay, was married to a Sikh. So was it fair to comment on Hindus in the manner that the *Jasarat* editorial had done?

The gathering was not only surprised to learn these details of cosmopolitanism in our First Family, they broke out in spontaneous applause. That, of course, did not change the Jama'at-e-Islami's line but at least it set these professional propagandists thinking.

Lifetime friends

My closest friends were a bunch of young men and women centred on Bina Muneer. She was married to Zaki, the son of one of Pakistan's tycoons from the Ayub era, the Hyeson Group, founded by his forefather, Abdul Hye. They had a stranglehold over the sugar business but were now in slow decline. Bina and Zaki made a lovely couple. I was still grieving the loss of my youngest brother Mukund, and as they were both of the same age, Zaki in my mind became the younger brother who had been cruelly snatched away.

Other close friends included Gulgee, Pakistan's great painter, and his lively wife, Zaro. They were murdered in their home some years after we had left Karachi, and a driver and a servant received life sentences for this awful crime. A painting by Gulgee, presented as a farewell gift when we left Karachi, as well as a portrait of me he did in 1989, remain precious souvenirs of my friendship with them. We were also very fond of Sadia Pirzada, the Pakistan People's Party (PPP) politician Hafeez Pirzada's wife, and the Tapals, Iqbal and Sabira.

It was through the Muneers that I met Akbar Liaquat Ali Khan, the son of Pakistan's first prime minister. The day after my arrival in Karachi, a fat envelope was hand-delivered at the consulate office, containing a booklet about the formidable Begum Ra'ana Liaquat Ali Khan. Idly flipping through its pages, I sat up on finding that her second son, Akbar, had been born on exactly the same day as me (10 April 1941). I immediately called her and asked to pay a courtesy call. She was graciousness incarnate. When I told her I had found from her booklet that I had been born on the same day as Akbar, she almost enfolded me in her arms. Akbar and I quickly became friends. Akbar earned the collective kudos of all of us when he arranged for Katy Mirza, an actress renowned for her exceptional physical assets, to visit Karachi, to the delectation of all!

The hanging of Zulfikar Ali Bhutto

The obsessive topic of discussion was Zulfikar Ali Bhutto. Many had known 'Zulfi' personally. Karachi was where he had gone to school, and many of those I met at the Sind Club were his contemporaries. The death sentence having been pronounced, Zia clamped down his '*Nizam-e-Mustafa*' (Rule of the Prophet) on the fourth day of Rabi-ul-awwal (1 February 1979), marking the further 'Islamization' of Pakistan.

The question was whether Zia would actually carry out the sentence. He had haughtily dismissed numerous pleas for mercy flowing in from every corner of the globe as emanating from a 'Trade Union of Politicians'. (Morarji Desai did not join the international chorus for mercy, and I for one – perhaps the only one – endorsed his decision.) I kept my counsel, but it seemed to me that the sentence would be carried out – and there would be little or no public reaction, at any rate in Karachi.

This unconventional assessment was not shared by many. What, above all, gave me pause for reflection was my conversation with the tailor we had hired to stitch the numerous curtains we needed. I asked him in passing one day which party he supported. He proudly pointed to his golf cap, akin to Mao's headgear, that Bhutto had popularized as the defining symbol of the PPP. 'What,' I asked, 'will happen if Bhutto sahib is hanged?' Scowling, the tailor replied, 'The streets of Karachi will run with rivers of blood.' That was a grassroots reaction and I had to take it at face value, but I was puzzled as I could not hear any rumblings in Sadar Bazaar nor among those who thronged our visa office.

Karachi had overthrown Bhutto in the 1977 elections. Not only had seven of Karachi's nine seats gone to the Opposition, the unending demonstrations at the crossroads of Lalukhet, labelled 'Stalingrad' by the demonstrators, had greatly facilitated Zia's coup. Even if the *muhajir* were not ready to forgive Bhutto his excesses, would not the native citizens rise in defence of a favourite son of Sind? Of course, most of Sind's leading PPP lights – Ghulam Mustafa Jatoi, Hafeez Pirzada et al. – were still in detention. But I was not hearing any threatening voices of rebellion from either the press or from the Sindhi friends I had started making, many of whom bore grudges against Bhutto.

My Sindhi friends included Elahi Bux Soomro, a *wadehra* (zamindar – large landholder) from Shikarpur abutting Larkana, who had been so close to Zulfi Bhutto that he found the one *qazi* (Muslim legal authority) willing to conduct the unorthodox marriage of the Sunni Bhutto to the Shia Nusrat. One day as Elahi Bux was driving around his lands, the SP in Shikarpur district drove up to his jeep and, saluting smartly, said he was under orders to arrest him. An astonished Elahi Bux asked why. The SP replied that he did not know, but his orders were to take him straight to Sukkur Central Jail. The SP soothingly added that Soomro would doubtless be informed of the reasons for his detention by the warder.

Of course, the first thing the bewildered Elahi Bux did on meeting the warder was to ask why he was under arrest. The warder shook his head and said he had been told to keep all three registers open – dacoity, murder and rape – and would be informed in due course which register to fill! Elahi Bux remained in confinement for months until one day he was suddenly informed that Bhutto had appointed him the deputy high commissioner to London. Such were the whims on which the government was being run.

Another old veteran of Sindhi politics was Ali Hassan Mangi, member of the National Assembly (MNA) of Sukkur. Apparently, he had publicly disagreed with Bhutto about some policy and had been bunged into Malir Jail outside Karachi. At 10 p.m., the warder came to his cell and said he was wanted on the phone. Mungo went to the warder's office and heard a familiar voice saying, 'Mungo, listen,' followed by the tinkling of a spoon against crystal. 'Do you want to spend the rest of the night in jail or would you rather have a nightcap with me? All you have to do is apologize.' Mungo had unleashed a string of expletives and banged the phone down. 'Such a b*****d deserves to die,' he muttered to me through clenched teeth.

There were other reasons for anger. The historian Hamida Khuhro, the daughter of the prominent Sindhi politician Ayub Khuhro, was my closest guide on Sind's politics and its opposition to Punjabi domination in Pakistan. She had been at St Antony's, Oxford, when the March 1971 crackdown in East Pakistan began and had published a letter in the London *Times* that caused a furore in Pakistan. She argued that the struggle was a bid by the 'overwhelmingly' Punjabi-dominated army and civil service to 'retain' their 'predominance' over not only East Pakistan but also the 'smaller provinces' of West Pakistan. She described Bhutto's role in the conflict as that of a 'political bastard' leading an 'increasingly fascist' party.

This led Zulfikar Ali Bhutto to write Ayub Khuhro a twenty-seven-page letter detailing all the 'humiliation' the Bhuttos had suffered at the hands of their Larkana neighbour. Berating Hamida 'who seems to have lost all sense of propriety', the letter boasted that 'at a time when my great ancestors were owning vast tracts of land' the Khuhros were 'nowhere in the picture'. He seemed to exemplify Hamida's description of Bhutto as 'a curious mixture of pique and pettiness'.

One final Bhutto story, one that I heard towards the end of my stay. I had accompanied Natwar Singh, our ambassador, to a meeting with Rasool

Baksh Talpur, the first minister of Sind. The minister was there when the lift's doors opened to welcome the Indian ambassador in his usual genial manner. Having seated us, the first minister would not let the ambassador get in a word edgewise.

'Main jaanta hoon, safir sahib, aap mujhse kyon milne aaye hain. Aap Bhutto ke baare main mujhse jaanna chahte ho na? Main bataoon. Itne bhaddu aadmi duniya ne kabhi nahin dekha, Hitler se bhi battar tha!' (I know, Ambassador *sahib*, why you have come to meet me. You want to know from me about Bhutto. I will tell you. He was the worst man the world has ever seen, worse even than Hitler!)

Natwar looked a little startled.

'Aap soch rahe hain ki Hitler ne chheh lakh yehudiyon ko jaan se maara. Main jaanta hoon. Lekin kisi ki gaand toh nahin li! (You are wondering how Bhutto could have been worse than Hitler. Yes, I know, Hitler killed six million Jews – but he did not get any of them buggered!)

This was a reference to the much-rumoured but unverified story that when Bhutto had arrested one of his closest confidants, J.A. Rahim, he had had his son violated in front of the father's eyes by a police sodomite.

I noticed the note-taker's hand stop in mid-air. Local protocol might have been best advised to not send in a spy disguised as a note-taker.

With all this animosity towards Bhutto, I could not see from where the momentum could come to fuel a major uprising against the general. February passed into March and March into April 1979 with suspense hanging over Bhutto's life.

At this time I received a telegram from Delhi informing me that the Indian chief of army staff (CoAS), General O.P. Malhotra, would be transiting through Karachi airport on his way back to Delhi from an official visit to Kenya. I informed my keepers, the Karachi Protocol Office of the Ministry of Foreign Affairs, and arrived at the airport well in time. I was distressed to find only a brigadier in attendance and comforted myself with the thought that perhaps a senior general would put in an appearance only after General Malhotra had arrived. That never happened. Our CoAS was the soul of courtesy, making polite conversation with the brigadier while I seethed at the discourtesy shown to our seniormost army officer and mentally composed the note of protest I would send next day to the Pakistan foreign office.

That note verbale never got sent. The next morning I learnt the reason why no high-ranking army officer could be spared to receive our CoAS. They were busy hanging Bhutto and arranging his burial before daybreak at his village of Garhi Khuda Baksh near Larkana!

While the papers were emblazoned with screaming headlines, the streets were subdued. There were no rivers of blood flowing. All was calm and quiet. I went around the city and returned to Hindustan Court and ran into my old friend, the *darzi* (tailor).

'What happened?' I enquired. 'You said the streets would run with rivers of blood!'

'No, sir, our leaders let us down. They did not give the call for us to rise. Cowards,' he spat out.

I persisted, 'Do the masses make the leader or do the leaders make the masses?'

'I don't know,' he replied dolefully.

'So,' I asked, 'why have you still got on your PPP cap?'

With infinite sadness, he responded, 'No one has asked me to take it off. If they do,' he added, taking off his cap, 'I'll do so.'

The revolution had choked. Zia had got away with murder.

A general view was that the silence was ominous for it betokened respect for the Islamic injunction that forty days of mourning must follow the death of a dear one. Come the end of the forty-day mourning period (the *chehlum*), perhaps all the pent-up anger would spill on to the streets.

One of the most ardent believers of this was Khushwant Singh, who had extended his patronage to my wife when she was just out of college. They had together (with her doing the writing and him as the supervisor) published an introductory book on the life and work of Guru Gobind Singh, whose tercentenary was celebrated in 1965. He had missed Bhutto's hanging but reached Islamabad in time for the *chehlum.* He rang Suneet and said he was flying into Karachi. We drove to the airport to receive him and he brushed aside all suggestions that we take him home, demanding to be driven around the city. My driver was happy to oblige. We wandered through boulevards and avenues, lanes and by-lanes, into slums and bazaars, all over the city. All was quiet. Khushwant was disappointed and finally gave up when we came across a group of boys playing cricket in the Bagh-e-Jinnah.

Encouraged by the absence of any public reaction to the hanging of

'Shaheed' Zulfikar Ali Bhutto, Zia started slowly releasing Bhutto's closest associates. Many of them flocked to Karachi. This was my golden opportunity.

Befriending PPP politicians

The first of the PPP leaders I cultivated, after their progressive release some six months after Bhutto's hanging, was Hafeez Pirzada, Bhutto's minister of law (who held several other portfolios). He had little to add about the muted reaction to Bhutto's hanging. But he had a great deal to say about the domination of the Punjabis and the need to ensure equitable power sharing among the four provinces.

After I got to know him better, I tried to probe into his plans to restore civilian authority. He was despairing. As the Bangladesh experience was then very much a 'lived' experience for every Pakistani, I was not entirely taken aback when one day, after we had become good friends, he sighed and said nothing could be done about military dictatorship in Pakistan without India. What, I asked, could India do? 'Sanctuaries,' he suggested. Because by then we had become fairly close, I replied, 'But where is your revolution?' 'Oh, first we need to be assured of sanctuaries,' he retorted. My response was, 'Hafeez, the only revolution you are capable of making is to stir the sugar in your coffee.' He laughed off the remark good-naturedly.

Through Hafeez and others I started widening my circle of political acquaintances, spreading in concentric circles to embrace virtually every persuasion. Strangely, for a group of politicians under a military dictatorship, they were all most forthcoming and uninhibited about expressing even to an Indian (much more, I discovered, than to my fellow members of the consular corps) their frank and frequently 'subversive' views.

Among them was Makhdoom Amin Faheem, the eldest son of the pir of Hala, one of Sind's most respected religious leaders. As the pir held a hereditary office, over the centuries the family had built an impressive palace at Hala and accumulated vast wealth which they used to reinforce their huge political influence. Amin was a modern-minded young man, very much a Bhutto man but wholly resigned to the hanging of their leader.

One memory that stands out is when I asked him whether his father had Hindu '*mureed*s' (in a throwback to my discovery on my first day in Karachi about our Hindu *sant*'s Muslim *mureed*s). He replied, 'But, of course, hundreds of them.'

I went on, 'Do they still keep in touch with him?'

He said, yes, they did. 'Every time there is a birth or a wedding or any other happy occasion like a son getting a job, their families write to my father and seek his blessings.'

'What!' I exclaimed. 'Even from India? After all these years?'

He seemed surprised at my surprise. 'Yes, from India too.'

Then, with some embarrassment, I went on, 'But I understand your father gives his blessings only after receiving his *nazrana* (votive offering).'

'Of course. Every blessing requires a *nazrana*.'

But how do they get it across?

'By the same route,' came the prompt reply, 'as they send their request. On camel-back through the smugglers!'

Thus does spiritual need outwit border control. To Makhdoom Amin Faheem, it was perfectly in the nature of things for his father's Hindu *mureed*s to seek the good offices of smugglers to send their *darkhwast* (petitions) for blessings on camel-back, along with a token *nazrana* (of five or ten Indian rupees) and receive in return, through the same smugglers' route, the pir's written blessings. I saw no reason to share this intelligence with my authorities.

Amin went on later to become the commerce minister of Pakistan and almost made it to prime minister. He was pipped at the post by the manoeuvrings of Asif Zardari.

Another PPP politician I recall with the greatest affection is Mir Hazar Khan Bijarani of Jacobabad. I was pleased but surprised when he invited me to visit his village of Karimpur in Upper Sind. 'It has a temple but no mosque,' he explained. I wondered if the authorities would permit me to go, especially as the anti-Zia Movement for the Restoration of Democracy (MRD) was gathering momentum. He waved away the problem, saying, 'Leave that to me.' And, sure enough, the permission came through. As we sped by the sparse landscape, I asked him whether he could tell me how much land his family held. 'Nothing much,' came his reply, 'just six thousand acres.' We went on for a while in silence and then he felt, in all politeness, he should ask me the same question.

'How much land do you own?' he asked.

I replied that my father had relinquished his share in return for the family house in the village but the family as a whole held perhaps twenty-five.

'Aap toh bahut bade rais honge,' he remarked. (So, you must be a very big landlord.)

I shook my head and explained, 'Not with just twenty-five acres.'

'Oh, I thought twenty-five thousand,' he replied.

That, I noted silently, was the difference between India and Pakistan: we had had land reforms and they hadn't, and perhaps that was the root cause for democracy in India as against dictatorship in Pakistan.

After a night spent in Karimpur where I woke to the sound of temple bells, he took me on a tour of several neighbouring villages. The villages were all decked out as for a political rally and people poured out of their huts to greet me as if I were a political leader. Cries of *'Jiye Bhutto!'* (Long live Bhutto!) rent the air and I rather suspect some of them thought I might be Bhutto himself. It was in many ways my political blooding and I have never forgotten the thrill of being mobbed, even under false pretences! I wonder what the authorities in Islamabad would have made of these shenanigans; as far as I could make out, they took it in their stride.

Of course, that drew me closer to Bijarani. We remained friends as he rose up the political ladder, making it to minister of interstate affairs in the Zardari–Geelani government. Learning that I was visiting Karachi for the Literature Festival in early February 2018, he called me in Delhi to invite me to stay with him and his recently acquired second wife, an utterly charming and very cultivated young woman. I do not know – no one seems to know – what exactly happened that evening, but their bodies were found in the bedroom next morning. Both had been shot dead.

In the autumn/winter of 1979, the PPP leader Ghulam Mustafa Jatoi was released. I was delighted to receive a dinner invitation from him. The entire consular corps was there. There was an Indus-like flow of alcohol being openly served by a host who had barely escaped the gallows himself. The police could have swooped down on him and taken him (and many of his guests) into custody for breaking the strict laws of the *Nizam-e-Mustafa*. I guessed the police were nowhere to be seen because they were under orders to make themselves scarce.

(Indeed, Zia himself had intervened when the police raided Amy Haque, the wife of one of Pakistan's star cricketers, and leaked to the press their find of a huge cache of liquor. Zia then added a coda to the shariat (Islamic law): a Pakistani's home is his castle, and the police must not chase alcohol into people's homes! The man was a religious fanatic – but a highly pragmatic one.)

I wended my way towards our host, having heard that he was at the bar (where else?). Jatoi greeted me effusively and, like every Pakistani I had met in Karachi, was more than willing to talk – and talk uninhibitedly – to an Indian diplomat of all people, at his first meeting. I asked him what it was he was demanding of the government.

'Democracy,' was his unhesitating answer.

Abandoning all caution, I went on, 'Within Pakistan or without?'

'Within Pakistan, if possible; without, if necessary!'

I then asked, 'What is it that you particularly have against Zia?'

'Mr Consul General,' he said, 'before this b****d came to power, I used to have twenty-four brands of whisky in my bar. Now I have only six!'

That seemed to be as good a definition as any of dictatorship in Pakistan.

Jatoi deeply disapproved Benazir's aspiration to dynastic succession, as did her uncle at one remove, Mumtaz Bhutto, and several of Bhutto's senior colleagues. It was an empty disapproval because Sind, in particular, and Pakistan on the whole, regarded Benazir as the only legitimate successor. Her senior colleagues might have the talent and experience of governance but only she had the charisma. The vote would be for her, not them. Yet, just as many were sensing the Zia dictatorship tottering, it was fascinating to witness the complete lack of unity in the country's principal Opposition party, let alone the Opposition as a whole.

Let me give an illustration. Driving through Jatoi's fiefdom of Moro in Upper Sind, my colleague visiting from Islamabad, Sati Lambah, drew my attention to a calendar adorned with Benazir's portrait hanging on the wall of a wayside tea shop. I mentioned this to Jatoi when I met him the same evening. He growled back, 'Must have been taken down by now.'

I was sometimes asked by Pakistani friends how I knew so much about Pakistan and Pakistanis, about their polity and their economy. I would draw them to one side and whisper my secret to them: 'You see, I walk my kids to school in the morning. Between my home and the Convent of Jesus and Mary falls the Bhutto home. So, on my outward journey, I pass by the front gate of the

Bhuttos and wish the guard on duty, '*Salaam Alaikum*'. On my return journey, I walk past the rear of the Bhutto household and wish '*Salaam Alaikum*' to the intelligence man on duty there. And by comparing the expressions on the two faces, I am au fait with the political situation in Pakistan before breakfast!'

Jatoi eventually left the PPP about a decade after I left Karachi. For a brief while, he became prime minister in the early 1990s, heading a coalition government – Islami Jamhoori Ittehad – in the company of a large number of bearded clerics, just about the last place one would have expected this bon vivant to find political refuge.

As for Mumtaz, I was once at a party attended by him and Benazir. Benazir, enthroned in the living room, was the cynosure of all eyes. He muttered to me in the hall, 'Just because the b***h made it to president of the Oxford Union doesn't mean she'll make it to president of Pakistan.' With friends like these why would the Bhuttos so assiduously cultivate enemies?

Expanding the political circle

I found my circle of political acquaintances rapidly extending beyond the PPP. There were independents, members of the Jamiat Ulema-e-Pakistan (JUP) and the Jama'at-e-Islami. The only place from where the Jama'at-e-Islami were able to return their MNAs, Khurshid Ahmed and Ghafoor Ahmed, was Karachi city. Whatever reservations India might have had about their public postures against India and their fanatical advocacy of militant Islamic tenets, it was they who had pressurized Zia to open the Indian consulate in Karachi without even waiting to reciprocally open the Pakistani consulate in Bombay. It was their constituents who were our principal visa seekers, the '*muhajir*'.

So, when a *muhajir*, Abdus Sattar Afghani of the Jama'at-e-Islami, won the municipal election to become mayor of Karachi, I was the first of the consular representatives he received to accept felicitations from. In sharp contrast to the PPP politicians I was consorting with, he was a homespun politician, a man of the masses, comfortable only in Urdu, a butcher by profession. At our very first encounter, he enquired whether I could arrange for him to be invited to visit Bombay. I said I certainly would and was then startled to hear him add that, as a butcher by profession, he primarily wanted to visit the Bombay abattoir, which he had heard was a model of its kind! I loved the innocence of the request.

In due course, he would ring me often to enquire about Indian precedents on issues troubling him. For instance, he was upset at having been pushed down the reception line when Prince Karim Aga Khan flew into Karachi. He wanted to know where, in the order of protocol, the mayor of Bombay was accommodated when distinguished visitors from abroad flew into the city. It would never have occurred to Mayor Afghani to ask the British consul general a similar question of the Lord Mayor of London, or the American consul general about the mayor of New York. It was India alone, and that too Bombay in particular, that was the only relevant precedent. On another occasion, Mayor Afghani said he had heard that Indian cities had invented manhole covers that were theft-proof. Could I get him the details? Of course, he could not have asked the UK or the US or even Chinese consuls general because manhole covers are not routinely stolen in their countries!

Notwithstanding his Jama'ati ideological affiliations, we became such good friends that when I visited Karachi many years later after losing my second election in 1996, he demanded to know why I had stood for election in India when I could have been guaranteed victory in any Karachi constituency. Goodwill more than confrontation can win many a heart – particularly a Pakistani heart.

Two other friendships helped me understand Pakistan and its history and politics better. My conversations with the great Sindhi politician Ayub Khuhro took place on his spacious lawns some two decades after he had ceased to be an active force in Pakistani politics. There was something piquant in his reminiscences. He was among those who went to London to persuade Jinnah to return to India to lead the All-India Muslim League.[9]

Another political aspirant who became a lifelong friend was Javed Jabbar. He was elected (or selected?) to the Senate under Zia-ul-Haq, minister in two Benazir governments, then emerged as a founder member of Farooq Leghari's political party after Leghari ceased to be president of Pakistan, and finally served as a minister under General Pervez Musharraf. His political trajectory

---

[9] For more about this colourful statesman who dominated Sind politics, in rivalry to the Bhuttos, for the best part of half a century until he passed away at age 80 in 1980, scan the QR code on p. 234. See also his historian daughter's biography of him, *Mohammed Ayub Khan: A Life of Courage in Politics* (Ferozsons, Lahore, 1998).

reflects the ground reality of political life in Pakistan. I admire his readiness for dialogue with India and Indians notwithstanding the gulf between his idea of a solution and ours. It is patriotic Pakistani politicians of intelligence like him who would make the best, if most difficult, interlocutors – 'foemen worthy of our steel'! We should have the courage to engage with them.

I also got to know extremely well the most honest politician in South Asia, Sherbaz Khan Mazari, the title of whose autobiography, *A Journey to Disillusionment* (Oxford University Press, 1999) says it all.[10]

Balochistan

The Government of India had initially sought to include Balochistan in my consular jurisdiction but Pakistan's agrément specified only Sind. So, although I could not visit Balochistan, whose borders began at the doorstep of Karachi, across the Hub river, I did try to gather what information I could from Baloch dissidents living in or visiting Karachi.

The leading Baloch revolutionaries, Ataullah Mengal and Khair Baksh Marri had escaped abroad to run their revolutions from exile which is why I never met them. (So it was with Murtaza Bhutto, the eldest son of Zulfikar Ali Bhutto, who, not without reason, was dubbed the 'Prince of Terror'.) However, I did get very friendly with the distinguished Baloch revolutionary Sirdar Akbar Bugti's younger brother, Ahmed Nawaz Bugti, and picked up something about the flavour of Balochistan's doomed past, present and future.

While I never personally met his elder brother, Akbar, we had a strange tryst with destiny. Akbar filched Hamida Khuhro's copy of my book *Confessions of a Secular Fundamentalist* (Penguin/Viking, New Delhi, 2004) from her drawing room, brushing aside Hamida's protest that hers was a signed copy, saying she could always get another copy from me. Then he went off to the cave in his homeland where he was gunned down by Musharraf's troops with my book pinned to his chest.

---

[10] For reasons of space, my publishers have not been able to include my extensive writing on several persons who made a long-lasting impression on me, including Mazari, Jabbar, Kamal Azfar, Sayyed Akhlaque Hussain, Zia Khaleeli, and Brigadier (retd) A.R. Siddiqi (to name but a few). The interested reader is invited to retrieve these deleted pages at this book's website by scanning the QR code on p. 234.

One day I received a visit from a Pakistani Malayali called B.M. Kutty. He was the personal political aide to the legendary Baloch leader Ghaus Bakhsh Bizenjo. Kutty whispered confidentially that Bizenjo wished to see me. He added he had arranged an unmarked vehicle to take me to the rendezvous at the home of a Baloch businessman, Akbar Mustikhan. I told him I would gladly come, not clandestinely but in my own official car with India's flag proudly flying. Kutty wondered whether local security would prevent me from reaching Mustikhan House, where Bizenjo was staying. I remained adamant saying I would either come openly or not at all. In the event, no restriction was placed on my movements within the city (although, as ever, I must have been followed). And I learnt to never set aside less than four hours for a meeting with Bizenjo sahib.

Bizenjo had a great deal to say. He began by presenting me with an English version of his speech in the lower house of Kalat's bicameral legislature in December 1947 in which he regretted Partition but said that now that it had happened, he preferred Kalat to be independent rather than accede to Pakistan. He then took me through the various phases of his eventful life.

Rather than join Jinnah's exclusivist Muslim League, he opted for the Indian National Congress in the late 1930s after graduating from Aligarh Muslim University, principally because, as an ardent footballer, he had learnt that it was possible for Indians of all races and religions to pull together as a team. It made him rubbish Jinnah's two-nation theory. In consequence, in newly formed Pakistan, he spent extended periods in jail, under both military and civilian governments, for the sin of consistently demanding democratic and civil rights.

He had dedicated his life to securing the rights of the 'nationalities', as he dubbed the linguistic/ethnic groupings of Pakistan. Although, or perhaps because, he was the only non-Sirdar to be prominent in Baloch politics and had spent decades trying to unite the tribal leaders to present a common front, he despaired of ever getting them to set aside their internecine quarrels. I came away feeling ennobled by his palpable concern for all oppressed people. I think I should emphasize that he never sought, or even hinted at, any help from India.

I also felt I should round out my impressions of Balochistan by meeting the 'other side'. Any interaction with army officers was, of course, impossible.

But I spent time with another Baloch, Mir Nabi Baksh Zehri, an onyx multi-millionaire who was convinced of the futility of the insurrection incited by Baloch tribal heavyweights owing to their ancient quarrels with each other. He had a soft spot for India. When his workers found a rough onyx stone that showed what he saw as a pre-Partition outline map of India, he begged me to get him an appointment with Indira Gandhi as he wanted to present it to her. Somewhat to my surprise, she agreed to receive him, and I later found him bursting with pride at a photograph taken of his presenting the onyx tablet to her.

Our attempts at projecting ourselves as potential saviours of the Baloch people, as, for instance, Prime Minister Modi tried to do in his Independence Day speech in 2017, is a dangerous fantasy. We have no physical access to Balochistan and, far more importantly, the Baloch are quite capable of and willing to settle their scores with Islamabad on their own. So, our best policy would be to let the Baloch get on with it instead of bumbling into the hideous complications – ethnic, linguistic and tribal – of the province. There are other more fruitful ways of countering Pakistan's blundering efforts at running a 'proxy war' in Kashmir.

What, above all, we need to understand is that Balochistan, as constituted by the colonial authorities and maintained in contemporary Pakistan, is not a homogeneous entity but a bewildering mosaic of linguistic and cultural identities, constantly rubbing against each other. First, there is Pashtun Balochistan, gratuitously grafted onto historical Balochistan by the British for their own reasons. It holds the bulk of the population, all the major towns – Quetta, Chaman, Mastung, Harnai, Ziarat, Bolan – and, till recently, almost all of Balochistan's modern industries. But Pashtun Balochistan does not speak Baluchi! Pashtu and, increasingly, Urdu, constitute the lingua franca of the region. The Pathans are also deeply religious, in sharp contrast to the easy-going ways of the authentic Baloch. This point of friction is admirably summed up in one sentence from Akbar Mustikhan's manuscript: 'The Pathan has more of God on his lips – and more of the Devil in his soul'!

Then come the Baluchi-speaking fiefdoms of the tribal Sirdars constituted by the British as a kind of buffer zone between directly ruled British Indian territory and the Khanate of Kalat, with the tribal territories of the Raisanis, the Mengals, the Marris and the Bugtis, among others, all under the totally unimpeded autocratic control of tribal leaders (Akbar Bugti once notoriously boasted that he had killed his first man when he was but twelve!). The Sirdars are much preoccupied with settling tribal blood feuds. Natural gas, which is largely appropriated by the federal government, accounts for much of whatever there is of Balochistan's wealth. It is sourced from the Sui gas fields that are part of this region.

The third element of the mosaic is Sindhi-speaking coastal Las Bela under its own Jam Sahib, tugging towards Karachi and mainland Pakistan rather than Balochistan and its secessionist sentiment. The fourth component is the further extension of Balochistan along the coast of Makran, where Baluchi and even Sindhi are not understood, and the spoken language is their own Makrani. The fifth element is the heart of Balochistan, centred on the dry, dusty, flea-bitten capital of Nal of the erstwhile Kalat state, Bizenjo's home town. It is a desert waste punctured by oases where camel riders gather to ask each other about '*haal*', the news of the day, in their language, ancient Brahui; according to some scholars (hotly contested by others), it has linguistic affinities with Tamil.

And now the Chinese have entered, basing themselves in Gwadar and extending their influence through Balochistan all the way to the Karakoram Pass. Where, in this heterogeneity, are we to find the entry point to combat the Pakistanis in Balochistan?

The Pakistan economy under Zia

When I had first arrived in Pakistan, dropping in on Islamabad for the ambassador's briefing, he said he had chosen me for the post as he had heard from K.B. Lall that I knew 'something of economics'. He, therefore, wanted me to study the working of the Pakistani economy and report back to him. Taking this injunction seriously, once I had sorted out the working of the visa office, I started spending hours in the library of the State Bank of Pakistan (the Pakistan central bank).

The problem was the difficulty in accessing statistics and information related to the western wing of undivided Pakistan. I, therefore, had to separate the figures for West Pakistan from those for East Pakistan in order to get a clear picture of how contemporary Pakistan, after the separation of Bangladesh, was faring in relation to what had been known, until 1971, as West Pakistan.

I somehow succeeded in wresting this information from the available tables and putting out a continuous narrative of the economic development of West Pakistan, over the quarter century from the partition of India to the partition of Pakistan, to provide a backdrop to the Bhutto years and the current performance of the Zia government.

Having completed the exercise, I began having serious doubts about the accuracy of my figures, given that I was so poor in mathematics that I had opted in my school-leaving exams for the higher Tamil paper in order to bypass higher mathematics! My consuls were graduates in history and physics respectively, and we did not have an economist or statistician among our officers in Islamabad. Where, then, should I go for a double-check?

I took a risk that I hope will not even now land me on the wrong side of the law. I had heard reports of a brilliant young economist, Hafeez Pasha, then heading the Karachi Centre of Applied Economic Research at Karachi University. I tore the statistical sheets out of my 'Top Secret' draft and took them to him, confiding I would be in serious trouble if it ever leaked out that I had shared these tables with him. But if he would be kind enough to look through them, I would like him to lunch with me at the Sind Club a week hence where he could tell me what needed correction. He smilingly agreed and, when we met a week later, effusively congratulated me on producing the first-ever continuous series on Pakistan's economy from 1947 to the present. He said no one else had even attempted this before. I was, of course, extremely chuffed.

Hafeez Pasha went on to become head of the Planning Commission and, for a while, federal finance minister before going on to the UNDP in one of its top posts. He then settled down as professor of economics at LUMS (Lahore University of Management Studies), arguably the best university in Pakistan.

Having received this unanticipated encomium from one of Pakistan's top economists, I returned to my draft with renewed confidence and got it completed in time for Ambassador Bajpai's visit to Karachi in September 1979. I proudly handed over to him my thesis titled 'Towards a Revival of the Pakistan Economy'. He baulked at the title since all his information was that the economy under Zia was tanking. Believing also that Zia's polity was on the brink of collapse, he did not like my opening paragraph that declared prognostications about the political future of Zia's regime should be refracted through the prism of the performance of the economy. My conclusion was that far from teetering on the brink, there was such evident economic resurgence that pessimistic forecasts would not hold water.

Remarking 'What's your game?', he put the paper aside and went to lunch with his friends. He returned looking far more cheerful. He had met Aurangzeb of Swat, son-in-law of Ayub Khan, and a nominated member of the board of governors of the central bank. The ambassador said Aurangzeb had told him the economy was in the doldrums, a hopeless mess. That, as far as the ambassador was concerned, was the end of the matter. Anyone who has met Aurangzeb will testify to his total innocence of economics. But as the ambassador did not explicitly restrain me from sending the study to the MEA and copying it to others who might be interested, I did. The only one who replied was Dr Arjun Sengupta from the PMO who sent back word: 'You are becoming an Ayatollah!' For the rest, it lay unattended in the cupboard until Mani Dixit had it pulled out and declassified it.

Unfortunately, I have not succeeded in getting it published and it is now hopelessly out of date; indeed by the early 2000s Pakistan's annual rate of growth exceeded ours. Yet, over the next two decades (and particularly under civil democratic rule from 2008 on), the economy has truly drifted into a morass of the politicians' making. My conclusion that the Pakistan economy under Zia was moving towards revival was borne out and, notwithstanding the fervent prayers of India's army of Pakistan baiters, shows even now that despite its huge problems, it is manageable provided US and IMF assistance is forthcoming, or China bails out Pakistan.

Businessmen and boxwallahs

My research gave me an opening to speak to businessmen about the economy. I began with the Karachi Chamber of Commerce that had a much-neglected foundation stone at the foot of the building saying the stone had been laid by Mahatma Gandhi in the early 1930s. It was not worn as a badge of pride.

The proceedings were marked by an exposition of grievances over India, but, once that had been put on record, they would mellow over tea and samosas and the folks would enquire about the price of *adrak* (ginger)! The fortunes of many of these traders were made by buying cheap in Singapore and selling dear in Karachi, especially those essential ingredients for Pakistani cooking that were unavailable in Pakistan and imported circuitously from India. Whatever the intention of the two governments, ingenuity triumphed, and smuggling and third country entrepôts (since shifted from Singapore to the Gulf) flourished.

The Karachi Chamber, and subsequently the Federation of Pakistan Chambers of Commerce and Industry, opened doors for me to meet individual businessmen, big and small. I most enjoyed my introductory meeting with Ahmed Dawood who regaled me with stories of his adventures on the cotton exchange of pre-Partition Bombay. He and his fellow cotton king, Ruia, decided one evening over a game of cards to buy up all the available stock of raw cotton in India, watched the prices shoot through the roof and then made a killing.

He and his family had lost a fortune when Burma was split from India in 1937 and many Indians had been thrown out. After Partition, Dawood shifted his base of operations to Dacca. There he recovered his fortune in jute several times over. Then, in 1971, he lost it all and moved to Karachi, much enthused by the advent of Bhutto. At his meeting with the business community, Bhutto assured them that he did not have any nationalization in mind; two days later, he nationalized almost anything that could move. Disillusioned, Dawood decided that he would go West.

I'm translating what followed from his Bambaiya Hindustani. 'I asked myself, "What are you going to do, Dawood?" If I go to Saudi, there is money but no honour. If I go to London, there is neither any money nor any honour. So, I decided I would go to America. "What, Dawood, will you do in America?" I was sick of the cotton trade. "But if you are sick of cotton, what else do you know, Dawood?" I set my mind on oil exploration! And I was so successful that I was on the verge of buying a Boeing 707 for my family when they hanged that bastard, Bhutto. And so, I came back to Karachi!'

Another entrepreneur friend was Sadruddin Hashwani, whose business interests ranged over cotton, rice and, above all, the hotel industry. His autobiography makes his opinion of Bhutto and Zia clear: 'I was used to speaking my mind and realized that if Bhutto felt I had crossed the line, he would put me on some negative list or blacklist.'[11] As for Zia, he recounts his first meeting, opening with: 'Mr Bhutto ruined the economy and you are rewarding the same set of bureaucrats.'[12] Next day, Sadru got a call from the chief of the IB: 'Sadru *bhai*, there is a message from General Zia. Please don't speak to him or bother wishing him socially. You are forbidden from doing so.'[13]

He exploded: '*Bhaad mein jao* (Go to hell). And please convey this to General Zia.'

Within a week, he and his entire family had been put on the Exit Control List. Bhutto or Zia, nothing had changed!

I also got to know rather well a hotelier called Sadruddin Gangji, who was putting up the Sheraton in competition with Hashwani's Holiday Inn and the Intercontinental. Gangji had entered my life within days of my arrival in Karachi when he called on me in something of a tizzy; he needed a ticket that night by Indian Airlines/Air India from Dubai to Bombay as the Karachi–Bombay flight was full. I walked him across to the apartment of the Indian Airlines manager, Desai, and a confirmed ticket was quickly given. Bursting with gratitude, Sadru asked me what he could do for me. I said, 'Nothing', and had to repeat it several times. He scribbled a number on a stray sheet of paper and said I could call 'Akbar at the Telephone Exchange any time I wanted, and Akbar would put me through to wherever I wanted to call'. I gave the chit to my staff and forgot about it.

Two years later when I was desperately trying to get through to Delhi, my secretary reminded me of Gangji and Telephone Exchange Akbar. He still had the chit. I asked him to get Akbar on the line and, when I gave my name, Akbar welcomed me with a warm '*Aapka bade din se intezar tha!*' (I have been waiting to hear from you for a long time) and within seconds put me through to Delhi. Saved! I had hardly put the phone down when Akbar called back, '*Ab bataiye, kahan milaoon?* London? San Francisco? Tokyo?' (Now tell me, where should I put your call through? London? San Francisco? Tokyo?) I

---

[11] Sadruddin Hashwani, *Truth Always Prevails: A Memoir*, Penguin, India, 15 August 2014.

[12] Ibid.

[13] Ibid.

laughingly put him off but confessed to myself there were uses for the Sadru Gangjis of this world.

Former high commissioner Rajeshwar Dayal visits

The president of the Indian branch of the Aga Khan Foundation, Rajeshwar Dayal, who had served in the city as India's high commissioner in the immediate aftermath of Ayub Khan's coup of October 1958, came on a visit to Karachi while I was there. He had overseen the Indus Waters Treaty of 1960, which has stood the test of time. He also arranged Nehru's last visit to Pakistan for the signing of the treaty. Above all, for me, it was Rajeshwar Dayal who, as special secretary in charge of administration, had stood steadfast at my side during my troubled and controversial admission to the IFS.

When he came to Karachi, I spent as much time as I could talking of his days there. He had a personal friendship with Ayub Khan going back to the late 1930s–early '40s when he was district magistrate, Mathura, and Ayub was posted in Agra cantonment. Ayub's brother, a police officer, was serving in Mathura as Dayal's SP. So, they had had many a convivial evening together.

Hence, Ayub dropped in at India Lodge unannounced. He asked Rajeshwar to convey a message to Nehru that he was ready to settle Kashmir on the same basis as the 1955 agreement between Italy and Austria on South Tyrol. There, the de facto division of the territory, including the key Adriatic port of Trieste, was accepted by both countries, with the de jure decision postponed to a future generation. The only condition Ayub laid down was that the matter should be settled within six months because, as he colourfully put it, 'At the moment, I have these bloody politicians by the balls, so there won't be a squeak, but only for six months; after that they will find their voices.'

Nehru, apparently, did not deign to even acknowledge the proposal. His deepest concern was that the 'Napoleon virus' might spread from Pakistani officers to infect their Indian counterparts with whom they had fought and won World War II. The fear was not unfounded as the rebellion of the Indian CoAS, General Thimayya, against Defence Minister Krishna Menon's obstreperous behaviour occurred at almost the same time. Preserving the Indian army's political neutrality was more important than legitimizing military dictatorship in Pakistan. Now, however, given that Ayub is long dead and so are almost all that generation of the Indian army, perhaps it is worth reconsidering the proposal?

One lakh visas in six months

The evening papers had taken it upon themselves to competitively keep count of the number of visas we were issuing (combined with some discreet leaks from our end). 'Fifty thousand' screamed the headlines about two months into the exercise. 'Seventy-five thousand' proclaimed the headlines two further months later. By September, within six months of our opening, we were edging towards one hundred thousand, a full lakh.

I called in ten Pakistani journalists, asking them to man the windows of our visa office so they could distribute the last ten passports that would take us to the 1 lakh mark. When it was reached, there was a loud roar of applause as the lucky recipient's passport was handed over to him (by a Pakistani newshound) and I presented him with a tin of Darjeeling tea.

The waiting audience burst into slogans: '*Hindustan ke consul general, zindabad, zindabad!*' (Long live the consul general of India!) Then, heart-warmingly, '*Yahan koi paabandi nahin, koi rishwat nahi!*' (No hurdles here, no bribes!). I was overwhelmed. So were the journalists. I had a field day in the papers that evening and the next. Little wonder that the two Jama'at-e-Islami MNAs were effusive in their thanks for us in having contributed to the fulfilment of one of their constituents' most keenly felt requirements, the open opportunity to visit India. I felt vindicated at having told my visa clerks not to regard their tasks as akin to issuing railway tickets; with every visa issued, we were buying goodwill.

Hostility vs goodwill

One of the most important lessons I learnt in Pakistan was that Indian hostility, or even the apprehension of such hostility, is what unites Pakistanis behind their government, military or civilian. So, any belief on our part that the frequently expressed disillusionment of Pakistanis with their leaders and their future reflects an underlying instability that will bring the country down is woefully mistaken.

Pakistan is an ineradicable reality and Pakistanis of every hue will fight to retain their 'New Medina'. Equally, as I wrote in my farewell dispatch from Karachi, the general populace will respond with the greatest outpouring of generosity to a 'blitzkrieg of goodwill' from our side. Pakistan is not going away; we can huff and we can puff but that's not going to blow the house down. But over four decades of plugging this line, I have found no takers for this view in India. It was dismissed by one of our best foreign secretaries, Mani Dixit, as a 'Pollyanna' [14] view of Pakistan. I have had to reluctantly conclude that the lobby for peace is far larger in Pakistan than it is in India.

Across a wide spectrum of Karachi opinion I found a clear willingness, indeed an ardent desire, to see differences with India settled. I searched for tell-tale signs from business barons to barbers and bootblacks; from society ladies in expensive chiffons and 'suited-booted' boxwallahs to butlers and domestic servants; from politicians who had held high office to purveyors of news and comment; from intellectuals to poets and writers; from artists of different genres; from street vendors to shopkeepers; from English-speaking pukka sahibs to die-hard Islamic nationalists; from the religious minorities, ranging through rich ones like the Parsis and Hindu millionaires, as well as, of course, the poor Hindu *haari*s (sharecroppers) of Sindhi *wadehra*s to a number of teachers in Karachi's reputed private schools and government schools; and from the sophisticates of Karachi to those who thronged the Indian visa area. All of them wanted peace; none was a warmonger, not even the '*Islam-pasand*'. Bhutto's 1965 call for 'a thousand years' war' with India had no takers. And later, no one wanted 1971 repeated in rump Pakistan.

Morarji's government falls

In mid-1979, I found myself summoned for consultations to Delhi to explain some inconsistencies the internal audit officer had claimed to have found in the accounts of our expenditure on repairing our long-neglected properties in Karachi. I had boned up enough on the details of the contracts to answer all the queries fired at me.

[14] Naïve, over-optimistic, ever cheerful.

I was far more interested in picking up all I could about the political crisis rocking the Morarji government. I went to Parliament and heard George Fernandes vigorously defend his government's record in the no-confidence motion the Congress-led Opposition had moved. It was a brilliant performance. A few hours later, I was in an aeroplane headed out to Karachi. On arrival there, I learnt that soon after delivering his stout defence of the government, George Fernandes had defected and joined the rebels to bring down the government! I was now the representative of an interim government.

I went to the Sind Club where my host shook my hand and then repeatedly muttered, 'Buckingham Palace, *yaar*, Buckingham Palace.' Buckingham Palace? I didn't get the drift. He went on, wonderstruck, 'The man loses a vote and goes immediately to the president to tender his resignation. Where does he think he is? Buckingham Palace? In our country,' he continued, 'we'd call out the army!'

I don't know of any tribute paid more succinctly to India and its democracy. It was almost on par with another backhanded compliment from a Pakistani: 'You guys build the worst motor car in the world – but at least *you* build them!'

India Lodge, the residence

It was not until September 1979, nine months after arriving in Karachi, that we were able to move into India Lodge, our palatial residence. The mansion was located on what was known as Clifton Road but the name had been changed to Shahrah-e-Iran in honour of the shah of Iran who loaned Bhutto a fleet of Huey Cobra gunships to commit a hundred Guernicas in Balochistan.

In December 1979, our residence was ready to throw a really big party. We called in everyone we knew, however disparate. So, there were the bon vivants, who constituted the majority of the guests, thoroughly enjoying the free flow of alcohol, and the two Jama'at-e-Islami MNAs for Karachi, who, after a while, took their leave, shaking their heads and muttering, '*Kitni zaleel hai hamari qaum!*' (How rotten is our nation!) It was the first of what were to become one of the most anticipated events on Karachi's social calendar. It also almost became the last. One of our guests, an artist of some repute, had consumed so much of the libations of Scotland that he crashed his car at the roundabout at the end of the road. Had that got around, severe restrictions amounting to a ban could have been placed on Pakistanis accepting invitations to India Lodge, especially under the drastic laws of the *Nizam-e-Mustafa*. Happily, the police covered up for us!

The Iranian consul general's home and office was located at the top of the road. Ayatollah Khomeini's revolution had started in mid-1978 when I was stationed in Baghdad, so I got a grandstand view from the west of Iran of its commencement. The revolution culminated in February 1979, so I got a grandstand view from the east as well!

But nothing prepared me (or the Pakistanis) for the young revolutionary sent as the Ayatollah's consul general to Karachi. He undertook his mission with zeal, going every evening to Karachi University to incite the students there to ecstasies of revolutionary fervour, including condemning inadequate Islamization in Zia's Pakistan. Unsurprisingly, the bulk of the police 'protection' deployed to keep watch over my residence was transferred to the Consulate-General of the Islamic Republic of Iran, an irony that brought a secret smile to my lips. It was not long before Iran and Pakistan came to an unpublicized understanding for the consul general to return to Tehran to expend his zeal on consolidating the revolution rather than exporting it!

Sana, our youngest

In October 1979, our youngest was born. The presiding deity was Dr Faridon Setna, who became world renowned when he attended to all of Benazir's pregnancies as she presided over the Permanently Pregnant Party, as the wits labelled the PPP! Dr Setna was very anxious that as this would be her third child Suneet should reach the hospital as soon as signs of labour set in. We rushed to the hospital at about 9 p.m. and Dr Setna followed hard on our heels. However, it was not till about 9 a.m. on the next day, 12 October 1979, that the baby arrived.

Suneet asked me to ascertain whether it was a boy or a girl. The soul of discretion, Dr Setna apologized about 'forgetting' to look. I then knew a third girl had been added to our family. We were both delighted, as were her three- and five-year-old sisters who wanted her named after a girl at school they admired – Sana. I learnt that the name, derived from a Quranic expression, '*Hamd-o-Sana*' – meaning 'Praise of the Glory of God'. We thought that most appropriate, not realizing that she would have to spend her adult life explaining to immigration and passport officers why, with an Arabic name and Karachi as birthplace, she carries an Indian passport and a Hindu caste surname! Sana is now a tenured professor of history at the Massachusetts Institute of Technology. We are very proud of her.

The siege at the Ka'aba

In November 1979, violence broke out in Mecca, at the Ka'aba. This provoked a siege of the US embassy in Islamabad and the American diplomats had to take refuge in the basement. While Indians of my generation are sceptical of Americans, and many dislike them, the Pakistanis hate them. So, when the Ka'aba was invested by armed Iranian rebels, the Pakistani mob, without further thought, immediately determined the US must be behind the desecration of Islam's most holy place and broke into the embassy to exact revenge. Such are the wages of bounty and benediction!

I called my US counterpart, Richard Post, whose chancery was quite close to ours, to enquire how he was. After finding he was all right, I heeded my secretary's warning that a crowd was heading towards our office and went down to investigate. It was a glorious early winter afternoon and most of my staff were taking in the sun on the lawns. If the crowd wished to attack us, we were sitting ducks. But they just ran right past us.

One of the old fogies on my staff was ambling back from lunch and an extended siesta. He stopped one of the boys and gently asked him where they were going. '*Hum kaafiron ko maarne ja rah hain!*' (We are off to kill the infidels!) But they did not mean us. Indeed, they waved cheerfully as they streamed past Bharat Bhawan (the official name of our consulate). It was for me a highly revelatory moment. Happily, they mistook the under-construction Holiday Inn for the US consulate and, thinking the job had already been done, went further to find an American office to burn down.

Indira Gandhi returns as PM

As 1979 ended, there were two developments of great consequence. One was the Soviet Union invading Afghanistan, albeit at the invitation of the Afghan communist government. The other was the decisive victory of Indira Gandhi and her Congress in an election that pushed the Morarji and successor Charan Singh governments into oblivion.

The arson at the US embassy in Islamabad was quickly forgotten as Pakistan resumed its role as the most faithful ally of the United States. The US entered the Afghanistan war, initially by providing critical armed help to the *mujahideen* (religion-inspired revolutionaries) to inflict defeat on the USSR. Many diplomats and commentators, particularly those based in Islamabad, believed that but for this fortuitous intervention, Zia would have been overthrown by popular resentment at his rule. I could not share this view from Karachi because there persisted a resigned acceptance of military dictatorship rather than any determined attempt at promoting civil disturbance. But, yes, it was true that deep concern at the possibility of a Soviet advance into Pakistan after they had overthrown the *mujahideen* resistance was a growing public concern. In the event, it quickly became clear that the Soviet Union had got bogged down in Afghanistan and that they would have to withdraw from that country sooner rather than later. There was no danger of their moving to the warm waters of the Indian Ocean that lapped the port of Karachi.

The other major churning was Indira Gandhi's return as prime minister following the elections of December 1979. I wondered what this presaged for India–Pakistan relations and, nearer home, for us at the consulate in Karachi. At first, it seemed the Morarji–Vajpayee initiative to work towards normalization would continue, especially after Foreign Minister P.V. Narasimha Rao reaffirmed in Parliament the decision to carry on with the earlier offer to hand over Jinnah House to the Pakistanis after the British lease came to an end.

But then, Zia, at his first meeting with Indiraji in Harare in April 1980, on the occasion of Zimbabwe's independence, presented her a gorgeously illustrated book on Pakistan of which he was immensely proud. The Indian PM idly flipped through the volume and discovered to her horror that Kashmir was shown as a 'disputed territory'. Then, Indian intelligence informed the Government of India that Pakistan's intention in taking over Jinnah House was to turn it into a memorial for the founder of Pakistan rather than use it for consular purposes.

This led to a withdrawal of the offer to lease Jinnah House to Pakistan. Unsurprisingly, there followed a downward sweep in our mutual relations, notwithstanding the visit to Pakistan of the Indian foreign minister, P.V. Narasimha Rao, in May 1981 (more on that later). It adversely affected cultural and social events at the consulate's auditorium and lawns because the Pakistani authorities intervened to stop such events where earlier they had been quite liberal, even encouraging such shows. This threw a shadow over my last days in Karachi.

Bhutto's first death anniversary

On the first anniversary of Bhutto's hanging, 4 April 1980, the PPP had called a large gathering of the party faithful at Bhutto's grave in his family village of Garhi Khuda Baksh, some 20 kilometres from Larkana. There was some expectation, particularly in diplomatic circles in Islamabad, that there would be trouble for the military regime. Karachi, however, as in the previous year, seemed tranquil. When, therefore, I was copied on a dispatch from our embassy describing in vivid terms the long-awaited uprising at Bhutto's grave, I went to see my PPP informants.

They were legion and they confirmed there had indeed been a little excitement when some in the crowd suggested they go to the Bhutto home and rescue Begum Bhutto from house arrest. The leaders quietened them explaining that it was not Nusrat Bhutto, but Zulfi's first wife who lived in the ancestral village. Nusrat was locked away in far-off Larkana. The only one not to understand the Sindhi language was General Tikka Khan, the Butcher of Dacca, who upbraided the gathering in Punjabi. At which, someone unhitched the horse from Tikka Khan's tonga and, after forcibly seating the general on the horse, whipped it to make it gallop off with Tikka Khan screaming imprecations!

I then rang my counterpart at the embassy and in the most discreet terms sought to know the source of their information. 'The BBC,' was his answer. I held my tongue. Years later, I asked the New Delhi correspondent of the BBC from where he had learnt of the uprising against the hangman at Bhutto's grave. 'Why, from the Indian embassy, of course,' he replied. The embassy and BBC had thus set up a perfect circle of mutual misinformation! Zia lasted an entire decade beyond the hanging.

A new ambassador arrives

The next major move on the chessboard of India–Pakistan relations was that Ambassador Bajpai was transferred to Beijing and on 16 May 1980 a new envoy, K. Natwar Singh, arrived. It was his birthday.

When Natwar's appointment was announced, I began worrying about continuity in consulate–embassy relations. The only time anything had gone wrong between me and Ambassador Bajpai was when he asked me to send him king prawns for a dinner he was hosting, and I mistakenly sent him tiger prawns (or was it the other way round?), not really knowing the difference! My colleagues at the embassy were laughing their heads off at what they thought Ambassador Bajpai would consider the ultimate gaffe. He, however, had contented himself with a 'Dear boy' reprimand, expressing astonishment that I should not, at this mature stage of my diplomatic career, know the world of difference between king and tiger prawns.

Natwar Singh was the highest flyer in the IFS and known to all as a personal favourite of the prime minister. His connection to the Nehru family stretched back to his schooldays and he had frequently breakfasted with Panditji himself at Teen Murti House when he was an undergraduate at St Stephen's where he had befriended the son of Nehru's sister, Krishna Hutheesingh.

How would I fare with such a prima donna? I anxiously called Shekhar Dasgupta who had served under Natwar in London. My worry was that I was in the newspapers in Karachi almost every day. I had heard that the incoming ambassador was a publicity hound. Would he not object? Dasgupta was most reassuring. 'So long as you confine yourself to the Pakistan media, he won't be bothered,' he replied, 'but be careful about getting into the Indian media. That he would wish to reserve as his domain.' As there was no possibility of any Indian journal being interested in my doings, I felt comforted.

Quite contrary to my forebodings, Natwar turned out to be a very pleasant, almost unassuming man, a great raconteur with a great sense of humour, easy to get on with and quite open-minded about everything I had to report. I was a bit startled to discover he was a teetotaller. 'Don't like the taste,' he explained. I returned to Karachi much relieved.

Natwar wanted to meet Nusrat Bhutto, Benazir being under house arrest. I arranged a clandestine meeting on his first visit to Karachi but he decided to forgo the opportunity. However, he did meet Benazir on a later visit and has recounted the encounter with zest in his autobiography, *One Life is Not Enough* (Rupa, New Delhi, 2014). His initial visit to the city was a huge hit, as indeed were his subsequent visits

Sanjay Gandhi

On 23 June 1980, I was sitting at my desk when my senior consul, Amitabh Tripathi, burst into the room lamenting that Sanjay Gandhi had been killed in an air accident. I turned my head to look out of the window and away from Amitabh, and thought to myself, 'Dear God, I don't believe in your existence, but if you do exist, thank you for rescuing us from catastrophe.' Within minutes, I received instructions from Islamabad that we were to lower our flags to half-mast and open a condolence book even if Sanjay Gandhi had held no official position.

Over the next several days, many Pakistanis streamed in to record their grief. The surprise visitor was Nusrat Bhutto. She was grace personified. She also asked me to personally convey her deep sorrow to the prime minister adding that as one who had only recently lost her son, she shared the loss of Sanjay as a mother. We talked a little over tea and quickly established a rapport. I escorted her to the porch. There was a mad scramble. The Keystone Cops had, it would seem, been taken by surprise when she veered into our chancery building, panicking them into thinking perhaps that she had taken diplomatic asylum in our premises!

The external affairs minister transits Karachi

I got home leave sanctioned in the summer of 1980. I went for a few days but quickly returned to my post. Suneet and the children, along with Nagamma, were still in Delhi in August. So, there was literally no one in India Lodge – no cook, no maid, no family member, no security guard – to pick up the phone if I went out. Unbeknown to me, Foreign Minister Rao was due to transit through Karachi and expected me at the airport.

His private secretary, Ramu Damodaran, tried every number and got the embassy in Islamabad to do the same. The office was closed for some holiday and no one answered there either. So, Rao passed through Karachi without anyone to dignify the transit. He was understandably furious and, when they returned to Delhi, Ramu rang to convey Rao's anger. My explanation was so bizarre it carried no conviction, not even to me. All I could say was that I would be on hand next time.

That happened soon enough, and I was at the airport dressed to the nines and had arranged with local protocol to be escorted on to the aircraft as Rao did not wish to use the transit lounge. I clambered on to see a worried-looking Ramu standing at the open door at the head of the stairs. He said the external affairs minister was sleeping and he was in two minds as to whether to annoy him by waking him up or risk being reprimanded for not doing so when he had been explicitly instructed to haul the elusive consul general on board. Ramu eventually decided that he must wake the man, and gently shook his arm. The minister woke up with a start, rubbed his eyes, looked at my unfamiliar face and bade me sit next to him. There followed a rather meandering conversation and I sensed I was being sized up. Happily, the seat belt signs came on and I could take my leave.

I could not make up my mind about how I had been assessed, nor what was the objective of his insistence on meeting a junior officer. On later reflection, I concluded that the government was re-examining whether or not to persist on the path of reconciliation. It took Mrs Gandhi a year or more to make up her mind. Mine was a tiny drop in the ocean of her reflection. Meanwhile, continuity was to be maintained.

That suited me and I made good use of India Lodge and the chancery lawns to celebrate anything remotely connected with India–Pakistan relations. Thus, I held a victory party for a Pakistani bridge team that had won an international tournament in Bangalore, even before Pakistan officially took cognizance of their achievement. A young UK-based Pakistani singer, Nazia Hasan, was riding the waves in both countries with a song recorded for a Bollywood film that had the line '*Aap jaisa koi meri zindagi mei aaye / Toh baat ban jaye*' (that a Karachi wit had twisted into '*Toh baap ban jaye*'!).[15] She declined to sing but

[15] 'Were someone like you to come into my life/We might be able to take matters to a conclusion.' When '*baat*' (matters) is replaced by '*baap*' (father) the meaning mischievously changes.

that was more than made up for by the chance presence of Shatrughan Sinha who never failed to make the ladies swoon.

I screened *Garam Hawa* at India Lodge for the Pak Hind Prem Sabha who loved the film as it touched upon that most important element of their lives: visas! We also received the almost unbelievable compliment that the kababs Suneet served up had met the highest culinary test of all: they melted in the mouth without having to be chewed.

We had the famed ghazal singer Shanti Hiranand, whose exquisite intonation of the most sophisticated Urdu allayed the fears of the audience that Partition might have killed the Urdu heritage. We had Ustad Asad Ali Khan who divinely played the rudra veena to an enchanted audience. We also had the famed qawwal group, the Sabri brothers of Pakistan, perform at Indian Lodge, our residence, as also the Pakistani ghazal singer Ghulam Ali, who was then beginning to make a name for himself, in the Bharat Bhawan auditorium.

To everyone's astonishment, Zia invited his history teacher at St Stephen's to visit Pakistan along with a small group of students. Professor E.R. Kapadia was Zia's favourite teacher despite I.H. Qureshi, the great propagandist of the Pakistan movement, teaching history at the college at the same time. Kapadia's son, who was in the IFS with me, told me his father was slightly puzzled at being the object of such an ardent *guru–shishya* (master–acolyte) relationship because he could only dimly recall the young Zia. The team arrived and were lavishly treated to the traditional overwhelming Pakistani hospitality with the added topping of being the president's personal guests. The tour included an evening in Karachi. So I took them out to Hawkes' Bay where we had a beach cottage and called the local YWCA to send a few young people to keep them company.

The most notable cultural event at Bharat Bhawan was the 1981 Independence Day sarod concert given by the incredibly talented (and incredibly handsome) Ustad Amjad Ali Khan. By that time, a patina of civilian rule had been given to the military regime through the appointment of civilian 'First Ministers' (in lieu of elected chief ministers) in Pakistan's four provinces. Sind saw the return of Rasool Baksh Talpur, once a close associate of Zulfikar Ali Bhutto and later a bitter opponent, one of those who had rejoiced at seeing Bhutto dangling from the gallows. He turned up at the concert and I, feeling deeply honoured, escorted him to the front row and seated him in the first seat to the right of the middle aisle.

I had just seated him when my consul rushed up to say that Begum Bhutto's advance security had just informed them that she too would be attending the concert and was, in fact, on her way already. I almost ran to the entrance to receive her. She arrived, her usual poised, almost regal self. I walked her down the aisle and seated her in the front row on the other side of the aisle from the First Minister. She sat down, looked around her and, on spotting Rasool Baksh, immediately put up her hand to shield her eyes from him. She continued in that pose through the whole programme. Rasool Baksh bitterly asked at the end of the concert if I'd seen and noted her 'uncouth behaviour'? I forbore to suggest that perhaps he should not have so openly celebrated her husband's execution.

Nagamma

I have earlier mentioned Nagamma, the young woman who helped Suneet in the kitchen and looked after the children. Nagamma never knew who her parents were as she had been abandoned as a child. She was bright as a pin, ever ready to learn and a wonderful person to have around. My mother paid her the highest compliment in her vocabulary when she decreed Nagamma 'must be of Brahmin parentage'!

Of late, Nagamma had been low and depressed. Pressed by Suneet to explain what was wrong, she said we had everything – a family, a home, a career – but she had nothing. Would anyone ever marry her? Suneet took an astounding step. A young man from Kerala, A.P. Bharathan, had been temporarily deputed from our embassy in Islamabad to help set up the consulate in Karachi. Suneet had heard on the grapevine that Bharathan had stopped by at our Hindustan Court apartment to say 'goodbye' to Nagamma at the end of the deputation. On this thin evidence, Suneet decided to write to Bharathan to ask if he would marry Nagamma!

Letters from Karachi to Islamabad and back went by diplomatic bag to Delhi from where they were sent on. It took several weeks for Bharathan to reply. He indicated his interest. I arranged for the whole family, including

Nagamma, to go to India on home leave via Islamabad, Attock, Peshawar and Murree, with Bharathan as our escort (courtesy Sati Lambah, who insisted on referring to Bharathan as my 'son-in-law', which indeed he was, in some surrogate sense).

At Murree, Bharathan confirmed his offer to wed Nagamma. On 18 August 1980, they became man and wife in the Ganesh temple my father had built on Irwin Road (now Baba Kharak Singh Marg). His parents were highly disapproving. The father was a Sanskrit scholar and the mother a headmistress, stern and learned. But they had been persuaded by their son to attend. The lady reprimanded Suneet, 'My son is not an orphan!' But the wedding went ahead as planned. Forty years on, they are happily together, living a retired life in the temple town of Guruvayur.

The Moradabad Eidgah riot

While we were in India, news broke of police firing at the Eidgah in Moradabad on the very day of Eid, 14 August 1980. Women and children had been shot. Communal rioting spread through western Uttar Pradesh, and then from city to city throughout north India. I was quite shaken. The minute I landed at Karachi, the Pakistan International Airlines (PIA) official sent to receive me said, 'All your good work is reduced to ashes.'

What regained some lost goodwill was Ambassador Natwar Singh's widely cited reaction to the riots: 'It shames us as Indians and diminishes us as human beings.' My day was spent receiving delegation after delegation who presented us with memoranda of protest demanding we guarantee the life, limb and property of our minorities. I received all of them in my office and gave them every opportunity to ventilate their grievances.[16]

Natwar himself reached Karachi while the rioting was still being brought under control. Brushing aside diplomatic practice and protocol that demanded

[16] There was one amusing incident. The mayor of Hyderabad Sind, from the Jama'at-e-Islami, asked if his delegation might take a photograph of me handing over their memorandum of protest. As the photographer was about to click, I stopped him and politely said to the mayor, '*Aise mauke par muskurate nahin hain.*' (On such occasions, one does not smile.) He did not take it amiss.

that hostile petitioners be kept at arm's length, he allowed me to usher in a delegation of really irate members of the JUP. And then he walked up the several flights of stairs to my third-floor office because the lift was not large enough to carry all of us up.

After they had been seated and coffee served, he courteously asked them to explain what was troubling them. One by one, they hurled their accusations and Natwar patiently heard them out. Then, one of them charged us with having massacred 90 lakh Muslims since Partition. Commotion set in, delegates arguing among themselves whether such exaggerations helped or harmed their cause. We just sat back and watched the shouting match. The rumpus ended and the delegation departed.

My worst apprehension had been about the reaction of the Pak Hind Prem Sabha. Vice President Abdul Khalique Allahwallah had been visiting his old haunts of Delhi's Jama Masjid and Chandni Chowk when the rioting broke out. I worried about the tales he might have carried. I need not have. When the Sabha met and someone started complaining, he was shushed with the admonition that Shia–Sunni riots were common in Pakistan every year, so why blame the Indians? Not a very convincing argument, I thought, but it worked like magic. Normalcy was instantly restored.

After the Moradabad riots, I found both the chancery and my home in Karachi surrounded by police who had pitched their tents and were cooking their meals and performing their ablutions on the pavement outside. I called in the SP and asked him if the tents outside our chancery could not be pitched on the other side of the road. He readily agreed. Opposite our chancery was the residence of the nawab of Junagadh who had seceded from India to Pakistan and fled to Karachi with all his dogs, leaving several of his begums behind. It was my personal revenge on him for this outrage!

In our home, I had numerous servants' quarters that the Government of India did not pay me enough to fill. So I suggested to the SP that rather than mess up the outside, why not send in his personnel to occupy the empty rooms I was happy to place at their disposal? The consequence was that when I took my morning stroll, the policeman on duty would present arms to me ten times a day, while I nonchalantly acknowledged the honour!

Life went on and soon picked up its former momentum.

'Shaheed' takes me to the brink

Through the year 1980, I had off and on received calls from someone calling himself 'Shaheed', asking to meet me. I had replied 'Shaheed' (meaning 'martyr') is not a name and I would not give him an appointment until he told me his real name and gave me an indication of what he wanted to talk about. He had declined.

On 25 December, the birthday shared by Jesus Christ, Muhammad Ali Jinnah, Atal Behari Vajpayee and Nawaz Sharif, I was at home. My doorbell rang. I opened the door, and there stood a young man who beamed and said he was 'Shaheed'. I was left with no alternative but to let him in.

Having seated ourselves, I asked him what he wanted to talk to me about. He began by explaining that he was an avid follower of 'Shaheed' Bhutto and after his martyrdom had abandoned his own given name to call himself 'Martyr'. He said he had heard a great deal about me from his fellow PPP workers and of my personal friendship with several PPP leaders, including Benazir and Begum Nusrat. His colleagues were planning a celebration on 4 January, Bhutto's birthday, and had asked him to invite me to be the chief guest. I thanked him but said he and his friends needed to understand that I was accredited to the hangman.

He said he understood perfectly, then settling himself more comfortably on the sofa, Shaheed said he had one more question to ask: did I think the Movement for the Restoration of Democracy (MRD) that Benazir had just launched would be successful? I replied I did not think so for two reasons. One, Benazir was trying to foist on MRD a multi-point agenda instead of fixing attention on a single point: the restoration of democracy. She did not seem to realize that she was joining hands with precisely those political parties that had banded together to oust her father; any diffusion of the agenda would tend to divide her from her partners, whereas focusing on a single point was more likely to keep them united. Second, I said, she must include all political parties in her movement, because if she left anyone out, Zia was likely to snap up that party or parties to give a civilian facade to his dictatorship. I pointed to her exclusion of the Jama'at-e-Islami as a specific mistake. (Eventually, Zia did co-opt the Jama'at-e-Islami.) Very politely and graciously, 'Shaheed' thanked me and took his leave, and I thought no more about this conversation than the dozens I had had on the same subject with others.

Three months after 'Shaheed' visited me, in March 1981 a PIA aircraft was hijacked on its way from Karachi to Peshawar and one of Bhutto's aides was shot on board. The hijackers took the plane on a circuitous route to various places, including Kabul, for several days while negotiating with Zia's government their demand that several named PPP activists be released from jail.

Eventually, the plane was landed in Damascus and a large number of PPP political detenus were released from jail and flown out of the country in exchange for the release of the passengers on the flight. Of course, immediately after the drama ended, Benazir was once again put under house arrest. Whenever my wife shook me awake in the middle of the night, it was to enable us to observe the goings-on in our neighbour's house from our bedroom balcony. The neighbour was the Bhutto household! Arresting, releasing and re-arresting the Bhutto ladies was par for the course, so I went back to bed and thought no more of it.

A month later – on 23 April, Shakespeare's birthday – I was in the shower when Suneet walked in and read out a news item in the Karachi *Morning News* which said the police, searching Benazir's house after her arrest, had found a letter which implicated a 'foreign diplomat' in encouraging the movement against the Zia government. The news item went on that the letter to Benazir was dated 25 December 1980 and had been sent from Karachi Central Jail to Benazir by a dedicated PPP activist, Sami Muneer (my friend Zaki's brother). The letter informed Benazir that Shaheed had come straight to Karachi Central Jail from the diplomat's home and asked Sami to urgently convey to Benazir some very important advice that he, Shaheed, had secured from the diplomat.

While the letter named the diplomat, the news report blacked it out. The letter went on to say that the diplomat concerned knew Pakistan well and his advice must be taken seriously as he understood Pakistani politics as no Pakistani did. The advice, in sum, was that the MRD should have a one-point/all-party programme if it were to succeed!

I froze in the shower. This undoubtedly spelt my end. A Bhutto admirer called Shaheed had indeed visited me to invite me to be chief guest at a function and we had spent some time talking frankly about Pakistani politics and Bhutto. The specifics of my advice on the MRD had been accurately conveyed by Samir to Benazir. It was thus only a matter of hours before I would be declared persona non grata; all my work would turn to ashes, and I would be revealed as a typical untrustworthy Indian. I steeled myself for the axe to fall.

It never did. Instead, poor Santosh Kumar at our embassy in Islamabad was declared *persona non grata* for allegedly making an un-notified and unapproved halt in Multan on his way back from Karachi to clandestinely meet a communist politician. This was about a year earlier. The Pakistan foreign ministry had kept the matter on the back burner for use when required. I, the palpably guilty one, was spared. I never ceased wondering why.

About a decade later, I learnt from a fairly reliable source (that I cannot disclose) that initially the authorities were extremely suspicious of me and followed me everywhere. They were impressed that I never turned my head to see if I was being followed. They were also impressed that I never hid from them. I travelled everywhere in my official car with the Indian flag flying. And dissecting my conversation with various interlocuters, the intelligence agents came to the conclusion that apart from a deep curiosity and interest in everything that pertained to Pakistan, I harboured no ill will. It was, therefore, decided that no action would be taken against me, but they had to show their disapproval. So Santosh was made the scapegoat. This is what I was told. I cannot certify the veracity of the explanation.

Foreign Minister Rao's visit

I also think they did not want to have a high-level diplomatic incident on their hands that might adversely affect the planned visit of the Indian external affairs minister to Islamabad and Karachi. He arrived in mid-May. I was part of the Indian delegation, and remarked that in travelling from Karachi to Islamabad I had covered a greater distance than those who had flown in from New Delhi. This was an illustration of how closely the two countries were geographically interconnected.

As for the emotional connection, P.V. Narasimha Rao put away his English speech at the Pakistan Institute of International Relations in Karachi after reading it, switched to Urdu – in which he was fluent – and recited from memory the famous lines of Jigar Moradabadi:

Unka jo farz hai
Ahl-e-siyasat jaane.
Mera paigam mohabbat hai,
Jahan tak pahunche.

[Whatever their compulsions,
I leave that to the people of politics.
My message is Love,
To wherever it might extend.]

He left the audience in ecstasy. The reception I had arranged in his honour was a thundering success. It was his Urdu verse that bowled them over.

Two memories of the Rao visit remain. One related to Lakshmi Puri, the undersecretary in the Pakistan Division. Pakistan protocol had advised spokesman Mani Dixit that arrangements were being made to serve Lakshmi dinner in a separate room because, they said, it was not Pakistan's traditional practice to have men and women dine together. 'Mani' blew up and demanded to know what the arrangements would be were Indira Gandhi to visit Pakistan!

The other incident was Foreign Secretary Ram Sathe informing me that I would soon be summoned back to headquarters to succeed Mani Dixit as joint secretary (external publicity) and official spokesman. Sathe then gently enquired what kind of qualities he should look for in my successor. Unhesitatingly, I replied, 'Only one, sir. A really strong liver.'

Sathe was astonished. Wasn't Pakistan under Zia a teetotal hellhole? On the contrary, I said, everyone drank like a fish and the police just looked away. I elaborated, 'I know the exact geographical location of the line that divides the *Dar-al-Islam* (Land of Peace/Land of the Believers) from the *Dar-al-Harb* (Land of Conflict/Land of the Infidels). It is the bar of the Sind Club, north of which is Ziadom and south of which is freedom!'

Notwithstanding the apparent success of the Rao visit, our relations sharply deteriorated, triggered by our government's repudiation of the commitment made by Morarji's government on handing over Jinnah House to Pakistan.

Relations were also deteriorating on account of Zia's blatant assistance to the Khalistan movement and the suspicion of Pakistan's hand in the previous year's Eid riots.

The impact was swift and sharp. We were forced to cancel a *mushaira* (poetry session) we had planned in association with the Pak Hind Prem Sabha. Indeed, the Sabha was ordered into virtual silence. We were told we had to take permission to use our auditorium for any cultural activities. My travel plans had to be put on hold.

Why we get Pakistan wrong

I have never really understood why Indian diplomacy has only rarely and fitfully considered mining this treasure trove of goodwill to promote good relations. While we are sure-footed in Paraguay, we stumble in neighbouring Pakistan!

Most of our diplomats and foreign secretaries, foreign ministers and prime ministers appear to regard Pakistani public opinion as irrelevant. Most seem ready to scratch at the scabs that have formed over old wounds and ignore the alternative of cultivating good relations with ordinary Pakistanis. Indeed, it is the ordinary Pakistani who is hit when we want to pummel the Pakistan establishment for its many excesses. The common or garden Pakistani not only speaks the same language as us, and shares much of the same *tehzeeb* (culture), they love Bollywood and its music and laugh at the same jokes and befriend us everywhere outside the subcontinent. Almost everyone who has served in Pakistan acknowledges their personal goodwill towards Indians.

Yet, we take it out on ordinary Pakistanis when we want to punish their government. Why refuse visas to Pakistanis when we want to reprimand their rulers? Do we really believe all Pakistanis are jihadis bent on wreaking havoc on our people? Why stop the Samjhauta Express when we wish to retaliate for some act of terror that has nothing to do with 99.99 per cent of the Pakistani population? Do we really think the Hurriyat will give up their call for *azadi* (freedom) if we stop Pakistanis meeting their relatives in India?

Does this not amount to punishing Indian minorities for having passed the 'loyalty test' to India when they did *not* migrate to Pakistan, as it is their relatives who are the principal visa seekers? Should we really stop cricket matches with Pakistan for fear of someone raising a Pakistani flag or cheering a Pakistani six? Is banning a Pakistani poet from attending an Indian *mushaira* worthy of a self-confident state? Why make it such a hassle to hold informal, non-official Track-II meetings? That Pakistan does the same is no argument. Why race with them to the bottom?

That is why I am flattered by this portrait of my days in Karachi from Ambassador T.C.A. Raghavan from his highly readable account of the socio-cultural dimensions of our political and military history of the last seven decades.

> Mani Shankar Aiyar was the first CG in Karachi from 1978 to 1981. At a time when public diplomacy was not a term used as frequently as it is now, he personified it in many ways. He was articulate, charming, considerate of Pakistani sentiments and indulgent, to a fault his detractors say. His tenure as consul general has acquired for many Pakistanis a larger-than-life character as he attempted to meet the pent-up demand for visas from the vast *mohajir* community. He did so with consideration and good humour that is recalled with warmth. No greater testimony to his functioning can be provided than by the fact that even some three-and-a-half decades later any Indian diplomat visiting Karachi from Islamabad will first be asked about M.S. Aiyar and then be regaled with stories about him.[17]

My disappointment is with the fact that the MEA regarded such 'public diplomacy' as an end in itself and failed over four decades to relate it to foreign policy.

My final dispatch

I locked myself at home in my last month to write a final dispatch from Karachi for the Pakistan Division desk officers at the MEA. The approach I

[17] T.C.A Raghavan, *The People Next Door: The Curious History of India's Relations with Pakistan*, HarperCollins, Noida, 2017. pp. 146–147.

advocated was perhaps too unorthodox.[18] For Delhi, it mattered little what Pakistanis thought or sought.

Conflict, and the management of conflict, is the realpolitik focus. And that is why people-to-people contacts, in regard to visas, films, media, trade, tourism or cultural exchanges or even pilgrimages, are the first to be sacrificed whenever governments want to bare their fangs. Sustaining distrust between governments is easier than the patient building of trust between people. As Mani Dixit put it, mine was a 'Pollyanna' view. Tough stands and tough action, not treacly sentimentality, is what the professionals believe, counts in 'diplomacy'.

While our governments played at ratcheting up tensions, our life started getting filled with farewell dinners, farewell lunches, then farewell teas, then even farewell breakfasts! In our last days in Karachi, Suneet and I ate almost nothing from our own kitchen. We made up for that with a really lavish New Year's Eve party at India Lodge to which all our friends came. Unfortunately, my professional photographer friend, who had taken a number of souvenir pictures, leaked the photographs to the press, causing a flutter in the dovecotes.

My real farewell had come a few days earlier. My faithful driver, Abdul Sattar, for once did not turn up in time one morning. When he arrived about a quarter of an hour late, I blew up. He explained he had been delayed because he had to go to a police *thana* (police station) to rescue his brother who had been arrested the previous night for illegally projecting Hindi films. He said he had gone to the *thana* and requested the duty constable to let off his brother.

The constable brushed him off, saying: 'Who the hell are you?'

Drawing himself to his full height, Sattar replied, 'Me? I am the driver of the consul general of Hindustan.'

'The consul general of Hindustan!' exclaimed the policeman. 'In that case, you are welcome to take away your brother.'

---

[18] For readers interested in my last thoughts from Karachi, I draw their attention to my *Pakistan Papers* (UBSPD, New Delhi, 1994). Foreign Secretary Dixit declassified my final dispatch from Karachi and allowed me to publish it as the dispatch represented my views, not the government's. The book contains a slightly redacted version of what I wrote in terms of a farewell summing up of my assessment of the constructive way forward. That approach has never been adopted.

I had never been paid a greater compliment. And over the last forty years, on my numerous visits to Karachi, Sattar is always at the airport ready to drive me to my old haunts and the homes of my friends. That's what I call fidelity!

On my last night in Karachi, as I lay awake in bed going over my memories of the last three years, I suddenly realized that I had, after all, held a post of great importance to the local populace and it was perhaps this, plus the hospitality embedded in Pakistani culture, that had led to the overwhelmingly warm and friendly reception I had received. But what of the junior staff? Had their experience been different?

So, the next morning after reaching my office for the last time, I sent for the official who had flown into Karachi from London on the night of the same day as I had. Reminding him of the fact that our stay in the city had been coterminus, I asked him how he had fared personally. He knew that I had been unusually feted, but how had his own treatment been?

He was slightly taken aback but said he had not had any problem. What, I asked, of his colleagues, the 120 or so low-profile clerks? He replied that none of them had had a problem or suffered any indignity. That, I remarked, might have been because in public places no one could tell whether they were Indians or Pakistanis. They looked alike.

But what about your wives? They wore saris, no? And a *bindi*?[19] And took the bus from outside Panchsheel Park, the Indian officials' ghetto, to do their daily shopping in Sadar. They were unmistakably Indian. How had they been treated? With a puzzled frown because he could not understand why he was being asked these questions, he said he had not heard of anyone staring or glaring at them, or being unfriendly or abusing them.

I was now ready for my final question. Reassuring him once again that his answers must be honest and would not go beyond the two of us, I asked whether it was true that the Indian staff would invariably be offered discounts when they went shopping. He hesitated, then nodded. Were they given these discounts because they were from the consulate, or because they were Indian? Because, he said, we are regular customers and because we are from India.

So, I summed up, you have been here exactly as long as I have been and we have both been treated with friendliness; your ladies have been treated with

[19] Coloured dot on forehead.

honour and you have received discounts in Sadar; none of you has ever been treated rudely. So, should we make friends with the Pakistanis? He looked utterly shocked. 'How can we, sir?' he replied. 'Are they not all Muslims?'

I ended the interrogation. This was the root of the problem.

I then went down to the auditorium where my colleagues had arranged a formal farewell, literally hours before our departure. They were in the middle of speeches, touching, sentimental and sincere, when there was a sudden disturbance. Mehdi Hasan, the great ghazal maestro of Pakistan, had arrived. He was reputed to never rise before the sun set. But had made the special effort, at the behest of his friend, Sadru Gangji, to rouse himself just for us. No greater honour could have been conferred on me and my family. As a quite exceptional parting gift, his golden voice wafted us on our way.

We left amid tearful goodbyes for Karachi port. I had booked myself and the family into a ship sailing from Kuwait to Bombay via Karachi. We arrived next day at Bombay's Victoria Docks – as if I were the last viceroy!

Had we spent three years in an enemy country? Forty-one years on, Suneet's puzzled question reverberates in my ears.

See detailed footnotes and endnotes by scanning the QR code above.

10

A Delhi Interregnum

1982–1985

My Pakistan proposal for Rajiv Gandhi

I took charge as official spokesman and joint secretary (external publicity) – JS (XP) – of the ministry on 12 January 1982. The perks included a chauffeured car. In the ministry, it was believed the JS (XP) only went to 'high-fliers' but I soon found as spokesman that I was just parroting the views of other officers with substantive portfolios. I thought I would much rather be heading a territorial desk than acting the role of a caged parrot. Hoping I could soon secure such an assignment, I got on with the job on hand.

One day I received a call from Vasant Sathe, minister of information and broadcasting (I&B), to attend a meeting on external publicity where 'Rajivji' would also be participating. Ministers and MPs were seated on sofas. Officers were seated opposite them on straight-backed chairs. Rajiv Gandhi arrived a little late. As he sat down, he started surveying the assemblage looking for a familiar face. I saw his eyes briefly light up when he spotted me.

I was still in Karachi in my mind. So, after the meeting ended, I went up to him and asked if I could set up a meeting with him as I had something important to impart arising out of my previous posting. He nodded graciously and asked me to get in touch with his private secretary, Vincent George.

Suneet and I fetched up at 1, Safdarjung Road. Rajiv joined us and I launched my crusade. I briefly summarized my experience of Pakistani public opinion and said I thought an emotional breakthrough was the prime necessity, what I called a 'goodwill blitzkrieg'.

Rajiv Gandhi, I said, held no formal office other than being a backbench MP but, of course, the whole world knew that he was the Indian PM's son. Hence, if he visited Pakistan, nothing he said would be binding on the Government of India; yet, as it was the atmospherics that needed to be set right, I gave him the example of Crown Prince Edward's highly successful personal visit to France that led to the Anglo-French entente cordiale of 1904.

I suggested that he ask to see Mohenjodaro, from where he should drive to Karachi via Sehwan Sharif or Bhit Shah or, best of all, both, for both promoted Sufi Islam that reconciled the two major communities. At both shrines, worshippers included Muslims and Hindus. One of the two *sajjada nashins* (managers of the shrine) of Sehwan Sharif was always a hereditary Hindu and it attracted a million worshippers every year. The Hindus revered the saint as 'Jhule Lal' (god of the waters – the Sindhu *dariya*, or Indus). Others revered him as 'Mast Qalandar', the inspiration for the immortal qawwali 'Dama Dam Mast Qalandar', which was the unofficial anthem of the PPP. Similarly, Bhit Shah, the shrine dedicated to Shah Abdul Bhittai, Sind's greatest poet, was revered by both communities and was famed for its evening qawwalis that combined high culture with deep spirituality.

It was the eclectic spirit cultivated at these shrines that had forestalled the outbreak of communal rioting in Sind until the *muhajir* from Uttar Pradesh arrived and provoked the exile of the Hindu community. Rajiv Gandhi's arrival in Karachi after visiting these two shrines, I assured him, would draw huge crowds and he would be received with wild enthusiasm. This rapturous welcome would be beamed into every drawing room in India and Pakistan and would open the way, through negotiations, to a possible entente cordiale between India and Pakistan. He seemed interested but non-committal. However, I think I did strike a chord that reverberated when he became, in 1988, the first Indian PM in twenty-eight years to visit our 'distant neighbour'.

Dealings with the press

Every afternoon, there was 'open house' for the press in my office. The standard fare was sweet tea, samosas and jalebis. During the day, I would call or personally meet with divisional heads to get the news. Briefings were on the record, but attribution could only be to the 'official spokesman', not the incumbent by name (happily, this has since been changed; I would have preferred not to be constrained by anonymity!).

I thought I built a good rapport with the journalists but that was for them to say. One of them – M.L. Kotru of the *Statesman* – said at my farewell that proof of their affection was that where they could have made a 'box story' of my offhand remarks every day they didn't, out of regard for my long-term career prospects. I could also host dinners in the smaller dining room of Hyderabad House for visiting journalists (a privilege now removed) and the foreign media guests would be duly impressed at being treated like quasi heads of government.

I started accompanying the foreign minister on some of his trips. I enjoyed returning to Hanoi, where I forced all members of the delegation to pay obeisance at the wooden bench where I had cried. I also recall a trip to Dhaka. I happened to be in the last vehicle and so got out in a leisurely manner to go into dinner. As I neared the veranda, I thought to myself that it was odd how all Bangladesh army officers looked like the president, General Ershad. When I mounted the stairs, I was astonished to find that waiting to welcome the last laggard was none other than President Ershad himself! Nothing can beat army officers in the extension of courtesies.

I wormed my way into Mrs Gandhi's entourage for Riyadh. Even the most humble of us were treated to lavish gifts. On the flight back to Delhi, I was seated just in front of the chief of protocol, M. Hamid Ansari. As we were required to surrender to the '*toshakhana*' (treasury) all gifts received above a certain value, I showed a watch I had received to Hamid and asked at what price he would value it. He looked at the insignia of the Saudi Kingdom on the dial and replied, 'Of no commercial value!' I retained the watch for years.

The NAM summit

I think it was in August or September 1982 that Ambassador K. Natwar Singh returned to Delhi from Islamabad, and it was announced that he would be secretary general of the forthcoming Seventh Summit of the Non-Aligned Movement (NAM); it was to be held in Delhi as Baghdad had opted out of being host because of its war with Iran. Iraq had had three years to prepare. We had only a few months. It was going to be a gigantic logistical nightmare come March 1983. And if everything was not tickety-boo, the press would have a field day reporting on our lack of preparation. The first step was to learn from Iraq what arrangements they were making or contemplating for hosting the event.

We arrived in Baghdad – not the shabby airport I had used four years earlier, but a spanking new one with all the mod cons. My marketing assistant, Mohammad Amin, was on hand to receive us. He took me to a corner and whispered that our locally recruited Iraqi colleague, Shahab Ahmed, had lost two of his young sons in the war but begged me to not offer Shahab condolences in public for fear that Shahab might break down. The Iraqi authorities were arresting anyone mourning in public and even hauling them off to the torture chambers!

I was greatly helped in my preparations for the NAM summit by a remarkably intelligent, practical-minded, hands-on deputy, Jaimini Bhagwati, who was designated officer on special duty (public relations). With him at my right hand, we were able to overcome all hurdles and be in full readiness to accommodate all the visiting media. I was able to leave it entirely to Jaimini to tackle any remaining glitches while I concentrated on my forbidding responsibilities as conference spokesman for the summit.

Perhaps the longest and most detailed, if not always unbiased, report on the summit was by Robert Shaplen of the *New Yorker*. He was granted all of eleven pages to make his assessment and there is something painfully resonant in his conclusion:

> The New Delhi Summit, more than any previous one, was in many respects a boastful fashion show, a gala costume party, rather than a serious forum. [My comment: Is that not true of the annual sessions of the United Nations and dozens of conferences that Shaplen's home country participates in and often itself convenes?] Its calls for peace and disarmament and for a new approach to development sounded brave and bold, but when the official planes had taken off from Palam airport nothing was left except tons of paper and a heavy silence. The beggars and the sacred cows were back on the streets, the summer heat had set in, and the flowers had begun to wilt.[1]

[1] Robert Shaplen, 'The Paradox of Nonalignment', *The New Yorker*, 15 May 1983.

To describe his assessment as racist and sneering would be too kind. But I had reason to be privately pleased. For, in the middle of this rant, he included one sentence: 'Twice-daily press briefings conducted by an amiable spokesman named Mani Shankar Aiyar were complete and informative.' Hurrah!

During the conference, Indira Gandhi said she wanted to visit the media centre. She arrived in the middle of my morning briefing. Uma Shankar Phadnis of the *Hindustan Times* languidly said they were getting nothing out of the briefings: he meant spicy stories. While I think he was attempting to be funny, that idle remark seems to have struck Mrs Gandhi as a serious complaint. I received urgent summons from her principal secretary, Dr P.C. Alexander, to meet him at his office in the main conference centre. He informed me that PM wanted the briefings to be done by someone senior. I was under the impression that I had built up a strong rapport with the press corps by telling the multilingual gathering: 'My name is Aiyar. To pronounce that correctly, remember it is the same as "eggs" in German or "elsewhere" in French!'

The senior person chosen to replace me was my boss, K.S. Bajpai, secretary (east). He took over reluctantly and gave it up almost instantly. He already had too much on his plate to set aside time to prepare for and hold two briefings a day. His substantive job was to steer the course in the main hall between India and Sri Lanka; between everyone and Kampuchea; between the proxies of China and the American proxies in South East Asia, including the issue of the South China Sea; and between Peter Sinai and Akbar Khaleeli, respectively the highly partisan Indian Ambassadors to Baghdad and Tehran! Bajpai went to the authorities and asked that the briefings be restored to me.

Foreign Secretary M. Rasgotra also intervened on my behalf. I also gathered that the secretary general, my old Islamabad boss, K. Natwar Singh, had prevailed upon the PM to let me back in, assuring her that there must have been some misunderstanding. All this was behind the curtains, as I moped around, miserable that the limelight had been stolen from me just when scores of journalists were congratulating me on a job well done. Within forty-eight hours, I found myself reinstated.

That was not the end of my travails. The Kampuchea issue was resolved at 3 a.m. and I summoned journalists still awake to an unscheduled briefing. Someone complained, 'Why does NAM come to consensus only at such unearthly hours?' and I, pert as ever, responded that the dove, which symbolized the movement, should perhaps be replaced by the owl! What I had forgotten was that in colloquial Hindi '*ullu*' for owl is commonly used to describe an idiot. So, one or two of the Hindi morning papers mischievously said I had described the delegates as *ullus*. The rumpus was, however, tided over.

I remember one light moment. I was headed for the gents as the *Times of India* correspondent, Mahendra Ved, was trying to squeeze a word out of me. He followed me into the gents and continued pestering me. When I had finished, the correspondent of *Time* magazine, Dean Brellis, who was in the stall next to mine, remarked, 'Now, I know why it's called a leak!'

All in all, for me and my team, the conference had been a huge success.

At the UN desk

Foreign Secretary Rasgotra, who knew I was not happy to be a mere spokesman, was so appreciative that he asked me which desk I wanted. Without hesitation, I replied, 'The UN desk,' as I knew my batchmate, Ramesh Mulye, would be relinquishing it to proceed to the Philippines as ambassador. The FS promptly agreed.

My moving to the UN desk resulted in the loss of my chauffeured car. Inflation had played havoc with the purchasing power of our salaries and, therefore, driving my personal car every day to office would place an intolerable burden on our limited family budget besides the inconvenience in terms of family chores like grocery shopping and ferrying kids to school. The only answer lay in slumming it by taking the bus to and from South Block. I soon discovered how hopeless I was at living the life of the common man. First, I left behind my lunch box; next, I had my wallet stolen. I was such an obvious target in my suit and tie.

My private secretary, whose attitude to me was that of a mother hen, took it upon himself to ring my undersecretary, Bhaswati Mukherjee, and beg her to find a way of getting me off the bus.

So I found a place on a Border Security Force (BSF) van that brought their officers to South Block. Bhaswati's problem was really to get me home after work, safe and sound. She decided to wait in the evening until I was ready to call it quits and drive me home although this added uncounted kilometres and litres of petrol to her own journey. Her father never stopped teasing her for her zeal!

Flight KL-007

On 1 September 1983, the Soviet Union shot down a Korean civil aircraft, KL-007, that intruded into Soviet airspace. The West went to town over this. For my part, I was more struck by the reports from the international press that went against the conventional grain and a press conference addressed in Moscow by Marshal Nikolai V. Ogarkov, chief of the general staff of the USSR.

While in the West politicians and some sections of the media concentrated on the undoubted horror of 269 ordinary passengers being shot down on a civil airlines flight, they ignored the very relevant question: What was Flight KL-007 doing wandering off for two and a half hours some 500–600 kilometres off-track, into clearly prohibited Soviet airspace?

The aircraft had flown close to Petropavlovsk on the Kamchatka peninsula. This was a well-known base for nuclear submarines and Russian Backfire bombers. The strategic importance of Petropavlovsk is that it is ice-free and provides direct access to the Sea of Okhotsk and the Pacific Ocean. This was a nerve centre for the Soviet navy, which was braced for tension since Japan had been demanding the return of the Kuril Islands occupied during World War II.

It seemed impossible that the Korean airliner accidentally wandered so far off course. The aircraft was 'fly-by-wire'. Course data was entered into three separate computerized navigation systems that, said the *Times* staff reporters were, 'virtually foolproof'.[2] In a flight of about 805 kilometres, the aircraft should (normally) be within a mile of the course preset by computers. The *Times* claimed, 'There is unlikely to be a disparity of 10 miles, never mind 300, after the flight from Anchorage to Sakhalin (where the flight was shot down).'[3]

Marshal Ogarkov said in his press conference that it had been proved 'irrefutably' that the intrusion had been a 'deliberate, thoroughly planned intelligence operation'. He added that 'a civilian plane' had been 'deliberately' chosen, 'disregarding or, possibly counting on the loss of human life', saying that US RC-135 spy planes were often in the area, and one 'rendezvoused' with the Korean airliner and flew side by side for approximately ten minutes. Thereafter, 007 did not respond even when contacted on the 'fixed international

[2] *The Times* (London), 6 September 1983.

[3] Ibid.

frequency, 121 megacycles'. Four rounds of 'warning shots', amounting to 120 cartridges, too did not get any response.[4]

Ogarkov underlined that even the US had admitted 'the grossest intrusion into the airspace of the Soviet Union'. And that shooting down the aircraft became imperative only as a result of the aircraft's 'ignoring of all warning and cautionary signals'.[5]

The International Civil Aviation Organization (ICAO), headquartered in Montreal, was convened in October and I was asked to represent the MEA. Before I left, Chinmaya Gharekhan, joint secretary (PMO), asked to see me. In front of him was a file with a noting in pencil by the PM. Carefully ensuring I did not read the note, Chinmaya told me the PM's instructions were that we should closely coordinate our stand on the incident with the Soviet delegation. I carried this brief to the FS. He endorsed the position that now carried the prime minister's imprimatur.

Perhaps I overplayed my hand. The US was infuriated, as were a number of other Western and even non-aligned delegates. Several Western ambassadors called on our foreign minister to protest the hard line I was taking. I was called from New Delhi at the official level and told to moderate my stand. So I let matters go. An enquiry was ordered by the ICAO but by the time their report came – a total whitewash – I was out of the MEA. But I was glad I put on record another perspective on the issue. Of course, when the US shot down an Iranian civil airliner over Gulf waters in July 1988, there was an immediate cover-up. Such hypocrisy and double standards are termed 'rules-based international order'!

International meets

I returned to a Delhi in the throes of organizing the Commonwealth Heads of Government meeting, or CHOGM, which a wit expanded to 'Chaps

[4] 'Transcript of Soviet Official's Statement and Excerpts from News Session Marshal Calls Flight 7 A "Provocation Perpetrated By U.S. Secret Services"', *The New York Times*, 10 September 1983.

[5] Ibid.

Holidaying on Government Money'. Nothing of note happened except for a sharp stand-off between the prime ministers of India and the UK over apartheid. Mrs Thatcher's principled stand in support of the unprincipled practice of vicious racial discrimination was to overshadow the Commonwealth as an institution and drive it into its present irrelevance. Perhaps, after Brexit, new life can be pumped into the Commonwealth, especially through the review and renewal of old Commonwealth preferences as much has happened since 1932 when tariff preferences for Commonwealth countries were agreed at Ottawa. I am reminded of a cartoon I saw in *Private Eye* when Britain initially sought membership of the European Common Market. The cartoon was a gravestone with an epitaph reading:

The Commonwealth,
Born of a sordid trade agreement.
Ottawa, 1932
Died of a sordid trade agreement.
Brussels, 1962

In my capacity as head of the UN Division, I made a token appearance in December 1983 at the UN General Assembly, attending a final meeting of the Sixth Committee – the Legal Committee – and found myself drawn by the argument most recently liberated member states were making that armed liberation struggles must not be confused with terrorism. The argument continues until today. And even today, we have not been able get the UN to move on an Indian initiative to define terrorism.

Between 1970 and 1989, during my postings at headquarters and from Brussels, and even subsequently, I represented India in a wide variety of international fora, including ECAFE/ESCAP, UNCTAD, GATT, UNESCO, FAO, IMF/World Bank, SAARC and UNWTO. I expected my handling the UN desk would involve visits to New York, Geneva and more exotic destinations. I was also awaiting my next assignment abroad which would doubtless be my first ambassadorial assignment. I rather fancied Dhaka although my wife preferred the alternative of Geneva. Unbeknown to me, I was coming to the end of my years in active diplomacy.

Operation Blue Star

On 5 June 1984, Indira Gandhi ordered our troops into the Golden Temple. I did not have an inkling this was going to prove a major turning point in my life. My wife and I had been invited to dinner at the India International Centre. As our driver dropped us, I saw a taxi parked at the side with the Sikh taxi driver bent over the radio in a posture of immense sorrow listening to the news over the radio. My wife, also Sikh, explained how badly this would be taken by her community. I tried pointing out that the Golden Temple had been turned into a terrorist hideout by Jarnail Singh Bhindranwale. She agreed but warned that the community would never forgive this act of sacrilege.

As she had anticipated, there was outrage at the 'invasion' of the Golden Temple, with the large Sikh diaspora most incensed. Foreign Secretary Rasgotra asked me to draw on my experience as JS (XP) to help contain the damage. I was inducted into something called the Special Publicity Group. My task was to escort the foreign press corps on daily Air Force flights to and from Amritsar for briefings by the very photogenic Brigadier Kuldip Singh Brar.

This would be followed by a round of the Golden Temple, gaping at the Akal Takht, Bhindranwale's headquarters, that had been totally destroyed. I would be trying to distract my wards by asking them to focus on the Harmandir Sahib that had been barely touched because, as I had been told to emphasize, the army were under strict instructions to not damage the sacred heart of the complex.

I don't know what credibility I carried, not being entirely convinced myself. My batchmate, Paramjit Singh Sahai, accompanied me on one of these flights, and although we bantered together with our usual levity, I could see how deeply distressed he was as a Sikh.

The FS also tasked me with reaching out to the Sikh diaspora, concentrated particularly in Canada and the west coast of the United States, and in England around Birmingham, but also scattered all over – from Hong Kong, Singapore and Malaysia to East Africa, parts of Europe and elsewhere. I was to send a daily report on what I was doing to the FS, copied to Joint Secretary V.C. Tripathi in the PMO. What I did not know was that the PM had asked her son, Rajiv Gandhi, to keep a watching brief on how external publicity was being handled. So, he received daily briefings from Tripathi, and sometimes the FS, where my reports received some prominence.

There were also frequent meetings of the Special Publicity Group under the FS's chairmanship. These were attended by many of the young people who had been drawn into politics by Rajiv Gandhi's position at the centre of national affairs. They included Arun Singh (Roon) and Romi Chopra, both of whom had been school friends of Rajiv (and were junior to me at school). They in turn would have been informing their friend Rajiv of what I was doing.

The arrangement was ad hoc and quite informal, and arguably not in keeping with standard protocol. The PM herself was being kept informed – although I didn't know this. I was simply doing my job as best I could. Imagine, therefore, my astonishment when the FS called me in and told me the prime minister had instructed him, in view of my 'outstanding performance' in the Special Publicity Group, to have me seconded to the (I&B) minister as his information adviser. I was stunned. I knew, of course, of punishments being inflicted for derelictions of duty but never punishment for 'outstanding performance'!

In all this, I also saw the hand of H.K.L. Bhagat, the I&B minister, who had been asked to visit Pakistan in July to make high-level contact with the Pakistan authorities to forestall their taking advantage of the strong dissatisfaction in our Punjab to infiltrate more Khalistani terrorists. Given my three years in Karachi, the FS had sent me with Bhagat's team on a five-day tour. The junior members of the team had great fun with the Pakistani offer of a Sahiwal stud bull as their present to the visiting dignitary. Of course, it was a great opportunity to introduce the minister to my numerous friends. He came back from Pakistan deeply impressed by my public diplomacy – and stuck a dagger into my back by asking the PM for my services in his ministry.

By early August, I found myself out of my parent ministry in South Block and in the I&B ministry in Shastri Bhawan with no work to do and a minister who really did not know what to do with me, yet proud as a peacock that he had got the PM to give him an IFS officer as an aide. S.S. Gill, the secretary, was courteous and correct but as unable to comprehend as anyone else, what I was supposed to do. None of the civil servants in the ministry had any liking for me. They jealously guarded their turf. The principal information officer, U.C. Tiwari, was particularly nasty in his trademark way. I was given a humongous room on the top floor and told I could appoint it as I wished, sparing no expense. But of regular work, there was none. I was just left to my devices.

One of my special privileges was to receive every morning a copy of the minister's programme for the day. I was intrigued to find that every afternoon, there would be twenty or thirty visitors listed to meet him at intervals of, literally, two minutes each. Thus, if A were listed at 2 p.m., B would be listed at 2.02, C at 2.04 and so on. Keen to know how this was being managed, I slipped into the minister's room one afternoon and watched the first petitioner come in. He had hardly begun speaking when the minister took the petition from his hands, pressed the bell on his telephone and asked his private secretary, '*Jag Parvesh se milaiye.*' (Get me Jag Parvesh. [Delhi's chief executive councillor])Then, turning to the petitioner, the minister signalled that he could leave as his petition would be receiving the personal attention of no less than the chief executive councillor of the Delhi Metropolitan Council. Impressed, the man would depart, to be followed by the next who would be given the same treatment, then the third and so on.

The gratitude of these petitioners was unmistakable but I was intrigued at Jag Parvesh not being brought on the line. So I slipped out to ask the minister's private office why they were not putting the councillor through. They roared with laughter and said they were under strict instructions never to put Jag Parveshji through. The whole purpose was to send the petitioner home satisfied rather than actually take action. If the problem could be solved, the officers concerned would take care of it; if it could not, that was destiny. The really telling point was that Bhagat had not only won his seat (East Delhi) by one of the largest margins, he seemed all set to return again.

There were other highlights of this miserable existence. One was the invitation I received from Urmila Gupta, head of the International Film Festival of India, to attend the opening ceremony followed by dinner at the Pragati Maidan exhibition grounds. She added there would be lots of film stars, including all my favourite actresses. I wandered around but recognized no one. Then I came upon someone I vaguely recognized wandering around equally aimlessly and opened the conversation with the salvo, 'There's no one worth looking at here except the director of the film festival.' He bristled and thundered, 'That's my wife you're talking about.' I beat a hasty retreat!

There was a more satisfactory perk. I could attend special screenings of any film I wished to see. I took my wife to such a private screening, just for the two of us, of *Mr and Mrs 55*, starring Guru Dutt and Madhubala, with Johnny Walker in one of his funniest roles. The film, seen after a gap of three decades, was hilarious. We thoroughly enjoyed ourselves. But I could not shut out the utter bleakness of my life outside the auditorium.

Another memorable incident – my moment of revenge, as it were – occurred when, with the general elections of 1984 in the offing, the minister decided to hold a series of dinner parties for the media, starting with cub reporters and subeditors and working up the media ladder. The first of these was held in Akbar Hotel. When the minister arrived, there was a rush to get as close to him as possible while I stood on the edges.

The minister preened himself, pleased as Punch with the fawning attention. Then, someone said, 'Congress is finished. The situation is so bad that Rajiv Gandhi is looking for a safe seat.' The minister was all ears. He hushed everyone else and focused on this one dissident.

'Where is Rajivji looking for a safe seat?'

The other said, 'Anywhere he can find it. But everyone knows there is only one guaranteed safe seat.'

'Which one?' asked my minister.

Pat came the reply, 'Yours, of course!'

The poor minister did not know which way to look. Should he be pleased that his East Delhi seat was regarded as the safest in all India? Or should he be alarmed at having to surrender it to the prime minister's son? I left the man to his dilemma.

I had been frequently calling the FS earnestly requesting that I be taken back into the ministry. He was sympathetic but pleaded that as it was the PM who posted me there, only the PM could have me taken back. I faced the dreadful prospect of no one having the courage to ask her and, since she barely knew me, the empty years stretched ahead of me with no hope of commutation of sentence.

At this low point, I turned to the one man I thought might be able to bail me out: P.V. Narasimha Rao, home minister, and my former boss, as minister of external affairs. I sought an appointment through his private secretary, Ramu Damodaran, everyone's friend! Ramu fixed it for 10 a.m. one morning the following week but asked me to confirm it with him before I left my office. I did.

He asked me in a hollow voice, 'Have you not heard?'

'Heard what?' I queried.

He lowered his voice. 'About the PM.'

'No,' I answered, not knowing what that had to do with my appointment.

'She's been shot,' came the reply, 'but there is no official intimation of her condition.'

The next several hours passed in a daze. Someone in South Block asked me who I thought would succeed her and, when I replied that, as in the past, there would be an interim PM – perhaps Pranab Mukherjee – before the party chose a successor, I was told not to be stupid, it would obviously be Rajiv Gandhi.

I was appalled. How could an utter amateur, a man who had been an airlines pilot until the other day, take over as PM? But within minutes it was confirmed Rajiv Gandhi had in fact been sworn in as the prime minister – and there was nothing 'interim' about it! The same evening, riots broke out but not as yet on the scale on which the pogrom would be carried out from next day onwards.

On TV that evening, we heard the new PM pleading for peace. He quoted his mother, 'Don't shed blood, shed hatred.' But it was such an amateur, hesitant, stuttering performance that it carried no conviction. (Later I learnt the short speech required over seven takes.)

In the morning, the TV cameras were focused on Teen Murti Bhavan where the late PM's body lay in state. Milling outside were Youth Congress thugs yelling, '*Khoon ka badla khoon*' (Blood for blood). Rajiv repeatedly emerged to calm them down. He admonished them to not talk of revenge. They quietened down but only to resume their slogan-mongering as other batches caught up.

Suneet and I decided to drive out to see what was happening. Our first stop was the petrol station in front of our house in the Moti Bagh government housing colony. There I heard the attendant stringing together the most obscene abuses targeting the Sikh community as he helped unload a consignment of iron rods a truck had just delivered. I was naïve enough to think this was a normal building contract! I realized later what those rods must have been for. My tank full, Suneet and I started down the Ring Road, saw the charred remains of shops and at least one petrol station gutted, and then reached the bridge beyond Ashram, from where we had a grandstand view of fires burning in the distance and nearer, in Bhogal. In the afternoon, I went to see Bhagat. He was huddled at home, seemingly paralysed into inaction. Later, he was accused of having organized the pogrom. As far as I could make out, he just hid – while the most vicious excesses were being committed in his constituency.

I had other concerns, principal among them being my mother-in-law who lived all alone in Defence Colony proudly displaying a nameplate that read 'Mrs Vir Singh'. The colony was full of her friends and family, and over the next several months the only greeting on morning walks was from members of the Sikh community anxiously checking with each other on departure for *sadda* (our) Punjab.

My mother-in-law remained adamant: Delhi was her home and she was going nowhere. Still, all it would take was for one nutcase to set her house ablaze. Fortunately, while some Sikh houses in Defence Colony were vandalized and a few Sikhs roughed up, others, including my mother-in-law, were spared the awful fate of thousands of their fellow Sikhs who were ruthlessly butchered.

On the evening of 1 November I received a frantic call from an old friend in Friends Colony. She said she was hearing calls from the nearby gurdwara blaring, '*Din tumhara tha, raat hamari hogi*' (The day was yours, the night will be ours). She wanted to know what I – as a senior civil servant – could do to help her. I had to shamefacedly confess there was nothing I could do and we must only hope that good sense would prevail before we were murdered.

But her call plunged me into another set of concerns. Since Suneet was a Sikh and I a non-Sikh, we were in danger of being attacked by either or both sides. At just this moment, the husband of one of our domestic staff burst into the house shouting, 'The Sikhs are coming, the Sikhs are coming.' We rushed across the wide lawn fronting our house to pick up our three young daughters – aged five, seven and ten – who had gone to play with a colleague's children and ran back home with them in the gathering gloom of a foggy November dusk. It was a completely false alarm; the group our man had seen was a vigilante squad, voluntarily formed to keep the peace, who had covered their heads and armed themselves with *lathi*s (stout staves).

Even as we drew our bewildered but highly excited daughters close to us in gratitude, the rumour-monger returned to say that trains were coming into New Delhi station with corpses in the bunks and those who were alive were set upon as soon as they descended. We dismissed the story, then learnt next day that our home-grown rumour monger had got it right: the horrors of Partition were indeed being revisited. Rajiv Gandhi once again came on TV and pleaded for peace. It fell on deaf ears. Not until 3 November, after the army had undertaken route marches, did the massacres start petering out. As a bystander, all I could do was make up my mind to vote against such an incompetent government.

Many years later, it was confirmed to me by Law Minister Shiv Shankar[6] that at 2.30 a.m. on 2 November, fed up with the government's paralysis, the new PM brushed aside security concerns and had himself driven to the worst-affected areas. Thereafter, he took matters into his own hands instead of leaving things to his far more experienced home minister and the lieutenant governor, who was a senior ICS officer. It was then that the pogrom began to scale down until it was brought under control by the 3rd.

I think this is the right point at which to evaluate one of the most sordid and controversial events of Rajiv Gandhi's premiership to dog his political legacy: the Sikh pogrom on the first three days of his term. First, I believe the new prime minister should have apologized to the Sikh community and taken upon himself and his colleagues the blame for the atrocities committed instead of letting others, including public opinion generally, pin the blame on him. An apology did come – from a Sikh prime minister, that too as many as twenty years later. It never sufficed.

Second, I have no doubt that the PM made a huge mistake in not dismissing his cousin, the commissioner of police, Gautam Kaul. The man deserved to be sacked and, when he wasn't, there was no escaping charges of nepotism.

Third, an impartial judicial enquiry should have been ordered immediately. It was not until the following April – six months too late – that P. Shiv Shankar announced an enquiry by Justice Ranganath Misra. It made no impression on those who were evaluating negatively the initial performance of the new PM – including people like myself.

Fourth, most importantly, the army was not called in immediately; this should have been done perhaps even before the pogrom began. I met, a decade or more later, Major General Jamwal who headed the forces stationed in the Delhi cantonment. He explained that in order to forestall the possibilities of a military coup, the Delhi contingent was always well below strength and so it became necessary in a crisis to wait until forces stationed in Meerut could come to the national capital to reinforce the Delhi contingent.

---

[6] Mani Shankar Aiyar (ed.), *Rajiv Gandhi's India: A Golden Jubilee Retrospective*, Vol. I, UBSPD, New Delhi, 1988, p. 27.

I am not a military man and cannot vouch for my own understanding of what happened but the surface evidence would indicate the army was not called in on time. It seems the home minister and lieutenant governor did not steel themselves to do this until it was far too late. That explains why it took longer for the army to move in from Meerut than it had taken for the rebel sepoys to cover the same distance in 1857. But none of this was explained to the general public and the widely held view was that the delay was deliberate.

Fifth, it bears emphasizing that in Home Minister P.V. Narasimha Rao Rajiv Gandhi had his mother's most trusted minister. Rao was a man of such vast experience that the Congress had no hesitation in pitching for him as prime minister after Rajiv's assassination in 1991. It might well have been that, with his own lack of any real political experience, Rajiv Gandhi felt that his sturdy home minister, in consultation with a highly reputed ICS officer as Delhi's lieutenant governor, would know better how to handle the situation. It was only when he discovered that they were quite out of their depth that he intervened personally during the intervening night of 2 November with decisive results.

Sixth, there was the infamous 'when a big tree falls' speech that has besmirched Rajiv Gandhi's name and reputation all these years. The fact is that the speech was *not* made on the day Rajiv Gandhi was sworn in as PM, as has been widely claimed and relentlessly propagated. A simple look at the record establishes this. Immediately after his swearing in as PM on 31 October, Rajiv Gandhi broadcast a brief message to the nation in which the key lines were:

> The foremost need is to maintain our balance. We can and must face this tragic ordeal with fortitude, courage and wisdom. We should remain calm and exercise maximum restraint. We should not let our emotions get the better of us, because passion would cloud judgment. Nothing would hurt the soul of our beloved Indira Gandhi more than the occurrence of violence in any part of the country.[7]

All-India Radio and Doordarshan broadcast this message in every language

[7] *Rajiv Gandhi: Selected Speeches and Writings, 1984–85*, Vol. I, Publications Division, New Delhi, 1987, p. 3.

to every corner of the country: there was no provocation; no excuses for what was happening; no call to revenge; and no mention of any tree falling.

He was back on radio and television on 2 November:

> Communal madness will destroy us. It will destroy everything India stands for. As Prime Minister of India I cannot and will not allow this. . .
>
> Tomorrow the mortal remains of Indira Gandhi will be consigned to [the] sacred flames. She had said, 'Do not shed blood, shed hatred.' Let this guide us.[8]

Rajiv Gandhi took into his own hands the responsibility of ending the pogrom – and he succeeded. Meanwhile, thousands of innocent lives were lost. That was the moment to apologize. That, he did not do. It damaged him irretrievably.

Sixteen days after the violence had ended, on 19 November 1984, that is, the sixty-seventh birth anniversary of the assassinated former prime minister, Rajiv Gandhi addressed a huge gathering on the lawns of the Boat Club.

He spoke in Hindi: 'In our retribution we must not be moved by anger or anguish ... Some riots took place in the country following the murder of Indiraji. We know the people were very angry and for a few days it seemed that India had been shaken.' And then came the fateful sentence: 'But, when a mighty tree falls, it is only natural that the earth around it does shake a little.'[9]

Taken out of context and blown out of proportion, that one sentence wiped from public memory everything else that Rajiv Gandhi said and did to halt the pogrom. That sentence has been portrayed as an exculpation of what had been done to the Sikhs in three days of mass madness. It was projected as justification of what the murderous goons perpetrated. Very soon it was claimed that the goons were Youth Congress thugs. And witty, witty Vajpayee caused vengeful mirth, when he reversed Rajiv's phrase and remarked, 'It is only when the earth shakes that a big tree falls.'[10]

Of course, much of what I have written in the preceding paragraphs came to light only subsequently. But I had heard all the speeches and also encountered the flood of misinformation. While what had happened to the Sikh community

---

[8] Ibid., p. 4.

[9] Ibid., p. 11.

[10] Tavleen Singh, *Durbar*, Hachette, Gurgaon, 2017.

was unforgivable and a lasting blot on the nation, the atmosphere was so divisive no one was willing to consider extenuating circumstances.

In the midst of this turmoil, the new PM decided to put his dynastic legacy to the test. Elections were announced and I, for my part, commended this as the right thing to do. Let the people decide whether they approved or condemned the young man. However, my personal decision to vote against the Congress remained.

Once a measure of normalcy had been restored, I went to see Dinesh Singh. He pronounced, 'Your generation's time has come. You must go and see Arun Singh.' Arun Singh had been appointed parliamentary secretary to the prime minister. I protested that I hardly remembered him. Pulling out the Doon School record, Dinesh read out that Arun Singh was no more than a year junior to me and, moreover, had been with me at both St Stephen's and Cambridge. For the life of me I could do no more than summon up a dim memory. Moreover, I had barely known Rajiv Gandhi at school or Cambridge. But, most important of all, did I really want to be associated with a leadership that had proved itself so thoroughly incompetent and, worse, inhuman during its first few days? Dinesh dismissed these doubts and advised me most earnestly to get in touch with Arun.

Slowly wending my way back to office, I decided to drop in on friends in South Block. There I ran into Dr Arjun Sengupta, an outstanding leftist economist who had been minister (economic) in our High Commission in Dhaka where I got to know him and had rapidly risen to the post of economic adviser to Prime Minister Indira Gandhi. Through the years that followed, he had been my mentor in socialist economics. His cheery greeting was 'Your time has come!' I was a little taken aback at this echo from Dinesh Singh's drawing room. He insisted that I must go and see Arun Singh.

It took me a few days to pull myself together to make the effort. What decided me was being told that notwithstanding the previous prime minister's passing, I could not return to the IFS until an approval was received from the new PM. Since the interim government was going in for immediate elections, that would have to wait until after the new elected government had settled in. I was also beginning to change my assessment of the new lot after Rajiv Gandhi opted for an immediate election to legitimize his inheritance. That was the right thing to do, the democratic thing to do.

Arun Singh was surprisingly friendly and cordial when I rang. He called me over immediately, and listened to my problem sympathetically and with great attention. He agreed with me that there was nothing constructive I could do in the I&B ministry and further agreed that if the government wanted me to become a spokesman for the whole government, as I had been for foreign affairs in the MEA, the obvious place would be to locate me in the PMO.

He suggested that I meet the information adviser to the PM, the redoubtable H.Y. Sharada Prasad, and, under his guidance, prepare a note for the new PM that he (Arun) would follow up on their return from the election campaign. The campaign was beginning the following day in Tamil Nadu, coincidentally in Thanjavur district where my ancestral village lay. With a twinkle in his eye, he promised to wave to my family as the helicopter flew over Kargudi!

I had not reckoned with the frosty reception I would receive from the information adviser. I had not known that the last thing he wanted was to be burdened with a deputy. He had had quite enough of the obstreperous U.C. Tiwari who served in that position before being designated principal information officer in the I&B ministry. He noted my desire to quit I&B but remained silent on the question of a transfer to the PMO. The possibility of a return to the MEA was also left hanging.

I was suddenly busy in I&B. The cabinet secretary ordered that, under the aegis of the Films Division, I should prepare a film on Operation Blue Star to reassure the Sikh community and, in particular, the Sikh units in our armed forces, that the Harmandir Sahib was unharmed and the country was one with them. To this end, Lieutenant General Gowri Shankar, security adviser to the Punjab governor, based in Chandigarh, had been assigned to take my team around and generally facilitate the filming. To this day, I do not know why I was picked for this bizarre task. I had neither any training to do the job nor had made a documentary before, nor was I given a brief, just asked to use my imagination. I had neither a scriptwriter, nor a director. My camera team and I were on our own, with logistics left to the general.

General Gowri Shankar first flew our merry band to Jalandhar, where he had laid on a generous *bara khana* (big feast) to introduce us to his officers and men. He then drove me to the Military Hospital to interview the severely injured second lieutenant, Gurvinder (his name and rank have been changed at his request), who straightened himself in his bed in a military salute and began peppering me with 'sirs' in typical army style. He agreed that I might interview him but wondered whether he could first have a word with me in private.

I shooed away the camera team and seated myself by his bedside to hear him out. He said that as an army officer he would do as he had been ordered to by General Gowri Shankar but asked me to bear in mind certain extenuating circumstances. He then went on to say that he was not afraid of being killed in the course of duty. His concern was for his parents, who were not in the army. The terrorists, he went on, had even attempted to climb the walls of the hospital to get to him in his sickbed. His parents were blameless and he was apprehensive that if his forthcoming interview with me were screened, the terrorists might target them.

I had never before faced such a moral dilemma. On the one hand, the interview would dramatically set the stage for the documentary. On the other, I had to weigh in the balance the real possibility of his parents being harmed, perhaps even killed. I told him I would really much rather not do the interview but as I was duty-bound to do so, I would finish the interview and then discuss with General Gowri Shankar and others whether we could leave it out.

The officer again straightened himself out in a military salute and indicated that he was ready. Interviewing him about the opening sequence of Operation Blue Star was one of the most moving experiences of my life. He answered all my questions cogently, fluently and fully, not having to be coaxed, nor with any hesitation in his voice. He detailed how he had been asked to put together his best jawans and told that all they had to do was carry some canisters of CN gas (colloquially known as 'mace') and fling them into the Akal Takht where Bhindranwale was hiding.

That retired General Shabeg Singh, one of the heroes of the Bangladesh War, was holed up with Bhindranwale had not been mentioned in the briefing he received. The terrorists, he understood, would not have an inkling of what the army was up to, and as the run from the entrance to the Akal Takht was only a few yards, he and his men would reach the target within minutes. Once the Akal Takht was overwhelmed by the fumes, the terrorists would surrender.

Instead, as they entered through the main gate, they were fired upon from apertures that gave on to the staircase sloping downwards and, once they were on the *parikrama* (the paths around the holy pools), there was a hail of bullets from the Akal Takht and all around that instantly killed almost all his comrades. He himself was seriously injured and knocked unconscious.

He had no idea how long it was before someone in the waves of jawans who followed his group noticed that he appeared to be still breathing and dragged him out. When he came to, he found himself in a hospital bed and learnt that his boys had been wiped out almost to the last. He had been incredibly lucky not to suffer their fate.

I walked out of the room, humbled. Two decades later, a smiling man, permanently injured but in high spirits, arrived for my daughter's wedding in November 2006. It was the same second lieutenant, earning an honourable living running a petrol station allotted to him by the Ministry of Petroleum and Natural Gas under the disabled servicemen's quota, accompanied by his wife and bearing a huge wedding present for my daughter. I think it would be fair to say that he was, for me, the most welcome guest. His parents, he assured me, were safe and the terrorist threats had ceased.

The film had still to be shot. Amritsar had then a very competent deputy commissioner, Ramesh Inder Singh, who had been specially deputed to handle the aftermath of Blue Star.[11] He was certainly about the best IAS officer I have ever encountered, cool, calm, collected, confident, fully focused on the job at hand, brave and unconcerned about any personal fallout from the decisions he was taking. His superb handling of what was a very difficult and dangerous assignment won my deepest admiration and, more importantly, showed me how wasted had been my career in diplomacy, spent largely on the cocktail circuit!

It was decided that we would not have a security detail as that would only expose us, and that we would film the Golden Temple and its surrounding areas in the early hours on the pretext of covering the *palki*, the sacred procession at dawn when the holy Guru Granth Sahib is solemnly carried in procession from its resting place in the Akal Takht to the sanctum sanctorum of the Harmandir Sahib. Our safety would be guaranteed by the Shiromani Gurdwara Parbandhak Committee (SGPC) who had been contacted and briefed by the deputy commissioner. Truth to tell, the briefing had been more fiction than fact.

---

[11] Ramesh Inder Singh has just published his memoirs, *Turmoil in Punjab: Before and After Blue Star* (HarperCollins, Gurugram, 2022). Essential and very disturbing reading.

It was biting cold that December morning when we arrived at the Golden Temple at about 3 a.m. We were given a brusque but not entirely unfriendly welcome. The SGPC assigned a liaison officer to accompany us. It was eerie walking around the *parikrama* in the dark. We surreptitiously filmed what we could and mounted the ramparts for long shots. We succeeded in getting snatches of information from our liaison man who had been in the vicinity when Operation Blue Star took place. We thought we had him fooled but one night, when we were in a pitch-dark alley, he whispered to me he knew we were from Doordarshan and were filming a story on Operation Blue Star. I froze, thinking this was it. But he carried on: 'Sir, can you get me a job with Doordarshan when you get back to Delhi?'

We were through, as I remember, in a couple of nights, perhaps three, and went back to Jalandhar to film an army recruitment camp that would answer a longer-term issue troubling the Sikh community. Punjab has long been one of the most important recruitment fields for the army and many Sikh families, especially rural families, are dependent on army recruitment for assured livelihood.

Rumours were rife that on account of the assassination of Prime Minister Indira Gandhi by her Sikh guards, the recruitment of Sikhs into the army had stopped. The filming we did at Jalandhar demonstrated that the rumours were unfounded and full-fledged recruitment of young Sikh men was continuing. Authenticity was imparted by focusing on the board that gave the date of the recruitment exercise: 3 December 1984. (The date remains etched in my memory because that was the day of the ghastly Bhopal gas tragedy.) That gave me the opening for the film eventually made, based largely on archival material at the Films Division library in Bombay.

I gave it the title *Saathi Saath Chalein* (Comrades, let's move ahead together), produced, scripted and voiced by me. I later found that the Films Division had not retained a copy and that the one copy made was sent to the Sikh Light Infantry but they misplaced it. Happily, after a test screening of the Golden Temple sequence for just five minutes, everyone agreed that the Operation Blue Star portions should be shredded. The interview with 'Gurvinder' never saw the light of day.

The ongoing election campaign was gathering momentum and the signs were that the Congress would score a big victory. Resolved to vote against the 'Hand' symbol to register my distress at the Sikh pogrom, I went to the nearest voting booth only to find that my name was not on the rolls. Indeed, not until I got to the booth did I realize that my residence in Moti Bagh was not in the New Delhi constituency, but in South Delhi where neither of the candidates had any attraction for me. So, in the end, my protest vote was never cast!

On the last day of the year, the results came in. Rajiv Gandhi had won a massive victory and my fate was now in his hands. The same day, I handed in to Sharada Prasad my petition, to be forwarded to the principal secretary to the PM, P.C. Alexander. What Sharada Prasad did not know was that I also took the precaution of dropping in on Arun Singh and giving him a copy, hinting that I did not think the information adviser was favourably disposed to my request.

About a week into the new year, Sharada called me in and gave me the doleful news that he had discussed my appeal with the principal secretary and they had agreed there was no need to trouble the PM. Instead, I could go to Khurshid Ahmed Khan, the newly appointed minister of state (MoS) for external affairs (the PM having retained the foreign affairs portfolio), and ascertain whether he wished to take me back into my parent service.

I trudged with a heavy heart to Khurshid sahib's office and was relieved to be let into his presence. He listened to me with great sympathy but regretted that as it was a PM (Indira Gandhi) who had sent me to I&B, only the current PM could let me return. I clutched at the proffered straw. Would Khurshid sahib be prepared to send the new PM a note in this regard? He said he would, adding the rider that I had to draft the note for him. I seized the opportunity. In the name of MoS external affairs, I could bypass the Sharada Prasads and the P.C. Alexanders, and get my petition straight into the hands of the one person who could get me into PMO. I readied the draft quickly and Khurshid sahib sent it off to the PM almost immediately, without any change, with his signature appended.

Pleased at having put one over the PMO mafia, I waited for the outcome. Meanwhile, Alexander had resigned after it was discovered that his private office had been a spies' sieve, with secret documents, including cabinet minutes, regularly sold by his staff to foreign diplomats for as little as a bottle of Scotch! Imagine my shock, therefore, when the note returned with Rajiv Gandhi's initials and a tick on the suggestion that I might be taken back into the MEA.

I carried the note forlornly to Foreign Secretary Rasgotra, who welcomed me back enthusiastically and expansively offered to appoint me to any post I wished to take. I consulted my colleagues and asked for the North America desk, which was falling vacant. I was promptly granted my request and I sat in my new office, downhearted.

It was then that I recalled the astrological prediction made by a cousin's husband, S. Srikrishnan, in 1983. As conference spokesman for the NAM, I was in the papers almost every day. He said this was 'nothing'. He had cast my horoscope and my life would be elevated to an altogether new level on 1 February 1985, turning me into a 'national figure'. I had dismissed the prediction as a load of mumbo-jumbo, quite opposed to my rationalist beliefs. But such was my despair at this point that I started writing a long letter to Srikrishnan telling him my hopes had been shattered and there was no way his forecast would prove true.

As the letter had to be written in snatches between bouts of official work, it was incomplete when I received an invitation to a reception at Hyderabad House on 31 January 1985 thrown by Foreign Secretary Maharajakrishna Rasgotra, on the eve of his retirement. As I entered the reception hall, I saw Sharada Prasad who greeted me with the somewhat ambiguous remark, 'You remember your note? It's been accepted.' He then turned away to speak to someone else. Not sure what the remark signified, I moved along to another part of the hall to congratulate the incoming foreign secretary, Romesh Bhandari. He was his usual ebullient self, effusively greeting me, saying, 'So you've returned to us only to drift off again.' That seemed to seal it.

The next day I was at a meeting with the FS when Gopi Arora, additional secretary in the PMO, rang to say, 'Welcome on board.' I had made it! Srikrishnan had been proved a prophet right down to the precise day, month and year. I was thrilled but continue to be sceptical of such predictions that come true so unbelievably.

There was the inexplicable chain of events that had led me to where I was: if the Golden Temple had not been stormed, and if that had not brought me into the Special Publicity Group, Rajiv Gandhi would have heard nothing of me. If Indira Gandhi had not parked me in the I&B ministry for my virtues, there is no reason I would have gone to see Arun Singh after her assassination; no reason for approaching the new PM for a post on his staff; no explaining away Alexander's removal from office; until we come to the last link: Gopi Arora's phone call.

'God' – whether you believe in Him or not – 'moves in a mysterious way / His wonders to perform.' Coincidences do seem to have played a decisive role in chalking out my destiny, assuming astrology had nothing to do with it. I think it was Albert Einstein who said that coincidences are God's way of not showing Himself to humans.

See detailed footnotes and endnotes by scanning the QR code above.

11

My Years with Rajiv Gandhi

1985–1991

1985: Rajiv Gandhi's 'golden year'

Rajiv Gandhi's first month in office as prime minister saw a whirlwind of new thoughts and initiatives from talk of taking India to the twenty-first century to securing a generous compensation from Union Carbide for the victims of the Bhopal gas tragedy, and passing legislation to put a stop to MPs and members of the Legislative Assembly (MLAs) switching sides at will – a phenomenon known in India by the expression '*Aya Ram, gaya Ram*' ('Ram comes, Ram goes', a play on the names – often including 'Ram' – of Haryana politicians who had proved to be prone to defection). It was a golden beginning to the golden year of his premiership. Even the highly partisan editor of the *Indian Express,* Arun Shourie, who was to turn into one of Rajiv's most vengeful critics, was all praise. And here I was, getting into the lift on the ground floor as his government took off.

Before I joined the PMO, however, I had one last job with the MEA. The young new PM had got the Americans to agree, against guarantees to be negotiated, that India would have access to dual-use technologies which could be used for either war or peace. It was this question of negotiating guarantees that was to be my last task in the foreign ministry. The new foreign secretary, Romesh Bhandari, requested me to delay joining the PMO until I had led a delegation to Washington, DC, to settle the terms under which the import of dual-use high technology might begin, 'for strictly peaceful purposes' and with cast-iron guarantees of 'no re-export to anyone' (read the Soviet Union).

My IFS senior, K. Natwar Singh, who was now a minister, more or less ordered me to first sign up with the PMO and then complete the assignment. This left me in something of a bureaucratic limbo. I had visiting cards printed for distribution in the US that contained only my name but no designation. My colleagues were amused at my chutzpah – the sheer arrogance of anyone imagining that just his name on a visiting card would suffice!

I went to Washington, DC, with a team of experts who were much taken by the bonhomie and easy familiarity we established with the Americans, particularly when I corrected the English of my US counterpart. A junior officer on the other side exclaimed, 'But the assistant undersecretary of state went to Harvard.' 'That's Cambridge, Mass,' I calmly replied. 'I went to Cambridge, Elite.' There was a gratifying roar of laughter and a round of warm applause. A couple of the US delegates remained in touch with me for years.

As soon as the agreement was signed, I rushed back to Delhi and formally presented myself at the PMO. That morning, Rajiv Gandhi was on his way to Moscow to attend Leonid Brezhnev's funeral and greet his successor, Yuri Andropov. So, as per the established protocol (which the PM later rescinded) the entire PMO was to go to the airport (technical area) to see him off. When we lined up outside the aircraft, Rajiv Gandhi gave me a quizzical look, trying to place me. I am not sure he did. But he must have enquired on the journey and was most friendly when he returned. It was the beginning of what turned out to be the decisive relationship of my career.

My relationship with Rajiv

I think this is the right place to clear up a persistent misunderstanding about the origins of my relationship with Rajiv Gandhi. True, we had been at the same school and at Cambridge together. But I was three years his senior at school – an unbridgeable gap in a school where the average stay was of five years. Moreover, it was a school that did not care for social distinctions within its ranks. So what if he was the grandson of the prime minister of India.

The only time I can remember running into him was at the swimming pool in the term after I had passed the school-leaving exam (Senior Cambridge). School rules allowed seniors of my venerability to swim at any time, but younger boys were required to take the permission of a 'senior' to swim outside the authorized hours. I recall a shy boy walking up to me and asking if I would let him swim, '*yaar*'. The normal Dosco[1] reaction would have been to say, 'F*** off.' Fortunately, something stayed my mouth, and I graciously gave him the required permission. I have often wondered whether if I had not, would he have appointed me to his PMO?

At Cambridge, we overlapped for a year. But he belonged to the high-spending class and I to the penurious, so nothing brought us together. Except that I remember him blocking my way as I entered the debating chamber at the Union for my first 'paper' speech (that is, my name was on the order papers to initiate the debate). Seeing that the white ducks I wore with my black *bandhgala*[2] were riding a little above my ankles, Rajiv smilingly enquired whether I was 'heading for the floods'.

That was the sum total of my acquaintance with Rajiv Gandhi before joining him in the PMO. I think that was to my advantage. Many of his other friends – Arun Singh being the prime example – fell by the wayside from carrying their childhood familiarity into the Prime Minister's Office. But in the PMO I always called him 'sir'.

It was an official relationship. The only time he came to my house (and was horrified at the state of my drawing room furniture) was when he called to condole the passing away of my mother. When we stepped out and he saw security hiding in the trees on surveillance, he remarked, 'They don't trust you an inch, do they?' And I was never invited to his home. I am sure Sonia Gandhi, who struggled to preserve the sanctity of her home, would have disapproved of my intruding on family privacy.

But the PM and I struck an immediate rapport, probably because he and I had so much in common in terms of our educational background and a shared idiom of conversation. I amused him and he enjoyed laughing at my quips. His most endearing quality was his upbringing: decent, unfailingly polite and

---

[1] In the school argot, a boy who was at, or had been to, the Doon School.

[2] Formal black jacket, closed at the collar.

deeply empathetic. Although I was never a friend, over the years I grew close enough to him to be just about his closest acquaintance.

This might also be the appropriate place to clear up a persistent, and perhaps deliberate, attempt to foist an elitist and nepotistic image of him as surrounding himself with sycophantic school friends. At the start, he did indeed appoint Arun Singh, whom he fondly called 'Roon', as his principal aide and parliamentary secretary. But at the same time he also appointed Oscar Fernandes and Ahmed Patel – neither of whom had even a whiff of Doon – as his two other parliamentary secretaries. Moreover, Arun Singh was soon moved to the Ministry of Defence, where he had a falling out with the PM over Operation Brasstacks and later Bofors.

Arun Nehru was a cousin – but was emphatically not a product of Doon but of a school and college in Lucknow. Chidambaram was from Madras Christian College, not from Doon, and went on to Harvard not Cambridge. Rajiv had inherited from his mother Wajahat Habibullah, an IAS officer from the Jammu and Kashmir cadre, also from Doon – but that was a regular administrative posting that ended within eighteen months of RG becoming PM when Habibullah's period of deputation ended and he moved, of his own volition, as administrator, Lakshadweep, an island territory for whose development the PM was preparing a major initiative.

That left only me as the one PMO officer with a Dosco background. Everyone else who mattered in the PMO – H.Y. Sharada Prasad, Sarla Grewal, Gopi Arora, Montek Singh Ahluwalia, Chinmaya Gharekhan, Ronen Sen, R. Vasudevan, Pulok Chatterjee – were not Doon alumni. And unlike them, I had no substantive portfolio – until the PM displayed an unusual but deep interest in Panchayat Raj, a subject that my colleagues in the PMO regarded with some disdain as an eccentric venture in which I had involved the prime minister. That's it. The club or coterie of Doscos is a myth.

I have tried hard to think of who in the political sphere might have had a Doon School connection. There was, of course, Kamal Nath – but he had been brought in by Sanjay Gandhi, and Rajiv Gandhi kept himself as far away as possible from Sanjay's friends. The only name I can think of is the former maharaja of Patiala, Amarinder Singh, a personal friend of RG's who, in fact, opposed RG politically and played a key role in sabotaging the implementation of his breakthrough Punjab Accord. So I hope this wholly unnecessary clarification will, once and for all, lay down the spectre of a naïve, nepotistic, blundering PM caught up in schoolboy manoeuvres, an image that was, and continues to be, thrust on him.

The PM's (political) men

The PMO was strictly divided between the political and the administrative – and woe to them who crossed the line. I was in the administrative half until my resignation from the IFS and induction into the party in late 1989, nearly five years later.

When I joined in March 1985, the political side was headed by Arun Singh, assisted by two other parliamentary secretaries – Ahmed Patel and Oscar Fernandes, as I have noted. We jokingly referred to the three as 'Amar, Akbar, Antony' (after the name of a Bollywood hit). After experimenting with this for about a year, the PM dropped the three without replacing them until, in his last year, he brought in Sheila Dikshit as his minister of state to deputize for him in Parliament.

At his residence on Race Course Road, Makhan Lal Fotedar initially kept court but was soon joined by Captain Satish Sharma, a buddy from Rajiv Gandhi's flying days (but not a Doon School boy, as often mischievously portrayed). Arun Nehru muscled in until he was finally disgraced for his nefarious role in the Babri Masjid affair – he is believed to have got the gates of the masjid unlocked – and possibly being the 'N' of the Ardbo diaries, as I recount in more detail below. R.K. Dhawan was brought in early in 1989 after helping in the reconciliation of ex-President Zail Singh with Rajiv Gandhi. While these political elements held sway at the prime ministerial residence, 7, Race Course Road, none had any locus standi in the PMO until end 1988. With the induction into the PMO of R.K. Dhawan and Sheila Dikshit as minister of state in RG's last year in office, 1989, the situation changed (for the worse) for reasons that I hope to make clear as we proceed with the narrative.

Let me now describe the key political figures. The two Aruns – Arun Singh (Roon) and Arun Nehru – who played such a large part in Rajiv Gandhi's premiership (largely to the PM's detriment) were as different as chalk and cheese. Whereas Arun Singh was sophisticated, agreeable and gentle, endowed with wit and a sense of humour, Arun Nehru was always the bull in the China shop: rough, brusque, dominating and a bully. While Roon was inducted into politics by RG, Arun Nehru was a holdover from Indira Gandhi's days. Also, while Roon was a friend, Arun Nehru was a relative. One can choose one's friends but not one's cousins!

Roon had entered politics when RG was testing the waters with considerable reticence and reluctance after Sanjay's air crash when he had been called in 'to help Mummy'. When I wrote about twenty-five years ago that Rajiv had called Roon to assist him, Sonia Gandhi had me called by her private secretary, V. George, to say I was misinformed: it was Roon who had thrust himself on Rajiv rather than having been requested to help. I stand reprimanded.

As I have recounted earlier, it was Roon who first welcomed the idea of my joining the PMO and later bailed me out when I ran into difficulties in the first few months of my assignment. I was, therefore, not surprised when he burst into my office (that was next door to the cabinet room) to tell me that the PM had transferred him from the PMO to the defence ministry. I congratulated him on his promotion, but he obviously thought otherwise. I do not know why Rajiv Gandhi took this decision. Perhaps it was because he did not like the projection Roon was receiving in the media as the ultimate insider; perhaps it was because he wanted to reward his friend by pushing him one step up the ladder.

However that may be, Roon clearly resented being 'kicked upstairs', as it were. That, I guess, was what psychologically fuelled his adversarial reactions to his erstwhile friend in Operation Brasstacks and the Bofors affair (as described elsewhere in this work and supplemented with detail in the forthcoming companion volume, *The Rajiv I Knew*). I have tried to engage Roon on or off the record on these questions, but he has politely turned me down saying he never talks about Rajiv Gandhi or his differences with the prime minister. I hope he will open up one day, but I rather suspect he prefers to let sleeping dogs lie.

Arun Nehru was a different matter altogether. Rajiv had inherited him from his mother; Arun Nehru ensured RG was sworn in to succeed his mother on the same evening as her assassination. Whether RG enquired and learnt the truth of rumours that Arun Nehru was the one who had instigated the pogrom against the Sikhs, I simply do not know. However, sitting in the office of the I&B minister, H.K.L. Bhagat, as his 'information adviser', I saw the terror on Bhagat's face every time a call came in from Nehru and the 'Yes, Sirs' with which he sprinkled his answers although he was much the senior in terms of party experience and loyalty as well as his unblemished record of electoral wins. Clearly, party hacks believed Arun Nehru was the fount of all power in the party and their futures depended on how pleased Nehru was with them.

I have recorded elsewhere the details of the influence Arun Nehru wielded for better or for worse – generally for worse – in the party, government and Uttar Pradesh affairs, and the encomiums paid to his importance by a fawning *India Today* cover story, which reflected the general perception that it was Nehru who called the shots and, in effect, decided what was what. But he overreached himself both in regard to opening the locks at the Babri Masjid and his alleged hand in the Bofors deal, both of which were unveiled by the internal investigations that the PM launched. Within a year of being 'elevated' as minister of state in charge of internal security in the home ministry, Nehru was out on his ear. He then became the single most important backer of V.P. Singh's revolt but faded from the public eye along with VP's ill-fated tenure of eleven months as PM.

R.K. Dhawan was born in Chiniot in west Punjab and moved to India at Partition. Chiniotis are reported to be sharp operators with an eye for the main chance. Dhawan personified this stereotype. Introduced to Indira Gandhi by his uncle, Yashpal Kapoor, her principal political pointsman, Dhawan soon rose to becoming her eyes and ears. Rajiv Gandhi viewed him with suspicion and scepticism as Dhawan increasingly grew into the most powerful political broker of them all. So when RG suddenly and unexpectedly became PM on the assassination of his mother, he swiftly acted to remove Dhawan.

For four long years Dhawan remained in the shadows, nursing his grudges, if any, in private, not a word escaping into the public domain. Then, the PM had a falling out with the president, Giani Zail Singh, and this soon snowballed into a serious political and constitutional crisis. Since Dhawan had had a major hand in bringing Zail Singh to PM Indira Gandhi's attention when she was casting around for a *rashtrapati* (an appointment that was often compared to the Roman emperor Caligula appointing his horse as consul!), Rajiv Gandhi turned to Dhawan to mediate between himself and Zail Singh.

Dhawan was quick to see this as an opening for a second innings and succeeded in persuading Zail Singh to visit the Gandhi homestead for breakfast. This, as Dhawan had foreseen, led to his induction into Rajiv Gandhi's PMO. My wife summed up the impact of the appointment by exclaiming to a bunch of us, 'You guys are now finished.' We indeed were. While Dhawan adopted a very low profile to begin with, even occupying a small room on the ground floor instead of his usual place – the anteroom to the PM's chamber – he quickly transformed the PMO: from an entity insulated from everyday politics, it became the front room of the Congress party.

In particular, he was instrumental in twisting the PM's perspective on the Ram Janmabhoomi–Babri Masjid issue from principled secularism to playing both sides off against the other by making the Congress party's plank the conservation of the mosque while starting the building of a grand Ram temple in the vicinity of the masjid. In the end, the Hindus turned against the Congress because the mosque was left standing, and the Muslims turned against the Congress because the foundation of the temple was laid under the aegis of the central government. The Chinioti thus scored a self-goal by being too clever by half. But, of course, Rajiv Gandhi was solely responsible for losing his self-confidence and turning over his fortunes to one he had earlier quite correctly spurned.

Dhawan saw me as an obstacle, however slight, to his goals and tried to thwart me at every turn. But I survived and even learnt an important lesson from him. He said: '*Maniji, zamaana aapke khilaf ho aur pradhan mantri aapke saath, toh aap jeet jayenge, lekin pradhan mantri aapke khilaf ho aur zamaana aapke saath, toh aap haar hi jaoge.*' (If the world is against you and the PM with you, you'll win. But if the world is with you and the PM against, then you'll surely lose.) I think that summed up his political philosophy. Later, he remarked at my praising Rajiv Gandhi in Narasimha Rao's presence: 'Doesn't the idiot know who the prime minister now is?'

Makhan Lal Fotedar, on the other hand, was the classical party apparatchik. He carried messages from the PM to party workers and leaders and from them to the PM. This gave him a larger-than-life reputation, but, as far as I could make out, it did not go to his head. He did not operate out of the PMO but a modest office at the PM's office-cum-residence at Race Course Road. He sat at the telephone most of the day and remained on call until late in the night when the PM went to bed. I don't believe he was particularly influential in determining policy; he was more a conduit or liaison between the PM and the party. Nevertheless, proximity to power bestowed a certain aura on him. He was generally pleasant and friendly, but on one occasion early in my tenure, he summoned me about a remark I had made that had been reported in a gossip column.

Fortunately for me, the phone rang as I entered and Fotedar embarked on a long and complicated conversation that kept him on the line for a long time. I looked across the table and spotted the offending line. It was both true and indiscreet. Some journalist had asked me what Rajiv Gandhi read in bed and I had answered, 'How would I know? I'm not there with him.' So, when the telephone call ended and Fotedar turned to me, I was able to summon up adequate righteous indignation and say, '*Chhee, chhee!* What rubbish these journalists write.' I got away with that! I have not read his autobiography but understand it is a modest effort. As Churchill is reported to have said of Attlee, 'A modest man – with much to be modest about.'

The PMO set-up

On the administrative side of which I was a part, RG ran a very compartmentalized PMO. Each of us were allotted his or her niche and we reported, for the most part, directly to the PM. There was little interaction among us, the one great exception (which weighed most heavily on me) being the PM's collegiate approach to the drafting of his major set speeches.

Thus, while Principal Secretary Sarla Grewal was his channel of communication to the cabinet secretariat and senior bureaucrats in other ministries, within the PMO she was more the coordinator than the leader of our team. In fact, she rather reminded me of a mother hen looking after her flock of chicks than the stern martinet she was reputed to be.

In contrast, Additional (later, Special) Secretary Gopi Arora bestrode the PMO like a colossus, but although we were all somewhat in awe of him, he let each of us be in our respective slots while focusing on his duties as the resident expert on domestic political affairs and defence and national security issues. However, he overstepped the mark when he deliberately held back a key note on Bofors that the PM had addressed to his minister of state for defence, which aggravated the crisis.[3] Had Arora not overplayed his hand on

[3] Please see the detailed section on Bofors in the forthcoming companion volume to these memoirs, *The Rajiv I Knew, and Why He Was India's Most Misunderstood Prime Minister*, Juggernaut, New Delhi, 2023.

the PM's relationship with one of his most important ministers, he might well have stepped into Sarla Grewal's shoes on her superannuation, as all of us and he himself expected. Instead, Gopi Arora was shunted out to the I&B ministry in late 1987 from where he continued to be consulted by the PM but had to wait for a change of government to reap his well-deserved reward of becoming secretary (finance), followed by a highly lucrative assignment with the IMF in Washington, DC, as the executive director for a group of South Asian countries that included India.

Foreign affairs were the domain of Ronen Sen, ably assisted by Meera Shankar, also of the IFS (both were later ambassadors to the US). Ronen had a mania for secrecy but that is probably what appealed to the PM about him. A thorough professional, with a deep insight into the Soviet Union in particular, Ronen went about his tasks largely in the dead of night when India slept but chanceries in the West and to our east and south were functioning. I sometimes think the PM trusted him more than he did anyone else in the PMO and the warm but confidential relationship persisted into the eighteen months that Rajiv Gandhi lived after demitting office as PM.

Montek Singh Ahluwalia was without doubt the economic czar. We were in transition between socialist India and LPG (liberalization, privatization and globalization) but Montek, who was very much a market man, did not allow his preferences to come in the way of no more than gently nudging the PM away from his socialist convictions. While Montek's moment came later with Dr Manmohan Singh's elevation as finance minister under P.V. Narasimha Rao, Rajiv Gandhi did lend him a willing ear and Montek restrained himself within the bounds of what, at that time, seemed feasible in terms of economic reforms. He was very ably assisted by Rahul Khullar. Low-profile Pulok Chatterjee, efficiently liaised with rural and human development ministries.

Holding the rather dull but crucial responsibility of vetting officers and others for promotion and transfer was R. Vasudevan, a model of efficiency and integrity. He always regretted never having been taken by RG on even one of his many trips within the country or abroad. His office was always chock-a-block filled with files which he went through meticulously before rendering his conclusions fearlessly to the prime minister. Thoroughly reliable, he was happily blessed with a wicked sense of humour. Of a line in a poem I had written of my wife lying in the crook of my arm, Vasu suggested it would be more accurate to describe her as lying in the arms of her crook! It was good humour like this that kept us going through the endless trudge of sixteen to eighteen hours that was the norm in the PMO.

Among the junior officers was Ajay Acharya, appointed to assist me around the midpoint of my years at the PMO. His most sterling contribution was researching old copies of the *Times of India* for the PM to be able to reveal at their sesquicentennial celebrations the sordid truth of the newspaper as first an imperial publication with dreadful colonial views and later a saffron rag when Ramakrishna Dalmia bought it over at around Independence. (It is now something of an Advertisers' Gazette.) That speech was among the best Rajiv Gandhi ever delivered.

The PMO had in young Jay Narayan Chaubey its expert on science and technology. And P.A. Hakim took up the thread of minority affairs when he replaced Wajahat Habibullah.

The key link between the PM and his officers was his private secretary, Vincent George. George had an enormous appetite for sustained hard work. It was sheer aesthetic delight to watch his fingers fly over the keyboard to invariably produce copy that did not require the least correction. Very pleasant in manner and crystal clear in conveying the PM's instructions, his rare combination of courtesy and efficiency elevated him subsequently to the position of Sonia Gandhi's most powerful personal aide – so much so that I ribbed him with a riddle. 'What is the difference between India under imperial rule and today's free India? Answer: We were then ruled by George V – and we are now ruled by V George!'

The PM's relationship with his officers was extremely cordial. He rarely, if ever, scolded or showed any annoyance. He loved a laugh and that is where I scored over some of the others. He treated us with respect and affection, but always expected us to deliver – and deliver on time.

The atmosphere in the office was open and democratic, with little pulling of rank. But the expectation was that at all times we would give of our best, there being no place for slackness or delay. One-on-one meetings with him would be sharp and succinct, but when required – as in drafting sessions – would extend over the time required. I once teased him when he asked to me to get something done instantly:

> There once was a lady named Bright
> Who travelled much faster than light.
> She went out one day
> In a relative way
> And returned on the previous night!

It was this air of good humour that powered the PMO; otherwise, the pressures of work might have had all of us tearing out each other's hair.

My assigned work

My first task at the PMO was to find a room. No one wanted to move into P.C. Alexander's room, considering that office 'inauspicious'. So I was edged into it. I soon discovered that Jawaharlal Nehru had used it for a year or so before moving into the PM's corner office in the south-west of South Block. I exulted at sitting in Nehru's chair and at his table – but I had almost nothing to do as no one seemed to know why I had been let into the PMO.

It was assumed that I would be understudying Sharada Prasad, but he seemed to be preoccupied and consciously distancing himself from me. I learnt the reason soon enough. He thought I was being groomed to displace him. But a few weeks later, towards the end of a meeting with the PM where both of us were present, RG told Sharada he had decided to give him an extension. Sharada was so relieved that he started humming, then singing a snatch of Carnatic music in the car as we drove back to South Block. His fears that I had been brought in to replace him had been allayed. So he started unbending and we soon established a working relationship.

To this day, many think I was the PM's press secretary and official spokesman, and hence minutely informed on the controversies in which he was caught. In fact, I never held either of those positions. I was, of course, much on TV screens because Doordarshan always accompanied the prime minister and I was almost always with him on tours and public functions. I also had a role to play in picking correspondents who would accompany the PM on his tours.

However, my asides to correspondents would often find their way into press commentary, more often than not to my disadvantage. What saved me was that the PM just shrugged off these snippets and let me get on with my job in my own way and sometimes enjoyed my slugfests with journalists. I drew what comfort I could from Vir Sanghvi describing me as the PM's 'lightning rod', drawing to myself barbs that in reality were aimed at Rajiv Gandhi. I am still not sure this was true but it certainly was one way of explaining my tangled relationship with the media.

Those responsible for keeping the media informed were, first, Sharada Prasad and, later, my bête noire G. Parthasarathy (not to be confused with Indira Gandhi's Polonius, G. Parthasarathi). They were principally required to brief the print media and instruct state-owned Doordarshan and All India Radio (until Rajiv Gandhi started giving the private sector marginal media space on audio-visual channels). But neither Sharada Prasad nor Partha was formally invested with the title of official spokesman. They got out what they wanted largely through subordinates in the Press Information Bureau of the I&B ministry or with privileged briefings to a select few.

Sharada entrusted me with tabulating the scores of media requests for interviews with the PM – and RG indicated he would accept all my recommendations. I then had to anticipate what questions might be thrown at him and write out answers, as well as sit in on these interviews. Sharada had done these tasks for Indira Gandhi for seventeen long years but was clearly not inclined to continue this into the Rajiv era.

Sometimes the interviews took wholly unexpected turns. The owner-editor of a US journal, *Leaders*, sought an interview. He declined to submit his questions in advance, as was standard practice. Nevertheless, the PM was ready to grant the interview. I sat in as usual. When RG indicated his readiness to start, the American plutocrat said he had nothing to ask and requested the PM to not only send his answers in writing but also to frame the questions himself! All he wanted was to chit-chat while his photographer took pictures. I had a ball preparing the questions and answering them myself, with an occasional, 'Yes, I see' or an 'Ahem' or an 'Ah, ha' thrown in to lend a touch of verisimilitude to the bogus interview. Rajiv was most amused when he saw the draft.

I particularly recall an interview he gave to Mario Cabral e Sa of *Goa Today* on the eve of the silver jubilee of the liberation of Goa. The PM ended by slapping his hands on the table and exclaiming, 'Okay, Mani, let's go.' I was a little taken aback to find Mario had included that exclamation in the interview.

There was one interview which had a fallout that continues to this day, and it poisons my relationship with the journalist concerned, Tavleen Singh, she of the quill dipped in hemlock. I had been quite friendly with her as the external affairs spokesman in the MEA. After Rajiv Gandhi became PM, I learnt (from her) that she was their confidante, with access to their home and a time-tested friendship with Sonia.

So, when she wrote in asking to interview the PM, I called to ask on whose behalf she was seeking the interview as I knew she was freelance. She confidently replied, '*India Today*.' So, without making further enquiries, as I really ought to have done, I just put up the interview request. A couple of days later an irate Aroon Purie, the magazine's chief editor and publisher, rang me, 'If the PM wants to give an interview to *India Today*,' he thundered, 'we will decide who will do the interview.' I stuttered my apologies and called V. George, the PM's private secretary, to cancel the interview.

Fortunately, it had not yet been scheduled. So, I was more than a little surprised when Sharada called me about a week later and, thrusting the *Sunday Times* of London into my hands, demanded to know why I had permitted Tavleen Singh to interview the PM. Did I not know that she was *persona non grata*? I said I really did not know that and recited the background.

At the earliest opportunity, I enquired with the PM whether he had in fact given her the interview. He smiled and said she was an old friend and he had. That should have been that, but Tavleen has since carried on her vendetta against the Gandhis, and, incidentally, against me for over three decades. I had to free myself from my bureaucratic shackles before I could give back as good as I got. It was Vir Sanghvi who wryly remarked in a quite different context, 'The best revenge is writing well.' The feud continues!

Besides assisting Sharada Prasad in press relations, I was given a more unorthodox job. Arun Singh called me in and asked whether I would be prepared to look after the PM's tour programmes, a task that in Indira Gandhi's time had been entrusted to a section officer. As a senior joint secretary, I was grades above a section officer but I took on the responsibility with enthusiasm, especially after I was also told I would be accompanying the PM on his tours, particularly to remote areas. This was like a dream come true. I started working out itineraries for the north-east, the jungles of central India, the western deserts, the high mountains and the 'Islands in the Marigold Sun'. Of course, all this threw me almost daily into the PM's affable company and we seemed to be on the same wavelength.

From riots and terrorism to reconciliation and secularism

However, my first trip with him, on 23 March 1985, was to nowhere exotic but to two sensitive hotspots: Ahmedabad, where vicious inter-caste riots had turned into Hindu–Muslim communal riots; and Hussainiwala in Ferozepur district, Punjab, within eyesight of the India–Pakistan border, to honour the memory of Shaheed Bhagat Singh.

The visit to Ahmedabad was occasioned by the social turbulence caused by the stunning election victory in March 1985 of one of the ablest chief ministers of the Congress, Madhvasinh Solanki. Solanki had put together a 'KHAM' coalition – of Kshatriyas, Harijans, Adivasis and Muslims – and announced a number of affirmative schemes in favour of the Other Backward Classes (OBCs). While it was the upper castes who had initiated tensions and violence in the run-up to the elections, the vote ended with a three-quarters majority for the Congress. The defeated BJP-led opposition then converted a caste war into a communal conflagration that required the army to be sent in on 18 March.

The PM arrived on 23 March, five days later, and, after touring some of the worst affected areas, sternly ordered Solanki to put down the disturbances, failing which he would have to go, notwithstanding the huge victory he had just handed the Congress. I will never forget the pained expression on Solanki's face as he saw us off. Alas, Solanki was unable to tamp down the violence and was left with no alternative but to resign in July 1985. Historians might date the rise of the BJP in the state, and the rise in the nation some thirty years later of Narendra Modi, to Solanki's resignation and the consequent collapse of KHAM. But this also signalled Rajiv Gandhi's policy of zero tolerance for religious intolerance.

From Ahmedabad, we went on to Punjab, much against the advice of the PM's security advisers, in view of Indira Gandhi's assassination and the anti-Sikh pogrom that followed it. All, however, went well – indeed, exceedingly well – with the PM publicly extending a hand of compromise to the disillusioned Akali Dal leaders. I listened open-mouthed to his speech on the anniversary of Shaheed Bhagat Singh's martyrdom. It contained no bitterness about his mother's killing but was full of sincerity in reassuring the Sikh community that they were a highly valued part of India.

On our return, a well-known Sikh journalist, Satinder Singh, visited me to register his disgust at what he called Rajiv Gandhi's 'hypocrisy'. I heard him out without arguing but my own impression was different: the PM really wanted to, and indeed had, initiated a process of reconciliation with the community. Satinder was unconvinced. He rejected out of hand the significance of the PM's visit to Hussainiwala notwithstanding the risks involved. Yet, within a hundred days, RG would show that he was not given to empty gestures.[4]

But before his outreach to the Akalis became public, terrorists struck in Delhi on 11 May 1985. Eleven transistor bombs went off simultaneously in eleven different localities in what was clearly a premeditated, coordinated terrorist attack. I happened to be with the PM next morning when he called each of his Delhi MPs. Firmly and unambiguously, he told them that if there was even one incident of retaliation in their constituencies, he would hold the MP concerned personally responsible. Miraculously, calm was maintained even as negotiations with Sant Harchand Singh Longowal, president of the Akali Dal, were being initiated by Governor Arjun Singh in Punjab.[5]

Visits to the Soviet Union

Soon after, the PMO busied itself preparing for the PM's first major visit abroad, to the Soviet Union. I had nothing to do with the visit, but was invited

---

[4] Narendra Modi as PM planned a similar visit to the martyr's memorial in Hussainiwala. in 2022. He baulked at moving ahead when his car-cade faced a farmers' agitation. He cancelled the visit and returned to New Delhi. My reaction to this cowardice, in contrast to RG's courage, may be seen at this book's website by scanning the QR code on p. 317.

[5] See Arjun Singh, *A Grain of Sand in an Hourglass of Time: An Autobiography*, Hay House, New Delhi, July 2021.

to attend a final briefing on the eve of the trip. At the briefing, the PM suddenly asked me, sitting in a distant corner, whether I was not accompanying him on the trip. I said, 'No, sir,' and he moved on. Then, as the meeting ended, he again said, 'I think you should come along.'

I was thrilled but my excitement was short-lived because after the meeting Sharada Prasad shot down the possibility of going along because he said I should be busying myself drafting speeches for the coming five-nation tour, including the US. I decided to acquiesce in Sharada's demurral, and buckled down to drafting half a dozen major speeches before the PM returned from the USSR. I was pretty chuffed with my efforts and proudly handed over my drafts to Sharada, taking care to also slip copies to Arun Singh.

A few days later, I was instructed by Sharada to sit in on a drafting session with Indira Gandhi's old warhorse, G. Parthasarathi, who took painfully long to dictate even the most banal sentence. Of my draft, there was no sign. I discovered I had been diddled out of Moscow and was going to be diddled out of the next trip as well.

Next stop: Cyclone-hit Bangladesh

RG's next trip, however, turned out to be not to Washington, but via Dhaka to a remote *char* (flood-prone islet) offshore. I had insisted on calling the PM while he was still in Kyrgyzstan (on Tavleen's suggestion – the snafu with her was yet to take place) to propose, in light of the cyclone that had devastated coastal Bangladesh, that he detour to our eastern neighbour before landing in India; I thought that would make a dramatic impact. The detour did not happen but the outcome of my intervention was a visit in early June to Bangladesh's worst-hit areas, along with President Jayawardene of Sri Lanka.

On the evening before the trip, I happened to be with the PM when the FS dropped in to enquire what aid or assistance he would want to announce in Dhaka. To everyone's astonishment, the PM replied, 'Nothing. You can announce what you like before I arrive, but I only want to demonstrate our solidarity with the affected people.' I was most impressed. Here was a truly different prime minister, who wanted India's contribution to be measured not in dollars or tonnes but in the scale of India standing by a neighbour in its hour of need.

As we took off for Dhaka, the PM came into our cabin and said he wanted to use the flight to read through the text of the speech he would be making to the US Congress. The Sharada–Parthasarathi draft was produced, titled 'First Draft'. Like a magician pulling a rabbit out of a hat, RG produced a paper and said, 'Since that one is headed "First Draft", let's call this one "Draft Zero" and work on it.' It was my draft! I was back in business.

The five-nation tour (June 1985)

On the eve of our departure a few days later on the five-nation tour that comprised Cairo, Paris, Algiers, Washington, DC/Houston and Geneva, Sonia Gandhi agreed to give her first-ever interview to Pushpa Bharati of the Hindi newsmagazine *Dharmayug*. The editor, K.L. Nandan, was there, as was the prime minister. I was not involved, being politely excluded at, I suspect, Sonia Gandhi's instance.

Late that night, at about 11 p.m. while I was finishing up at the PMO, Nandan rang to say he had forgotten to ask one key question: 'Did the prime minister believe in God?' I replied that it was far too late in the night to trouble the PM, but I was certain he didn't because he was a modern, rational, intelligent man. Next morning, as the engines were revving up, I went into the PM's cabin and informed him of the answer I had given. He was astonished. 'But I do believe in God!' he exclaimed. I rushed into the cockpit and demanded to be connected to the tower. Someone came on the line, and I asked him to take down Nandan's number and convey my urgent message: 'Rajiv Gandhi believes in God.' And then we were off into the blue, blue skies!

I carry but one memory of our one-day stopover in Cairo. The PM was taken to the museum, the rest of us shuffling along in his wake. We came upon a mummy wrapped cosily in its shroud with its eyes firmly closed. My only thought was, 'You lucky thing. You've been asleep for five thousand years and I have not had a wink in weeks.'

Next stop, Paris. We had great fun at the Festival of India on the Trocadero and it was pleasing to hear the PM read at UNESCO the speech I had drafted. From there, we went to Algiers (where, to our horror, we learnt the Algerian authorities, as a measure of abundant caution, had locked up all the Sikhs!) and I was able to show off my French, translating questions and answers at the PM's press conference. We then landed in Washington, DC, for the pièce de résistance, the grand State visit.

There I was told of the concern in the Indian press corps about which six journalists would be allowed into the US president's banquet. With his vast experience, Sharada refused to let himself be dragged into this witches' brew and I, in all innocence, volunteered for it. I said two of the six places would, of course, go to the two agencies, PTI and UNI, leaving four spots. These, I suggested, might best be filled by the editors accompanying the prime minister. I had noted in my mind that, by happy coincidence, these four editors comprised a Sikh (Rahul Singh), a Muslim (M.J. Akbar), a communist (R.K. Mishra) and Narendra Mohan (a deeply believing Hindu), the owner-editor of the widely read *Dainik Jagran.* Together, they could project at the banquet table the composite face of India.

There was an angry growl of protest. To calm things down, I said it was after all a banquet and there would be nothing more newsworthy to report than the speeches of the two leaders, which would be covered by the agencies. As the state banquet was to be followed by a violin concert, all that remained for me was to check – ha, ha – if there was a music critic among the assembled press corps. At this point, the American liaison lady intervened to exclaim, 'Oh, there'll be dancing too.' Balu of the *Hindu*, who was possibly the seniormost of the Indian press corps in Washington (he had served for years with PTI, before being picked up by the *Hindu*) gave vent to his acute dissatisfaction with my selection.

I then made one of the biggest mistakes of my life. I chided him – witty, witty me – 'So, you want to dance with Nancy Reagan?' That broke up the meeting, but the consequences of my sarcasm were not long in coming. The press corps went in a body to complain to Ambassador Bajpai and also to Sharada Prasad. I was haunted by the thought that this was the end of the line for me, and I had screwed up a great opportunity. But on our last stop in the US in Houston, Arun Singh told me to forget about the rumpus. It was par for the course. I was partially reassured.

Vice President Bush accompanied Rajiv Gandhi in the US president's plane, Air Force One, on the last leg of the US visit, DC–Houston. The rest of the delegation, including my successor in the North America Division who had been on the advance team, followed in the PM's Air India plane. After the brief visit to space laboratories in the city, we were to fly to Geneva where the PM was scheduled to address the ILO. As we drove to the departure lounge of Houston airport, I heard my successor at the North America desk, Siddharth Singh, enquire about his luggage that had been sent on earlier in the PM's aircraft. He was parting ways with the rest of the group and flying to Ottawa. The assistant confessed he had forgotten to offload it from the PM's plane. Siddharth was furious: he was due to fly to the meeting in Ottawa of the India–Canada Joint Commission, an important meeting.

The Government of India had decided the previous year (1984) to freeze relations with Canada because of the Canadians' reluctance to deal with Khalistani terrorists based in their country. It was only the bomb attack on Margaret Thatcher in Brighton earlier in the month Indira Gandhi had been assassinated (although the two were unrelated) that brought the Canadians to their senses, and they started making amends. The meeting of the India–Canada Joint Commission – one of the last things that I arranged in my time at the MEA – was the first sign of a thaw in that relationship.

Siddharth was naturally upset; he couldn't possibly attend this important event in the clothes in which he was standing. From Ottawa, he was booked to fly back to India by an Air India flight from Montreal. Instead, he decided to fly to Geneva first, and personally collect his baggage, which had been dropped off there, before returning home. Meanwhile, the flight on which he had been booked out of Montreal – the *Kanishka* – had on board a terrorist bomb that exploded as it was approaching Ireland. The assistant's negligence saved Siddharth's life. Another instance of Yama (the Hindu messenger of death) not calling before the appointed hour.

We landed in Geneva and were lodged in the fancy Beau Rivage hotel. For security reasons, the Swiss authorities decided that the PM would be safest at the ambassador's residence several kilometres out of the city along the lake. Next morning, I got an urgent summons to see the PM. I feared that this might be to tell me I had been dismissed from the PMO, for the sin of having ribbed the Indian press corps. The PM suggested that we take a stroll on the lawns. Once we were outside, he whispered that he thought the Swiss might have bugged the ambassador's home. I wondered why my imminent sacking was a secret that needed to be withheld from the Swiss eavesdroppers.

Once out on the open lawn came the explanation. At the state banquet in

Washington, DC, Reagan had informed Rajiv Gandhi that he had decided, as a personal gesture of friendship, to release from detention Rajiv's childhood friend, Adil Shahryar Khan. Adil Shahryar was the son of Mohammad Yunus, a nephew of the Frontier Gandhi. Yunus had refused to move to Pakistan at Partition and had been accommodated in the IFS. Adil had been caught red-handed in an insurance fraud that might have led to great loss of life at sea. As a special gesture of goodwill, Reagan used his presidential powers to pardon the offender.

Rajiv Gandhi was deeply worried that news of this would reach India before we did, and he would be put on the mat by the press who would demand to know why the prime minister had not pressed the US president to release many other Indians held on far less serious charges. What, he asked me, was he to do? I replied that the PM had missed the beat. I said he should have told Reagan, 'Mr President, I represent a developing country. You, sir, represent a developing civilization!' For the president had not reckoned with the sensitivity of the Indian PM's delicate position on this issue. RG laughed, all tension gone. The question he was apprehensive about was never, in fact, posed. Adil Shahryar passed away soon after his release.

My dismissal was not even tangentially on the cards. But the relentless attack on me in the press continued for several weeks with the *Hindu* even taking me on editorially by name. I survived but remained a media target for the rest of Rajiv Gandhi's term.

Rural tours

After this, the PM embarked on visits to the geographic and social periphery of India. For his first visit to the tribal areas of Madhya Pradesh, the PM dropped everyone but me from his entourage, even the amiable Vincent George. We stayed in modest forest and dak bungalows except for one night in the historic Jahaz Mahal at Mandu. Congressmen were intrigued at the presence of this IFS officer on domestic tours.

My principal task was to take notes of the PM's encounters with ordinary villagers to ensure follow-up action on return. I was also charged with collecting the hundreds of written petitions with which the PM would be swamped on these tours, and, on return, sorting these out, collating them and sending them on to a large secretariat located in Rail Bhawan – which I never saw but was told housed a number of clerks with considerable linguistic diversity and experience who would pass them on to the right authorities. I personally took charge of the few requests or complaints that the PM had flagged; for the rest, I left it to the secretariat to process. On the whole, the system worked well as we received few complaints of there being little or no meaningful follow-up.

But this might well have been an illusion. The PM explained to me how, as a backbencher, he had often wondered what became of the thousands of petitions thrust eagerly into his mother's hands as she went through the ritual of the morning '*darshan*' – the round of meeting people gathered in her garden that she undertook as an earnest duty at the start of the day's work. RG said he decided to walk behind her to find out. She would very briefly interact with each petitioner, take the petition from his or her hands, then pass it on to R.K. Dhawan who walked a few steps behind her, and then move on to the next petitioner.

As RG had positioned himself to the rear of Dhawan, he had a clear view of the petitioners' expression as Indiraji walked up to them. The petitioners' eyes would light up in anticipation, their hands coming together in a respectful 'namaste'; they would mumble a few words while handing over the petition, then step back with a beatific expression as Mrs Gandhi went on to the next person. What struck Rajiv was that the petitioners rarely had any expectation that their requests would actually be fulfilled. The petitioners were content that the very busy prime minister had taken a few seconds off to listen to their woes; they had experienced a moment to treasure with the prime minister.

The point of this story, RG emphasized, was to understand that while his mother's generation were content with *sunwai* (a hearing), the new generation expected not just a hearing but results as well. My job was to ensure that petitioners were informed that their request was under process – and with whom – even if ultimately there were reasons why the request could not be met. This stress on a 'responsive administration' became the core rationale for his Panchayati Raj, that is, participatory democracy at the grassroots, as the only way of ensuring inclusive governance for inclusive development. All this, of course, evolved over time and did not spring full-blown from his head in the first year. But from the very start, these tours were never acts of 'rural tourism'. Rather, they were tours of self-instruction and systemic rectification that eventually led to the conceptualization of Panchayati Raj.

Of this initial tour of the tribal areas of Madhya Pradesh, then chief minister Motilal Vohra has often since laughingly complained that although he talked to me until dawn broke, he was unable to get a commitment that his state would get the massive financial package RG had allegedly pledged when he was no more than a general secretary in the Congress. Note was also taken of the budding friendship between me and the young, thirty-four-year-old Madhya Pradesh party president, Digvijaya Singh. So much so, that when I returned to Delhi, Madhavrao Scindia, Digvijaya's deadly rival in state politics, asked me to dinner only to warn me against the 'machinations' of Digvijaya.

This was followed by a visit to the perennially drought-ridden Kalahandi region in Odisha. There RG announced an innovative 'area development package' to encourage the cultivation of hardy ragi, which was more suitable for the region instead of water-guzzling rice. This transition from rice to ragi was to be achieved by heavily subsidizing the price of rice for household consumption, helping to wean the farmer from growing thirsty paddy in a rain-shadow area.

This model not only operated in Kalahandi for years, but also became the model by which other coarse cereals (jowar/bajra), pulses and oilseeds were encouraged in rain-deficient areas in the rest of the country. One of the enduring but not oft-mentioned successes of the Rajiv Gandhi era was the 'Technology Mission for Oilseeds' that resulted in the doubling of oilseeds output over the 1980s. This was an extraordinarily important contribution to our balance of payments since edible oil was second only to crude oil in our overall imports. However, this steady, sustained increase in oilseeds output virtually ended with RG and edible oil still remains amongst the top four in India's list of imports.

The night we landed in the Kalahandi area, someone informed RG that the tribal populace was distressed they had not been there to welcome him at the helipad. He sent me off in the pitch dark to make enquiries. When we woke the sleeping inhabitants to ask what happened, it turned out that they were more disappointed at having been denied a glimpse of the *udan khatola* (the magic flying palanquin of legend) than at not seeing Rajiv Gandhi! I settled that by assuring them that the next morning they would be taken to see the *udan khatola* rise into the skies from the helipad. They sounded gratified and did not enquire whether they would also be seeing the PM. When I informed RG of this, he did not feel slighted – only amused.

We then found ourselves in the arid deserts of Rajasthan, where Rajiv Gandhi began conceiving his plans for 'drought-proofing'. In the two following years, Rajasthan suffered its two worst successive droughts since Independence. After gruelling road journeys where I would get off the advance jeep covered in dust and sweat, the PM would immediately go into a huddle with senior ministers of the state and their top officers to discuss the details of the drought relief required. He never seemed to need rest or even give himself the luxury of a wash. RG's purpose was first-hand acquaintance with the problems on the ground. The PM ensured more funds were sanctioned for relief and 'drought-proofing' in Rajasthan than in all the previous forty years put together.

This was the basic approach he adopted in the following year, 1986, when the climatic phenomenon known as El Niño resulted in drought hitting several states of India. The PM visited each of these states, drove around by road talking to the people, landed by helicopter at obscure, hidden locations, and generally acquainted himself with ground conditions, before convening ministers and officers in the evening to discuss at length what needed to be done. The *Indian Express*, which was involved in a corporate war with Nusli Wadia, in which they thought the PM was leaning towards Wadia, satirized these tours without caring to understand what they were about. From this, they went on to be viciously critical of everything else the PM did. This peaked with their treatment of the Bofors story. So biased was their reporting that RG's school friend, Suman Dubey, decided to resign in protest against editor Arun Shourie, who was his brother-in-law.

The first Rajasthan tour was followed by a visit to the lovely fishing villages of Kerala, and its Silent Valley (saved from destruction by India's foremost environmentalist, Indira Gandhi) and then the wonders of Lakshadweep and Minicoy. It was there that one of RG's most telling initiatives, the Island Development Authority (IDA), was launched. It provided for all cabinet ministers concerned, few or none of whom had visited these islands, to, in turn, attend annual meetings of the IDA, alternately at Port Blair (Andamans) and at Kavaratti (Lakshadweep), to discuss schemes for the sustainable development of these island territories. In this exercise, he pulled in an environmentalist of note, Romi Khosla, who was a personal friend besides being a thorough professional much sought after by the UN.

A temporary move to Parliament House

When Parliament convened in July 1985 for the monsoon session, Gopi Arora called me in to say that I was required to shift my office to Parliament House, a door or two away from the PM's Parliament office, to be on call at a moment's notice. I suspected this was not because I enjoyed any special status with the PM, but because my duties were nebulous, unlike everyone else's.

At Parliament House, I discovered that my room was the most convenient waiting room for those calling on the PM; so, instead of twiddling my thumbs, I found myself entertaining the high and the mighty of the Congress establishment. It burnished my image as a confidant of Rajiv Gandhi (although I was there only in my capacity as the PMO's spare tyre!).

One of the more frequent visitors was Arjun Singh, then governor of Punjab. We hit it off largely because he was under the wholly mistaken impression that I could wheedle out of the government a crore or so for one of his favourite projects – Bharat Bhavan, a cultural complex in Bhopal. The Bhavan blossomed but my contribution was nil.

Punjab Accord

Then, I learnt why Arjun Singh was such a frequent visitor. On 24 July 1985, the PM announced in Parliament a settlement between the government and the Shiromani Akali Dal:

> About 20 minutes ago, Sant Harchand Singh Longowal and I have signed a Memorandum of Settlement. This will bring to an end a very difficult period through which the country has passed. It will be the beginning of a new phase of working together to build the country, to build unity and integrity in the country.[6]

The House erupted in thunderous applause and wild cheering as he proclaimed the 'Punjab Accord' to resolve an issue that had been burning

[6] *Rajiv Gandhi: Selected Speeches and Writings, 1984–85*, Vol. I, Publications Division, New Delhi, 1987, p. 38.

for seven years and had thus far defied all attempts by the best brains in the country to defuse it.

Tragically, less than a month later, on 20 August 1985, Rajiv Gandhi's forty-first birthday, Sant Harchand Longowal, was shot dead. Unfazed by this grim setback, just three days later, on 23 August, the prime minister announced in Parliament that elections would be held in Punjab, as provided for in the Accord, explaining as he did so that on the step he was taking 'hinges the fate of the democratic system in India'.[7]

He went on to underline his basic philosophy: 'How individual parties fare is of little consequence. It does not matter who wins and who loses. What matters is that the lamp of democracy is not extinguished, what matters is that India wins.'[8]

While I consider this one of his best speeches (I made no contribution to it), many of his Congress colleagues saw this as a squandering of the party's assets. It was clear that the Akali Dal, and not the Congress, would prevail at the polls. The nation was deeply impressed that national interest was being put above the party's but the knives were being sharpened in the PM's own camp. They were to be plunged into him the following year.

Assam Accord/ Mizoram Accord

Rajiv Gandhi believed the need of the hour was not public relations gestures but resolute action. This was seen not just in Punjab, or in his dealing of the Delhi terrorist attacks. I was in the audience on Independence Day when he proclaimed from the ramparts of the Red Fort:

> I am happy to tell you that last night, or, rather, today at 2.45 am, an agreement was signed between the Assam students and the Government of India. We hope that with the signing of the agreement, another element of tension [besides Punjab to which he had alluded earlier] will be removed and the country will be able to address itself to rapid development.[9]

---

[7] Ibid., p. 48.

[8] Ibid.

[9] Ibid., p. 47.

There appeared to be no end to the miracles the young PM could perform. In June the following year came the Mizoram Accord that ended twenty years of vicious insurgency and rendered Mizoram the most peaceful state of the Indian Union.

Bhutan, a major reshuffle and another multi-nation tour (September–October 1985)

At this stage, I went through a major health issue. On returning from the Punjab election tour, I found myself writhing in the throes of duodenal ulcers. After treatment, my doctor, seeing how keen I was to join the tour to Bhutan, allowed me to go, perhaps against his better medical judgement.

As we flew into Thimpu by helicopter from Hashimara, my troubles began again and by next evening in Paro I was so seriously ill that I passed out in the middle of the night. I recall the dread with which I crawled in the pitch dark from the bathroom to my bed, feeling my way along the freezing floor. I somehow recovered by mid-morning, but on returning to Delhi was sternly forbidden by my wife and doctor from joining the next tour to the UN, via London and Cuba.

Before embarking on that tour, the PM undertook the first of his frequent shake-ups of his ministerial team. The two most significant changes he made were to have a profoundly adverse impact on him politically, although no one foresaw this at the time. Both were disguised as 'promotions', not demotions. Arun Singh was dropped as parliamentary secretary to the PM and 'raised' to minister of state for defence. Arun Nehru was shifted from minister of state for power to minister of state for internal security in the home ministry. These changes sowed the seeds of Rajiv's eventual ouster. But all this was in the future.

At the time, it seemed like a routine ministerial reshuffle after a year in office, with Arun Nehru's decisive role in party affairs being given due recognition, and also as a sign of the PM's desire to be seen as independent of Arun Singh, who was widely believed to be his closest adviser. In any case, as RG retained the defence portfolio, Arun Singh's elevation from parliamentary secretary to minister of state to work directly under the PM in the defence ministry could be seen as a promotion (although Singh undoubtedly felt demoted from his earlier perceived position as the prime minister's eyes and ears). There was little to divine that either Arun would be as lacking in team spirit – I cannot put it more delicately – as events would prove.

The visit to London, Havana and New York went ahead. It was on that trip that, in London, Margaret Thatcher broke protocol to be present at Heathrow to receive Rajiv Gandhi. What made it even more memorable was the headline given by editor R.K. Karanjia of *Blitz*: 'Britannia waives the rules'!

Despite Mrs Thatcher's widely appreciated gesture, she and RG had serious differences over apartheid in South Africa. So serious that when RG went to his first event in Delhi on return, I heard him greet his minister, Margaret Alva, with the words, 'Nice Maggie!'

The Doon School Golden Jubilee

A few days on came the Golden Jubilee Founder's Day at our school to which the PM was invited as chief guest. RG, dressed in his old boy's blazer, was at his photogenic best but there was no want of carping critics who portrayed this as elitism at its worst. Indeed, I unwittingly contributed to some of the worst media mocking by sharing with RG my Hahn story about the Lamp of Knowledge on the breast pocket: 'A pity they didn't light it when you were at school.' Rajiv enjoyed the sally so much he included it in his Founder's Day address, being careful to preface it by saying the incident happened 'to a friend of mine'. But the humourless, scornful critics presumed Gandhi was speaking of himself!

My most vivid memory of this visit is, however, unrelated to the quip. The wife of J.A.K. Martyn, our headmaster, had recounted in her biography of Martyn the story of Pandit Jawaharlal Nehru's visit to the school in the mid-1950s to see his eleven-year-old grandson. Ms Martyn said Rajiv was nowhere to be found on the 72-acre Chandbagh estate. Then one boy said that when they played hide-and-seek, a favourite hiding place was the large wicker baskets kept for laundry in the bathrooms. Sure enough, Rajiv was found hiding in one of those – out of sheer embarrassment at having the headlights shone on him.

I asked RG if the story was true. He replied tangentially, saying it was not true that he did not have opinions, but he found that, if he expressed them, he would be sneered at either for parroting his grandfather or for not being in line with Nehru if they were different. So, he said, he had preferred to keep his opinions to himself. Hence, the dark room of the school's photography lab was the only place where he distinguished himself and where he could think his thoughts through. He just hated being thrust into the public eye.

Perhaps it was because he had contemplated national issues in this manner that when he suddenly burst upon the public scene, he arrived with so many innovative ideas.

Speechwriter to the PM

Soon after the Doon School jubilee, the PM added weightier matters to my somewhat ambiguous range of duties. RG was required to make public speeches, some major, mostly minor, that often ran to several a day. He was not satisfied with the quality of speeches drafted by various ministries and fine-tuned by sundry PMO officers. He wanted to centralize the function of speechwriting in one officer to impart an element of consistency and coherence to his spoken word.

The PM asked me to take on this position. I was thrilled. It gave me an operational niche and a platform to watch close up as the PM handled a bewildering variety of issues. It compelled me to bone up on and learn about numerous things where my knowledge ranged from sketchy to utterly deficient. Above all, it was a creative outlet.

My first job was a marginal involvement in the drafting of one of the most consequential speeches of RG's prime ministership: his address to the Congress centenary session at the Brabourne Stadium in Bombay on 28 December 1985. The draft had been under preparation for months in the capable hands of the additional secretary (PMO), Gopi Arora, under the overall direction of the two Aruns, Arun Singh and Arun Nehru. Many of us had been present when the PM rejected the first draft, precisely explaining the message he wanted to convey, essentially signalling a transformation of the 'old' politics to the 'new', especially in the moral dimension. The team had then produced a substantially altered version that more accurately reflected what he wanted to say.

There was little, therefore, for me to contribute other than getting an insight into the working of his mind. My main recollection is thus of a table tennis match, played as a break from the tensions of the drafting work, which pitted Arun Nehru and me against Arun Singh and RG. Our side was comprehensively defeated. The drafting process went on, however, even during the flight to Bombay.

At the centenary session, RG said: 'Millions of ordinary Congress workers are full of enthusiasm for the Congress policies and programmes. But they are handicapped, for on their backs ride the brokers of power and influence, who dispense patronage to convert a mass movement into a feudal oligarchy.'[10] It was a sensation. However, while RG's speech went down well with the general public, the wielders of influence in the party were disapproving. Girilal Jain, editor of the *Times of India*, sternly warned the prime minister that he was playing with fire in describing those who had spent a lifetime serving the party as 'brokers of power'.

The audience, ranging in their thousands around him, consisted precisely of these 'brokers of power'. The English-speaking middle class cheered but most of the Brabourne Stadium audience were not English-speaking. When they learnt the insults hurled at them, they turned against their leader even while thunderously applauding him. I was as guilty as anyone else in not having anticipated this, but we were far too buoyed by the enthusiastic reception to the speech by the drawing room middle class to notice that the praise came from those who habitually despised politicians and political parties, and not from those steeped in politics.

So no one in our team heeded Girilal Jain's prescient warning. It was a gamble by the PM. He did not consult any of the old school except Arun Nehru precisely because he was attempting to craft a type of politics very different from what had been in vogue until then. Perhaps he should have run his ideas past the Congress Working Committee (CWC), but had he listened to the veterans, the speech would have made no impression at all for it would have been along conventional lines.

From Bombay, RG and his family departed for a holiday in Ranthambore.

[10] *Rajiv Gandhi: Selected Speeches and Writings, 1984–85*, Vol. I, Publications Division, New Delhi, 1986, p. 85.

The country did not take well to this. They were not used to prime ministers taking vacations, however routine this might be in other democracies.

With V.P. Singh in Pakistan

A minor fallout for me of the centenary celebrations was a trip to Pakistan. V.P. Singh, finance and commerce minister, sidled up to where I was standing below the platform and asked whether I would accompany him to Pakistan, where he was shortly headed to tie up a trade agreement. He had heard that from Karachi I had written a paper, 'Towards a Revival of the Pakistan Economy' and made a speech on the potential benefits of a full-scale resumption of India–Pakistan trade titled 'An Indian View of the Pakistan Economy'. I was delighted at this possibility of revisiting all my old friends there but said the PM would have to approve. He said he would himself ask the PM. Happily, RG agreed.

We left for Islamabad in an Indian Air Force plane in early January 1986. The visit was most fruitful in terms of its objectives achieved. The Pakistan side were delighted to accept our suggestions to significantly augment our mutual trade. As something of a veteran of India–Pakistan encounters, I would hold that V.P. Singh's visit was not only one of the smoothest and most productive I have seen, but also a signal to the Pakistan establishment that the new prime minister wished to make a new beginning. RG later wondered aloud whether Indian ministers could not make it a practice to stop off in Pakistan on their way home from foreign tours. But this never happened. For my part, I had a most enjoyable time introducing V.P. Singh to my numerous friends in Islamabad and Karachi.

V.P. Singh was a curious case of contradictions. He was ruthlessly ambitious but quite eccentric. His son was at school with a cousin of my wife's and would generally air his view that his father's head was not quite screwed on right. For my part, I was extremely impressed initially with his apparently scrupulous integrity, especially in keeping fat cats at arm's distance as finance and commerce minister. And, of course, I remain grateful to him for the trust he reposed in me personally for what he believed was my expertise and experience in handling Pakistan.

My personal relations with him were cordial but those between RG and him broke down in 1987. VP resented being shifted from finance to defence in the wake of a raid his officers conducted on an industrialist, Lalit Thapar (that eventually led nowhere). VP took it that his move out of finance was on account of the Thapar raid. The PM held that tc lighten his load he needed to entrust the key portfolio of defence to someone senior and respected. I leave it to the reader to make what they he will of the real cause for the change of portfolio.

But immediately on moving from North to South Block, V.P. Singh began a witch-hunt, starting with a submarine deal with West Germany that had been concluded in Indira Gandhi's time. The PM objected. V.P. Singh resigned in April 1987 about three months after his change of portfolio, and then started a campaign to oust RG. He left the Congress and went on to create the National Front that won the election of November 1989, principally by his spreading the canard that he had in his pocket a chit on which was written the number of the Swiss bank account held in favour of Rajiv Gandhi which would put RG in jail within a fortnight of VP becoming PM.

That claim was revealed as hollow – so perhaps VP's protestations of being clean as a whistle were equally hollow. In any case, within eleven months of being sworn in as PM, V.P. Singh was thrown into the dustbin of history, failing to manage the numerous contradictions of which he claimed to be the 'master manager'. Had he remained true to his party, he might well have become the PM instead of P.V. Narasimha Rao after RG was assassinated. But hubris overcame him, and he will be best remembered as a prime minister who is not remembered.

The golden year ends

The Congress centenary celebrations marked the end of Rajiv Gandhi's golden year when every step he took attracted public approbation. There was some restiveness in the party because he seemed so willing to gift away state governments to non-Congress parties and, in some circles (read Arun Nehru), because of his refusal to touch tainted sources of party funds.

Over the next four years, RG's prime ministership was rocked by controversies that wrecked his reputation: Shah Bano; Babri Masjid; Brasstacks; the Indian Peace Keeping Force (IPKF); Bofors. Public disenchantment grew and significant sections of the party turned against him. Through all of these, I had no active role to play, but watched and wondered as a concerned citizen and a well-wisher of the prime minister. At the same time, the many constructive steps he took – including the Technology Missions, a beginning with economic reforms, the zonal cultural centres (ZCCs) and, above all, the constitutional amendments that brought in Panchayati Raj, in addition to his bold openings in foreign policy to China and Pakistan, as well as the presentation to the UN of his Action Plan for a Nuclear Weapons-Free and Non-violent World Order – did not receive the commendation they deserved.

The general impression that I was privy to everything that went on is completely erroneous. Because we had such a compartmentalized PMO, headed in each section by just about the best talent available in the civil services, there was little or no scope for individual officers to interfere in, or even get to know about, issues that were rocking the headlines but were none of their official business. In fact, because my own duties kept me so tied up, I hardly even got to study and absorb news stories and press comments. My non-involvement officially in almost all the issues that marked the Rajiv years, combined with my deep involvement in some of his innovative measures, particularly Panchayati Raj, means I am unable to give a personal account of how RG tackled his many crises – except in retrospect after studying the available papers.

That is why I have had to read up on and converse with those involved in the issues that led to Rajiv Gandhi's electoral defeat in 1989 (and the steps he took to prepare himself for the never-to-be second term). This has persuaded the publisher and me to write the companion volume, *The Rajiv I Knew, and Why He Was India's Most Misunderstood Prime Minister*, which is based on political analysis and research; therefore, they do not quite fit into these memoirs which are about my own experiences.

It is also astonishing to see how little of what RG was thinking on controversial issues actually entered the public domain. This was principally because he did not have an official spokesman to put out his line, but also because on controversies like Shah Bano and Bofors there is almost nothing on record of his personal rationale. Whatever I know of this has been picked up by eavesdropping on his private conversations with others and building on hints thrown out in passing conversations with me. This absence of effective public relations harmed Rajiv Gandhi.

I am convinced that it was this lack of proper press briefings on a daily basis that contributed in large measure to the vicious uncontested media attacks that he had to endure at the hands of an extremely biased media – uncontested because the PMO did not believe in polemical contestation with the press. Also, the PM himself did not avail of the opportunity he could easily have created of fireside chats on radio that would reach hundreds of millions, or personal appearances on TV to present his point of view on deeply contested matters.

Although I was little involved in the ups and downs of the PM's political life, I was struck by the quiet confidence with which he conducted himself through this time, concentrating on the issue at hand, and not letting triumph or tribulation disturb his attention span. Life at the PMO flowed on at an easy, steady pace. We got on with the job. The turbulence was in the headlines.

Shah Bano, Babri and Bofors

Even though I wasn't directly involved in Prime Minister Rajiv Gandhi's three biggest domestic crises, I want to write a little about them here and in more detail in the companion volume. I believe he was innocent of the allegations and charges made against him, charges that continue to stain his reputation. Let me begin with the Shah Bano controversy and then proceed to the fracas over the opening of the locks at the Babri Masjid, concluding with the Bofors contretemps.

Other controversies – such as the unravelling of his accord with Sant Longowal on Punjab and the rumpus over Operation Brasstacks, and the disaster of the IPKF's deployment in Sri Lanka – are dealt with in the companion volume. The Sikh pogrom in the immediate aftermath of his being sworn in as PM has been dealt with at some length earlier in these memoirs (pp. 248–53). I would, however, caution critics, of whom there are bound to be many, that the following paragraphs are merely a summary. It would be best if they would have the patience to await the companion volume before opening up their guns. Of course, that is their choice.

The basic question that endures is: If Rajiv Gandhi was blameless, why have these controversies stuck to him, through all these years? First, he knew his hands were clean – and believed this would eventually be established, as it was after more than a decade of persecution in the guise of prosecution. In this, he underestimated the public fascination with political sensationalism. Also, as I have said earlier, no attempt was made to deal with why he was thinking and acting as he did either through press briefings or press conferences or even party statements. He also did not allow me and others concerned to elaborate on the controversies in drafting his speeches or party documents like the Congress manifestos of 1989 and 1991. He seems to have believed that it was enough to have the issues debated and sorted out in parliamentary debate. In doing so, he seemed not to have reckoned with Parliament proceedings receiving scant attention after the Emergency whereas, in Nehru's time, newspapers assigned their best correspondents to the Parliament beat and regularly devoted at least a full page to what was happening in both Houses.

Shah Bano

In April 1985, the Supreme Court awarded maintenance to a divorced Muslim woman, Shah Bano, under the vagrancy provisions of the Criminal Procedure Code, overruling the processes of divorce settlement provided for in the sharia, or Muslim Personal Law. To almost everyone in the country, it appeared self-evident that if an aged woman is abandoned by her uncaring husband, it follows that the husband must be brought to account. That 'obvious' conclusion has clouded all discussion on the steps Rajiv Gandhi took to resolve the conundrum with which he was faced.

These steps essentially involved long personal discussions with individuals and groups who were agitated (one way or the other) by the subject, including Muslim MPs who spoke eloquently and forcefully over a six-month period in Parliament on the subject, such as the polar opposites, Arif Mohammad Khan and Z.R. Ansari; leaders of the Opposition, particularly the leader in the Lok Sabha, Madhu Dandavate; civil society activists of different persuasions; feminist groups; jurists of eminence, beginning with the highly reputed law minister Asoke Sen; students, journalists, opinion makers and a miscellany of others. RG's moves were not dictated by M.J. Akbar, as is often wrongly portrayed, but through a nationwide, objective appraisal of the situation.

Above all, he deeply pondered the shariat provisions on marriage and divorce. Liberal and Hindutva opinion joined hands in portraying the shariat laws as barbaric remnants of desert existence in seventh-century Arabia that disregarded the rights of women, particularly divorced Muslim women. The PM, on the other hand, came to the conclusion that the shariat in this regard was far from barbarous.

The shariat in Islamic law made elaborate and equitable arrangements for the economic security of divorced Muslim women by devolving this responsibility on the male members of her family of birth. If this were to fail, the relevant state's Waqf Board was charged with maintaining the divorcee, at least until the woman got married again, which, one survey showed, happened within two years in 78 per cent of the cases studied.[11] The fault lay not in the shariat per se but in the fact that only mullahs, muftis and maulanas could interpret the shariat and only petty local clerics were charged with implementing the provisions. RG believed that the answer, therefore, did not lie in rejecting the shariat, but in incorporating its provisions in our jurisprudence, so that interpretation and implementation were placed in the hands of our civil courts. To this end, the law minister in May 1986 introduced and had passed the Muslim Women (Protection of Rights on Divorce) Bill which sought to bring within the ambit of India's civil law the processes of maintenance decreed in the shariat, with the additional provision of the magistrate being authorized to 'order' the relevant state's Waqf Board to look after divorced Muslim women who were neglected by the male members of their family of birth.

Critics described this as unwarranted 'appeasement' to garner minority votes. But this reconciliation of Muslim Personal Law and the nation's civil law was accepted by hard-core Muslim MPs and the community as a whole, including Muslim clerics and theologians, as a solution that both respected the constitutional right of all Indians (both majority and minorities) to their respective personal laws and the humanitarian need to ensure that no woman was inhumanly abandoned to her fate.

Nevertheless, a renowned leftist Muslim lawyer and jurist, Daniyal Latifi, filed a writ petition in the Supreme Court in September 1986, four months after the passage of the Act, challenging its legitimacy. The 2001 judgment of the Supreme Court on this writ petition commended the former prime minister for giving effect to the 1985 Supreme Court judgment while meeting

[11] Abusaleh Shariff and Syed Khalid, 'Unimportance of Triple Talaq', *The Indian Express*, 29 May 2017.

the concerns of the Muslim community. In particular, the Supreme Court's 2001 judgment held that no fundamental rights of divorced Muslim women had been abrogated by the Act of 1986.

Yet, Rajiv Gandhi has been portrayed – and continues to be portrayed – as pandering to backward-looking clerics to keep the Muslim vote bank with the Congress ('minority appeasement').

RG remarked to me in passing:

> Where was the electoral advantage to me in all this? I knew I would be losing many of those who had supported me until then and giving an impetus to those who opposed me. I still went ahead to preserve the secular ethos of our nation. According to my opponents, half the electorate – women, whether Muslim or non-Muslim – will vote against me for this. So will men of all other faiths. So too will those Muslim men who regard themselves as 'modern' or 'liberal'. That leaves only Muslim clerics and the hidebound orthodox on my side. So who am I appeasing?

That perhaps best explains his rationale. What remains unexplained is why he restricted his views to personal asides instead of making them the core of a blistering attack on those who bitterly opposed him (which, in effect, was virtually everybody). Had I been his press adviser or spokesman, that is what I would have advised.

Babri Masjid

Next only to Shah Bano in the denigration of the former PM is the shadow of the Babri Masjid issue. In October 1985, Arun Nehru was made minister of state for internal security. This was widely seen as evidence of his huge political clout. *India Today* of 31 October 1985 described him as 'the fastest rising star in the firmament of Rajiv Gandhi's government'.

After the resignation of Narayan Datt Tiwari as chief minister of Uttar Pradesh on his being elevated to the Union cabinet, Arun Nehru personally picked and promoted the relatively unknown Vir Bahadur Singh as the state's chief minister in September 1985. There was, said *India Today* (31 October 1985), an 'awed realization' of Arun Nehru's hold over party affairs. For his part, Arun Nehru believed that the best route to winning the Hindu vote was by opening the locks that had been placed in December 1949 on the gates leading to the Babri Masjid. This sixteenth-century mosque had become the focus of a localized dispute over ownership rights dating back to the mid-nineteenth century, based on the claim that the mosque had been built on the birthplace of Lord Ram – Ram Janmabhoomi. At the time (1985), this local dispute had no national reverberations despite the gates being locked up thirty-five long years earlier. But Arun Nehru, with his local roots, having studied at a Lucknow school and college in proximity to Ayodhya, had an awareness of the potential of this issue that barely registered, to begin with, on Rajiv Gandhi's consciousness.

The new chief minister visited Ayodhya in December 1985 and stirred up a hornets' nest by ordering that all files relating to the closure of the gates be reviewed. Meanwhile, a case was filed by a private party before the sessions judge, Faizabad, to reopen the locks. The gravamen of his plea was that the locks had been placed in December 1949 by executive rather than judicial order. The sessions judge scheduled an immediate hearing; after the local police and district magistrate testified they did not apprehend a law and order problem if the locks were opened, the sessions judge ordered their reopening. Within minutes of the order being passed in Faizabad, the locks at Ayodhya, closed for over thirty-five years, were broken open and, in what appeared to be an orchestrated move, huge numbers of Hindu devotees poured into the masjid premises. Clearly, the administration was in cohorts with the district sessions court.

The judgment was quickly challenged by a private Muslim party before the Uttar Pradesh High Court, and the state government impleaded itself into the court proceedings. For the saffron forces, wilting in the penumbra after their massive defeat in the 1984 elections, this was the opportunity to stir the communal cauldron to make a political comeback.

It has since been held by most public opinion that it was at the PM's behest that the locks were opened, whereas RG maintained that he was completely in the dark about this conspiracy to open the locks and learnt about it only after it was an accomplished fact. There has always been intense speculation as to how such a momentous change in the status quo could have been undertaken without his knowledge and explicit sanction. Commentators reasoned then – and their argument continues till today, nearly four decades later – that Rajiv

Gandhi, having got the Muslim vote in his kitty through the Shah Bano matter, had now decided to also grab the Hindu vote bank by opening the locks at Ayodhya. RG always maintained that he had no prior information about what Arun Nehru was up to, and this is confirmed by Wajahat Habibullah in his *My Years with Rajiv: Triumph and Tragedy* (Westland, New Delhi, 2020).

There was no executive order by which the PM could reverse the order to open the locks since it was a judicial order. Huge communal tension would have built up had he gone to the High Court. In any case, a petition against the sessions judge's order had already been filed in the High Court and was soon followed by the Sunni Waqf Board and the government of Uttar Pradesh impleading themselves as affected parties. But going to the courts is invariably a time-consuming business.

So the PM ordered an internal party enquiry into the respective roles of Arun Nehru and M.L. Fotedar in the imbroglio. The enquiry exonerated Fotedar but pinned the responsibility on Arun Nehru. Accordingly, Arun Nehru was first sidelined and then dropped summarily from the Council of Ministers in October 1986. For him to fall so precipitately within a year of being hailed as the power behind Rajiv Gandhi's throne was punishment enough. Indeed, he had had a heart attack at Dachigam in Kashmir in April 1986 and the first sign that all was not well between him and his cousin was that the PM pointedly declined to go to his bedside and sent just his physician instead. (There was also Arun Nehru's nefarious interference in the Bofors matter, touched upon in the next section on Bofors, and further elaborated in the companion volume.)

Once the immediate kerfuffle was over, it seemed through most of the succeeding two and a half years (mid-1986 to end 1988) that the political turbulence over Babri Masjid–Ram Janmabhoomi simmered rather than boiled over. It was only once V.P. Singh's National Front emerged as a strong contender for the 1989 elections that its partner, the BJP, stoked the dispute into a national matter. By 1989, it was evident that the issue was going to play a major role in determining the outcome at the hustings.

At this point R.K. Dhawan was brought into the PMO. Also, Sheila Dikshit was appointed minister of state for parliamentary affairs, with an office in the PMO and became the channel through which partisan party considerations began flowing into decision-making. Moreover, the firewall provided by Gopi Arora was absent as he had been shifted out of the PMO in late 1987. The political advisers were brought in because it was believed that it was their absence from the scene over the past four years that was the precise reason for the growing dissidence in the party and Rajiv Gandhi's tumbling image in the media and public opinion. As Suneet had warned us, with Dhawan's entry, things really changed. Once decision-making in policy got entangled with party and electoral considerations, the PM's standing only deteriorated further.

The most egregious example was the *shilanyas* (ground-breaking and foundation stone-laying ceremony) at the Ram Janmabhoomi site in the middle of the election at the behest of the Dhawan–Fotedar duo; it did nothing to attract the hard Hindu vote to the PM but definitively alienated Muslim and left–liberal opinion. While the PM's own commitment to not allow the demolition of the mosque remained firm and consistent, the *shilanyas* he arranged amounted to imitation of the saffron forces and appeasement of the majority community. He stepped on to the ground prepared by the Opposition and the rationale of his action (saving the mosque but promising a grand temple) was lost on those who wanted the mosque gone and even on those who desperately wanted the mosque saved. It was a classic case of being hoist by his own petard – and the persons fundamentally responsible for this were the 'politicos' inducted into the PMO in early 1989 to allegedly lend political heft to the PM.

Yet, at the end of the day, only Rajiv Gandhi was responsible for accepting irresponsible advice that was anathema to his moral principles and enduring belief in secularism. Because he imitated the Opposition instead of confronting them, all his many positive initiatives were lost in the electoral tornado that blew across the country. It was the only time I saw him looking shaken and jaded, his normal self-confidence and smiling demeanour having deserted him. He knew he was fighting a losing battle.

What conclusion does one draw from this sad tale? Had Rajiv Gandhi stuck to his basic values and fought the 1989 elections on his secular convictions and his many constructive nation-building initiatives, such as Panchayati Raj, and not allowed himself to be led to fighting the elections on turf prepared by his opponents, he might have prevailed. Of course, he would have lost his commanding lead of 1984 but would probably have emerged in end 1989 with a majority, however slight. By allowing himself to be misled by Dhawan & Co – for which, of course, he had only himself to blame – he allowed calumny to triumph over constructive nation-building. He also opened the door to the majoritarianism and authoritarianism now being inflicted on the nation.

Perhaps neither hubris nor assassination would have overwhelmed him had he not had such a large and assured parliamentary majority on becoming prime minister. A humbler victory in 1984 may have made him more cautious and circumspect, and more obliged to consult sidelined party veterans. But that was not how it turned out – and he eventually paid with his life.

Bofors

On 16 April 1987, a Swedish radio broadcast alleged that the Swedish arms manufacturer Bofors had paid substantial bribes into a number of Swiss bank accounts to secure a large order – in fact, the largest single order – from India for armaments. The story goes back to January 1985 when the newly elected prime minister declared that middlemen and their commissions would be banned in all defence deals. The announcement was widely applauded. However, a coterie of Congressmen led by Arun Nehru, the party's principal fundraiser, were upset at this rejection of their strategy of eschewing small domestic donations and replacing them with a grand creaming-off of international defence deals.

Later that year, the PM would meet President François Mitterrand and Prime Minister Olof Palme, the heads of government of the two main competitors – Sofma of France and Bofors of Sweden – involved in the forthcoming Howitzer deal. His aim was to emphasize at the highest level his message of 'no middlemen' at the highest level. While some observers portrayed these parleys as an elaborate feint, party dissidents, led by one mysterious 'N', hatched elaborate plots to ensure that the winning bidder paid them their *hafta* (colloquial Hindi for 'share' or 'bribe').

As part of this, an agreement for commercial espionage was signed in November 1985 between Bofors and 'Bob' Wilson of AE Services who was a long-standing clandestine collaborator of Martin Ardbo, managing director of Bofors. This clandestine agreement became operational two weeks after the two prime ministers had announced that all agents and intermediaries must be called off to facilitate a straightforward contract between the Government of India and the competitor offering the better deal. The arrangement was for AE Services to conduct industrial sabotage at rival Sofma to keep Bofors ahead in the negotiations but under two rather unusual conditions: that AE's commission of some $35 million would be paid only if Bofors were awarded the contract before 31 March 1986; and the payment would be in five instalments of around $7 million each simultaneous with the five payments from the Indian government.

Bofors were in fact awarded the contract a week before the expiry of the deadline of 31 March 1986. This might have been considered a coup de main but was in fact the inevitable consequence of the finance minister having to accommodate the unprecedentedly high payments to Bofors in his forthcoming budget by the last day of March. The budget had to be discussed and passed at the resumed sitting of Parliament the following month (April 1986). The deadline of 31 March had not been arbitrarily but deliberately chosen bearing in mind our well-known and long-established parliamentary procedures with respect to the tabling and passage of the budget after due debate.

Accordingly, the first instalment of AE Services' dues, amounting to some $7 million, was paid into a Swiss account designated by them in September 1986, following the payout by the Government of India in August 1986 of the first advance instalment for the Bofors guns. Then, abruptly, the payments to AE stopped and were never resumed, although some $28 million remained due. This coincided with Arun Nehru's fall from grace and his removal from the Council of Ministers in October 1986. I leave it to the reader to connect the dots.

The next stage in the drama arose out of a Swedish parliamentary committee investigation into the shenanigans of Ardbo, Bofors and AE Services in a Middle Eastern defence deal. A sidelight was the revelation that Bofors had made several payments into secret bank accounts in Switzerland that might have a connection to the Howitzer deal with India. Swedish Radio latched on to this and broadcast the story that opened Pandora's box.

Prime Minister Rajiv Gandhi promptly requested the Swedish authorities to investigate the matter. It needs to be underlined that the Swedes undertook the investigation neither suo motu nor because of media sensationalism nor the demands of India's Opposition, but at the express request of India's prime minister, conveyed through proper diplomatic channels. Why would a guilty

PM have sought an investigation in a foreign land over which he would have no control unless he knew he was innocent? He also set up a Joint Parliamentary Committee (JPC), which included prominent leaders of the Opposition, to jointly investigate the alleged scam. Finding themselves unable to prove their allegations and innuendos, the Opposition, at the last stage, boycotted further proceedings. The final JPC report cleared Rajiv Gandhi and his government of all charges. (A dissent note prepared by one member was annexed to the report.)

Yet, sections of the media and the Opposition continued to allege that the government and the PM in particular were covering up a major scandal involving the payment of Rs 64 crore as bribes. They received a boost when in April 1989 the comptroller and auditor general (CAG)'s report was leaked to the press. These findings were at sharp variance with the JPC findings and should, according to set procedure, have been vetted by Parliament's Public Accounts Committee (PAC), chaired invariably by a leader of the Opposition, where indicted persons are given the opportunity for clarifying matters. Only thereafter are the findings made public and the report is debated on the floor of the House. Instead of allowing this standard procedure to move forward, almost the entire Opposition resigned their seats in the Lok Sabha, which meant that there was no PAC to examine this report and therefore, it was not properly examined in Parliament. The CAG, T.N. Chaturvedi, was rewarded by the BJP with a seat in Parliament and a major governorship thereafter.

The Opposition's moment finally came when V.P. Singh became PM after the elections of November 1989. In the debate on 28 December 1989 Rajiv Gandhi, by then leader of the Opposition, demanded of the new PM that all the files on Bofors in the PMO be placed on the table of the House. Why, I wondered, would RG insist on papers that might establish his guilt be made public? Unless, of course, he knew that he was completely innocent of all the allegations levelled against him by the Opposition and a vicious media over the previous two and a half years.

The V.P. Singh government through its additional solicitor general, Arun Jaitley, presented the Swiss authorities with the required letter rogatory in February 1990 to access all the information they sought on the Bofors matter. The letter rogatory was, however, rejected by the Swiss authorities in July

1990 for the casual and incorrect (indeed, farcical) manner in which it was presented. The V.P. Singh government began tottering a month later and fell on 7 November 1990. Rajiv Gandhi, the target of the VP government and the butt of all their propaganda, was assassinated a few months later. With his death, all further proceedings against him should have lapsed – but did not. He was to be persecuted beyond the funeral pyre because, as Jaitley (law minister in 1999) disarmingly explained in Parliament, there was no point in prosecuting the case without naming Rajiv Gandhi as an accused. They were clearly less interested in unearthing possible corruption than pursuing a vicious personal political agenda.

It was not until 1997 that the Government of India was able to meet all the requirements of Swiss law to persuade the Swiss to part with the Bofors papers. The trove amounted to over 600 documents. The pleadings of the Central Bureau of Investigation (CBI) passed muster in the lower court, then went in appeal to the Delhi High Court. On 4 February 2004, Justice J.D. Kapoor of the Delhi High Court pronounced his definitive judgement on the matter, holding that there was not a 'scintilla'[12] of evidence to prove these allegations.

The principal conclusions might be summarized as follows: nowhere had the allegation been proved that 'payment made by AB Bofors by way of commission constituted a bribe to the public servants'; the public servants are 'completely absolved of all the allegations'; 'there is no evidence on record to suggest that either Rajiv Gandhi or Bhatnagar (Defence Secretary) used any direct or indirect influence on anybody'. Therefore, all charges against them were to be 'quashed'. Alas, the judgment delivered in February 2004 never received the attention it deserved because the country was distracted by the Vajpayee government's almost simultaneous announcement of general elections six months before they were due.

Soon after, Srichand Hinduja and Others (i.e. Bofors), against whom Justice Kapoor had ordered further proceedings, appealed against the order before Justice R.S. Sodhi of the Delhi High Court. Justice Sodhi, in his judgement of 31 May 2005, damned the CBI for 'launching a persecution based on a

[12] 'Kartongen Kemi Och Forvaltning AB ... vs State Through CBI on 4 February, 2004', Indian Kanoon. https://indiankanoon.org/doc/561739/?type=print.

political agenda'. He went on to hold that the 'remuneration payable to the Hindujas was for market expenses . . . (and) has obviously nothing to do with securing the Bofors contract'– the precise point that Rajiv Gandhi, as PM, had been making. Before quashing 'all proceedings against the Hinduja brothers', the justice expressed his 'disapproval at the investigation that went on for 14 years' and 'cost the Exchequer nearly Rs 250 crores'. He added: 'During the investigation a huge bubble was created *with the aid of the media* [emphasis added] which, however, when tested by court, burst leaving behind a disastrous trail of suffering . . . Careers – both political and professional – were ruined . . . Many an accused lived and died with a stigma.'[13]

Possibly, Rajiv Gandhi's reputation was the worst victim of these shenanigans. He was innocent of every charge laid against him by the Opposition parties, V.P. Singh and Arun Jaitley, the CBI prosecutor, and, above all, the biased media.

The Modi government appealed against this High Court judgment in the Supreme Court. On 2 November 2018, a three-bench order helmed by the Chief Justice Ranjan Gogoi , with the concurrence of his two colleagues, Justice Joseph and Justice Hemant Gupta, rejected the CBI petition because 'we are not convinced with the grounds furnished by the petitioner for the inordinate delay of 4522 days in filing the present Special Leave Petition'.[14] Accordingly, the petition was dismissed and High Court Justice J.D. Kapoor's and Justice R.S. Sodhi's conclusions remain the final judicial findings on the subject.

Tragically, justice was delivered when the principal person indicted had been cruelly assassinated thirteen years earlier. Justice delayed is indeed justice denied.

Panchayati Raj (A personal story)

The initiative with which I was most closely associated personally, and which has become the metronome of my political life, is Rajiv Gandhi's constitutional initiative on local self-government, which goes by the Indian name of 'Panchayati Raj'. This too deserves the detailed treatment I have attempted

[13] 'Srichand P. Hinduja vs State Through CBI', Indian Kanoon, https://indiankanoon.org/doc/230231/.

[14] 'Petition Against Hinduja Brothers: SC Dismisses CBI Plea in Bofors Case, Cites Inordinate Delay', *The Indian Express*, 3 November 2018.

in the companion volume, but is here summarized to lend balance to the tale of controversies that has been recounted.

Professor Balbir Singh taught the 'Indian Economics' paper at St Stephen's College when I was a student there. It was he who introduced me to the subject of Panchayati Raj. He was deeply enthused by Prime Minister Jawaharlal Nehru inaugurating Panchayati Raj at Nagore, Rajasthan, on Gandhi Jayanti, 1959, which created a three-tier Panchayati Raj system: Gram Panchayat at the village level, Panchayat Samiti at the block level and Zila Parishad at the district level. As his eighteen-year-old student, I, too, was much taken by the essential idea of enabling people to take charge of their own lives instead of depending helplessly on the bureaucracy.

Then I was sent to Brussels on my first posting in the IFS. Belgium has, perhaps, the most effective system of local self-government in the world. The city of Brussels, then comprising a mere million people, was administered by no less than nineteen self-reliant and self-governing communes (municipalities). I was most impressed with the effective communication this established between residents and the local commune on a wide range of issues, including even passports.

I also learnt that local self-government in western Europe and the United States preceded full-fledged democracy at higher levels of government. This is what accounted for the smooth running of the administration even in the midst of political upheaval (acute in the case of Belgium, racked as it was by linguistic and social differences between French and Flemish speakers). Later I saw in Pakistan that military dictators like Zia allowed elections at local levels even while denying elections at higher levels. So when Rajiv Gandhi became the elected PM of India, I was thrilled by his emphasis on 'responsive administration', an expression he often repeated and included as the final point of the new twenty-point programme he presented to the nation on Independence Day, 1986.

He addressed many of these ideas at length extempore, in a speech to the All India Panchayat Parishad on 24 September 1986. I was staggered to find my own thoughts on the subject reflected in his observations. He and I, it seemed, were on the same wavelength and, when he chose me to carry forward his plans for Panchayati Raj, I fell in with his goals in a frenzy of deep conviction.

RG put me in charge to work out, with the Department of Personnel that supervised all categories of civil servants, a programme for five workshops with district heads of administration at venues around the country. At the first of these, in Bhopal, he asked me at the end of the proceedings whether I had noticed that the bright ones were all asking for elected local representatives to help them with administration and development, while the dimmer ones asserted that local elected representatives were a nuisance. I confirmed that I had.

At the second workshop in Hyderabad, he indicated that it was perhaps Gandhiji's concept of Panchayati Raj which could be the foundation for his own ideas; at the third and fourth workshops, in Imphal and Jaipur, he evolved his 3R formula (Representativeness = Responsibility = Responsiveness)[15] and at the last workshop, in Coimbatore, he added planning[16] to his schema.

On our way to Imphal on 2 April 1988, he indicated to me and P. Chidambaram, the minister of state for personnel, that he intended to make Panchayati Raj the principal plank of his election platform for the next general elections, then some eighteen months away. From June to December 1988, he sounded out his own party and chief ministers – both Congress and Opposition party – on his ideas. He also instructed me to arrange sectional seminars with disadvantaged categories of the population, such as women, Scheduled Castes (SCs) and Scheduled Tribes (STs). In all, he must have interacted with about 25,000 delegates at different conferences. I was privy to this evolution in his thinking – and perhaps also contributed to the process.

All these deliberations led to his decision to introduce a constitutional amendment that would give constitutional status to the Panchayati Raj institutions that had been created in 1959 and allow them more powers and scope for self-government. It was, if I remember correctly, in January 1989 that he set up a committee at the Department of Rural Development, which fell under Minister Bhajan Lal, to draft the amendment.

---

[15] *Rajiv Gandhi: Selected Speeches and Writings, 1988*, Vol. IV, Publications Division, New Delhi, 1989, p. 136.

[16] Ibid, pp. 162–63.

I was named his liaison to the committee, which was chaired by Vinod Pande, secretary (rural development), and included the law secretary, P.C. Rao, and the legal secretary, Rama Devi. The drafting work was fuelled with mounds of samosas and jalebis that Pande ordered and which I think sparked my diabetes! I was constantly reporting progress to the PM and carrying his points of view to the committee. The most important of these was that there should be no attempt at supplementing the constitutional order in which local self-government was firmly placed in the State List of the Constitution, which delineated the separate responsibilities of the Union and the states, in addition to a Concurrent List where responsibility was shared between the Union government and state governments. The committee had to see how constitutional sanction, sanctity and safeguards for Panchayati Raj might translate into conformity state legislation, thus leaving local self-government firmly in the state government's domain.

RG was also very particular that responsibility for law and order must continue to vest in the district administration and not be devolved to the panchayats. Panchayats were to be conceived for purposes of economic development and social justice, and endowed with the powers to be the first rung of development planning for the nation. The PM's attention to detail was such that when we presented him with an illustrative list of subjects for devolution to the panchayats, which included 'bridges', he asked why not 'culverts' as these were by far more important to rural folk.

We were ready with the draft amendment by April, and I got down to writing the speech that would introduce it in the Lok Sabha. As usual, my initial draft was subjected to the minutest and most pernickety corrections and suggestions by the PM. We wrestled with words for the better part of a fortnight before we had down on paper the precise thoughts in the precise language that he wished to convey.

The exercise ended past midnight on 14/15 May. He was scheduled to speak in the morning. Once the draft had been finalized, the PM left for his residence. I stayed on to put the finishing touches. The phone rang. It was about 2 a.m. As George was unavailable at the time, I answered and an astonished Rajiv Gandhi exclaimed, 'What are you doing so late in the office?' I responded, 'While the world sleeps, India awakes to life and freedom!' He laughed and ordered me to bed.

The speech went off with a minimum of interruption. In the Officers' Gallery, I was the recipient of congratulations all around. It was among the proudest moments of my life.

But the work was not over. For at a meeting of chief ministers on 7 May, ahead of presenting the draft amendment to Parliament, Narayan Datt Tiwari, chief minister of Uttar Pradesh, had enquired why we were not extending constitutional local self-government to urban areas. The PM immediately fell in with the suggestion. We, therefore, began a similar exercise with a committee constituted under the chairmanship of K.A. Sivaramakrishnan, the urban development secretary.[17] The 65th amendment took much less time to ready than the 64th, and the minister, Mohsina Kidwai, was able to introduce it in July 1989 at the start of the monsoon session. The PM replied to the debate before it was put to the vote. It was passed with virtually no negative votes, the Opposition having largely walked out.

The real problem was not in the Lok Sabha but the Rajya Sabha where, in sharp contrast to the position in the Lok Sabha, the government had only a wafer-thin chance of securing two-thirds approval. RG had decided he would have the legislation settled, one way or the other, by Independence Day, 1989. To this end, he instructed me to empty the VIP/diplomatic corps space in front of the ramparts of the Red Fort to accommodate anganwadi workers from all over the country who were to be his honoured guests to hear his Panchayati Raj announcement during the 1989 Independence Day address. However, at the last moment, his political advisers prevailed upon him not to make this announcement as the Upper House verdict hung in the air.

Dhawan & Co did succeed in getting a number of Congress dissidents removed from the Rajya Sabha and replaced with loyal hands, but they failed to secure passage. Eventually, after much drama, on 13/14 October, the motion was defeated, falling short of the two-thirds majority required by three votes. The eventual passage of the two Bills in December 1992, by then numbered 73rd and 74th, is told in the sequel to this volume which comprises my memoirs after RG's assassination on 21 May 1991 (*A Half-Life in Politics*).

[17] K.A. Sivaramakrishnan has furnished a detailed account in his book *Power to the People? The Politics and Progress of Decentralization* (Konark Publishers, New Delhi, 2000). It contains hilarious references to my role, as the senior officers were never sure whether I was disrupting their work with my ideas or really conveying the PM's views!

The immediate fallout of the defeat of the Bills in the Rajya Sabha on my own life was that I determined to ask the PM permission to resign from the IFS to join him in politics. He reluctantly agreed after making me wait for some six weeks in the hope that I would change my mind. It eventually led in 2004 to my appointment as the first-ever Union minister for Panchayati Raj.

Panchayati Raj over the past three decades

While the mandatory elements of the 73rd and 74th amendments – essentially the creation of an election process for Panchayati Raj institutions and their urban counterparts – have been complied with, the attainment of the operational aims and objectives has been left to the state. This has resulted in a great variation in the practice of Panchayat Raj[18] in different parts of the country and over time.

What, then, are the successes, on the one hand, and the work in progress, on the other?

I would rate as the greatest of the successes the constitutionally guaranteed establishment of nearly 3 lakh institutions of local self-government to which have been elected some 32 lakh representatives. Not only has this vastly increased people's representation and participation in governance, especially at the level that matters most to most people much of the time – the local, neighbourhood level – Panchayat Raj has this been made ineluctable, irreversible and irreplaceable. Potentially, this fulfils Jawaharlal Nehru's expectation that 'Panchayati Raj was the most revolutionary development in India because behind it are all the forces which, when released, would change the structure of the country'.[19]

And it is perhaps the awareness of this that has resulted in state governments dragging their feet. They are comfortable with the status quo, especially as most MLAs are the pillars of the existing social structure and among its major beneficiaries. They are unprepared for 'revolutionary development', but comfortable with a third tier of governance so long as the third tier remains

[18] Hindi grammarians are divided over whether the correct expression is 'Panchayat Raj' or 'Panchayati Raj'. I tend to use the two expressions interchangeably.

[19] In a speech to chief ministers on 9 December 1960, cited by Sarvepalli Gopal in his monumental biography of Jawaharlal Nehru (Oxford University Press, Bombay, 1976).

limited in devolved powers. However, for all their reluctance to meaningfully allow for devolution, they have gone far beyond what the Constitution envisaged when it comes to the representation of women. Whereas the Constitution stipulates a minimum of one-third representation of women, as many as twenty-one states have increased the share of reserved seats for women to 50 per cent.

This is a reflection of the relatively similar performance of men and women representatives in the panchayats despite sneers that women are no more than stand-ins for their husbands. A survey[20] I commissioned for the internal use of the Ministry of Panchayati Raj by the well-known polling firm A.C. Nielsen (and written up by Professor Niraja Gopal Jayal of Jawaharlal Nehru University) gave the lie to this cynical impression most bruited about by those who are sceptical of Panchayati Raj itself. As a result of the women's reservation system, which incorporates SC/ST/OBC women, the number of women elected to panchayats and municipalities now constitutes around 14 lakh. *There are more elected women in India alone than in the rest of the world put together.*

I have put the last sentence in italics because, amazingly, this astonishing achievement features hardly at all in the articulated national narrative. This is probably because most of the women elected to local government institutions come from the lower middle class and the really poor. While they have been accorded a measure of political empowerment in their villages and *mohalla*s, their sisters in the upper echelons, who aspire for similar women's reservations in the state and central legislatures, are being unfairly and unjustly denied their due. The share of women in the Lok Sabha has rarely exceeded double digits. I am wholly in favour of raising the share of women in Parliament and the state assemblies to a full 50 per cent. Perhaps when that happens, due recognition will be accorded to their less educated, less economically well-off and lower-social-status sisters in the panchayats and municipalities than is the case at present.

---

[20] A.C. Nielsen ORG-MARG, Niraja Gopal Jayal and the Ministry of Panchayati Raj, 'Study on EWRs in Panchayati Raj Institutions', Ministry of Panchayati Raj, 2008. The current government (2023) has commissioned another similar study led by Dr Nupur Tewari, my former senior research officer.

Equally successful have been reservations for the SCs. The essential confrontation between Dr Ambedkar and Mahatma Gandhi on the question of Panchayat Raj was that while Gandhiji wanted Indian democracy to be built up from village panchayats upwards, Ambedkar held that villages are 'the ruination of India . . . a sink of localism, a den of ignorance and communalism'.[21] He believed Panchayat Raj institutions would only lead to 'elite capture' (to use a term now in vogue), and the perpetuation of the sins of the terrible centuries-old, scripturally sanctioned discrimination against SCs. Therefore, despite Gandhiji's unflinching commitment to Panchayati Raj as the very foundation of Indian democracy, Ambedkar adamantly opposed inclusion of any reference to village self-government in the Constitution, but eventually relented to allow a brief reference in the Directive Principles of State Policy, a non-justiciable part of the Constitution.

Rajiv Gandhi's genius lay in reconciling these apparently irreconcilable views through the system he (and he alone) devised for SC reservations. This, in essence, was based not on national or state averages of the share of SCs in the population but on evolving a wholly new system of SC reservations based on the share of SCs in each panchayat, block/taluka, and district in his three-tier system of local self-government in rural India. This resulted in SCs being privileged in representation in areas of their concentration, and in panchayat, intermediate and district presidencies. We thus have about one lakh local bodies where higher-caste representatives work *under* the leadership of SC chairpersons, both men and women, which many would have considered inconceivable till it was demonstrated in practice in the local bodies set up under the Rajiv Gandhi system. This, in my view, substantially reconciled the Ambedkarite and Gandhian views, and accounts for the stable national consensus on SC reservations. Similar arrangements have been made for urban bodies.

As for STs, the constitution amendments exempted states where they are in a majority (such as Meghalaya, Nagaland and Mizoram) – unless, as in the exceptional case of Arunachal Pradesh, the ST majority state itself wishes to join the constitutionally established Panchayat Raj system. Instead, they are encouraged to energize traditional tribal systems of village governance, as

[21] Kavita Krishnan, 'On Constitution Day, the Modi Government Is Exacting the RSS's Revenge on Ambedkar', The Wire, 26 November 2022.

Nagaland, in particular, has done with stunning success. For states with small ST populations, similar reservation provisions were made as for SCs. But in areas where they live with substantial non-ST populations, identified in the Fifth Schedule of the Constitution, the amendment, as finally drafted and approved, provided for Parliament to devise a special law for tribal areas in the nine identified Fifth Schedule states. Such a law was framed and entered the statute books in December 1996 as the Provisions of the Panchayats (Extension to Scheduled Areas) Act (PESA), the best piece of conformity legislation on Panchayat Raj with the potential to truly liberate tribal populations from the impositions of the state.

Tragically, the Act has been observed mostly in the breach by the nine states concerned, with Maharashtra being the major exception. This, in my view, constitutes the fundamental reason for the spread of Maoist Naxalism in the jungles of central India which Dr Manmohan Singh described as the 'single biggest internal security challenge'.[22] The present government has by brute force driven out the guerrillas from many of their hideouts, but while the law and order issues might be under control, the essence of the problem – self-governance for tribal communities – remains the basic cause of tribal discontent and can only be solved by the sincere implementation of PESA.

As for the Sixth Schedule areas, largely in the north-east, where STs are almost 100 per cent, these were totally exempted by Rajiv Gandhi from the constitutional provisions for Panchayat Raj in view of tribal practices of local self-government; these traditional practices are nearly parallel to the basic conception of Panchayat Raj. If, however, any Sixth Schedule state wishes to come into the national panchayat system, it is free to join, as Arunachal Pradesh has done. Tribal systems of local government have gained international recognition with the UN in 2007 rewarding the Nagaland system as the best in the world.

Hence, as far as equitable representation is concerned, Panchayat Raj has been a spectacular success. But when it comes to real systemic administrative and economic/social justice empowerment, women, SCs and STs are empowered only to the extent that the panchayat system as a whole is genuinely empowered. Unfortunately, with the exception of really progressive states

---

[22] 'India's Deadly Maoists', *The Economist*, 26 July 2006.

like Kerala and Karnataka, the extent of effective empowerment remains inadequate. The Devolution Index initiated in my time as minister shows that while all states continue making some progress with respect to inclusive growth through inclusive governance, the pace varies enormously between the front runners and laggards like Uttar Pradesh, with other states falling in between, and hill states like Sikkim and Himachal doing exceptionally well.

District planning has fallen by the wayside, aggravated by the abandonment of planning at the national level by the central government. The panchayats are funded directly almost exclusively by untied central Finance Commission grants; this has the downside of making panchayats vehicles for patronage and privileging instead of functioning as robust instruments for economic development/social justice and grassroots planning, as envisioned in the Constitution.

My own assessment is that not until the panchayats are integrated into the political hierarchy are we going to see the earnest implementation of the system envisaged in the Constitution. Hope, however, lies in the fact that elected panchayats cannot now be abolished without amending the Constitution. The political fact of their existence will gradually extend the ambit for real Panchayat Raj.

I recall that Rajiv Gandhi said to me that he expected 'at least one generation to pass' before his goals for Panchayat Raj were substantially realized. After three decades, I place the accent on 'at least', for another generation or two will perhaps be required.

My life after the golden year

Meanwhile, what of my own life in the years following the golden year?

My primary duty remained acting as 'Manager, Tours and Travels' (the opprobrious title given me by *India Today*) and accompanying the PM within the country and abroad. At home, his tours during his golden year had involved journeying to remote corners of the country to connect with the social and geographic periphery. In 1986 and 1987, the accent shifted to touring drought-hit and flood-afflicted states.

As virtually every state suffered from drought or floods in those climate-disaster years, we were in one part or other of the country on many days each month, with PM urging his chief ministers to take measures for long-term drought-proofing or flood protection, as the case may be. Some of these measures fructified, others did not. And certainly there were few electoral dividends to be reaped from such intensive interaction with people in distress. The disconnect between real problems and voting preferences grew increasingly apparent as the Congress lost more and more states.

Occasionally, these trips occurred suddenly. I remember RG's visit to Rajahmundry in Andhra Pradesh to apprise himself of flash floods there. We left before lunch and returned by teatime! There was another occasion when I was asked to escort the Dutch crown prince and princess to Allahabad on a daytrip that began with elevenses and was over by the sunset hour.

Then there was the flurry of election tours, particularly the three bunched together in the spring of 1987: Jammu and Kashmir, West Bengal and Kerala. It was during these gruelling election tours that the PM noticed and commented on my enthusiasm for election work. He charged me with climbing to a commanding view at each venue and rating/ranking the public reaction at the different venues at which he spoke. He was quite enthused about the reports I gave him of his many election tours, particularly in West Bengal where he was challenging the long-reigning Comrade Jyoti Basu.

When that election ended with a sizeable increase in the Congress party's vote share but an even more significant augmentation of the CPI(M)'s, his eyebrows shot up as he asked how our expectations had gone wrong. I replied, 'We only get to see the people who come to see us. We do not see those who do not come. And it seems their number was larger.' The PM nodded.

From the end of 1987 onwards, many tours were connected with the five workshops he had us arrange around the conceptualization of Panchayat Raj. Of course, when he was on tour for these workshops, the chief ministers or Pradesh Congress Committee (PCC) presidents concerned would insist on his incorporating local tours in his programme. So we would often be on the road from dawn to dusk and then attend rallies in the gathering darkness before he made it to the workshops.

I particularly recall his arriving at the fifth and final Coimbatore workshop well after midnight and his interacting for hours with exhausted district magistrates until 3 a.m. He never seemed to tire or make up for lost sleep. Perhaps it was his pilot's training that made him attune his body time to whatever was the local time. It was an exciting, unusual way of life that exposed me not only to a wide spectrum of IAS civil servants but also to political dignitaries from a variety of parties and stoked my desire to become part of their politics.

Towards the end of 1988, the Tamil Nadu Congress leader G.K. Moopanar succeeded in persuading Rajiv Gandhi that with MGR having passed away and Jayalalithaa still to find her feet, RG should take on the DMK's Karunanidhi in a straight fight in Tamil Nadu. This resulted in his mounting no less than thirteen day-long road trips throughout the length and breadth of the state. But Moopanar had hopelessly misread political opinion in his state, and a full year's repeated tours ended with the Congress winning a miserable twenty-six seats in the assembly. I did not let on that many of these twenty-six seats were in constituencies that the PM had not visited.

There was also a series of road tours in Haryana with deadly rivals Bhajan Lal and Bansi Lal packed together like sardines in a jeep driven by the PM in a false demonstration of unity. It became quite clear as the campaign wound to a conclusion that none of this was bringing the fractured Congress together in the state and, in consequence, defeat was certain. When, after the last rally in Ambala, we were flying back to Delhi, I mentioned this to Bhajan Lal. He readily agreed that the Congress would be beaten at the hustings but continued with a twinkle in his eye as the biggest operator of '*Aya Ram, Gaya Ram*' politics in the state: '*Ab dekhen ki kaun banayega sarkar!*' (Now let's see who forms the government!).

When I was not preparing RG's tours or accompanying him, my time was often taken up in setting up and encouraging the ZCCs on which he was so keen, as well as generally supervising the organization of two giant inter-zonal festivals, Apna Utsavs, in Delhi (1986) and Bombay (1989). The PM was deeply convinced that the performing arts held the key to the emotional integration of the nation and that these had to be taken to the people rather than being concentrated in cities and elite connoisseurs. To this end, the primary duty of the ZCCs was to take troupes of folk, tribal and classical artistes to the countryside and improvise stages on which to have the artistes perform. This spawned all manner of innovations, including the rejuvenation of the *guru–shishya parampara* – the traditional system of maestros training younger novice artistes – to engage senior artistes in the training and teaching of upcoming talent. It was a most rewarding experience.

I also remained busy with speechwriting, often taking my steno with me to dictate the next load of speeches in the aircraft. My rough calculation is that I prepared speaking points for about a thousand speeches in the four years I was tasked with this duty. The PM spoke several days a week and often twice or thrice a day at different venues, not to mention election speeches.

The most time-consuming and stressful were the grand set speeches at the UN, the Commonwealth and NAM summits, and during visits to key countries like China and Pakistan, the Soviet Union and the US which also included an endless round of banquet speeches; these had to pass muster with my peers before submission to the PM. There were also academic orations at Qing Hua University in Beijing, the Jodi Lecture in Harvard and gatherings like the annual Science Congress in India. There were, finally, his interventions in Parliament and keynote addresses at party forums. I would obtain the raw material from the ministry concerned, then weave it into the broad sweep of his ideas for India. All this meant, on average, a sixteen-hour day, sometimes extending to eighteen or more.

I was young enough, enthusiastic enough and energetic enough to do this almost day after day. But it also meant neglect of the family. My office preoccupations were a source of deep disappointment for the children for which I was reprimanded later by my eldest daughter, Suranya, who exploded, 'You were never there when we needed you!' I have not recovered from that slap in the face – because it was true. Fortunately, Suneet stepped into the breach, devoting all her time and energy right through the 1980s to looking after the growing children. It was only in the '90s that we started travelling together as a family at home and abroad.

See detailed footnotes and endnotes by scanning the QR code above.

12

The Transition from PMO to CPO

Taking the plunge

After the prime minister's colourless Independence Day address on 15 August 1989, when he should have been proclaiming Panchayat Raj as his banner for the next election but did not, he flew out to Karnataka on 17 August and to Andhra Pradesh on the 18th. I travelled with him. It struck me that this was a golden opportunity to discuss my personal future. If I spoke to him on the flight from Karnataka to Andhra Pradesh, when politicians from either state were not in the helicopter, I would get a clean hour and a half to talk to him without interruption – a rare window.

As we flew from Haasan to Mysore on the 17th, I walked up to him and said I would like to talk to him about something important the next day. Hc was intrigued and asked why not now. I replied I would rather wait until the morrow. He was so intrigued that when the day's events were over, the Special Protection Group (SPG) knocked on my door and said the PM was awaiting me. Rajiv Gandhi once again enquired what it was that I wanted to talk about. I once again demurred because I was trying to make up my mind whether to consult my wife. The PM let it go, and I spent much of the night wrestling with myself over whether or not to sound out Suneet, then decided it would only complicate my resolve if she were to ask me to think it over.

Next morning, at first light, we got into the helicopter and the PM motioned me to the seat next to him even before we quite took off. But before our conversation began, I first had to fulfil my usual role of acting as the prime minister's right hand – literally – as I was required to wave from the window across the aisle at the cheering crowd (without showing my face) while RG handled the crowd from the window next to him.

Immediately after take-off, the PM looked at me enquiringly. I cleared my throat and began by saying I wanted to quit the IFS to join him in politics. Rajiv Gandhi looked stunned. Why on earth did I want to leave an assured job in which I was doing very well for the uncertainties of politics? I reminded him of our Cambridge days when I had run for president of the union. I said ever since I was in school, my dream had been to enter politics, but I had no constituency, nor the required linguistic skills, nor my own resources. I wanted to leverage this opportunity to make the transition. Rajiv looked sceptical.

He himself believed, I continued, that he would win the coming election and I certainly hoped he would, but everyone I knew – including my wife who was running a journal, *India Speaks* that furnished English translations of language journals – was convinced that the Congress would lose. So my request was to hitch my star to his wagon, win or lose, and this appeared to be the right time. He did not reply immediately. Either he did not agree with me or he wondered why he should take me on as an additional political burden. In any case, he asked me to think things over. But as far as I was concerned, the die was cast.

I then turned to another consideration that I regarded as germane. I said I knew he was on the target list of assassins. There was always that danger. But I did not think anyone would get him in Delhi where he was well protected; things were more uncertain when he was on the move. 'However, as I am always in the open jeep that travels ahead of you, any assassin would mow me down before they get you.' He listened sombrely.

We landed at Cuddapah (now Kadapa) without a decision. On the way from Cuddapah to Delhi, he did not resume the conversation, and from then on, I found him deliberately avoiding my eye. I decided to bide my time.

I then broached the subject with my family. Suneet, always my support, immediately fell in with my plans. The children looked concerned when I said it might be difficult to finance their higher education if things went wrong. My brother, Jam, stepped into the breach. He pledged to take care of their college education in the event of my coming a cropper. His worry, he said, was altogether different. He was certain that Rajiv Gandhi would be jailed after losing the election; so why did I want to go to Tihar when I had not benefitted by even one *khota paisa*[1] from Bofors? I brushed off the question.

Finding that I was sticking to my guns, the PM waited for over a month and then asked his principal secretary, B.G. Deshmukh, to take me in hand. Deshmukh discovered I was impervious to argument and, moreover, I had the backing of my family. I had thought through the entire issue and my mind was made up. I was finally ushered into the PM's presence on 10 October, Suneet's birthday.

RG began by saying he would never be able to make me a minister. As I had heard that Dhawan was telling anyone who cared to listen that my ambition was so overweening that I would not be satisfied being made foreign secretary and was aspiring to be foreign minister, I took this opening gambit in my stride. I said I was ready to never be made a minister.

The PM then emphasized that the 'system' would never accept me, just as it had accepted neither 'Roon [Arun Singh] nor even Arun [Nehru]'. (I have sometimes wondered whether he was also thinking of himself as 'not having been accepted by the system'.) I nodded, saying that while I entertained no false hopes of a ministership, I did hope he would be able to fulfil my lifelong desire to be an MP. He said he had been reflecting on that and had come to the conclusion that he could get me into the Rajya Sabha from one of the three seats available to the moribund Municipal Corporation of Delhi (MCD). Although this would be equivalent to being born out of the womb of a corpse, I gratefully accepted the prospect. (This was never fulfilled because immediately after the Lok Sabha elections, the MCD was deservedly put to sleep and a new Delhi legislative assembly was put in its place; however, very few Congress MLAs were elected.)

Having clarified matters, he agreed that I might put in my papers and, after my voluntary retirement was agreed to by the government, I could join the Congress. He then said he required something else from me. He wanted me to continue with him in the PMO as an officer on special duty even after resigning. I promptly agreed, but he seemed to think further explanation was needed.

'I want you with me because you never come back to me on any task that I

---

[1] 'Not even a brass farthing' would, I think, be the right English translation.

assign to you except to say the task is done. And you often seem to comprehend my thoughts better than I do.' What greater compliment could I receive? I walked out of his study floating on cloud nine.

On Foreign Minister P.V. Narasimha Rao's instructions, the paperwork at the MEA took virtually no time. On the afternoon of 13 October, I handed over to the PM my letter of resignation and asked him to sign it. Is that necessary, he asked? I said, 'No – but for me it would be a historical record.' He smiled and appended his signature.

R.K. Dhawan, who was present, asked whether I would be prepared to take the Congress ticket from New Delhi to contest against Lal Krishna Advani! I immediately recognized the ploy as a subtle attempt to ground me before take-off. Dhawan made one more attempt to nobble me. I asked Rajiv Gandhi whether I might designate myself 'Special Assistant to the Congress President' but Dhawan wanted to know why I needed a designation at all. Fortunately, Rajiv Gandhi overruled him and said I could call myself his special assistant. No one else ever called me that!

My kids were appalled that I had chosen for my transition to politics the inauspicious date of Friday the 13th. I dismissed their apprehensions as superstition – but there is no denying that, at least in hindsight, it was a very bad start.

The news of my voluntary retirement from the IFS to pursue an alternative career in politics caused a mild flutter. Ajoy Bose, the journalist, was to tell me later that my former classmate Arun Shourie, editor of the *Indian Express* and a vitriolic critic of Rajiv's, scoffed when Ajoy handed him his copy, 'Don't you guys have anything better to write about than Mani Shankar, Mani Shankar. . .!'

Pritish Nandy, editor of the *Illustrated Weekly of India*, had me on the cover, following Rajiv at a pre-election meeting in Kizhakkarai, Tamil Nadu, with a bundle of petitions under my arm, and the heading 'Mani Friday'. Within was a long interview with me introduced by Nandy and laced with his hallmark sarcasm:

> The Tamilian brahmin with the odd sense of wit first came into prominence when, within weeks of his joining the prime minister's office, he had a brush with the press in Washington, DC . . . Aiyar never lived down that

> confrontation, and the Indian press . . . found in him an excellent opportunity for target practice. . .[2]

Then came the rather perceptive assessment that I understood what my PMO colleagues had not, that is, Rajiv Gandhi's priorities, and that I took my work seriously, 'despite the silly witticisms for which he is best known'.

Nandy went on to explain that although I had 'harmed' the PM's image with the speeches I wrote becoming 'more and more provocative' and 'facetious', yet when I 'teamed up' with rural development secretary Vinod Pande, I presented the PM with 'two of his finest political weapons, the Panchayat Raj Bill and the Jawahar Rozgar Yojana, followed by the Nagarpalika bill'. Granting that 'Aiyar's contribution towards the schemes were brilliantly conceived, a fact which no one seemed to notice since the air was too thick with Bofors and HDW', he ended by asserting that 'Aiyar's contribution towards drafting the bill(s) remains the single biggest achievement of his bureaucratic career'.

It was, I think, on the whole a fair assessment of my time in the PMO.

Lok Sabha elections, 1989

To my astonishment and that of most people, Rajiv Gandhi announced the next general election on 16 October – three days after I had quit the IFS.

I got down to the task of drafting the Congress manifesto – which came to be called the Mani-Festo, not in praise but in denigration of me, many journalists delighting in the comeuppance that was about to be delivered to the Congress.

I then travelled with the PM to Haldia, Narora and Trivandrum. He had tentatively enquired, at the start of the journey, whether instead of accompanying him on the election tour, I would prefer to man the press room along with M.J. Akbar. I baulked at this suggestion. In any case, the idea came to an abrupt end when Akbar was given the Congress ticket to contest from Kishanganj in Bihar. 'Watch out,' counselled Akbar, 'Dhawan is trying to shaft both of us.'

RG was busy with fraught discussions involving the allocation of 542

---

[2] Pritish Nandy, 'Mani Friday', *The Illustrated Weekly of India*, 29 October–4 November 1989.

tickets for Lok Sabha seats to Congress candidates. Aspirants were legion, many getting their applications and biodata typed out by the itinerant typists who had set up shop at 24, Akbar Road, the Congress headquarters. One enterprising entrepreneur, who had an electronic typewriter, advertised his services by claiming that applications typed on manual typewriters could not be fed into computers. He was literally besieged!

My first 'political charge'

One night at about 2 a.m., when RG's office at 7, Race Course Road was still buzzing, he phoned to say he was entrusting me with a delicate task. There were two women from Andhra Pradesh, Geeta Reddy and Uma Gajapati Raju, to whom he had promised tickets, but he was facing heavy opposition in the Congress Parliamentary Board (CPB). Would I call and persuade the women to choose any assembly segment in their proposed parliamentary constituencies and he would ensure that they were at least allotted the assembly segments of their preference?

I rang Geeta Reddy who burst into tears but told me the segment she desired, even as she sobbed uncontrollably (she went on to win it and became a state minister several times over). Uma was a different proposition. She had a large vocabulary of colourful abuse and, when I gave her RG's message, she used it to shattering effect. She adamantly refused the PM's offer of a seat in the state assembly and, cursing him in language worthy of a stevedore, turned her ire on me. She continued calling me through the night – much to Suneet's annoyance – blasting her stream of off-colour expressions.

I returned to Race Course Road at 5 a.m. to be told the PM had gone to bed only a few minutes earlier. His diligent private secretary, V. George, having been up all night, looked a little dishevelled, unlike his normal dapper self, and took himself off. I picked up an atlas and, covering myself with it, put up my legs and went to sleep.

I woke to hear Makhan Lal Fotedar, Rajiv's political adviser, confidentially whispering to George that the ticket for Visakhapatnam had been awarded to a well-known Andhra industrialist. Fotedar was worried. As steel minister, he had ordered an enquiry into the business baron's affairs. Hence, the award of a Congress ticket to a man under formal investigation might reflect adversely on him. I went still behind my atlas. I came out from behind it only after

Fotedar had left and, going to the lawn, stationed myself at a point RG would have to pass on his way from an early morning meeting on the lawns to the conference room.

As RG walked up to me with a questioning look, I whispered that I needed a moment to inform him of the reaction of the two Andhra ladies and what I had overheard Fotedar saying this morning; I thought it gave the PM an opportunity to fulfil his pledge to Uma. He told me to get it in writing from Fotedar, which I did, and Uma fought and won the seat.

The 'Ram Rajya' plank

On moving out of the PMO to the Congress President's Office (CPO) in mid-October 1989, I was immersed in working out the complexities of the PM's election tour itinerary with its intricate logistics. The tour, as decided months earlier, was scheduled to kick off in Nagaur, Rajasthan, where Jawaharlal Nehru had gone on Gandhi Jayanti, 1959, to inaugurate his version of Panchayat Raj – the principal proposed plank of our campaign.

I was discussing the tour programme with the PM when Sheila Dikshit, his minister of state, entered the room and said she had come on behalf of her colleagues; they wanted her to emphasize that Panchayat Raj could not be the main issue as all attention was fixed on the Ram Janmabhoomi–Babri Masjid controversy. She and her colleagues wanted him to begin his campaign in Faizabad on the outskirts of Ayodhya. She also said the PM should stop driving his own vehicle on these tours.

After she bustled out, I reminded him that when Margaret Thatcher won an unexpected election victory after the Falklands war, he (RG) had presented me with the book *Campaign!* by Rodney Tyler; my main learning from it was that no campaign must be fought on a turf of the Opposition's choosing. I was, therefore, of the view that we should stick to our long-planned intention of making this election about Panchayat Raj, not fall into the trap of making the BJP's principal issue our issue. He nodded but made no comment.

RG later sent me a message saying that the first meeting of the election campaign on 3 November 1989 should be in Faizabad. Nagaur could come later. At the Faizabad airfield, I busied myself on the hotline with arrangements for the next stop. I was, therefore, not on the platform when Rajiv Gandhi mentioned 'Ram Rajya' in his first election speech, which the Opposition later made into a whiplash to lacerate the sitting PM's campaign, portraying him as an opportunist hunting with the hounds and running with the hares to appeal to the Hindu vote while appeasing the Muslim vote.

I knew that 'Ram Rajya' was not included in his speaking notes, and he had not asked for it to be included. So somebody on the stage must have asked him to refer to it. I have, therefore, studied the news reports to unravel what happened. Here are my findings.

The Hindi-language *Hindustan* (4 November 1989) had the most detailed report. It does not even mention the words 'Ram Rajya', whereas the Calcutta *Statesman* of the same date headlined its brief report 'PM pledges Ram Rajya' and ran a story that claimed his 'promise was greeted with cries of "*Har, Har Mahadev*", "*Bajrang Bali ki Jai*" and "*Jai Bharat Mata*". The *Statesman* correspondent appears to have been the only one to have heard these BJP/VHP (Vishva Hindu Parishad)-associated slogans. I certainly had not – and no other report I found mentioned this.

The mystery was cleared by the following day's *Economic Times* which reported that 'Leaders of the National Front and BJP, at simultaneous evening briefings, ridiculed the Prime Minister's claim for [*sic*] bringing about a "Ram Rajya"'. Obviously, the Opposition had cottoned on to the phrase often used by Mahatma Gandhi to run their campaign of calumny.

I think it was there and then that Rajiv Gandhi lost the election. If only he had stuck to his two-year resolve to make Panchayat Raj the main plank of his platform, perhaps the margin of defeat might have been narrowed. Nevertheless, his campaign for re-election was going quite well when unmitigated disaster struck a week later.

As I have noted earlier, his political advisers, led by Dhawan and Fotedar, had persuaded the PM to facilitate the *shilanyas* of a new Ram temple on the land identified by Home Minister Buta Singh as 'undisputed'. This was a gross misrepresentation on Buta Singh's part because a piece of the so-called 'undisputed' land was in fact part of the dispute. On the basis of the Buta Singh report, Rajiv Gandhi's political advisers were able to persuade the PM that not only should he authorize the *shilanyas*, but he should also schedule it within the election period, not before or after, and, to that end, suddenly announce elections to squeeze the maximum political benefit out of the ritual.

I was not part of this discussion and was, therefore, startled to hear this sudden call to elections. The Dhawan–Fotedar belief appeared to be that such a dramatic announcement would not only take the wind out of the sails of an increasingly belligerent Opposition, it would also enable Rajiv Gandhi to make the building of the Ram temple (along with the physical preservation of the Babri Masjid) his main election platform. This cynical, unprincipled, opportunistic strategy was put in play.

The very idea of playing off both sides – guaranteeing the continued existence of the Babri Masjid to the Muslims while offering the Hindus the prospect of a grand Ram Mandir –appalled me. But there was little I could do as I had entered politics only a few days earlier. In any case, I was still imbued with a strong belief that Panchayat Raj, not Ram Janmabhoomi, was going to be our key issue.

The *shilanyas* and its consequences

On the day of the *shilanyas*, I was told to cancel his scheduled tour programme for him to stay in Delhi to monitor developments. By the late afternoon it appeared that there had been no negative fallout of the event, so I was asked to immediately arrange for him to fly to a Jammu rally that evening and to route him from there to Goa at night. The following day, he was due to campaign in coastal Karnataka before returning to Delhi and heading for the Fursatganj airfield, from where he would travel by helicopter to Sultanpur, the district headquarters of his own Amethi constituency. I slotted three hours for his road journey from the Sultanpur election rally to Tatarpur, where he was to spend the night, to give time to the cheering crowds expected to line the road.

When we reached Chikmagalur, next stop Udipi where Oscar Fernandes was contesting, the PM received a call that all hell had broken loose in Sultanpur district, and it would be advisable to return at once to Delhi. It fell to my lot to call Oscar and inform him of this. I must say he took this last-minute cancellation well.

Back in Delhi, Rajiv Gandhi listened to the bad news of communal riots in his own constituency in the thick of election season and decided to proceed to his election meeting in Sultanpur. As dusk had fallen, we could not take the chopper from Fursatganj airport to Sultanpur and reached the election meeting ground by road hours behind schedule. It was all but empty. I counted an audience of about 186 people. Nevertheless, RG delivered a full speech.

We then drove to Tatarpur in darkness. It took us less than forty-five minutes compared to the three hours I had set aside. The roadside was empty. For the first time in my five years with him, he was silent, withdrawn, his brow furrowed with worry, his famous smile wiped off his face. At the Tatarpur rest house, I busied myself with reorganizing the next day's programme while RG, Dhawan and Fotedar gathered in the garden outside and plunged into earnest conversation at which my presence was obviously not desired.

Next day, we helicoptered to rallies in Hardoi, Sitapur, Pilibhit, Mau, Jaunpur and finally Allahabad, reaching Allahabad before sunset. RG had heard that the BBC were repeatedly reporting the unfounded rumour that the Babri Masjid had been razed to the ground. So, at each stop, he urged the Congress candidate to hire a bus and take local Muslim leaders to see for themselves that the masjid was standing where it had for the past 500 years, untouched and as stolid as ever. The only one to follow his advice was Kalp Nath Rai in Mau. He was one of the two Congress candidates to win from the many hundred constituencies scattered between Amethi and the Bangladesh border. (M.J. Akbar was the other, from Kishanganj.)

The Nehru centenary address

In the Allahabad circuit house that bleak evening, RG pulled out his laptop and opened the first page of the draft I had prepared for his Nehru centenary address in Vigyan Bhawan on 13 November. The source of the draft was a memo of thirty pages, translated into Russian and hand-delivered to Gorbachev in response to a request made by Gorbachev to RG to explain how such a diverse country as India, beset by separatist movements, had been held together.

To Gorbachev, this seemed a miracle and he wanted to know how. It was obvious that Gorbachev was feeling the stresses that were to bring the Red Revolution to a close a few months down the road. The PM was flattered at his request. He handed over the responsibility of preparing the draft to his intelligence chief, M.K. Narayanan. Narayanan did a thorough policeman's job of it. Rajiv read through it, called me in and asked, 'Is this the way we have held the country together?' Of course, it was a policeman's report and comprehensive and thoroughgoing as far as it went. But it talked of no dimension other than thumbscrews on the nails of rebels!

My instructions were to prepare another draft to which Narayanan's contribution was to be attached as an annex, to give a fuller picture of how we had ensured the unity of India. I had never before penned a more detailed or lengthy account of the 'miracle' of India's unity in diversity. The PM had my draft loaded on to his computer and for about a month or more travelled with it everywhere, availing of every spare second to peruse the draft with a toothcomb to make or suggest the changes he wanted. It was only when he was fully satisfied the draft included everything important that final clearance was given. The official translator was summoned from our embassy in Moscow to render the memo into the Russian language, so that we could control the version that Gorbachev would read in his native tongue.

Soon after the memo to Gorbachev had been dispatched, the question of who was to be invited to deliver the Nehru centenary lecture in Vigyan Bhawan, New Delhi, was raised. I insisted that it could not be anyone other than the prime minister of India. 'Who, me?' was RG's response. 'But I am the man's grandson. Would this not stink of nepotism?' It took me a while to persuade him that it would be absurd to call a foreign dignitary to speak on this historic centenary. I reminded him that there were no living persons of adequate distinction who had worked with Panditji or who could be described as Nehru's comrades-in-arms. (I had in mind the precedent of Khan Abdul Ghaffar Khan having been invited as chief guest for Mahatma Gandhi's centenary in 1969.) Even though he was the grandson, I believed the prime minister – none other – should pay this tribute.

Rajiv Gandhi must have consulted others. But I prevailed when I said the draft Nehru centenary speech was ready. What did I mean, he asked? The memo to Gorbachev, I replied. He himself had spent so much time on it that it could be considered his contemporary interpretation of Jawaharlal Nehru's idea of India. What could be more befitting than a modified version of that memo as his draft centenary address? I think that persuaded him. The draft of the address was readied and he once again uploaded it on to his personal laptop and kept fiddling with it whenever he was undisturbed.

After dinner that night, I sat with him in his suite, and we went through the draft, as modified by him, word by word and phrase by phrase. My memory is that we finished in the early hours, around 2 or 3 a.m.

It turned out to be his last public speech as PM. There was one remaining hitch. Ronen Sen had objected to a phrase scoring the atrocities inflicted on

Red Indians (now more correctly called 'Native Americans'). I was adamant that the phrase was necessary to make the point at which we were driving. Ronen felt it gave needless cause for complaint. RG gave no decision on the question. So Ronen and I waited tensely as the PM approached that part of the address. He used it! In the event, the speech made no impact as Rajiv Gandhi was to be ousted a few days later.

Defeat looms

Our hurtling towards defeat was greatly aggravated by Sanjay Singh – the raja of Amethi who was a principal aide to Rajmohan Gandhi, Rajiv Gandhi's main opponent in his constituency – becoming the target of an assassination attempt. Sanjay Singh had been brought to a Lucknow hospital by his wife, Garima, and RG put aside the campaign programme to make an unscheduled visit to the Lucknow Raj Bhawan to meet Garima. We waited a long time, but Garima did not turn up and we overheard stories that she had refused to come to the Raj Bhawan because she and her husband's supporters believed Rajiv Gandhi or his associates were complicit in the assassination attempt. There was not an iota of truth to that rumour but no one was looking for the truth.

The only thing left to do was to fly to Gorakhpur airport (which had night-landing facilities) and proceed to Gopalganj in Bihar by road. It was way beyond midnight when we reached the almost empty and very cold Gopalganj election meeting venue. We then went on a futile road journey to Patna with almost no one on the road or at meetings. It did not take a pollster or soothsayer to see the end was nigh.

As the campaign was winding its way to a conclusion, we found Gopi Arora, M.K. Narayanan and B.G. Deshmukh waiting to board the PM's plane at Calcutta. They had not been summoned but had come to Calcutta of their own volition. They went into a huddle to tell him the only way of saving the election was for him to announce that no place of worship would ever be demolished for whatever reason. I was told later that RG's argument was that even in Saudi Arabia shrines had been demolished to make way for highways, so how could he in all conscience make the statement they had come all the way to Calcutta to plead him to make. (I did not then, and do not now, believe that such a statement would have made any difference to the outcome.)

On the very last day of the campaign, we flew back to Delhi from Varanasi. All of us were aware, I think, that this was the last of the hundreds of journeys we had made in that aircraft.

The following evening, I was at a reception hosted by K.K. Sharma, correspondent of the London *Financial Times*, in his very elegant Chanakyapuri home, to discuss election prospects. Yashwant Sinha was among the guests. I had known him for decades because we had both served in Delhi on trade matters and, later, he was consul general in Frankfurt reporting on European Community issues to our common boss, Ambassador K.B. Lall in Brussels. He drew me aside to confide that his incoming government would allow Rajiv and Sonia to go to Italy, if they were so inclined. I was livid. Whatever made him think they were planning to flee to Italy? Rajiv Gandhi knew he could answer all the bogus charges levelled against him by V.P. Singh and his cohort. He and his wife were not going anywhere, they were staying put!

The results came in sluggishly. There could be no doubt that a majority, however reduced, eluded Rajiv. In the end, the number of Congress seats was slashed by over half from over 400 to under 200. Yet, the Congress was the single largest party. I was unable to see Rajiv or learn his intentions despite leaving messages with his staff.

My phone rang. It was a very indignant Aroon Purie of *India Today* who had been at school, indeed, in the same class, as Rajiv: the two had tied at a low second-class position in their school-leaving examination. Purie demanded to know why Rajiv Gandhi was going to Rashtrapati Bhavan to meet the president when he had quite evidently lost the election. By what right was he staking his claim to cobble together a government? I heard him out until he calmed down.

Then I asked, 'You know everyone at school stole compasses from other students' geometry boxes. Did Rajiv ever steal your compass – or anyone else's?' Rajiv Gandhi, I said, was going to the top of Raisina Hill only to tell the president that as he had lost the election fair and square, he would not be asking to be invited, as head of the largest single party, to form the government. He would be content to sit in the Opposition. I did not know this for sure. I was only guessing from what I knew of the man's innate integrity. I guessed right!

I was summoned to the PM's office in South Block one last time. He was back to his usual cheerful self. We got on with recording his farewell message.

From there, we went straight to Central Hall, where a meeting of the Congress Parliamentary Party had been convened. We marched in, me right behind RG, to the thunderous sound of Arjun Singh leading the thumping of desks. I proudly stood by Rajiv Gandhi's side and slightly to his rear, as he delivered his extempore address to his defeated colleagues. There was nothing tearful about the event. It was an expression of determination.

It marked the end of one of the most decisive phases of my life, and it was the start of a whole new chapter.

Special assistant to the Congress president (1989–91) and a columnist

Elections over, much of that first month in the Opposition was filled with setbacks for me. Far from grooming me as his V.K. Krishna Menon, as I had hoped, I hardly got to see RG as he was very busy personally conducting an introspection process with Congress leaders. I was pointedly excluded. Suman Dubey tells me it was perhaps at this juncture that I remarked to him, 'I am the only rat I know that has jumped on to a sinking ship!'

One day, on a now rare private moment, just as we were boarding an aircraft, RG suddenly asked, 'Am I arrogant?' I replied, 'I don't think so, but people resent your having been born with a silver spoon in your mouth that you have turned to gold.' Obviously, there was a great deal of churning going on in his head, heart and soul.

Left on my own, I scouted around for something to do. It was Vir Sanghvi, editor of the Calcutta-based *Sunday* magazine, who inducted me into an altogether new vocation as a columnist. In a *Sunday* box item during the elections (he was certain Rajiv Gandhi would be defeated), Vir famously predicted that Captain Satish Sharma would find himself 'unemployed and unemployable'! As for me, his prediction was that I would become a *Sunday* columnist, although I had given him no hint I was interested.

I leave the rest to him by reproducing this passage from an introduction he wrote for a book I published a couple of years later:

> I still remember his first column for *Sunday*. Published . . . when the media were singing the praises of V.P. Singh, it accurately presaged the end of the Janata Dal government. . .

> Abusive letters from Disgusted of Jabalpur and Hysterical of Bangalore poured in. Many readers threatened to cancel their subscriptions...
>
> At *Sunday*, we were stunned by the response. The anger of some of our readers did not surprise us – Mani went out of his way to provoke them. What staggered us was first, the large number of letters and second, that to be provoked by Mani you had to first read him. Clearly, all those who loathed his column nevertheless turned to it as soon as their copies of *Sunday* arrived to find new reasons to hate it. He was probably the most widely read columnist in the history of *Sunday*.[3]

Although my first piece, which caused such a furore, was a 'guest column', Vir's boss, Aveek Sarkar, quickly moved to make me a regular with a most generous remuneration, along with permission to place the column, after initial publication, wherever I liked. Within a few months, I had secured publication in many journals – in English, Hindi, Tamil, Gujarati, Marathi and others – that would take my income well above my last government salary. I remain astonished that I was not taken to court, for not only did the column display an astonishing chutzpah in not taking the electoral defeat lying down but it also dripped with sarcasm and often contained an abusive strain in its critique of personalities and policies.

One incident remains in my memory. Pinki Virani was at Bombay's *Mid-Day* evening paper which carried my column after publication in *Sunday*. One day, I found the column in *Mid-Day* had been cut off arbitrarily in full flow before going to the end. I rang in high dudgeon to complain. Pinki answered. After listening to my rant, she patiently explained, 'I am sorry, Mr Aiyar, but half our subeditors hate your column and half of them love it. One of the former must have been on duty when your column was aborted.' I think that neatly illustrates the public reception to my writing.

My college friend, IFS colleague and keen phrase maker, Shekhar Dasgupta suggested the standard disclaimer at the end of the column be amended to read, 'The views expressed in this column are not even those of the author'! Another good friend, Steve Weisman of the *New York Times*, who had been transferred from New Delhi to Tokyo, wrote back to say I had 'an amazing

[3] Mani Shankar Aiyar, *In Rajiv's Footprints: One Year in Parliament*, Konark, New Delhi, 1993, pp. x–xi. For the full article, please scan the QR code on p. 362.

talent to abuse and amuse'. That, I think, was the column's USP. It was also the same USP that led to many arrows being shot into my back.

My wife Suneet was annoyed with some of my columns where she thought I was being petulant. So when I ended my second column with the news account of L.K. Advani asking his taxi driver to take him to the PM's residence and the driver bringing him to the doorstep of RG's home, I quipped that it showed who the ordinary people of India thought the real PM still was. She called Vir and insisted that the punchline be deleted. To keep the peace, Vir assented.

An IFS colleague, Jitendra Daulet Singh, asked me bluntly to stop making a fool of myself and gracefully accept defeat. Others, such as S.S. Ahluwalia, were also gunning for me. Just as I was despairing, Vir told me to hang in there, as in a few months I would be hailed as a prophet who had foretold the demise of the V.P. Singh regime. That, indeed, is what happened. Yet, I thought it prudent to check with Rajiv Gandhi whether I might persist. He replied that he had not read any of the columns, but Rahul had and said they were fine. Thus, Rahul Gandhi at age nineteen became the patron saint of *Mani-Talk*!

If finding a regular source of income was my first concern, finding suitable private accommodation was my second. As a retired government servant, I was entitled to six months' continued occupation of my government house. However, I sneered at Urban Development Minister Murasoli Maran in one of my columns saying his 'government that works' functioned so inefficiently that months after my resignation, his ministry had not got around to sending me an eviction notice. He promptly sent it. My mother-in-law had a couple of rooms to spare in her Defence Colony residence. We stayed with her, in extremely cramped conditions that interfered with the children's studies, until my fortunes changed.

In the meanwhile, Suranya, my eldest, went to St Stephen's and the other two, Yamini and Sana, quickly adjusted themselves to the changed circumstances. Indeed, Suranya got so involved with the anti-Mandal students' agitation that she and Yamini were detained at the Parliament House police station. That did not faze them so much as the prospect of confessing to their parents that they had been in police detention. When I heard that Suranya had achieved at seventeen what I was to still achieve at nearly fifty – police detention – I quite startled her by enthusiastically congratulating her on her achievement. It somewhat melted the ice that had grown between her and her parents in her early adolescence – one of my most painful personal memories.

Failed attempts at Rajya Sabha membership

As I have mentioned, RG's promise to get me into the Rajya Sabha from Delhi had gone awry with the incoming government dissolving the moribund MCD (whose members constituted the electorate) and upgrading it to a regular elected state assembly. I had also lost the opportunity of coming in from Uttar Pradesh, which the state's chief minister Narayan Datt Tiwari had arranged for me, when RG delayed accepting my resignation from the IFS to the very eve of the general elections. I decided to try my luck from Pondicherry, but that too was ruled out by Jayalalithaa. I was left with little option but to rely on Jayalalithaa's benevolence to come in from Tamil Nadu. This seemed on the cards for a while and RG deputed my old boss, Dinesh Singh, to persuade her to let us have the seat in exchange for support we were extending to her in Pondicherry. But this fizzled out. RG encouraged me to try my luck in Arunachal Pradesh but that too proved illusory. I was on my own, stranded and without any prospects.

I moved into my tiny office in the All India Congress Committee (AICC) where I was given a small room adjacent to the ladies' toilet. The smell was unbearable. I made the mistake of mentioning this at a dinner party and soon enough the story had wended its way to the media who greatly enjoyed me getting my comeuppuance.

What rescued me was a poor joke I cracked at a Congress demonstration where I remarked that it was clear to me that RG had not taken the Bofors money for my room did not even have an AC. Pritish Nandy published this remark in his gossip column at the *Illustrated Weekly of India*, adding that my lack of an AC was not because RG had not taken the Bofors money but because I had ceased to matter. To my surprise, the Congress treasurer, Sitaram Kesari, barged unannounced into my office demanding to know where the AC was to be installed. It seems Nandy's article had been shown to RG and he had ordered the treasurer to rectify matters without delay. If I did not melt in the heat of that summer, it is only because Nandy, as was his nasty wont, had decided to take a swipe at me!

Convention against communalism

Under the Jammu and Kashmir rubric of my companion volume, I have described at length my involvement from end January to mid-March 1990 in RG's concerns over the alarmingly deteriorating situation in the Kashmir Valley. After our return from Srinagar, RG concentrated on organizing an AICC 'Convention against Communalism' in May 1990, and on measures to whip a demoralized Congress back into shape.

The convention, to be held in Talkatora Stadium, was scheduled for 19 May, about five and a half months after the electoral reverse. The newly elected Congress MP for Kishanganj in Bihar, M.J. Akbar, and I were asked to prepare the draft theme paper. We were asked to meet the senior leaders P.V. Narasimha Rao and V.N. Gadgil before putting pen to paper. When we arrived for the meeting, I, for one, was quite taken aback by both Rao and Gadgil being not only unenthusiastic about the idea, but just barely stopping short of opposing it. Rao had scraped through the 1989 elections, standing from Ramtek in Vidarbha, Maharashtra. Gadgil had, in fact, lost in Pune.

After Akbar and I briefed the two veterans on the course we had planned, they began, almost offensively, denigrating the traditional Congress line on secularism, saying people were not interested in listening to standard cliches. They were seeking answers to questions about the *tushtikaran* (appeasement) of the Muslim minority. They listed the questions they had faced in their respective campaigns and asked us how we proposed to answer these.

I took down the questions and said we would return with draft answers. Akbar seemed a little shaken and, to the best of my memory, took little further part. A sampling of the questions:

- Why should we not have a uniform civil code?
- What justification was there for negating the Shah Bano judgement by an Act of Parliament?
- What is the logic of persisting with Article 370?
- Why should Hindus adopt family planning when Muslims resist it?
- Why build a Haj Manzil in Bombay for Muslim pilgrims embarking for Jeddah when there is nothing similar for Hindu pilgrims proceeding to Nepal?

- Why does the Government of India subsidize Hajis when it does not similarly subsidize Hindu pilgrims?
- Why should we make such a hue and cry over secularism when no Muslim country practises it?
- Does not a religion which talks of '*kafir*' (non-believer) and '*jihad*' (holy war) pose a special threat?
- Why do Indian Muslims cheer Pakistani teams at sports events?
- Does not the demand for *azadi* on the part of Kashmiri Muslims show that a Muslim can never be a patriotic Indian?
- Why are Indian Muslims so worried about the Al Aqsa mosque when there are so many dilapidated mosques in India?
- There have been cases of Muslim shrines being shifted to other locations in Islamic countries such as Saudi Arabia. Why not in India?
- Why do Muslims object to singing the national song 'Vande Mataram'?
- Why do Muslims seek a separate identity in India when they do not do so in countries like Indonesia?
- Why do foreign missionaries proselytize in India?
- Why should we permit Christian missionary activity?

When I took my draft answers to these questions to Narasimha Rao, he pouted and, without reading the draft, enquired whether these were the official views of the Congress. I stuttered, saying I did not know, I was only providing tentative answers to the questions he and Gadgil had asked. I was dismissed. It was my introduction to the mind of the person, P.V. Narasimha Rao who, as prime minister, was to facilitate the dismantling of the Babri Masjid. I seem to remember the convention being held without a theme paper. But I was not done and so titled my paper 'Secular Answers to Communal Questions: A Catechism for Communalists' and sent it off to Pritish Nandy who happily published it in the *Illustrated Weekly of India*.[4]

The success of the convention, and my startled discovery of opposition to it in the top echelons of the party, led me to accept an invitation I received from Iqbal Hasnain, a professor of geology at Jawaharlal Nehru University, to

4 The text is included in my book, *Confessions of a Secular Fundamentalist* (Penguin Viking, New Delhi, 2004).

become president of an organization he proposed to set up, called the Society for Secularism.

With plenty of time to spare, I travelled to west Uttar Pradesh – Bijnor, Saharanpur, Muzaffarnagar, Moradabad, Meerut, Bulandshahr, Kanpur, Fatehpur (V.P. Singh's constituency), Aligarh (town and university), Ghaziabad – and farther afield in Haryana (Panipat, Kaithal, Faridabad); Indore and Jabalpur in Madhya Pradesh; Pilani and Churu in Rajasthan; Bangalore, coastal Andhra Pradesh (Guntur), Hyderabad city and Trichy (Tamil Nadu) in the south – spreading the message of secularism, largely based on the paper Rao had rejected.

The Uma Shankar Dikshit report

Meanwhile, Rajiv Gandhi, synthesizing all he had learnt from older, more experienced colleagues, decided the answer to revitalizing the party lay in a report prepared at his instance by a veteran Congressman, the octogenarian Uma Shankar Dikshit, which stressed the imperative of organizational elections at all levels within the party. So the Congress president set about convening an 'extended' meeting of the CWC, which meant that besides the twenty full-time members, Congress chief ministers, PCC presidents and other senior Congress leaders, including general secretaries and other office bearers, would be invited. I too was slipped in.

The gravamen of the proceedings was the adoption of the Dikshit report and the resolve to implement its recommendations. (Extraordinarily, no copy of the report could be found in the Congress archives at 24, Akbar Road, despite Priyanka Gandhi Vadra's attempts on my behalf at tracing a copy. Not even Sandeep Dikshit, the grandson of the author, has been able to locate a copy in the family's personal papers. Viswajit Prithvijit Singh was reported to have possessed a personal copy. But his wife, a retired IFS officer, has, at my request, searched and reported back negatively. That, I think, reflects the state of the party now.)

It was decided to convene a plenary meeting of the AICC to debate and endorse the extended CWC's resolution. They convened in July 1990 in Mavlankar Hall and passed, after debate, the required resolution. Just over six months of his electoral defeat, RG had found a consensual road to the rehabilitation of the party – through the Uma Shankar Dikshit report. Thirty years later, as the Congress struggles to find its feet after two resounding electoral reverses, in the ninth year of Modi Raj, the most useful lesson the party could learn from Rajiv Gandhi's brief leadership was the speed and conviction with which he moved to resurrect and rejuvenate the party.

The descent and fall of V.P. Singh

Alas, the recommendations of the Uma Shankar Dikshit report were never implemented. The principal reason for this was that within weeks of the Mavlankar Hall AICC session, V.P. Singh, who described himself as a master 'manager of contradictions', destabilized his own government by announcing his acceptance of the long-pending recommendations of the Mandal Commission on reservations for OBCs.

Singh found himself caught in the claws of the worst contradictions within his own government. On the one hand, there was the internal pressure to act on the Mandal Commission recommendations for OBC reservations in educational institutions, government employment and representation in the panchayats – which could result in deepening fault lines along caste contours in Hindu society. On the other hand, the BJP sought to thwart such salami slicing of the Hindu community by promoting, as the alternative, the vicious 'othering' of the minority Muslim community as the basis on which to unite the majority.

Rajiv Gandhi initially took a hard line, based on the stands taken by his grandfather, Jawaharlal Nehru, and mother, Indira Gandhi, on, respectively, the Kakasaheb Kelkar report (1956) and the Mandal Commission recommendations (1980) on reservations for OBCs. He felt, like his predecessors, that any implementation would not only prove deeply divisive but would privilege the freezing of caste over its dismantlement. But several of his advisers, led by Arjun Singh, persuaded RG to moderate his opposition. So, while Advani got on with organizing his '*rath yatra*', the country was consumed in the double fire of communalism and the fierce opposition against reservations for OBCs, including self-immolation by a student.

From the day V.P. Singh made this announcement in Parliament on 7 August 1990, his government began to totter. It fell when Advani's *rath* was stopped at Samastipur in Bihar by Chief Minister Lalu Prasad Yadav, one of the central government's supporters, for spreading communalism in a state that had a substantial Muslim population. The BJP reacted by withdrawing their outside support from the central government and V.P. Singh's government was left dangling in mid-air. It lost a vote of confidence on 7 November 1990, eleven months after it was sworn in. Attention then focused on whether to call another general election or to try to cobble together an alternative government.

I wrongly thought RG would plump for a general election. By then, I had concluded that the Rajya Sabha option was closed, and I should try my luck in open electoral contest. I went to see President Venkataraman on my own, banking on his having known my parents when he was a member of the Constituent Assembly. I wanted to leverage this family connection to secure a ticket to contest from the president's former constituency of Thanjavur, which is also where my ancestral village lies. He was totally unsympathetic (I later learnt that he had in mind his former constituency right-hand man, Tulasiah Vandiyar). I was sternly rebuked that we were a poor country and could not afford frequent general elections. Leave alone endorsing my electoral ambitions, it was essential, he said, that an election be altogether avoided. I was out on my ear within minutes of being ushered into his august presence!

Instead of pressing for another election to return to power, RG chose the alternative of extending the Congress party's outside support to a government led by Chandra Shekhar – a classic case of the tail wagging the dog.

The erosion of secularism

I was disappointed at this development, but much more distressed at the impact of Advani's *rath yatra* on the Congress mind. Staunch Congressmen of the ilk of Narayan Datt Tiwari – who had just lost his chief ministership to long-term opponent Mulayam Singh Yadav of the Samajwadi Party, a hard-line Mandal proponent – were looking at the Ayodhya (read Hindu) card as the road back to power despite their left-wing orientation (socialist, secular). Dinesh Singh too seemed to be drifting in the same direction, telling me in some wonderment that food was not being cooked in Lucknow households because the womenfolk were out on the streets beating pots and pans to voice their support for a Ram temple to replace the Babri Masjid. I had earlier experienced the reactions of P.V. Narasimha Rao and V.N. Gadgil.

I, therefore, took myself off to the Nehru Memorial Museum and Library to research how Nehru had stared down a similar challenge to his unflinching secularism when religion-based prejudice raised its ugly head within the party back in 1949–51. The flagbearer of that revolt was Purushottam Das Tandon, who contested and won the September 1950 Congress party leadership election at Nasik, with the support of Sardar Vallabhbhai Patel, against the much-respected Gandhian, Acharya J.B. Kripalani. In 1950 there were a number of other factors pulling the Congress away from its anchoring in Gandhi–Nehru secular values, including intra-party opposition to the Nehru–Liaquat pact on the treatment of minorities in India and Pakistan. There was also the controversy over the president, Dr Rajendra Prasad, wanting to be officially present at the inauguration of the rebuilt Somnath temple; Nehru and his cabinet opposed this as being incompatible with the constitutional requirement that the State must be above all religions and not demonstrate affinity with particular faiths.

My research led to the discovery that Nehru had succeeded in ridding the party of Tandon by the expedient of getting members of the CWC to resign, thus forcing Tandon's hand. Jawaharlal Nehru then took up the presidency of the party and, in a memorable address at Ramlila Ground on Gandhi Jayanti, 2 October 1951, proclaimed: 'If any person raises his hand against another on the ground of religion, I shall fight him till the last breath of my life, both as the head of the government and from outside.'[5]

A fortnight later, Syama Prasad Mookerjee founded the Jana Sangh.

I wrote up my research and sent it for publication in the *Hindustan Times*. When it was printed, I took it to RG and said this was a private letter to him published in the guise of a public article to warn him against those in his own ranks who had lost trust in the bonding adhesive of secularism. I warned him that the main threat secularism faced was from within, not without the party. RG told me not to worry. He would remain true to his basic beliefs. I was not entirely reassured.

[5] N.L. Gupta (ed.), *Nehru on Communalism*, Hope India Publications, New Delhi, 1965, p. 217.

My apprehensions were soon put to the test. RG thought up the novel idea of leading a *padayatra* (journey on foot) from Allahabad to Ayodhya as a way of publicly demonstrating the contrast between the methodology and objectives of Advani's *rath yatra* and the proposed Congress *yatra*. He went deep into the details, and summoned the PCC chiefs to discuss arrangements and fix dates. Asking me to brief the PCC presidents, he sat with his senior colleagues. I was feeling very buoyed at being put in charge of conveying RG's plans to the PCC chiefs in the conference room at 24, Akbar Road, little knowing that in the higher-level meeting RG had convened next door at 10, Janpath, he was being persuaded, perhaps even pressurized, to abandon his plans as needlessly provocative and potentially counterproductive.

So, when I emerged from the meeting I was chairing, I was informed in a whisper by Murli Deora that I had been wasting my time and those of his colleagues as it had been decided at 10, Janpath, not to go ahead with the counter *yatra*. The Congress was fleeing the field of battle.

Rajiv Gandhi's Sadbhavana Yatra

Then Rajiv Gandhi, reverting to type, decided on a 'Sadbhavana Yatra' (communal harmony journey – literally 'pilgrimage') as the alternative. The *yatra* began at Rajghat, Mahatma Gandhi's samadhi, on his birth anniversary, 2 October, with a pledge in Jawaharlal Nehru's words: 'to dedicate myself to building a secular India, where every religion and belief has full freedom and equal honour, where every citizen has equal liberty and equal opportunity'.[6] Instructions were sent to the PCCs to repeat the pledge at exactly the same time and in the same words by knots of Congress workers and party sympathizers in each of the 5 to 6 lakh villages. The yatris then set out for Delhi Gate and down Daryaganj before wheeling left into the teeming lanes of Shahjahanabad that housed a concentration of Delhi's Muslim citizens.

Over the next three weeks, I walked in the wake of Rajiv Gandhi through Fatehpur and Faizabad; down the narrow *gali*s of Ayodhya; in the by-lanes of Ghaziabad and Modinagar; late through the night past the crowded tenements of Hashimpura – scene of some of the worst communal atrocities

---

6 *Independence and After: A Collection of the More Important Speeches of Jawaharlal Nehru from September 1946 to May 1949*, Publications Division, New Delhi, 1949, p. 36.

in 1987 in Meerut; from the famed Charminar in the old city of Hyderabad to Gandhiji's statue in the twin city of Secunderabad. I was in a procession that took seven hours to wind past him and Jayalalithaa taking the salute, as it were, at Spencer's Point in Madras; and then accompanied him on a deeply evocative pilgrimage to the temple of Vaikom in Kerala, where Gandhiji had thrown open the temple doors to Harijans.

Further *yatra*s by Rajiv Gandhi included going from Bhagalpur in Bihar, site of the horrendous rioting on the eve of the 1989 general elections, to Dhubri in Assam; then Calcutta and Bhubaneswar; from Raipur by train through Chhattisgarh and Mahakoshal to Bhopal; by the Garib Nawaz Express to Ajmer and Pushkar; then on to Ahmedabad and Bombay. Everywhere he went, there was love in the air in sharp contrast to the hate spewed through Advani's near simultaneous *rath yatra* leaving a trail of scores of lost lives and hundreds injured. To the multitudes that thronged his addresses, Rajiv Gandhi's message was of harmony and peace, of the ending of strife and the binding of wounds, of our unity in diversity.

The slogans that rent the air were:

Hindustan ke char sipahi:
Hindu, Muslim, Sikh, Isai

Hindustan ka yeh hai nara:
Hindu hamara, Muslim hamara

Awaz do:
Ham ek hain.[7]

Alas, the sounds of hate drowned out the sounds of love.

Search for solutions

On the question of the masjid/temple at Ayodhya, Rajiv Gandhi closeted himself with a cabal of advisers to work out an alternative plan for dealing

[7] The English translation would be something along the lines of 'Four soldiers of Hindustan / Hindu, Muslim, Sikh, Christian / This is the slogan of Hindustan / Hindus are ours, Muslim are ours / Raise your voices / We are one'.

with the Ram Janmabhoomi–Babri Masjid crisis. Siddhartha Shankar Ray, the statesman-jurist, was the strongest voice of those making the argument that the crux of the issue lay in determining whether Babar's general, Mir Baqi, had, in fact, destroyed an extant Ram temple to erect the Babri Masjid or whether he had only built the mosque on unused land that was now being claimed as the birthplace of Lord Ram. He suggested that it be left to the Supreme Court to pronounce its view on this limited but crucial question after hearing the historical and archaeological evidence from respected experts.

Siddhartha Ray further argued that there were two ways of securing the Supreme Court view on this 'key question': either under Article 142 or 143. Under Article 142, the Supreme Court view would be expressed in court as an order that 'shall be enforceable throughout the territory of India'.[8] If raised before the Supreme Court as a presidential reference under Article 143, the court's finding would be a non-binding 'opinion' addressed to the president. Ray preferred raising the issue in the Supreme Court under Article 142 as that would result in a 'binding' order.

Another alternative that was considered related to requesting the Supreme Court to convoke a commission of inquiry under Section 3 of the Commission of Inquiry Act, 1952, comprising five sitting judges of the Supreme Court, selected by the chief justice of India, to determine the question of fact as to whether, at the site of the dispute, a Ram mandir was in fact destroyed to build a masjid in its place. If it was held that such a commission could not be established owing to the same question pending before the Allahabad High Court, an ordinance or law might be passed under Article 138 enlarging the jurisdiction of the Supreme Court.

These alternatives were put to PM Chandra Shekhar by Rajiv Gandhi in writing and others were conveyed orally. Chandra Shekhar finally decided on Article 143, a non-binding opinion on a presidential reference. That could not, by definition, have definitively ended the matter. This caused RG considerable annoyance.

---

8 'Part V: Article 142', Constitution of India. https://www.constitutionofindia.net/articles/article-142-enforcement-of-decrees-and-orders-of-supreme-court-and-orders-as-to-discovery-etc/.

The invasion of Iraq

Another thing that caused him annoyance was the approval accorded by PM Chandra Shekhar to the US to refuel American warplanes en route to Iraq on bombing missions without full UN sanction and certainly without an approving vote from India. I was in Fatehpur for my Society for Secularism when the news broke. I was summoned back by V. George. When I protested that I was, in any case, scheduled to return the next day, George said nothing doing; RG wanted me back the same evening. So I was driven helter-skelter to Lucknow airport with barely minutes to spare for boarding the flight. I rushed to 10, Janpath, to find a somewhat distraught RG indignant that such a major decision had been taken by PM Chandra Shekhar without consultation with the principal party supporting the government.

Saddam Hussein was not only a leading member of the NAM, he was also a staunch friend of India. The firm championing of non-intervention by a military superpower, which had been a core principle of NAM, had been violated and the 'coalition of the willing' put together by the US was outside the pale of international law. Moreover, I was told by RG that at the intervention of RG's great friend, the crown prince of Jordan, Saddam had agreed to withdraw from his unwarranted intrusion into Kuwait and it was only the US military intervention that had stalled his voluntary withdrawal of forces.[9]

At this stage, another favourite of RG's, Ronen Sen (who had continued as principal foreign policy adviser in the PMO to both V.P. Singh and Chandra Shekhar), drew RG's attention to the standing instructions that any military aircraft overflying India (unless the passengers included heads of state/government and, sometimes, foreign ministers) had perforce to land in India. They were also entitled to refuel before taking off. These were instructions which RG himself had endorsed.

Ronen contended PM Chandra Shekhar was only following standing operating procedure in agreeing to let US military aircraft refuel at Indian airports. Ronen also strongly felt that our self-interest would be affected if India withdrew permission to the American military aircraft to overfly or refuel in India as we might be denied overfly rights by Pakistan and others

[9] See also Chinmaya R. Gharekhan, *Centres of Power: My Years in the Prime Ministers Office and Security Council*, Rupa, New Delhi, 2023, p. 209–210.

as a consequence; this would disrupt the frequent sorties that our Air Force undertook to Soviet destinations to pick up munitions, spares and equipment. He apprehended that this would jeopardize our relations with the West and other members of 'the coalition of the willing'. (I countered that our Air Force could easily cross the Pamirs into Kazakhstan, then part of the Soviet Union, without overflying Pakistan, but I made the argument to Ronen long after the Iraq war was over.)

Ronen was also not sure that banning US military overflights on their way to bombing Iraq with whom we had no quarrel would be adequately appreciated or endorsed in either the UN or even NAM. Finally, he had no doubt that US and Soviet intelligence agencies were closely monitoring developments, perhaps even in touch with each other, so that no US military step caught the Soviet Union off guard. I have learnt all this from Ronen Sen only decades later; neither RG nor anyone else in Congress circles (like Natwar or Romesh Bhandari, my erstwhile senior IFS colleagues) told me about these arguments.

My guess is that RG continued to denounce Chandra Shekhar's approval to US warplanes refuelling in India because RG had agreed to such landing and refuelling of military aircraft in peacetime, not in a time of war where India would implicitly become a collaborator in US aggression. Ronen does not agree. We have agreed to disagree.

A Lok Sabha opening for me

In the aftermath of the dust-up between RG and Chandra Shekhar over Iraq, my attention was distracted by a potentially life-changing occurrence in the last days of January 1991. I had been invited to a joint meeting of all Rotary Clubs of the Bangalore region to speak on secularism. I had to return post-haste next morning to Delhi by the first flight from Madras, but the usual road route to Madras from Bangalore had been blocked at the call of a *hartal*[10] by Jayalalithaa of the All India Anna Dravida Munnetra Kazhagam (AIADMK), then in the Opposition. So I had to find my long way around via Andhra Pradesh in the middle of the night, which meant running the gauntlet of dacoits. The chief minister, S. Bangarappa, provided me a police

[10] Stoppage of all work and movement; a common form of protest in India.

escort and we fetched up at Madras airport at about 5 a.m. to catch the 6 a.m. red-eye to Delhi. At the airport, we found that the flight to Delhi had been delayed until the evening. So I dossed down at the nearby apartment of one of the party and slept until late in the morning.

On awakening and opening the *Hindu*, I discovered that the serving Congress MP for Mayiladuthurai, E.S.M. Packeer Mohamed,[11] had passed away the previous night. This presented an opportunity of finding a seat in Parliament through the by-election this would necessitate. I rang my cousin in my ancestral village of Kargudi and ordered him to carry the biggest wreath he could find to the hospital to express my condolences.

On reaching Delhi, I made a beeline for RG's office. I told him I wanted to fill the Tamil Nadu vacancy that had arisen. Rajiv looked quite startled. He remarked it would mean my fighting an election. Of course, it would – but that was just the point. I would, I told him, much rather be in the Lok Sabha than the Rajya Sabha and was confident I could win if I were given the ticket. He enquired if my ancestral village, which he had visited three years earlier, lay within the constituency. I said it didn't but lay only 15 kilometres from the western edge. 'Near enough,' Rajiv said and seemed ready to go along with the suggestion. I floated on air. This was why I had quit the foreign service.

RG seeks to end the Iraq war

Meanwhile, RG was wondering if a direct appeal from India to Saddam might not result in a compromise that ended armed hostilities and spared Iraqi civilians the horrors of war. He decided to make his way to Baghdad via Moscow and Tehran to meet Saddam. I was included, along with Natwar Singh and Bhandari, in the accompanying team.

In Moscow, RG asked me to accompany him to the Kremlin for his pre-dinner meeting with Gorbachev. He wanted me to be at hand when the conversation turned to the thirty-page letter he had sent Gorbachev in response to Gorbachev's query as to how the Government of India had kept

[11] In the Tamil script, 'F' does not exist, and 'P' is substituted in its place. The pronunciation of the late MP's name would have been 'Faqir Mohamed'.

together a country even more diverse than the USSR. Rajiv Gandhi went into Gorbachev's chambers and I sat in the anteroom, awaiting the call to join them. However, within just a few minutes of going in, RG and Gorbachev walked out, RG signalling me to come up to him. He whispered that I should go back to the dacha and await him.

I went back somewhat disconsolate and accepted the invitation from our chargé d'affaires, Alfred Gonsalves, for a spin around town to catch a glimpse of Moscow by night. I was astonished to see a long queue outside the Baskin-Robbins outlet because the Russians used to be inordinately proud of their ice cream. Why then were they queuing up to eat American ice cream? Alfred said it was a symbol of the crumbling Soviet system. The Russians waiting patiently in line for their Baskin-Robbins ice cream were demonstrating their disenchantment with the Soviet regime. He gave another example. Apparently, no one referred to Leningrad by that name any more. They were not quite ready to revert to the Czarist name, St Petersburg, but were content to call it 'Peter's'.

When Rajiv returned to the dacha, he was frustrated on two counts. One, Gorbachev had not even glanced at the letter over which RG had toiled so hard. Moreover, while agreeing with RG that his permanent representative at the UN, Vorontsov, should take a strong stand on Iraq, Gorbachev had requested Rajiv to instruct Vorontsov as he, Gorbachev, was not in a position to do so! After all, Gorbachev pleaded, Vorontsov had been a long-serving Soviet ambassador in Delhi and would, therefore, heed any advice tendered by India at a sufficiently high level. Nothing could have more effectively evidenced Gorbachev's crumbling hold over his country. And next morning, when it proved impossible for the former PM to get through to the current PM in his country retreat of Bhondsi, because if the Indian PM's communications network was so poor, it was also clear that Chandra Shekhar's hold over his administration was as tenuous as Gorbachev's. In RG's time as PM, the hotline, as I well knew, never failed even from the remotest regions.

We proceeded to Frankfurt to catch our connection to Tehran. In the lounge at Frankfurt airport, we saw the television coverage of the end of Operation Desert Storm as the US road-roller swept through the disputed oil-rich desert dividing north Kuwait from south Iraq, burying alive the elite of Saddam's formidable army and the Revolutionary Guards. It was evident that Saddam had lost the 'mother of all battles' and little purpose would be served by Rajiv Gandhi driving out to meet him in his hideout.

We landed in Dubai preparatory to proceeding to Tehran. Royal protocol were waiting at the bottom of the front ramp to receive their distinguished visitor, even if he was no longer a serving head of government. They fell into utter confusion as Rajiv, Sonia and the entire delegation descended from the rear ramp, as we had all been booked in economy!

We landed about an hour later in Tehran. The next morning, RG asked me to accompany him to his meeting with President Ali Akbar Hashemi Rafsanjani. I trotted along. RG opened the discussion by asking, 'After Saddam, who?' Rafsanjani came up with a startling answer: 'Saddam.' Rajiv was certain there had been a mistranslation somewhere. He began patiently explaining that what he meant was that as Saddam had been abjectly defeated on the battlefield, who did Rafsanjani think would succeed Saddam?

With equal patience, Rafsanjani explained that he had fully understood the question the first time round and his answer remained the same: 'Saddam would succeed Saddam.' He went on to explain that the Kurdish problem was common to Turkey, Iraq and Iran. As Turkey had the largest number of Kurds, this NATO ally could not brook any secession and so the Americans had to keep Saddam in office because he was the only one of the three (Iran, Iraq and Turkey) who had the ruthlessness to keep the Kurds in check. He freely confessed that Iran could not do more. And so, the Kurdish problem would require Saddam remaining the president of Iraq, notwithstanding his crushing defeat at American hands, to serve US long-term interests in keeping the Turks – who guarded the underbelly of the Soviet Union – satisfied.

Saddam, in fact, remained president, and rained chemical weapons on the Kurds, until President George H.W. Bush's son invaded Iraq a second time about twelve years later. But along with Saddam, US sanctions also remained, leading to half a million Iraqi infants and children dying of starvation, malnutrition and hunger-related diseases. It was the kind of callousness I had seen first-hand in Vietnam.

After that conversation, there was a somewhat romantic interlude. It was RG's and Sonia's wedding anniversary and they had not been allowed by their personal security detail to eat out together since one outing in London at the start of his premiership. The Iranians said they would handle the security (and, by God, they did!) and so Rajiv and Sonia (for the last time, as it turned out) were able to visit a restaurant together to celebrate twenty-three years of marital bliss.

The following day, we landed in Dubai and found that Shaikh Zayed, the ruler of Abu Dhabi and head of the United Arab Emirates (UAE), horrified at the prospect of his distinguished guest flying out of the UAE in economy, had placed his personal plane at RG's disposal to return to Delhi. It was the only time I washed my hands under taps made of solid gold!

The mess in the economy

Soon after our return from Tehran, I called on an old friend, Deepak Nayyar, chief economic adviser in the finance ministry, to get some statistical information for an article I was writing comparing wholesale prices of foodstuff in 1947 with prevailing wholesale prices. The required data was furnished soon enough but Deepak motioned me to continue sitting. He then filled me in on the details of the economic crisis facing the country, particularly in respect of the balance of payments tottering in the wake of Gulf remittances having dried up. There was a great deal else also wrong with the economy.

I rushed to 10, Janpath, to apprise Rajiv Gandhi and found that he was about to join a CWC meeting that was just starting. I made bold to request him to spare me a moment before the meeting commenced and he obliged by walking to the window on the far side of the room for me to speak to him in confidence. After hearing me out for a few minutes, he interrupted to say I should be informing the whole of the CWC about this impending disaster and invited me to address the senior leaders present.

I did so as briefly as I could. RG then asked me to wait in the anteroom until the CWC meeting ended. The meeting was soon over and, when I returned, he laughed, saying that virtually no one had understood the gravity of my disclosure. He wanted me to immediately visit Dr Manmohan Singh, who was then serving as chairman of the University Grants Commission, to request him to come by and see him.

I drove over to Manmohan Singh's Pandara Road residence and asked to meet the good doctor. His wife, Gursharan Kaur, came out to say Dr Singh was very ill with some kind of flu and could my message wait? I replied that I had come from the former prime minister with an urgent message to be delivered personally. Could I, therefore, be permitted to meet doctor sahib? All I needed was a nod. With great reluctance, Gursharanji let me in. Doctor sahib was lying prone, obviously drained of energy. I conveyed my message to him as succinctly as I could and asked him only to indicate by a shake of the head if he would be prepared to meet RG when he was better. Dr Manmohan Singh pulled my head down towards himself and whispered hoarsely in my ear that he would call on RG as soon as he felt a little better. That was enough, and I took my leave. This call was to have profound consequences, unforeseen by any of us at the time.

Intimations of assassination plots

In early February, Ramesh Dalal, a social activist and trade union leader from Haryana, called on RG to say that Chandra Shekhar had sent one Mahant Sewa Dass to London, all expenses paid, to contact Jagjit Singh Chauhan – who was coordinating the different militant factions of the Khalistan movement – apparently to persuade Chauhan to call off the Khalistanis. To combat the London cold, Chandra Shekhar even loaned the mahant his personal overcoat.

The mahant had told Ramesh Dalal that in London he soon found himself caught up in a plot being hatched by representatives of the Babbar Khalsa, JKLF, ULFA and LTTE gathering together under Chauhan's tutelage to coordinate the assassination of Rajiv Gandhi. Not wanting any further part in these murky goings-on, the mahant had returned post-haste to India and informed Prime Minister Chandra Shekhar, but the PM dismissed him and seemed disinclined to take the threat seriously. Therefore, Ramesh Dalal had sought an appointment with RG to apprise him of the plot.[12] I ran into Dalal outside RG's office and found him somewhat down at the mouth. He said he had told RG of the plot, but RG had shot back that there was nothing he could do about it. It was for PM Chandra Shekhar to take the required steps.

---

[12] See Ramesh Dalal, *Rajiv Gandhi's Assassination: The Mystery Unfolds*, UBSPD, New Delhi, 2001.

RG was right. He had personally conceived the SPG and empowered it to overrule even the local district magistrate, if necessary, to provide the required level of security. Unfortunately, despite lacunae in the legislation being pointed out to the minister of internal security, P. Chidambaram, in the debate on the SPG Bill, no steps had been taken to provide for SPG cover in the event of the person protected ceasing to be prime minister without any diminution in his threat perception.

V.P. Singh had, therefore, withdrawn the SPG from RG saying only serving PMs were entitled to that kind of security. In RG's view, it was only that level of security that could provide an iron-clad guarantee of his life. However, as Chandra Shekhar had not seen fit to restore SPG cover to RG, he knew his life hung by a thread. But he refused to be intimidated, or to curtail his tour programmes, or his RG-to-people contacts.

Intimations of my first election

Within days of our return from Iran, two Haryana constables, Prem Singh of CID Narnaul and Raj Singh of CID Rohtak, were caught maintaining vigil at the edge of the Congress office at 24, Akbar Road, overlooking RG's residence at 10, Janpath, next door, ostensibly 'to keep a watch on terrorist activities at 10, Janpath/24, Akbar Road'. RG was furious that the very government that was dependent on his goodwill for existence should have had the gall to set spies on him. He demanded the chief minister of Haryana be asked to resign; Chandra Shekhar, who relied heavily on Haryana chief minister Chautala, would not agree.

Accordingly, the Congress withdrew its support from Chandra Shekhar on 6 March 1991, the day the budget was to be presented. The prime minister tendered his resignation that evening to the president but was asked to continue as head of an interim government.

For me, this meant, I would be fighting in Mayiladuthurai in a general election, not a by-election. I expected to win, both because of the past record of Congress wins in the constituency but also because Jayalalithaa had signalled to me her enthusiastic support – *if I got the ticket.* This latter condition surprised me as I thought that with the support of RG, getting the ticket might be taken for granted. But she was clearly on to something that had missed my eye.

The principal opponent to my Congress candidacy for Mayiladuthurai, I found, was none other than G.K. Moopanar, the strongman of the Congress in Tamil Nadu. I thought I had built an excellent rapport with him in the thirteen gruelling road journeys RG had undertaken in Tamil Nadu during the run-up to the state's assembly elections in January 1989. I particularly prided myself at having persuaded the Congress president to name Moopanar as our chief minister-designate at a public rally in Madras. There was a much-photographed moment when I hugged Moopanar on the sands of Marina Beach as RG broke the tension by making the announcement. That Moopanar had been utterly wrong in predicting a win for the Congress if we were to go it alone after MGR's death was another matter, but throughout the thirteen long months of that campaign, I had stood shoulder to shoulder with Moopanar to ensure that every detail of every tour was worked out to his entire satisfaction.

What I did not know was that two of Moopanar's three principal homes were in the Mayiladuthurai constituency and that the great kingmaker could not abide the thought of anyone other than a designated puppet representing the constituency. Hostilities were initiated when I attended a buffet lunch hosted by Moopanar in Delhi for RG and the host refused to greet me as I entered the venue and studiously ignored me throughout.

His antennae were alerted when I made a special trip to Kumbakonam (the main town of the constituency) in February 1991 with the excuse that I was paying my condolences to the bereaved family of the deceased MP when it was perfectly clear to everyone that I was casing out the constituency. I had even used the cover of my Society for Secularism to address a public meeting in Kumbakonam.

My most challenging moment there came in the Q&A session when a girl dressed in the standard black of the Dravidar Kazhagam asked how I dare speak on secularism when my caste was emblazoned in my surname. Sometimes, spontaneity comes to one's rescue. Instead of being fazed by her question, I told her that the first time my name had been printed in the newspapers was when I stood first in Delhi University in the Economics Hons exam. I then slyly added that if there had not been an 'Aiyar' dangling at the end of my name, the credit would have gone to Uttar Pradesh – where 'Mani Shankar' was a common enough name! I stressed the 'Aiyar' in my surname was not a caste name in the north where I had been raised, but an identity tag pointing to my Tamil origins.

The problem of the division of the Cauvery waters between Tamil Nadu and the upper riparian state, Karnataka, came to the fore at this time. The three-man commission to resolve the dispute was visiting the Cauvery delta and their tour was scheduled to begin near my ancestral village. When I joined the members of the commission, they seemed relieved to have an English speaker among them. We journeyed in a cavalcade from the banks of the Cauvery near my ancestral village to my hoped-for future constituency.

My first political engagement was at the village of Govindapuram, about midway between Kumbakonam and Mayiladuthurai, where the commission broke journey for their first interaction with the farmers of the delta. I had written the Tamil equivalents of some of the technical terms on a prompt card and, after briefly making my points in Tamil, referring frequently to my prompt card, I said I would explain what I was saying in English as the members of the commission did not speak Tamil. This led to my principal DMK opponent-designate mistakenly campaigning on the theme that I knew 'no Tamil at all'. This redounded to my benefit because the electorate were pleasantly surprised to discover that, however halting and incorrect my pidgin Tamil, it was untrue to say I knew no Tamil at all. The tour also gave me the opportunity to join a public demonstration at Sirkazhi, in the far north-east of the constituency, to demonstrate my solidarity on the Cauvery waters issue with the delta farmers who constituted four-fifths, if not more, of the electorate.

It was in the CPB that final decisions were taken on the distribution of tickets. Dinesh Singh, a member of the board, filled me in on the details of the CPB proceedings. Moopanar had vigorously opposed my candidature for the Mayiladuthurai constituency. RG had then remarked that if Moopanar did not want me to have the ticket, would he contest the constituency himself? Moopanar, who had barely scraped through the assembly election, threw up his hands in horror and refused point-blank. 'Then why,' enquired Rajiv, 'are you so opposed to Mani being given the ticket?' Moopanar shot back, 'Because he'll lose.' At that point, P.V. Narasimha Rao intervened to say, 'Then let him lose. After all, in politics, you have to learn to both win and lose. Let him learn by losing first.'

And, thus, on the assurance that I would be defeated, I was selected as the MP candidate for Mayiladuthurai (which means the 'bank of the river on which the peacock dances' – a reference to a legend that Lord Shiva had arrived in the guise of a peacock to dance with the other peacocks on the banks of the Cauvery river). But Moopanar made the condition that my candidacy would not be officially announced until candidates for all our twenty-nine Tamil Nadu seats (out of a total of thirty-nine, ten of which would go the AIADMK) had been decided.

This left me biting my fingernails when I came to know that Jayalalithaa would be campaigning in Mayiladuthurai on 22 April. It was imperative that my candidacy be officially announced by then as I would not otherwise be able to legitimately join her on her campaign trail. As it turned out, the official spokesman, Janardan Dwivedi, persuaded All India Radio to announce my name in its 10 p.m. broadcast on the evening of 21 April. I caught the evening flight to Madras and the overnight train to Mayiladuthurai to reach the constituency before Jayalalithaa.

Before leaving Delhi, I paid one last call on Rajiv. Brushing past others waiting to go in to see him, I told him I was leaving for the election campaign, but I did need to tell him that my colleagues in the local Congress insisted on referring to me as RG's '*iniya nanbar*' (close or dear friend). I thought it necessary to warn him before he fetched up in the constituency. He smiled and replied, 'Are you not my friend?' Those, as it turned out, were the last words he spoke to me.

Electioneering in Mayiladuthurai

That same evening, I stood on the side of the highway hoping Jayalalithaa would recognize me and stop her vehicle. But her car-cade rushed past me at high speed. And that is when S. Rajakumar, an ordinary Congress worker, then twenty-three, demonstrated his presence of mind and quick reflexes that eventually led to his becoming my principal aide in the constituency. He rushed to the open jeep that followed which was carrying the candidates and shouted to them that the MP candidate was waiting to be picked up. They stopped and, at the first halt, I clambered on to the stage. In acknowledgement of my presence, Jayalalithaa gave me a curt nod.

I was dreading the prospect of being asked to speak, but that, I was relieved to find, was not on the agenda. My fellow MLA candidate signalled to me that all I was expected to do was stand at the rear of the platform and keep my head down and my arms crossed over my chest in prayerful respect to the Leader and to only put my hands together in a '*vanakkam*' (greeting in Tamil, respectful) when she mentioned my name as the Lok Sabha candidate.

First lesson learnt, we moved to the next stop. A police constable was precariously perched on the step at the rear of the jeep on which I was travelling. Suddenly, our jeep braked to let a pig amble past. The vehicle right behind us screeched to a halt but not before it smashed into the constable. I shall never forget the spectacle of his ankle dangling from the edge of his leg or the acute pain etched on his face. We continued in the car-cade as the constable was taken first to the local hospital, then to Thanjavur and finally to Madras; sadly, he died there the same night. (I caught a return flight from Trichy to Madras and back the next day to condole with, and give some money to, the old grief-stricken parents.)

In the wake of 'Amma' (Mother) – as Jayalalithaa liked to be called – we covered the entire constituency, east to west, stopping at every town on the way, the throngs of people on both sides of the road only increasing as we continued the journey. I learnt that in Tamil Nadu, candidates were not expected to wave but to bow in the direction of the audience with hands folded.

One major problem I had to deal with was that my *veshti* (equivalent to a 'dhoti' in Hindi but differently worn), which I had wrongly tied across my potbelly, kept slipping and I had to frantically stop my assets from being fully revealed to the voting public! I learnt to tie the knot at my waist and to keep the top of the *veshti* well above my heaving stomach at just under chest level. The other problem was language. The structure of my mother tongue had been built into my mind by my mother. But my vocabulary was limited. However, I was endowed with a quick ear and soon started picking up the words and sonorous alliterations used by the 'orator' who kept up a steady commentary on my varied virtues and those of our alliance from the front seat of the jeep as we drove through the constituency.

What I found almost impossibly difficult to cope with was the burning heat of the sun. I tried to overcome that by asking that my tour programmes start as soon after dawn as possible and take a break at noon until the afternoon sun became bearable around 4 p.m. My colleagues, who had no difficulty with the scorching temperatures and high humidity, were a little puzzled but soon adjusted themselves to what they saw as my weird timings. But as there were no Seshan-imposed restrictions[13] on the closing time of the campaign, my fellow MLA candidates would keep the vehicles moving till well past midnight. I feared I would die of exhaustion before the results came in!

I also found my mood oscillating between wild optimism and, more realistically, deepening despair, as the campaign gathered steam. The optimism sprang from the growing realization that the electorate wanted Jayalalithaa to form the next government; my pessimism from my obvious inadequacies in an unfamiliar milieu, a strange land, among people with whom I had just got acquainted and speaking a language I barely knew. What kept me going was the assurance from almost everyone that once Rajiv Gandhi arrived and spoke, I could consider the election sealed and delivered.

In the meantime, I received the endorsements of Muhammad Ali, the nawab of Arcot (important, I thought wrongly, to tie up the 15 per cent minority vote); Maragatham Chandrashekhar who had earlier represented the constituency (important, I thought wrongly, to tie up the 20–25 per cent SC vote); Tamil Nadu Congress Committe (TNCC) president Vazhapadi Ramamurthy; and, most important of all, G.K. Moopanar who, I was told, had been sternly warned by Rajiv Gandhi that he would be held personally responsible if I were to be defeated. I must say Moopanar was his charming old self and soon whipped his many followers into at least not publicly displaying their hostility to my candidature. There were, besides, a few AIADMK leaders who came canvassing, including R.M. Veerappan, the cine moghul.

[13] T.N. Seshan was the chief election commissioner who earned a nationwide name for himself for bringing in various restrictions on candidates that the chattering classes highly approved of. Sadly, Seshan destroyed his reputation for integrity by standing as the Shiv Sena candidate for the post of president of India – which, of course, he lost.

Moreover, my shaking legs slowly found the stamina to put up with the strain. My self-confidence grew as I got to know my fellow campaigners better. And as I progressively found my voice, I even tried out a couple of jokes. I had been a month on the road without a break. Rajiv's visit would be at the cusp of the election campaign and the vote. Overall, the signs were encouraging.

The assassination of Rajiv Gandhi

Rajiv Gandhi's visit was first announced for 19 May but soon postponed to the 22nd at the somewhat awkward time (for crowd gathering) of 9.20 a.m. I spent most of 21 May writing up a draft speech for RG and converting it into speaking points. I then faxed it to S.V. Pillai, an assistant and stenographer in RG's office, who, in turn, sent it to the TNCC president, Ramamurthy. At Madras airport, Rajiv put the speaking notes in his pocket and set out for Sriperumbudur, beckoning to Neena Gopal of *Gulf News* to get into his vehicle.

She poignantly recounts his last moments:

> There was a sea of flags fluttering . . . it was just open ground with a few hundred people milling about within the bamboo barricades. The lighting was poor.
>
> In my mind's eye, I can still see Rajiv Gandhi's gentle smile that showed not the slightest irritation . . . Stepping out from the front seat, Rajiv Gandhi had said, 'Come, come, follow me,' . . . A suicide bomber, let alone the first female suicide bomber on Indian soil, was the last thing on anyone's mind as Rajiv Gandhi plunged into the crowd of supporters.
>
> But as the huge explosion went off a few minutes later and I, standing about ten steps away, felt what I later realized was blood and gore from the victim splatter all over my arms and my white sari, a nameless dread took hold – something terrible had happened . . . The heat, searing, singeing, knocked me back with its strength.[14]

---

[14] Neena Gopal, *The Assassination of Rajiv Gandhi*, Penguin/Viking, New Delhi, 2016. (I have rearranged the sentences to give coherence to this eyewitness story, which has been accepted by the author vide email dated 23 May 2023.)

The bomb went off at 10.21 p.m. At 10.21 p.m., I was making up for time lost in drafting Rajiv Gandhi's never-to-be-delivered speech and supervising arrangements for the rally the next morning. I went in the late evening to remote villages in the Kuttalam assembly segment to garner a few last-minute votes, finishing the campaigning well past midnight.

We clambered out of our jeeps and threw our exhausted limbs into the chairs laid out in a semicircle in a friend's coconut grove under the star-spangled sky. Talk turned inevitably towards the morrow's great event. Pon. Govindarajan asked me how long it had been since I had last seen Rajiv. I counted. 'Thirty days,' I said. 'That's the longest I haven't seen him since I joined the PMO in March 1985.'

We finished our fresh tender coconut water and stood up to leave. I asked the driver to take me straight to our election office in the city bazaar. Waiting for me in the bazaar was the teenaged son of one of my principal campaign managers. Stumbling over his sentences, he conveyed the news: Rajiv Gandhi had been assassinated a few hours earlier in Sriperumbudur.

I couldn't believe my ears. I rushed to the rally grounds. There, in the dark, I thought the workers were busy putting up the stage, the sound system, the barricades. (They were, in fact, dismantling them.) I turned around thinking to myself that this was a silly, thoughtless, cruel rumour being spread.

I arrived home. Suneet, who had accompanied me to the campaign along with our three daughters, met me at the doorstep. Sawani, superintendent of police, Thanjavur, and previously on Rajiv's SPG detail, had been on the phone to her. The news was confirmed. I went to one of our fleet of campaign cars that was fitted with a car radio and asked for the BBC to be switched on. And over the radio waves came the information that would not be denied: Rajiv Gandhi was, indeed, no more.

We woke the children and told them to get ready. We had to leave for Trichy almost immediately as it was generally believed that Pattali Makkal Katchi (PMK) workers would soon begin their protests in the usual way: cutting down trees and laying them across the roads to block all traffic. From Trichy, we could catch the overnight train to Madras and from there fly to Delhi.

We arrived in Delhi and, while the family went home, I set out for Teen Murti Bhavan to say my last farewell to my friend, patron and mentor. Sitting stoically beside the casket was Sonia Gandhi. When we were told in whispers to get up to make place for the myriad others who wanted to pay their last respects, Sonia signalled to security to let me be. It was a gesture of compassion I have never forgotten.

The following day I went to 10, Janpath, and a new guard asked me in stentorian terms, '*Aap hain kaun aur aapka kaam kya hain?*' (Who are you and what is your business?) Other security personnel on duty recognized me and hustled me past the entrance. But, clearly, a new age had begun.

At the funeral, I sat apart. Vir Sanghvi came up to me as the rituals were drawing to a close to ask if I would do a special column for *Sunday* by noon the next day. I woke at 5 a.m. and began to write. As I arrived at the last paragraph, the emotional dam burst:

> In my mind's eye, I see Vazhapadi Ramamurthy handing over the fax message to Rajiv at Meenambakkam airport. I see Rajiv glancing at it, tucking it into his shirt pocket. I see it travelling with him as delirious crowds wave him on through Villivakkam and Poonamallee to his tryst with destiny at Sriperumbudur. I see the woman with the garland bending down to touch his feet as Nathuram Godse did to Mahatma Gandhi. And I hear the deafening explosion that carries Rajiv and my speech away to eternity.
>
> Goodbye, Sir. We'll meet up again, up there. I'll never forget what you've meant to me. Goodbye, Sir. 'Good night, sweet prince.'

And the tears coursed down my cheeks to stain the paper on which I had written.

My first election victory

I returned to the constituency. It was apparent that the shock of Rajiv's assassination – and that too on the sacred soil of Tamil Nadu – had altered the entire milieu. I shall never forget one old woman on a distant village road coming up to my jeep and, putting her head on a poster of Rajiv's, crying her eyes out. Victory was certain. The only question was the margin. I was hoping against hope for 35,000; the actual margin was over 1,50,000.

Fittingly, the results were declared on 17 June, my late mother's eighty-first birth anniversary. If it had not been for her drilling Tamil into my unwilling ears, this moment would have never come. I, therefore, dedicate my parliamentary life of nearly a quarter century to her memory. And to my father, whom I called Appa, I say: 'It was because of your Brahmin identity that you had to leave the banks of the Cauvery. Now, sixty-five years later, I have brought the family back.'

There was an analysis done in 2007 of my dark horse election win by Professor M.M.S. Pandian of the Centre for the Study of Developing Societies, New Delhi. In his magnum opus, *Brahmin and Non-Brahmin*, he presented an interesting take on how I became one of the very few Brahmins in at least a generation to win a Lok Sabha seat from rural Tamil Nadu:

> As we have seen, Brahmins were steadfastly preoccupied with authenticity during the colonial period and claimed the Brahminic as the national. In the 1990s, the political context had so dramatically changed that the chances of a Brahmin's political survival hinged on his denial of his Brahmin identity . . . Mani Shankar Aiyar was carefully demonstrating in public that his Brahmin identity was essentially false.[15]

That is true. I was born a Brahmin, but since my early adolescence I had denied my 'twice-born' caste. It is that denial which enabled me to make it to Parliament.

I found myself in a confused state of mind and emotion. On the one hand, I had fulfilled my life's ambition of making it to Parliament. On the other, my benefactor who had wrought this miracle was dead. I did not know how much further I could get without his patronage. At the same time, I was determined to make the most of this opportunity. That I was on my own from now was a challenge; there was no one to help if I stumbled. I knew there

[15] M.M.S. Pandian, *Brahmin and Non-Brahmin: Genealogies of the Tamil Political Present*, Permanent Black, New Delhi, 2007, p. 235.

were very many in my party who considered me an upstart. At the same time, I knew the aura of having been closely associated with Rajiv Gandhi would be my biggest asset. I also knew Sonia Gandhi would be around to help me *in extremis*. I had the self-confidence to expect that I would make it. It was thus for me 'the best of times and the worst of times'.

Meanwhile, I must hoe the field my father had been compelled to abandon. I had to work towards my mother's earnest hope that I would learn the Tamil language that she had loved. I also had before me the example of the times without number I had seen Rajiv Gandhi trudging the rural roads and interacting empathetically with villagers and farmers, prioritizing solutions to their problems over his own comfort or convenience.

I could perhaps use these memories as a beacon to signal my own way forward in this still unfamiliar rural milieu in a language in which I was woefully deficient and with a people I knew only as voters. I had now to rediscover them as living, breathing human beings with problems that I barely understood and had certainly not lived through, and do what I could to alleviate their suffering. Above all, I had to replicate the sincerity, honesty and integrity I had seen and experienced in RG. So long as I kept in mind his example, I would not walk alone.

I also knew Suneet would always be there, and so would my hugely talented daughters, Suranya, Yamini and Sana.[16] More than anything else, it was this which gave me the confidence to soldier on.

I had just turned fifty. Apart from about twenty years as an infant and then a student, I had been a diplomat for a quarter century. I was now embarking on a new, unfamiliar path for which I had no training, no experience. I knew I had to succeed, if only to get my daughters educated at Oxbridge and beyond, and my own and Suneet's life steadied and on an even keel. I little anticipated the roller-coaster ride that lay ahead. I took what came in my stride and hoped it would all work out.

---

[16] Suranya, in a recent social media post, has written: 'Mani Shankar Aiyar does not have three daughters. He has three lionesses!' Never was a truer word said.

What actually happened, my rising and falling like a wave in a stormy sea, is the story of the rest of my life. I call it a 'half-life' in politics, much like the radioactive half-life discovered by Ernest Rutherford, the father of atomic physics – that is, the phenomenon of radioactivity growing for a while and then slowly petering out. In a similar way, my life in politics rose in spurts to its highs and then spluttered out to the point where I find myself sidelined by Rajiv Gandhi's heirs and marginalized even in the party. But that is another story for another book.

See detailed footnotes and endnotes by scanning the QR code above.

Index

A Note on the Author

Mani Shankar Aiyar was educated at Welham, Doon, St Stephen's and Cambridge before joining the Indian Foreign Service after a brief entanglement with the Intelligence Bureau. He served for twenty-six years in posts abroad, ranging from Brussels to Hanoi to Baghdad and Karachi, with ambassadors who alternated from being outstanding mentors to nasty sticks-in-the-mud, besides two postings at Headquarters in as many as three different ministries. In 1985, Rajiv Gandhi inducted him into the PMO from where he migrated four years later into politics and Parliament. His special interests include Panchayati Raj and Pakistan.